GIRL INTREPID

PREVIOUS BOOKS:

The Little House
by Leslie Armstrong

Space for Dance: An Architectural Design Guide
by Leslie Armstrong with Roger Morgan

GIRL INTREPID

A NEW YORK STORY OF
PRIVILEGE AND PERSEVERANCE

LESLIE ARMSTRONG

EPIGRAPH BOOKS
RHINEBECK, NEW YORK

Girl Intrepid: A New York Story of Privilege and Perseverance ©2020 by Leslie Armstrong

All rights reserved. No part of this book may be used or reproduced in any manner without written permission from the author except in reviews and critical articles. Contact the publisher for information.

Earlier versions of sections of this book appeared in *The Coachella Review, Flumes Literary Journal, The Poydras Review, Slippery Elm Literary Journal,* and *The Smart Set Literary Magazine.*

Hardcover ISBN: 978-1-951937-24-9
Library of Congress Control Number: 2020903680

First Edition

Book design by Colin Rolfe
Jacket design by Anthony Russell
Production and distribution by Epigraph: www.epigraphps.com

Epigraph Publishing
22 East Market Street, Suite 304
Rhinebeck, NY 12572
(845) 876-4861
epigraphps.com

For Johnny

Contents

Introduction by Emily Arnold McCully ix
Dramatis Personae xi
Prologue – Carol xix

Part 1 — BREARLEY GIRL

1. Beacon Hill to Bloomingdale's 3
2. Brearley Girl 20
3. First Flights 36

Part 2 — SEXED

4. Sexed 51
5. Wicked Step 69
6. Foggy Bottom 75
7. Step II 92
8. Hans's Haus 112
9. Hamlet and Henchard 134

Part 3 — HOWARD'S END

10. Harrods	165
11. Sin	176
12. My Funny Valentine	191
13. Sacrificial Anode	198
14. The Andrews Sisters	219
15. Howard's End	238

Part 4 — LA VITA DOLCE-AMARA

16. Post Mortem	255
17. Decisive Moments	264
18. Unhappy Returns	285
19. Spoleto Redux	296
20. Der Spiegel	311
21. Getting On	334

Part 5 — CHARRETTE

22. Repeating Patterns	365
23. Huey	384
24. Two Out of Three	404

Epilogue – Barbara Song	416
Acknowledgments	425
Index	428

Introduction

BY EMILY ARNOLD MCCULLY

One spring weekend four years ago, Lale and the friends she calls the Andrews Sisters gathered on the Brown campus for the 55th reunion of the Class of 1961, of which she is an honorary member.

When the formal festivities were over, four of us set out for the Diggs/McCully home in eastern New York State, a three-hour drive across Massachusetts. Lale had the latest of her zippy little cars, this one a spirited Mini convertible. I admired it, and Lale, always willing to share the treasures of a beautifully curated life, said, "Don't you want to drive it?"

Turned out she meant drive it all the way home. I was tickled, but nervous. Lale wasn't at all concerned about her baby. She settled into the passenger seat and launched into the story of her young life, much of it new to me. Much of it sounded painful, if highly entertaining, thanks to Lale's astringent wit and a familiar cool distance that both insulates and frees her. When, at the end of the three hours, she said she was making it all into a book, I was enthusiastic. If she could write the way she talked, there was no limit to its appeal.

She could, and she did. This engrossing coming of age story

might have been titled *An Unsentimental Education*. It spares no one, most especially its author and protagonist.

"Give me the child when she is seven, and I will give you the woman," says filmmaker Michael Apted in his series *Seven Up!*. Lale's life from seven on up was a clash of privilege and deprivation. The settings for her odyssey range from Upper East Side New York (cramped walk-up and luxurious apartments) to New Jersey hunt country, the Maine coast, Chicago, Providence, London, Paris, Vienna, Rome, Spoleto, Tel Aviv.... Yearning for the love of her monumentally selfish parents, she forgave her father's absences, rages, and betrayals (up to a point) and adopted her preoccupied mother (defanged) as a role model. Mostly, she faced the larger world alone, armed with an indomitable spirit, a powerful will, multiple talents, a sponge-like capacity to absorb, and, eventually, some sympathetic assistance from family connections and those she attracted by force of her personality. For the Andrews Sisters, Lale was our urbane New York society girl given to Bohemianism, our collaborator in fun with her amusing affectations (mostly Britishisms), and her why-give-a-damn attitude.

Lale tells us of her decision to become an architect at an early age in order to measure up to her view of her parents' expectations. Some hard times in the pursuit of this career have been weathered with grace. But because the book ends when Lale is in her mid-thirties the reader will have to visit her website[*] to see how brilliantly she has executed her commissions.

Very much later in life, fate smiled on Lale, when she met and married John Bowers. But that is another story, and possibly another book. This one is about how Lale found herself.

---

[*] www.lesliearmstrongarchitect.com

Dramatis Personae

The names in italics have been changed to protect the privacy of those individuals.

Immediate Family of My Father, Sinclair Howard Armstrong, Jr., "Howie"

Sinclair Howard Armstrong, Sr.	Howie's father, "the Admiral"
Katharine LeBoutellier Armstrong	Howie's mother
James Sinclair Armstrong	Howie's younger brother, "Sinc"
George Alexander Armstrong	The Admiral's younger brother
Mary Armstrong Eustis	George Armstrong's daughter
Elizabeth Howard Armstrong	The Admiral's and George's younger sister
Charles LeBoutellier	Katharine's father, "Grandpop"
Sinclair Wallace Armstrong	The Admiral's, George's, and Elizabeth's first cousin, "Sin"

Charlecote—the Armstrong family house in Washington, Connecticut, built in 1916 by Charles Le Boutellier and inherited by his daughter and son-in-law, my grandparents

Immediate Family of My Mother, Barbara Lewis, "Barby"

Clarence McKenzie Lewis	My mother's father, "Gaffer"
Annah Churchill Ripley Lewis	My mother's mother
Helen McKenzie Lewis, née Forbes, later Helen Naomi Salomon	Clarence Lewis's mother, "Grannie"

Hyman Philip Lewis	Clarence Lewis's father
William Jones Salomon	Clarence Lewis's stepfather, "Uncle Willie"
Clarence McKenzie Lewis, Jr.	My mother's older brother, "Mac"
Louise Fitzpatrick	My mother and Mac's governess, "Mrs./Granny Pat"

Skylands—the Lewis family house and estate in Ringwood, New Jersey, designed by John Russell Pope and built by Helen Salomon and her son Clarence Lewis in 1928

Distant Family of My Mother

Harmon Goldstone	My mother's half cousin, architect
Shirley Faulkner-Horne Simmonds	My mother's third cousin, equestrienne
Vernon Churchill Simmonds	Shirley's husband, farmer, and Battle of Britain pilot

Manor Farm—the Simmonds farm in the New Forest, Burley, Hampshire

Family of My Mother's Second Husband, Hans Handforth Zinsser

Hans Zinsser	Hans's father
Ruby Kunz Zinsser	Hans's mother, "Minghii"
Gretel Zinsser Munroe	Hans's sister
Nancy Drinker	Hans's first wife
Judith Phaigre Zinsser	Hans's and Nancy's older daughter, "Judy"
Katherine Jo Zinsser	Hans's and Nancy's younger daughter, "Pago"

Brearley Girls

Katharine Martin Le Boutellier	My grandmother
Barbara Lewis	My mother
Allison Coudert née Moore	My mother's best friend, "Babe"
Nina Galston née Moore	Babe Coudert's older sister
Judith Zinsser	My stepsister, two grades below me
Katherine Zinsser	My stepsister, ten grades below me, "Pago"
Vanessa Lale Cortesi	My daughter
Allison Pierce Coudert	Babe Coudert's daughter, "Eo"
Camilla Cahill	Classmate and aspiring writer who died too young
Claire Albrecht-Carrié	Classmate, musician, and foodie
Lucinda Childs	Classmate, dancer, and choreographer, "Cindy"
Linda Livingston	Classmate
Emily Manheim	Classmate
Dorothy Sokolsky	Classmate who died too young, "Dodo"
Marilla van Beuren	Classmate and equestrienne

Grey Craig—the van Beuren family's house and estate in Middletown, Rhode Island

The Andrews Sisters

Emily Arnold	Actress, illustrator, and writer
Mary Honoré Clark	Freshman and sophomore roommate
Elizabeth Diggs	Playwright, "Liz"
Gael McManus	Graduate school roommate

Joyce Reed	Actress and academic administrator
Deena Rosen	Actress and sophomore roommate
Susie Ross	Dancer who died too young

Boys Becoming Men

Gordon Dennis Bok	Guitarist and folk singer, "Denny"
Alexander Benjamin Bull	Musician and son of Daphne Hellman, "Sandy"
Andrew Bullmore	Classics student and corporate executive
Clark Coolidge	Poet and drummer
Tracy Coudert	CIA operative and son of Babe Coudert
Alvin Curran	Musician and composer, "Al"
Manuel Gerade	Architect
Robert Claro Johnston	Poet and artist, "Johnst"
Oswald Johnston, Jr.	Academic and older brother of Johnst
Hillary Parterre	Fashion photographer, "Hill"
Eddie Roberts	Musician
Ralph Watson	Corporate executive

Spoletini

Samuel Barber	Composer, "Sam"
Margherita Boniver	Politician, "Marghe"
William Crawford III	Festival administrator
Giada Franchi	Scenic and costume designer
Giulietta Franchi	Journalist and Giada's younger sister
Roger Fritz	Photographer

Fiorella Mariani	Scenic designer
Gian Carlo Menotti	Composer and festival artistic director
Federico Roccati	Engineer, "Freddie"
Marcia Stillman	Actress
Luchino Visconti	Director
Deric Washburn	Playwright

Teachers

Anne L. Basinger	Middle School Head, the Brearley School
Sheila Biddle	English/History, the Brearley School
Heinrich Brunner	Medieval Art, Brown University, "Henri"
Mary Carpenter	Art, the Brearley School
Jocelynn Gibson	English, the Brearley School
Percival Goodman	Architecture, Columbia University
William Jordy	Architectural History, Brown University
Alexander Kouzmanoff	Architecture, Columbia University, "The Kouz"
Jean Fair Mitchell	Head, the Brearley School
Juan Lopez-Morillas	Comparative Literature, Brown University
Henry S. Millon	Architectural History, MIT
Adolf Placzek	Head, Avery Library, Columbia University, "Dolf"
Jan Hird Pokorny	Architecture, Columbia University

Huey, Louie, and Dewey

Alexander Cortesi	Computer software salesman, "Huey"
Llewelyn Jones	Writer and architectural critic, "Louie"
Dewey Oehler	Pulmonologist, "Dewey"

Very Significant Others

Kirsten Ann Childs	Interior designer and business partner
Hans Lehfeldt	Obstetrician/gynecologist
John Lippmann	Advertising executive, "Lipp"
Henry Potter	Film producer and director, "Hank"
Alexandra Walcott	Metalsmith, "Sandy"
Vanessa Cortesi	My older daughter
Sinclair Smith	My son
Helen Priester	My younger daughter, "Hellie"

And all I can do is keep on telling you
I want you, I need you,
But there ain't no way I'm ever gonna love you.
Now don't be sad
'cause two out of three ain't bad.
Now don't be sad
'cause two out of three ain't bad.

— Meat Loaf

Prologue — Carol

CAPE PORPOISE, MAINE — AUGUST 1954

Stone Horse Light at anchor.

Tuesday was another grey morning on the coast of southern Maine. A gentle breeze rippled the water's surface. While we waited for the big Zenith to warm up and give us the latest marine weather broadcast about the progress of Hurricane Carol, Howie cranked up the Primus stove in preparation for breakfast. We soon heard that Carol had hit the Connecticut shore around 8:30 a.m., somewhere around New London. He primed another burner and started to make batter for a giant batch of his extra thin and super delicious crepe-like pancakes.

"High tide is around noon today. Carol will be hitting the coast at high tide, so she'll bring floodwaters. We'll need a big breakfast. It might be our last chance to eat for a while." How could this be? We were always going below for hot soup or something solid to eat in even the roughest of weather. And today we weren't even leaving the harbor. I felt a prickle of worry but I trusted Howie and didn't complain. I loved those pancakes and ate more than my share.

Howie was mid-height, slightly barrel-chested, with curly dark hair graying at the temples, sparkling green eyes, an aquiline nose, and a radiant smile. He was handsome and eccentric. But except for our long faces and olive skin, we didn't look much alike. I had adored him in early childhood and had been thrilled to be reunited with him two years before at the age of twelve. He animated a panoply of stuffed Teddy bears, one of which, Bear Bear Armstrong Bear, sometimes accompanied him to dinner with his adult friends. Howie wore a coonskin coat in winter and drove a series of American-made convertibles, the top down in all seasons. He recited Milton and Robert Service with equal gusto. He was a horrific snob and was sure that he was the smartest guy in any room that he entered and he probably was. In response to his high Episcopal upbringing by teetotaling parents, he spewed forth streams of lewd limericks and combined curse words in kaleidoscopic cadences. He was catnip to women, drank too much, sometimes smoked a pipe, was proud of rarely bathing and took pleasure in all bodily functions. Unlike my elegant, intellectual, and emotionally guarded mother, he was earthy, warm, funny, and even sexy despite the beginnings of a gut and a receding hairline.

By the time we finished eating and cleaning up, a fine rain was falling. We donned our oilskins and went on deck to make final preparations for the day. The wind had picked up and was kicking up some chop in the harbor. Howie told me to get out a pair of lanyards, five-foot lengths of hemp with an eye splice at one end and a snap hook at the other. (I'd done the splicing myself.) If you were on deck in a storm and had to go forward to trim a sail or clear a line, you would tie the line snugly around your chest and clip the snap hook onto a stay or stanchion so you'd be attached to the boat. The wind speed was increasing with every minute and the rain was beginning to feel like nails driving into our faces and hands.

Prologue — Carol

"This is getting nasty!" Howie yelled over the wind. "We've got to set the Yachtsman now." I was a wimpy girl of fourteen but used to the heavy lifting as Howie had had surgery on his back the year before. I went forward and hauled the super-heavy Yachtsman anchor out through the forward hatch and set its shaft and cross bar at ninety degrees to each other. Then I went below after the massive coil of line which was tied in several places with marlin so its loops wouldn't become tangled. I hauled its huge mass up on deck, untied the bits of marlin, slipped one end through the big ring on the anchor's shaft, and secured it with a bowline. Then I tied the far end of the huge coil around the main mast, as I'd done with the Danforth line the night before. I carried the anchor forward onto the bowsprit, braced myself against the head stay, and turned to face the stern with the anchor in my right hand off the port bow. At Howie's signal, I let go of the anchor, but the heavy line got caught on a forward cleat. I bent to clear the jam but instead of the line slipping through the chock as the wind pushed us back, the whole coil of rope pulled out of my hands and went overboard in a huge splash. As it sank below the surface, I saw one of the marlin ties still holding the loops of the line in a tight coil. I had blown it. Howie came forward to check the set and when I told him what happened, he went white.

"We can't set her if we don't have tension on the line. We have to dig those flukes in and be sure they're solid. With the marlin around the coil, we can't get tension."

"It's okay," I shouted, "we still have the far end of the line around the mast. I'll just pull the whole coil and the anchor up. You'll drive her forward again. We'll reset the anchor and then dig her in." It was too late. Howie returned to the cockpit and threw the throttle to full speed ahead. The wind and waves had become so powerful that we could make no headway through the water at all. The line to the Danforth was as taut as piano wire, the line to the Yachtsman as slack as knitting yarn.

Stone Horse Light was named for the light ship that marked the end of the shoal off the elbow of Cape Cod. She was more beamy than sleek. Her decks and hull were steel so she was relatively spacious below. She drew five feet. However, the wind speed was close to forty miles per hour and higher in the gusts, and we were only at the beginning of this storm. Howie made sure I understood that thanks to my little mishap all we had between us and the destruction of the boat and possible loss of our lives were one thirty-pound Danforth anchor, fifteen feet of chain, and a diesel engine.

While I stood paralyzed by shame, self-pity, and fear, there appeared to starboard one of the fishing vessels from the inner harbor, with a craggy-faced Yankee at the helm.

"Saw you out there," he shouted over the howling wind. "Want to come into shore? It's going to get pretty bad out here."

"Thanks, but got to stay with the boat," Howie shouted back.

"How about the girl?" shouted the fisherman.

Howie turned to me "Pooch, you go. Leave this to me. It's not going to be any fun out here." I thought about this for a second.

"No," I bellowed to my would-be rescuer. "I'm staying. He might need me." And I put my arms around Howie's belly, wet oilskin to wet oilskin, and pressed my face against his big oil-skinned chest.

"Up to you then. Good luck to you!" he shouted, shaking his head as he gunned his powerful engine and turned back to the inner harbor.

Conditions steadily worsened. The wind speed kept increasing, blowing the tops off the waves that were bearing down on us. There was no going below for shelter. Lashed by rain and sea spray, our eyes, stinging from salt, were peeled for anything that might break loose or crack and endanger us. We held on tight to the cockpit

Prologue — Carol

coaming and to each other while *Stone Horse*, with her engine at full speed forward, bucked and reared against Carol's fury. As we fought the storm, Howie kept an eye on the distant shoreline to be sure the Danforth was holding. But the shore was becoming harder and harder to identify as the height and frequency of the waves inside the harbor increased.

Then the shore disappeared.

At high tide, most of the sand and mud flats and meadows of kelp that define Cape Porpoise's outer harbor are underwater, and only the string of tiny islands is visible. The weather forecast had told us that Carol was a compact and intense storm. She would strike at high tide, pushing ten to fifteen feet of tidal flooding ahead of her. The eight little islands on which we counted for protection were now submerged, leaving the ocean free to batter us to bits.

My job was to keep the engine running. The propeller whined and whinnied with every wave that swamped our bow and kicked our stern out of the water. Howie inched forward to check the anchor lines, snapping his lifeline to a different stay or stanchion as he progressed.

"What's up?" I shouted when he returned.

"The line on the Danforth is still taut," he yelled. "But it would be even if we were dragging. I can't tell. No land to gauge by. But at least it hasn't snapped. And guess what, Poochwoman," he said. "The line on the Yachtsman is also taut. Good work!" I got a huge wet hug. Phew! Somehow the marlin tie holding the line to the Yachtsman anchor had broken, and it was free to contribute its fifty pounds to the task at hand!

We endured another terrifying hour of merciless assault, and then, almost as quickly as the winds had risen, they stopped altogether. So did the rain. The sky was a sickening yellow. The big ocean swells flattened out. The surface of the water seemed greasy.

We were anchored without any protection in what was effectively the middle of the ocean, but in relative peace. Who cared about pus-colored skies? Our ordeal was over. I was ready to celebrate.

"We're in the eye," said Howie. "We've got the second half to get through and it'll be just as bad. So go get us some crackers, and I'll check out the boat."

We looked aft and were pleased to see our dinghy still with us. We'd left it to trail behind us on a fifty-foot line so it could respond to the waves in its own rhythm. And in the calm of the eye we were able to see, to the east, the high point of Trott Island, the largest in the Cape Porpoise archipelago and the only one not totally submerged.

I had just enough time to go below, grab the crackers and put on a dry shirt and sweater under my oilskins before the whole show resumed, as quickly as it had subsided, and with what seemed even greater force and vengeance. Sheeting rain and shrieking winds gusted over one hundred miles an hour. The bow of our small boat was completely submerged by each twelve-foot wave that smashed over us, with a cacophony of stays, halyards, sheets, and canvas vibrating, howling, screeching, and slapping, smacking, and flapping in protest against the assault. Powerless to resist the storm's might and consumed by terror, I hunkered down on the cockpit floor and whimpered.

Then we started to heel to starboard. The main mast made an alarming creaking sound. The jib had broken its stops. The strips of canvas with which it had been furled had come untied. The wind was filling the sail and driving it up the forestay, causing us to heel way over. The waves were filling the bottom of the sail with water. There was no way the mast could carry a sail driven by such wind. Nor could the anchor lines handle the additional stress. If the mast didn't snap and kill us, the wind and water in the sail could capsize us.

Steel boats filled with water don't float.

"I've got to go forward and cut her loose," Howie shouted.

"No. Every wave puts the bowsprit underwater. You'll be swept overboard and drown. I'll go," I cried. Terrified as I was, I was more terrified of losing him.

"No, you stay here."

Howie grabbed some line and put his heavy-duty marine jackknife around his neck and began the crawl forward, clipping and unclipping his lifeline as he crept along. By the time he reached the main mast I could hardly see him through the water breaking over the bow. He still had to make his way to the bow and then out onto the bowsprit, a bare, slender, five-foot length of painted oak that projected from the bow, with no handrails, no guard rails, and no safety netting. I knew the routine well. I'd ridden the bowsprit many times in fair weather. Holding the forestay in one hand, he was going to have to step out onto the sprit, reach forward five feet with the other hand to grab the head stay, then work his way along the sprit until he could secure his position while being alternately plunged under water, bucked into the air and knocked about by the brute force of the flapping jib. He'd then have to secure the jib or cut it free.

At some point, I could no longer watch. I turned my eyes down to the cockpit floor and resumed whimpering over the near certainty of my impending loss.

Then *Stone Horse* righted herself. I stood up and scanned the bow. The jib was no longer flapping, but there was no sign of Howie either. In a panic, I attached my own lifeline to the guard rail and started to crawl forward. I soon saw him, drenched and on all fours, snapping the lifeline as he worked his way toward me.

"It's done," he shouted, "and we didn't lose the sail!"

"Where were you? I couldn't see you. I was terrified!" I sputtered.

"I was exhausted. I lay down on the forward deck. I had to rest."

The storm moved on around 5:30 that afternoon. Although the floodwaters remained, the tide was on the ebb and the high points of several of our little islands had reappeared, affording us some protection from the still raging seas. When we looked aft, we saw that the dinghy was gone. We went over the boat from stem to stern to assess our other losses. There were none.

As the wind subsided and the water in the harbor settled down, our craggy Yankee fisherman came out to check on us.

"You folks okay?"

"All we lost is the dinghy," Howie said. The fisherman looked impressed.

"That's amazing. It's sure a mess on shore. Boats smashed up, trees down, power out, flood damage, though I s'pose it could have been worse. I'll have a look round for your dinghy tomorrow morning. It may have washed up on one of the flats." As an afterthought he called out, "Either of you like to come ashore? There's a phone line still working at the end of the town wharf." We accepted his invitation and found conditions much as he had described. While some fishing boats and pleasure boats had broken loose and ended up on the shore, most were still at their moorings, having suffered very little damage. Trees were down but not many more than after a nor'easter. Yes, it could have been worse. I phoned my mother as I figured she might have heard about Carol and been worried. From her response, I don't think she understood the furious intensity of the storm. Probably better that way. Howie phoned his father, who followed him about both on land and at sea, much to Howie's annoyance, showing up in this or that port unannounced and expecting to be invited aboard for a few days of cruising. He was glad to know we and *Stone Horse* had weathered the hurricane safely.

The fisherman ferried us back to *Stone Horse*. Seeing her at a distance, riding peacefully on her anchor lines, took me aback. She looked slightly disheveled, with lines hanging from her booms and stanchions at odd angles, but otherwise unscathed. She was rock solid.

We gave the ocean a day to calm down and ourselves a day of rest before pulling up the anchors and setting off for Marblehead, our next port of call on the way to Martha's Vineyard. There we knew we could use the Eastern Yacht Club launch to get ashore, and there we would purchase a replacement dinghy from one of the marine supply stores along Cliff Street. However, true to his word, our fisherman had searched for our dingy; he found it washed up in the kelp off Trott Island and towed it back to us. Howie offered him some remuneration for his trouble but he accepted only our thanks and we said our goodbyes.

Howie switched on the engine and we powered forward over the Yachtsman to break her hold so I could haul her up. Her fifty pounds were dug in deep, and it took several passes at increasing engine speed to dislodge her. Her flukes were caked with mud as she finally broke the surface. But the lighter Danforth wouldn't budge. She had held fast against a building sea and become too embedded to wrangle loose. After many tries, Howie gave the order to cut her loose.

Our only loss: a thirty-pound Danforth and fifteen feet of chain.

Marblehead may have been the only harbor on the East Coast that could, at that time, compete with Oyster Bay, Long Island, for the size of its fleet of cruising, racing, and motor yachts. Marblehead could boast of four yacht clubs, of which the Eastern Yacht Club was the most upscale and Howie's favorite. Amongst its members were many friends and drinking buddies from my parents' days in Boston. The harbor is a long narrow rectangle which opens to the northeast, making it a rough anchorage in a nor'easter for those boats closest to the mouth of the harbor. But the Eastern Yacht Club is tucked halfway down Marblehead's eastern shore and its waters are somewhat more protected. Though we had thought that Carol might have given the Marblehead fleet a bit of a thrashing, we were completely unprepared for the devastation and destruction that met our eyes as we sailed between Fort Sewall and Lighthouse Point. The sleek hulls of eighty- and one-hundred-foot-long sailing yachts were smeared like slabs of butter along the full length of both rocky shores. Between, on top of, and beneath these behemoths lay the hulls of smaller boats in varying degrees of fragmentation. Everywhere we looked there were broken masts of all sizes and materials held at odd angles by tangles of steel stays and rigging. Tatters of fabric that had once been sails looked like rolls of unfurled toilet paper caught in the branches of a forest. There were no signs of life on the water, no little boats scurrying around to assess the damage, probably because no little boats had survived the storm. Marblehead was a wasteland, a nautical cemetery.

By the grace of some God or a combination of good fortune, Howie's good judgment, and the seaworthiness of *Stone Horse Light*, we had survived Carol's rage unscathed, for which I felt grateful and humbled.

The next day we motored across Massachusetts Bay, then hugged the Eastern shore, passing Scituate, Duxbury, and Plymouth as we headed for the entrance to the Cape Cod Canal. I had wanted to take the outside route to the Vineyard: around Cape Cod and past the lightship, the anchored vessel that served as a floating lighthouse, after which *Stone Horse* was named. But Howie was bushed.

We powered through the Canal and out into Buzzard's Bay. We waited for the slack tide so we would have an easy run east through Woods Hole. We passed West Chop, then East Chop, and headed south into Edgartown Harbor, *Stone Horse*'s port of call, where Howie had learned to sail as a kid.

We were home.

Boats and shore properties in Edgartown had also been badly damaged by Carol. But Edgartown Harbor was better protected than Marblehead so the damage was less, although everyone was making comparisons between Carol and the great hurricane of 1938, which may have been even more destructive.

Two days after we picked up our mooring in Edgartown, I flew back to New York and to my mother's and my little apartment on East 62nd Street. Over the next four days Howie readied *Stone Horse* for the winter, and then he returned to Chicago.

Howie probably should have never been a father, but he was mine.

Part I.
Brearley Girl

1. Beacon Hill to Bloomingdale's

145 East 62nd Street—the top four windows were ours.

NEW YORK CITY — AUGUST 1947

I had turned seven in May. My first journey from our new apartment in New York to the Brearley School on opening day was terrifying. I boarded an enormous silver Campus Coach school bus at the corner of 62nd Street and Lexington Avenue, which was then two-way. The trip up Lexington was familiar territory, but the bus then turned east on 79th and rolled past blocks of tenements and slums that I had no idea existed there or anywhere. At the end of 79th Street, the bus turned up East End Avenue, which was a canyon of burned-out warehouses with smashed windows, home only to thousands of pigeons, incongruously interspersed with pre-war apartment houses, not unlike those on Park Avenue. At 83rd Street, there was a pair of outdoor tennis courts on the northeast corner, and the bus turned east again, in sight of the East River, and pulled to a stop in front of 610 East 83rd, which looked to me almost as forbidding as the old Charles Street Jail, near which we had lived in Boston.

Part I: Brearley Girl

As we children entered the Main Hall, I was deafened by the piercing shrieks of girls of all ages reconnecting after the long summer. Above the acoustic bedlam, I was directed to Miss (Margaret) Lawrence's homeroom, on the second floor: up the cold and dismal fire stairs, down the wide corridor with its dreary brown and black tile floor, brown doors, and walls lined with grey metal lockers, and into a large sunny room with high ceilings and big windows overlooking the Pier, a large concrete playing field encased in high chain-link fencing perched atop the Esplanade that ran parallel to the river.

It was apparent who was new and who was not by the stiffness, fit, and color of one's uniform. If it was a soft faded blue, very short, and maybe slightly too small, you were an old girl and belonged. I, with my rigid blue tunic just above my knobby knees, was clearly a new girl, further hampered by a broad Boston accent and a big chip on my shoulder about having to repeat second grade while the friends I had made at camp the previous summer had moved on to third.

Miss Lawrence looked like a female version of Stewart Granger in *The Prisoner of Zenda*. I didn't like Miss Lawrence. Why should I? I belonged in the class above. I craved sympathy for my undeserved demotion. Miss Lawrence wasn't keen on any girl who indulged in self-pity and who didn't measure up. As the year got underway, we were in a stand-off. In addition to reading *Dick and Jane* in all its variations, which bored me to tears, we studied food groups and began French as well. I had not done badly at the Woodward School in Boston, but I did not do well at Brearley.

The previous summer I had been packed off to Sky Hollow Farm in Rochester, Vermont. Owned and run by a former lower school teacher from Brearley, Sky Hollow had twenty-five campers, several bunk houses (no plumbing–only chamber pots in the bunkhouses and privies in the woods), a barn with horses to ride, hiking, and singing around the camp fire. My mother had insisted I would love it.

Most of the campers were Brearley girls from New York City. In my age group, each was in every way stronger, braver and more self-confident than I. Along with the wrong accent— Boston, no r's—I had the wrong clothes: pinkish red denim jeans, shorts with pleats like mini culottes that my mother thought very fashionable, and shirts with collars. The other girls had real blue jeans and gabardine shorts with white stripes down the sides and panel fronts with double rows of buttons like sailor pants. And they had T-shirts. My fellow campers taunted me relentlessly, and when I capitulated, they gave me a bigger dose. As if either to build my resistance to further torment or to punish me for my weakness—I never knew which—my counselor made me empty the chamber pots in our bunkhouse for weeks on end.

My mother knew I was miserable and sent me long letters full of sweet endearments. One such letter was headed "Dearest Laley Princesse Cublet Darling Bunny Gaga"—all her affectionate nicknames in a row with "Gaga" added for good measure. One of my bunkmates got hold of the letter, and for days all I heard from all corners of the camp was the sound of little girl voices derisively chanting "Laley Princesse Cublet Darling Bunny Gaga" shattering the sweet intimacy of my mother's letter.

Early in August, I received another long letter from my mother. This one told me that at the end of the summer I would not be coming home to Boston. Instead, she and I would be moving to New York City, and my father, Howie, would be moving to Chicago— wherever that was. He would come to New York to visit me at least once a month, she wrote.

My mother's latest "friend" (she had had several in Boston, as had my father) was finding us an apartment, she wrote. Her "friend" may have been a very distinguished lawyer, but to me he was just a strange old man whom I called MR (short for "Mr."). I was to go directly to my new home from camp, but not to worry. Everything had been arranged for my safe travel to Rutland and from there to make my first airplane flight, unaccompanied, to New York. In September I would be starting at Brearley, and wasn't it great that, thanks to being at Sky Hollow, I already knew so many people who would be in my class?

Actually, I was quite pleased with this news. A new start and my mother all to myself, even if MR was hanging around. He was so old. He couldn't last forever. And Howie once a month, all to myself, as well. I'd rarely seen him more than that in Boston so that was okay too. I wasn't dismayed about my parents' pending separation. I didn't know better.

The first challenge of my new life in our little apartment on the fourth floor of a walk-up on East 62nd Street, then a working class Irish/Italian neighborhood, was getting used to the deafening rumblings of the Third Avenue El, less than a block away, and the emotive swell of dissonant song emanating at all hours, not just on Sundays, from the Rock Methodist Church four doors to the east of us. Next, I sought to conquer my terror of the shabby stores that lined Third Avenue's unlit sidewalks below the imposing structure of the El overhead. Some were pawn shops. Others displayed a horrifying array of hernia belts, artificial limbs, and other prosthetic devices in their grimy windows. Drunks staggered in and out of the dingy Irish bars lining both sides of the avenue. Bloomingdale's was two blocks to the south. But my mother declared it a store for the working poor and not for the likes of us. I was not allowed to go there.

My mother hired a stocky middle-aged woman, Anna Peterson, to look after me and the house. Anna was gentle, Swedish, and very kind. For the first month or two of our new life in New York, my mother was very much in evidence. She spent her days looking for work as a lawyer. Despite being third in her class at Columbia and having eight years of legal experience in Boston, she found that the only positions open to her were secretarial. She kept looking. I asked my mother incessantly when Howie would be making his first visit to see me. No answer.

During that first fall and winter in New York, my mother and I made several trips to her childhood home at 1000 Park Avenue to visit her father and Mrs. Fitzpatrick. Mrs. Pat, as she was called, had been installed as my mother and her brother's governess when they were little by my mother's mother just before her untimely death. Mrs. Pat was still in residence. Although Mrs. Pat and my grandfather, whom I called Gaffer, were not married, Mrs. Pat was very much the lady of the house and not a servant. I liked Granny Pat. She had wavy white hair clinched in a chignon, a soft bosom, and a slight lilt of Irish in her voice from her Dublin days. She knitted me lovely sweaters, one decorated with a Chow dog with real black fur, like the Chows my grandfather had. Granny Pat smelled of Jean Marie Farina Eau de Cologne, which she liberally shared with me on our visits.

There was nothing soft or friendly about Gaffer. He was very deaf and wore a large hearing aid behind one ear, which was held to his head by a thin metal band. A wire connected the device behind his ear to an even larger device, about the size of an old-fashioned calculator, that he kept in his breast pocket. This controlled the hearing device. He turned it on and off at will, sometimes while someone was speaking to him were he displeased with what he was hearing. He had a bulging colostomy bag under his waistcoat, thanks to a past bout of colon cancer. The bag gurgled and rumbled on its own. He seemed to take particular pleasure in berating

Part 1: BREARLEY GIRL

my mother for bringing shame on the family by failing to keep my father in line, and by her subsequent divorce. He badgered her to give up her ridiculous little apartment on 62nd Street, her silly stab at independence, and move back to 1000 Park, where I could be raised under his and Granny Pat's supervision. He didn't care that I was taking in every cruel and hurtful thing he said. If anything, he seemed to relish it.

Later in the fall, my mother and I spent a weekend at Skylands, Gaffer's enormous baronial mansion in northern New Jersey. There was no one there for me to talk to except Mary and Julia, the Irish maids, who were spinster sisters. Gaffer had cut back on staff and brought the maids from New York to Skylands when he and Granny Pat went up on weekends. I liked visiting Mary and Julia during their off-hours in their Spartan but cozy rooms at the top of the house. When Granny Pat discovered that I was spending time with them, beyond having my meals with them in the kitchen, I was forbidden to go to their rooms again, and Mary and Julia were reprimanded.

On a later visit, when I was allowed to sit at the dinner table, Gaffer began taunting my mother during the meal about what he deemed her obsession with her appearance, and she fled the room in tears. I ached to follow and comfort her, but Gaffer commanded me to stay put. After those episodes, I didn't want any part of Gaffer or Skylands

By Christmas, the visits to 1000 Park ceased, and my mother announced that we were broke and alone. She took increasing numbers of pills to help her sleep. Her health deteriorated rapidly and she took to her bed, emerging only for her thrice-weekly appointments with her psychiatrist, Herbert Spiegel. She received no visitors except her carriage trade internist and, of course, MR. The double doors between her room and the short hallway to mine were always closed.

My mother got up from time to time. I saw her briefly before and after school. I don't remember how we celebrated Christmas or Easter or either of our birthdays. Apart from some good times with Anna Peterson and her husband, my primary remembrance of that first year was of being alone again, much as I had been in Boston. I missed my old school on Marlborough Street, and my few friends. I missed the sounds of music from the Victrola and of grown-ups having drinks in our big living room on the backside of Beacon Hill. I missed Howie, who neither came to visit nor wrote nor called. Neither, as my mother was quick to tell me, did he send the fifty dollars per month he had legally agreed to contribute towards my support in exchange for freedom from my mother, married life, and me.

Late that spring, when I got off the school bus at the corner of 62nd Street and Park, my mother, rather than Anna Peterson, was waiting for me. I couldn't believe my eyes. My mother had actually gotten out of bed and walked the block and a half to meet me!

"I'm back," she said, leaning against a lamp post to gather her strength. "I'm back for good." We were both in tears as I put my scrawny arm around her slender waist, and we slowly negotiated our way back home, in step with one another, as on outings in Boston, and never walking on the cracks. True to her word, she spent less and less time in bed each day. She got up in the mornings and made me breakfast just as she had in Boston, and she spent time with me in the evenings. She even took me roller skating in the park and insisted on roller skating herself—in short shorts, which were just coming into fashion abroad but were as yet unheard of in the States.

My father's uncle George Armstrong and his remarkable maiden aunt, Elizabeth Armstrong, became periodic visitors and our only connection to family. The Armstrongs were a furry lot and Aunt Elizabeth, born in 1898, was no exception. She had been short and

Part I: Brearley Girl

squat to start with, and because she did not develop normally as a teenage girl she had been treated with hormones, an inexact science in those days, which resulted in her developing male secondary characteristics, including a beard that grew quickly enough that she had to shave twice daily. To describe her as plain would be a kindness. Between the permanent five o'clock shadow and her general heft, Aunt Elizabeth was a sight to behold. But thanks to her fine mind, biting wit, and warm heart, her appearance did not define her. Aunt Elizabeth had graduated from Barnard, made a career for herself in the State Department, and lived in an apartment on Q Street in Washington, DC. Uncle George, retired from the Consular Service, was living in New Jersey. They both loved my father and each apologized to me for his absence. But they also liked and admired my mother and wanted me to connect to my Armstrong roots. I was always excited to see them and learned from Uncle George, at age nine, how to make very dry martinis straight up, just as the Armstrongs and my mother liked them.

One late spring weekend my mother took me out to Oyster Bay, Long Island, where I met her friends from Brearley and Columbia Law School—two sisters who each had her own house on a large estate owned by their father, Louis de B. Moore, president and part owner of Tiffany & Co. Nina had been in my mother's class at Brearley (1931) and then again in her class at Columbia Law School (1938). She was about to get divorced. Her younger sister Allison, known as Babe, had also gone to Brearley and then to Vassar, after which she married Nina's and my mother's law school classmate, Alexis Coudert. At the time, I didn't realize how grand it all was in Oyster Bay, perhaps because Nina's and Babe's houses were relatively modest compared to Skylands. What so impressed me then was that these houses had fathers and mothers and children who all seemed to like one another and were predisposed to like me. In addition, each had a television set, a piano, and a dog, all of which I aspired to own.

Back at Brearley (with a slightly less stiff and slightly smaller blue tunic and a non-regulation white shirt underneath), I began third grade, only to find that Miss Lawrence and I had been promoted together and I would be in her homeroom for a second year. I was not happy. According to Miss Lawrence, I was still not living up to my potential. But at least I had stayed clear of the special reading group.

That year I acquired my school nickname of "Layo," a variation on "Laley" (and later "Lale"), which I was called at home. I hated the name Leslie, especially when it was pronounced Less-lee. At that time, the name Leslie was most often associated with the English actor Leslie Howard, and Armstrong was linked with Jack Armstrong of the radio program "Jack Armstrong, the All-American Boy." I wanted a proper girl's name and I also wanted to have a middle name, like everyone else. So I kept trying on middle names to feminize Leslie. Eventually, I put my mother's name in front of my name and called myself Barbara Leslie Armstrong, but only on paper.

Money was a serious problem. Gaffer, my grandfather, was trustee of an inheritance left to my mother by his mother, her Grannie (my great-grandmother). He refused to release it until my mother mended her ways and returned to live at 1000 Park Avenue, which she refused to do. In desperation, my mother went to court and sued her father for part of her inheritance in my name. She won. The court appointed a Guardian ad Litem, who had jurisdiction over how this money was to be spent. At age eight, I wasn't sure what that meant. I imagined my guardian to be an elderly man with black robes, a wig, and wings sprouting from his shoulders.

Part I: Brearley Girl

Over time, I learned the broad outlines of my mother's situation: whereas she had next to no money of her own other than her meager freelance earnings, winning her lawsuit meant there was a source of income that could be spent on my well-being. In short, I was solvent, but she was not.

In the meantime, my mother continued looking for work as a lawyer. Despite having graduated third in her law school class and been elected to the Columbia Law Review, the establishment New York firms wouldn't touch her. She wrote articles for various publications, including *Fortune,* in hopes of garnering attention. She eventually met younger, more progressive lawyers who had smaller firms and were open to working with women of her caliber. She rekindled her connections with old friends from school and cultivated new acquaintances amongst New York's literati in hopes of developing her own client base. She decided it was better for business to work out of some sort of office rather than from home. And so she rented space from one of the smaller firms where she had contacts.

On the home front, Anna Peterson was replaced by a fiftyish, tall, stout, imposing Brunhilde type called Dagmar Knudsen. On the plus side, Dagmar was smart, a good cook, and occasionally fun and affectionate. She loved the radio, which my mother disdained, and together Dagmar and I spent hours listening to "Life with Luigi," "Beulah," "Amos and Andy," and "The Arthur Godfrey Show," in addition to afternoon adventure programs like "Sky King" and "Jack Armstrong," and soaps like "The Romance of Helen Trent." On the minus side, Dagmar was, most of the time, mean and dangerous. She attributed her mood swings to "the change." When she would light into me with a resounding whack for some small infraction after school, I would try to keep crying until my mother got home so she could see how I was abused. I rarely succeeded.

At Brearley, it was important to be a good student and be good at gym. I was neither. I was a slacker and, later, a cut-up. I did have a few friends whom I ventured to invite over after school. On these rare occasions, if Dagmar were in one of her moods, she would meet us at the school bus stop at 62nd Street and Park Avenue, take each of us by the ear, literally, and drag us the whole block and a half past Lexington to our house, up the stairs and then shut us in my room. Few girls elected to return.

Fortunately, Dagmar had weekends off. When we didn't visit the Couderts in Oyster Bay, my mother thought up activities for us in town. I didn't make this easy. After a few excruciating visits to the Museum of Modern Art, the Met, and the Museum of Natural History, I declared that I hated museums. More successful were our outings to see musical comedies. My first was *Miss Liberty*, and then *Where's Charley*, with Ray Bolger. *South Pacific* and revivals of *Oklahoma*, *Carousel* and *Showboat* followed. Sometimes we went to the ballet at City Center on West 55th Street. We always had to walk there and back, and I complained nonstop. Once we went to *Mme. Butterfly*. In the last scene, just before Cho Cho San was about to commit hara-kiri, her little boy appeared on stage, demanding her attention. He pointed to a teddy bear high up on a cabinet to Mme. Butterfly's left that he couldn't reach. She stopped in mid-stabbing, reached for the bear and handed it to her son, He clutched it to his chest and exited stage right, and she completed the task. This undid me. The gesture of buying him off with the teddy bear and the selfishness of her abandoning him because of her own grief was more than I could endure. I sobbed all the way home.

On Saturday nights my mother was almost always out—unless she was having a party. But Sunday evenings we spent together on the carpeted floor by the fireplace in our tiny living room. Although I longed for meatloaf and mashed potatoes, fried chicken, and

Part I: BREARLEY GIRL

Franco-American spaghetti, we always had cold meat and salad (diet food). My mother sat with her long, tapered legs stretched out to one side of her plate and her back against the easy chair, and I sat with my back against the sofa opposite her. We talked about family and money (and our lack of each), friends (hers and my lack of them), clothes (hers and mine), work (hers), school (mine). Every so often she stacked another pile of LPs on the Vic, as she called the record player—Bartok, Bloch, Hindemith, Poulenc, Ravel, the Razumovsky quartets, most of which I found pretty grating. But at least we were together.

In fourth grade, we studied the explorers and the exotic geography of their wanderings. The drawing, coloring, and labeling of maps and charts was the first bit of school work I really enjoyed. I would get lost in the effort required to control the lettering and to color carefully along the edges of countries and continents. But still I was not doing well. Mrs. Payne, our homeroom teacher, thought that because my mother was myopic, I might be as well, which might account for my difficulties. Initially, I hoped that the long, annual bus ride up to the Eye Institute at Columbia Presbyterian would result in my having my first pair of glasses so I could be more like my mother. But by fourth grade, I felt I was homely enough and didn't need glasses to make things worse. Late that fall, when Dagmar took me up to the Eye Institute yet again, Dr. McNee placed me in his big examining chair, turned down the lights and asked me to read the letters on an illuminated screen that seemed miles away. Carefully and confidently, I read out the first four lines. When I was done, Dr. McNee asked me to go up to the screen and take a closer look. The letters were Hebrew. Busted.

My new frames were a bright and cheerful red, but they did nothing to enhance my performance. I continued to do barely acceptable work. My report cards still stated that I wasn't "living up to my potential." What potential? I was just ten years old, wimpish, and trapped in a homely body. I was my own worst enemy when it came to self-promotion. I felt stigmatized by having a working mother who was divorced. Then there was the tyranny of Dagmar. Still, in addition to Allison and Tracy Coudert, I did have one or two other good friends.

One was Dorothy Sokolsky, who lived on the West Side—which, at the time, was likened by my mother to the far side of the moon—so we didn't see each other much out of school until I was old enough to travel to her neighborhood on my own. Dodo's father, George Sokolsky, was a gnarly rightwing journalist who wrote for the *World Telegraph and Sun,* the evening tabloid, and was an enthusiastic advocate of Senator Joseph McCarthy and his witch hunt. G. David Schein and Roy Cohn were regulars from mid-afternoon through dinner at the Sokolskys. Dodo was precocious and thought Schein was cute, but both Cohn and Schein gave me the creeps.

Dodo distinguished herself in fourth grade by being the first in our class to develop breasts and pubic hair. Dodo reported regularly on the progress of her passage through puberty and held periodic viewings in the toilet cubicles of the Lower School student bathroom. It must have been tough to be so far ahead of the rest of us, but she made the best of it, and going to her house was always fun if you could steer clear of her father and his coterie of Fascist friends. Eventually, even the old man softened towards me. I attended my first Seder at their house and was schooled by him in the asking of the four questions as the youngest at table. Later, as a teenager, I visited their house in the Berkshires, and Dodo told me that when she first saw me come into school in the second grade, she thought I was the ugliest child she had ever seen. I had to agree.

My most important friend was Marilla van Beuren, who entered

Part I: Brearley Girl

Miss Lawrence's second grade homeroom a week after I did. She was tall and leggy with long dark braids and all the self-confidence and assurance that I lacked. She was a good student and a star at sports, which counted for lots at Brearley, even in the early grades. And she seemed to have a real family of formidable parents, two brothers, a sister, and a stern but warm-hearted Swiss governess, Miss Schill, whom Marilla called Schillum.

Marilla lived only four blocks north of us at 66th Street and Park, but she hailed from a different world. Her father was the publisher of *Cue Magazine*, the *Time Out* of the time. Her mother was a tall, dark, and imposing woman whom I remember more or less from the ground up because I was always looking abashedly at the floor in her presence. She stood or walked duck-footed on small feet with arches so high that her feet looked as though they were about to pop out of the dark, high-heeled pumps in which they were encased. Her ankles were trim and her shins narrow until they met ball-like calf muscles close to her hemline, just below her knees. Then came the long shaft of her generally straight skirt, which hung off a somewhat distended belly, on top of which rested her sizable bosom, usually decorated by a large brooch sporting some serious rocks. Emerging from this compressed mass was a long neck, supporting a small head. Her face was fleshy and bejowled, marked by a gash of bright red lipstick, and topped by a head of short and tightly permed dark brown hair. In one hand, she generally clutched a martini glass, in the other she fingered a glowing cigarette.

The van Beurens occupied the entire eighth floor at 640 Park Avenue. The layout was not unlike my grandfather's apartment at 1000 Park, with the public rooms on Park Avenue facing east and the bedrooms along the side street facing south. But their apartment was twice as big and full of light, and it had a giant servants' wing that housed the butler, Carl, various kitchen and chamber maids, and a handyman. Miss Schill had her room and bath next to Marilla's. Like Mrs. Pat, governesses of Miss Schill's caliber were always housed with the family and not with the servants.

The family spent winter holidays at Mr. van Beuren's parents' compound in Boca Grande off the west coast of Florida. They spent summers at Sonnenhof, their picturesque semi-sprawling house on Newport's Third Beach. When Mr. van Beuren's parents died, the family moved to Grey Craig, a large estate on Paradise Avenue that overlooked Newport's Second Beach across a huge expanse, more like a park than a lawn, and an equally large pond full of ducks, geese, and gulls. Grey Craig was up there with the best of the huge Newport mansions, with its nine-hole golf course, cutting and formal gardens, outdoor theatre, stables and carriage house, ten-car garage, ballroom, game room, gun room, Chinese room, plus the usual bedrooms, bathrooms (with parquet floors), and servants' quarters interconnected by gracious glazed galleries, flying staircases, and wide corridors flooded with sunlight. It took me several years to obtain an invitation to Grey Craig, because living, as we did, a block from the El, we were not in the van Beurens' league.

In the city, we generally played at 640 Park, as their front hall or foyer was the size of a small gymnasium, and we could practice runs of cartwheels, headstands, and handstands, at which Marilla excelled and I attempted and failed. At Marilla's, the library where the van Beurens and informal guests congregated for cocktails, as well as the drawing room, the music room, the dining room and a door to the servants' wing, all opened onto the foyer. The music room was centered between the huge dining room and the even larger drawing room, where no one ever sat. Marilla and I banged out *Chopsticks* endlessly on the Steinway baby grand, but more importantly, when the van Beurens were out, we were allowed to watch TV, which was the main attraction of this room. We would

Part I: Brearley Girl

not have a television set at our house until I was sixteen and, even then, its screen was the size of a pot holder.

In fourth grade, many of us started going to dancing school—ballroom dancing school. This was the only opportunity for boys and girls to meet—unless you had a brother, which I did not. There were three main dancing schools for children in Manhattan at that time: Barclay's, which was held in the ballroom at the Cosmopolitan Club on East 66th Street; de Rham's, which was the most exclusive, was first held in the ballroom at the River Club on Beekman Place, and then moved to the Colony Club on 62nd Street and Park and actually taught kids to dance. And then there was Miss Viola Wolff's, about which I don't know much, as it was the dancing school for Jewish kids, though we really didn't distinguish Jewish from not-Jewish until later on in middle school, and even then, very little was made of the distinction, at least not within the walls of the school. What mattered at Brearley were athletic skills and, most of all, smarts.

How my mother parlayed a place for me in de Rham's is beyond me, but despite her lack of cash, she was determined that that no social doors should be closed to her daughter. On Thursday afternoons, I got home from school, removed my glasses, stripped off my grubby blue tunic, bathed, tried to do something with my stringy hair, got buttoned into one or another organdy or taffeta dress with puff sleeves, a Peter Pan collar, and a big broad sash, and donned white anklets and black patent leather Mary Janes. White gloves, a dress coat, and a hat trimmed with velvet completed the outfit. Boys, too, wore white gloves, along with dark suits and ties. Boys and girls were collected from near their apartments or houses and driven down to the River Club in little yellow school buses. We checked our hats and coats near the door, descended to the entrance to the ballroom, and lined up to be received by the elegant and fiercely upright Mr. William de Rham and his blowsy dancing partner, Miss Vera Chapin, who was always decked out in flowing chiffon trimmed with rhinestones and a deep décolletage—there were lots of jokes and tittering about the décolletage. If one of us failed to shake hands firmly or speak our greeting clearly, or if we did not curtsy to the proper depth or bowed without purpose, Mr. de Rham cracked the offending child on the head with the mariachi he kept in his left jacket pocket.

There was no fooling around at de Rham's. You were there to learn to dance: Viennese waltz, foxtrot, samba, tango, rumba, and even the Lindy on special days. Mr. de Rham and Miss Chapin would demonstrate a sequence of steps and then pick one of the more accomplished boys and one of the better girls to replicate what they had done. If they messed up, out came the mariachi. Crack! Boys got whacked more than girls because we were taught that boys led and girls followed, so the probability of a mistake being the boy's fault was high. But we girls got our fair share of cracks on the head too, especially if we were perceived as leading, as was frequently the case with tall and athletic Marilla, whereas I, ever mousy, stayed under Mr. de Rham's radar. Almost all of us learned to dance well, and some, like Arthur MacArthur (son of Douglas), Harold Talbott (who became a Tibetan Buddhist monk), and George Hamilton (the actor), were brilliant. In the four years we took classes with Mr. de Rham, we made friends who would stand by us through our upper school years and the Christmas and spring dances that were once again our principal vehicle for meeting, greeting and otherwise pressing our young, nubile female bodies against hard and wiry male bodies. But that was still some years away. When we started out at de Rham's we were still very much children.

2. Brearley Girl

SEPTEMBER 1950

The Brearley School — seen from the East River.

The Brearley School was founded in 1884 by Samuel Brearley, an Englishman and Oxford University graduate who believed in equal education for women. He died of typhoid fever two years after its founding, but his name lived on. Brearley was never a finishing school for the daughters of New York's aristocracy. It was a serious seat of learning which, even before the turn of the century, admitted Jewish girls as well as gentiles from the many strata of New York society whose families wanted them to have a first-class education. My mother graduated from Brearley in 1931, went on to Bryn Mawr, and then, at her father's insistence that she pursue a profession, went to Columbia Law School where she excelled. Brearley was New York's bluestocking school and she was determined that I should follow in her footsteps.

In fifth grade, we entered middle school. It was the first year we really felt part of the corpus of the Brearley School. On Monday mornings, just after attendance was taken, decked out in our blue tunics of varying shades and lengths and our blue or white shirts, some twenty-four of us lined up in pairs at the door to our homeroom, filed down the hall and the nearest of the two fire stairs, and descended many flights to the double-height Assembly Hall on deck C. Substantial wooden folding chairs that could be reconfigured or removed when the room was used for dances, fairs, and alumnae day luncheons were arranged in three sections, with a cross aisle just under the edge of the balcony where the teachers sat. There was a raised stage behind a simple Art Deco proscenium at the west end of the room. On the short diagonal walls flanking the proscenium was a bronze relief portrait of our short-lived founder, Samuel Brearley, in profile, on one side, and on the other, an oil portrait of Millicent Macintosh, who had been the headmistress until 1947, when she became dean (and later president) of Barnard College. She was succeeded at Brearley by Jean Fair Mitchell, the remarkable headmistress of my day, who stayed on until 1975.

In a *New York Times* obituary that appeared on August 6, 1998, Miss Mitchell was described as "a violin-playing, jig-dancing Scottish-born educator who guided the venerable Brearley School for girls from the white-glove 1940s through the armband 1960s without missing a beat...[She] was a short, husky woman of verve who declaimed the poetry of Robert Burns in authentic dialect and Scottish burr... She lost ... little time in putting her own stamp on the school. Brearley had made social history by welcoming Jewish students as early as the 1880s, but Miss Mitchell promptly advanced its commitment to social diversity by recruiting its first black students, an effort aided by a Rockefeller Foundation grant to provide scholarships for needy minority students."

Short and husky? Miss Mitchell was the closest thing to a man in a skirt that any of us had ever seen, other than Miss Edna Carling, the head of the gym department, who had been there in my mother's day. Miss Mitchell's full head of greasy dark hair was cut short and held off her high forehead by an array of unmatched bobby pins. She wore earth-toned gabardine suits over the regulation short-sleeved nylon blouse, opaque stockings, and heavy, gum-soled shoes. To add gravitas to her appearance when presiding over our assemblies, she donned a mid-length academic robe over her suit, as students on scholarship do at British universities. When all the classes were seated, she would stride into the Assembly Hall to take her place in the short row of chairs by the lectern. Mr. (Louie) White, head of the music department (and one of our few male teachers), played the introduction to the first hymn on the mid-size Steinway, and we would grab the hymnal from the seatback in front of us, turn to the hymn whose number was posted, as in church, and burst into song. Following the hymn, we would all recite the Lord's Prayer in unison. Then Miss Mitchell, in her mild Scottish burr, would read a passage from the Bible and deliver a ten-to-fifteen-minute lesson. At its close, she would recite a prayer. We would all sing the final hymn and file out of the Assembly Hall and back up to our homeroom for the start of the academic week.

All this Christian ritual, despite a good third of the student body being Jewish! However, if we hadn't sung those hymns, and if not for Miss Mitchell's recitation of those prayers and reading and speaking to those Biblical passages for eight years running, I would have known nothing of the Christian aspect of the culture into which I had been born.

American history, long division, and more advanced fractions were our main subjects of study in fifth grade. But I spent as much time as I possibly could making geometric designs using an ordinary swing-arm compass and as many colors as my set of Prismacolor pencils allowed, coming up with designs for all sorts of clothes for female paper dolls, and best of all, developing detailed floor plans of houses and apartments. My mother loved clothes and had been offered a job to train as a buyer for Bergdorf Goodman before her father compelled her to select a profession. ("Who has ever heard of the department stores of ancient Rome?" he had said to her.) I expressed my interest in fashion by designing clothes for paper dolls. But it was the floor plans that really set me dreaming. I lost myself planning endless variations on these residential interior spaces, how they worked together, how each resident got from one room to another and what each room looked out on.

As usual, my grades were poor.

Grown-ups constantly ask what you want to do or be when you grow up. While I wasn't sure I would ever grow up, because childhood was passing so slowly, if I did, I was surely not going to be a nurse, a teacher, or a ballet dancer (however much I longed for ballet lessons). Van Gogh's reward for being a famous painter was the self-amputation of his ear. Beethoven's reward for being a great composer was deafness. Both died young. Clearly being any sort of artist was out. There was a lot of talk in our small household about the virtue and dignity of having a profession. It had been required of my mother, so if I was going to measure up, I reckoned I should go this route as well.

What were the professions? The only ones I knew about were law (out; no competing with my brilliant mother), medicine (out; no competing with my brilliant but absent father), engineering (out; I could barely memorize the times tables, and fractions were killing me). I didn't know about prostitution, but even if I had, it wouldn't have been an option.

Then there was architecture.

Maybe.

In the years following my mother's return to New York, her

Part I: BREARLEY GIRL

"nervous breakdown," her recovery and her quest for a career in the law, she cultivated a very active social life. She had many gentlemen friends. But she was not looking for a meal ticket, just a meal, and preferably one served at Henri Soulé's Le Pavilion on 54th Street, just east of Fifth Avenue, at The Colony on East 61st Street, or at the '21' Club just west of Fifth Avenue on 52nd Street. Some of these gentlemen were old friends from her Boston days. Others were friends and former professors from Columbia Law School. Still others were "confirmed bachelors" like Charlie van Rensselear (who wrote for the society gossip column, Cholly Knickerbocker), the furniture designer Edward Wormley, and the Frank Lloyd Wright aficionado Edgar Kaufmann, Jr. These men were safe, smart, and entertaining.

Harmon Goldstone, an architect, was another one in this category. He was tall, gentle, and avuncular, with a head of thick, wavy black hair streaked with silver; a big nose; and a kindly smile. He spoke softly, but clearly, with what I soon came to recognize as an aristocratic New York accent. Harmon and my mother were voracious readers and loved to talk about books—fiction, biography, history, political commentary, thrillers, and trash. They commiserated about their professions. My mother was struggling to find work as a lawyer and Harmon, employed by the firm of Harrison & Abramovitz, was working on the master plan for New York's Lincoln Center, and felt underappreciated. Eventually, my mother and Harmon got to talking about their families. My mother learned that Harmon came from an old and revered Jewish family. His father, Lafayette Goldstone, had been a distinguished architect. His mother, Aline, with whom Harmon still lived, was an intellect and published writer. He could trace his mother's family on her mother's side, but no one knew much about her father, who died in 1881 before she turned three. His name was Hyman Philip Lewis.

Was he the same Hyman Philip Lewis who left my mother's

grandmother, Grannie, stranded and with child following their whirlwind romance during the Philadelphia World's Fair in 1876? When my mother told me about this coincidence, I must have been about ten. I reveled in the possibility that Harmon might be related to us. We might have some family after all!

Harmon's mother dug out the family books and records. The dates seemed to work. Gaffer had been born in Jersey City in October of 1876. Harmon's mother, Aline May Goldstone, née Lewis, had been born in New York City in November 1878, and her brother, Harold Lewis, had been born in November of 1880. My mother had thought Philip Lewis died in June of 1880. Apparently not.

Harmon's mother, Mrs. Goldstone, became quite excited on learning that she had a previously unknown older brother and told her son that she wanted very much to meet him. How ironic that they lived only a few blocks apart on upper Park Avenue! I hoped that discovering he had a long-lost sister might make Gaffer a friendlier person.

My mother, who was still not on good terms with her father, told him of her and Harmon's discovery and the existence of his half-sister, who desired to meet him.

Gaffer refused.

Why?

My mother thought it was because Gaffer suspected there had been no divorce after Philip Lewis abandoned Grannie—and that for all he knew, there had been no marriage either. The existence of Aline Goldstone née Lewis meant that she or he himself was illegitimate. My mother sensed that her father was unprepared to deal with this so late in his life.

It must have been around 1950 that Mrs. Goldstone, then in her early seventies, took to waiting mornings or evenings at the southwest corner of 84th Street and Park to catch a glimpse of her older half-brother walking Ling, the last of his Chow dogs. Being rebuffed and thus reduced to the equivalent of a geriatric stalker so humiliated Mrs. Goldstone that she dug further into the family books and records and, over a period of several months, found entries reflecting sequential payments by her mother's family to Helen Forbes Lewis, my mother's Grannie, in exchange for removing herself and her son from their and Philip Lewis's lives.

Subsequently, Helen Forbes Lewis met and fell in love with William Jones Salomon, a successful banker. To marry into his distinguished family, she had to take instruction and covert to Judaism. She and Uncle Willie, as he was known, wed in 1892 and lived at the height of luxury in a large house at 1020 Fifth Avenue that he built for his new bride, renamed Helen Naomi Salomon, while he continued to increase his fortune underwriting the development and construction of new railroads. My grandfather, Gaffer, worked for Uncle Willie, first as an engineer, and then was taken into his banking firm, Blair and Co. (not to be confused with Salomon Brothers). Uncle Willie had no children of his own, and when he died in 1919, he left his estate to his wife and her son, my grandfather. My grandfather was without religion and my mother and her brother Mac were raised accordingly. However, my mother said that her father insisted that if either were asked if they were Jewish they answer in the affirmative out of respect for Uncle Willie. My mother was rarely asked, but her brother Mac, with his dark wavy hair, olive skin, and prominent nose, looked Semitic. He was asked regularly by his fellow classmates at St. Bernard's School and in the early 1930s was frequently beaten on his way home for being a Jew.

My mother's and Harmon's friendship survived Mrs. Goldstone's acrimony, although my mother could never acknowledge Harmon as family. Maybe she felt that if her father was illegitimate, then so was she. Maybe she didn't want to be part of a family that was so clearly

Jewish, given the discomfort of her and her brother's tenuous and often painful connection to Judaism in their childhood. Whatever the reason, I loved it whenever Harmon came to take my mother out or stayed for dinner with us. He always had time for me. If someone as warm and kind and bright as Harmon could be an architect, maybe I could be one too. Though I had no idea what architecture was, I figured it had an element of art to it. Drawing house plans and figuring out how people might live and what they might do in the various rooms that I laid out was something I really enjoyed.

I talked about being an architect with Harmon. He said there were very few women architects—in fact, there were even fewer women in architecture than in law—and the prejudice against them ran deep. If I wanted a go at it I would have to study longer and get better grades at school, then work harder and do better than my fellow males at whatever job I would be lucky enough to land, just as my mother was having to do in the law.

"Are you prepared for that sort of effort, Leslie?" Harmon asked. (He didn't start calling me Lale until I was older). "It will be very, very difficult.," he added.

"Sure," I replied.

What did I know at age ten?

One thing was for sure: when people asked me what I wanted to be when I grew up and I replied, "an architect," they stopped dead in their tracks and actually paid attention to me for a few seconds. In retrospect, selecting a career path at age ten on the basis of knocking people's socks off was probably unwise. But once I had identified my chosen métier and announced it to whomever would listen, there was no going back. I had a goal to strive for. My life was going to have direction and meaning, however poorly I was doing at school.

Part I: Brearley Girl

In June of 1951, it was back to Grand Central Station and onto the overnight train to Lake Placid for my second full summer at Camp Treetops while my mother went abroad yet again, allegedly in search of new business. That year I was assigned to a smallish cabin with a bunch of girls at the edge of the woods overlooking the senior camp grounds. The common outhouse was to leeward. It was damp, dark, and home to many spiders and mosquitos. There was mandatory swimming in Round Lake twice a day, rain or shine (too cold, and I was a weak swimmer), hiking at least three times a week (too much uphill, and I was a wimp), and riding twice a week (which I loved!). The barn and the horses were managed by Roy Reed, a commanding riding instructor who spoke few words, smiled infrequently, and had a pate as smooth as a crystal ball. We campers had to pitch in—mucking the stalls, feeding and grooming the horses, sweeping the barn and cleaning the tack—in exchange for two sessions a week in the ring or on trail. I wasn't as crazy about horses as many girls were, especially my friend Marilla. In fact, I was terrified of being bitten, stepped on, or ejected from the saddle as a result of my mount's shying, bucking, rearing, or simply deciding it was time for a roll, with me still on board. But despite my fears, I loved covering ground on the back of a horse and moving to his or her gait. I still do. So keeping Roy Reed's barn shipshape was well worth the effort, though Mr. Reed himself never gave me the time of day. I learned what I learned from his underlings and the horses themselves.

Treetops was probably as good a camp as exists. Yet, riding notwithstanding, I didn't want to be there for eight weeks while my mother sashayed around Europe. However, the difference between the first year and the second two years was that I had fallen in love with a gorgeous blond boy I had first seen when we got on the train at Grand Central. I lived and breathed for the occasional glimpse of this older Adonis who was my first serious crush. My obsession with him provided me with yet another context in which I could agonize over my inadequacy.

My other gnawing obsession was what my mother was doing in Europe. I lived for mail call and the hope that one of her colorful postcards or long descriptive letters would be waiting for me. From these, and from having already met several of the principals, I developed the following model for her spring and summer trips: London was her starting point. There she had an old friend, Lady (Ann) Peek, who had just remarried Sir William Rootes of Rootes Motors whom I had met in New York. Billy worshipped Annie for her elegance and beauty, and Annie enjoyed having serious money in her purse.

From London, my mother and Annie might go to Paris together for the collections, but as often as not my mother would go on her own, as she was fast cultivating a coterie of Parisian friends thanks to her connections with the Paris office of Coudert Frères (the law firm of her friend Alexis Coudert and his family) and with her old friend Odile Raymond, whom she and I had met through my Aunt Elizabeth Armstrong on a trip to Washington in the late 1940s.

Odile, who was even more elegant and beautiful than Annie Rootes, had recently returned to France with her American husband and was pleased to see my mother on French turf. Odile, née Pathé, was born to the famous film family. She had been educated in France and England and had a ton of interesting and fashionable friends in Paris, Monaco, and Beirut whom she happily shared with my mother. What's more, Odile's friends sent her on to their friends even farther afield. My mother was in her element. Thanks to her grandmother, Helen Naomi Salomon, my mother loved all things European and especially French, and spoke excellent French as well. She was well versed in politics and international affairs and, as a lawyer practicing in New York, she had much more cachet in Europe and the Middle East than she had at home. In spite of being continually short of money, she maintained that she had to keep up appearances, which meant she had to stay at the Plaza Athenée in Paris, the Hassler in Rome, the Grand Bretagne in Athens, Shepheard's in Cairo, and, of course, Claridges in London. And she had to be well dressed.

In those days, there was no prêt a porter. Each fashion house presented a spring and fall collection, which you had to be invited to see. If you wished to order something, they took your measurements and made you a "toile," a three-dimensional canvas pattern replicating the unique shape and size of your body. They used this pattern as the basis for constructing whatever you had ordered from the collection. If you were a regular, you had your own "vendeuse," or sales assistant. My mother's heart belonged to Dior, where she had Mme. Suzanne and her own toile. For at least seven years running she would show up, select her fabrics, and put down her deposit. In those post-war years, the U.S. dollar was desirable currency, so she received a fourteen percent discount. Knowing that Maison Dior wanted to make an inroad into the American market, she had the cheek to ask for an even larger discount, explaining that she was a prominent American lawyer who often argued cases in the highest courts, where her Dior clothes would be observed by a new and elevated market. In fact, my mother hated to litigate and, as a matter of principle, never appeared in court if she could help it.

In addition to the summer trips, my mother was often absent around my birthday in May, attending meetings of the boards on which she served at the American Farm School in Salonika, and Robert College in Istanbul. In her view, these institutions, like the American Universities in Beirut and Cairo, founded by worthy

Protestant American captains of industry, promoted the best of Western ideas and education in countries that were shackled by archaic traditions of belief and learning. She felt it her duty to contribute to that effort. I was not convinced. It meant she was unable to attend any end-of-the-school-year events in which I might be participating. Shepheard's Hotel in Cairo burned to the ground during one of her spring trips. I was certain she had perished in the fire and cried hysterically until Babe Coudert produced her copy of my mother's itinerary which showed that she had been in Morocco at the time.

Our principal subject of study in sixth grade was Greek mythology, but I was much more interested in the arrival in our classroom of Cecile Miller, a pretty, smart, and shy little girl of Jamaican origin who was the first African American student ever to be admitted to a New York City private school. But Cecile was soon swept up by other, more popular kids. So I spent much of sixth grade focusing on learning to draw horses (to attract Marilla's attention), and making friends with another new girl, Emily Manheim.

Emily transferred to Brearley from Friends Seminary downtown following her parents' divorce. Her father was a lawyer and had a fair amount of money behind him—owing to some connection with Welch's grape juice. Mr. Manheim had wanted out of the marriage in order to marry his girlfriend, so Emily's mother and her three children, Martha, Tony and Emily, had moved uptown to a bright, open-plan apartment in the brand-new Manhattan House at 200 East 66th Street. My Armstrong grandparents had also moved to Manhattan House, but I rarely saw them. My grandfather, known affectionately as the Admiral, did occasionally take me out for lunch, but I'd never been to their new apartment, and if

Part 1: Brearley Girl

it was anything like the pigsty they had lived in on East 90th Street, I didn't want to go.

Manhattan House was fashioned following the architectural principles propagated by Le Corbusier. The site is an entire city block. And the building itself, the first in New York to be clad in white brick, is divided into five sections, each with vertical strips of cantilevered balconies and its own core of elevators, fire stairs, and related services. The building is set back from the streets and avenues that border it, and has a glazed lobby that used to run the whole length of the building. Each of the five elevator banks went up to a series of glazed roof pavilions opening onto a huge open roof deck that also ran the full length of the building, all for the communal use of the tenants. For someone with my architectural aspirations, the freedom to run around the lobbies and roof terraces of Manhattan House was exhilarating. Emily's sweet and sorrowful mother, Kate, who was way overweight and had some sort of illness relating to drink, medication, or both, spent most of her days in bed, so we had the run of both the apartment and the building.

When I told my mother about my new friend, she wasn't enthusiastic. The problem seemed to be that Emily and her family were Jewish.

"But, Ma, I thought we were part Jewish. Didn't Grannie convert to Judaism when she married Uncle Willie? Isn't her name Helen Naomi Salomon, and isn't Naomi a Jewish name?"

"That's different, dear," my mother replied.

"What's different? And why does Emily and her family being Jewish matter? You've always been so proud that you and I have never been christened, that we have no religion."

Silence.

I was confused and indignant about this unfair slight to my new friend. All I knew about religion was that we had none. I didn't know what it meant to be Jewish other than Hitler had killed millions of Jews, which had been wrong, and so how could there be anything bad about being Jewish? I liked Emily and was not to be dissuaded from pursuing our friendship.

Second on my list of sixth grade achievements was to get into as much trouble at school as the system would tolerate. My attention span was lousy, as was my attitude. I knew I wasn't stupid, but I felt dense, thick, as though my mind was filled with a viscous syrup. I couldn't make myself perform as others seemed able to do. I was never elected even to the lowest positions in Self Government, and I was the last to be chosen for team sports. I cheated. I stole, sometimes from my mother or friends, sometimes from neighborhood shops. I lied and forged excuses to get out of gym, study hall, even to leave school early. My sins gave me no pleasure. I was riddled with guilt.

One afternoon, early in the spring of sixth grade, my mother came back from the office much earlier than usual. She called me into her bedroom and closed the double doors.

"I was at school today," she announced. My mother at school? She never, ever came to school, and on the few occasions where parents were invited to watch their children perform, she was always late.

"Miss Basinger asked me to come in," she continued. "She wanted to have a talk with me." Miss (Anne) Basinger was the head of the Middle School. She was very tall and wore her long dark hair scraped back from her round face into a severe French twist. Despite her authority, her smile, defined by bright red lipstick, was kindly. And unlike Miss Mitchell and Miss Carling (and many other members of our faculty), Miss Basinger didn't dress as though she wished to be

Part I: Brearley Girl

a man. Though she, too, wore suits and tailored dresses and fairly sensible shoes, hers seemed slightly stylish. And she told funny stories in Assembly about a fictional Brearley girl called Pickle, who was always getting into trouble. So far I had not had a direct run-in with her, but she was formidable in demeanor and I knew she was a force to be reckoned with.

"Miss Basinger told me that you have been acting up." My mother continued, "She told me about your stealing, and forging excuses, and your disruptive behavior in class." I reddened with shame. How come Miss Basinger knew all this and hadn't called me in or kicked me out?

"I had no idea all this had been going on," my mother continued.

Of course you didn't, Ma. You have no idea about anything that I care about or that hurts me or how miserable I am. I said nothing.

"Miss Basinger said that she and the school felt that addressing these transgressions was the school's responsibility, not the parents'. However, Miss Basinger wanted me to be at least aware of what is going on in your life at school in the event that I could be of help."

The school was willing to take responsibility for my rotten behavior and was not suggesting that my mother punish me? Was that what Miss Basinger was saying to my mother?

This conversation had an extraordinary effect on me. Brearley and Miss Basinger were willing to take the heat for me? Why? Never mind why. I had to do something to prove myself worthy of their belief in me. Somehow I had to try harder. Somehow I had to stop cheating, stealing, and lying, and try to fit in.

Several years later, I told my mother how much her conversation with Miss Basinger had meant to me. I asked her then what Miss Basinger had actually discussed with her. It was that Howie had been due to come to New York and to see me for the first time in two years, and at school I had been overexcited and out of control in anticipation. Then, when he cancelled the visit, I had become so devastated that I fell apart to the point that my teachers could not contain me. Miss Basinger had wanted my mother to know what effect Howie's impending visit and its subsequent cancellation had had on me and to encourage her to give me more support during such times. That was it.

My turnaround took years; but Miss Basinger started the ball rolling.

3. First Flights

CODY, WYOMING — JULY 1952

SS Andrea Doria, *after her 1953 maiden voyage.*

At last, when I protested against going to summer camp for the seventh consecutive year, my mother relented. She arranged for us to go to Deer Creek, a small dude ranch outside of Cody, Wyoming, for the month of July. My mother had grown up riding and seemed to be looking forward to the trip. In another stroke of good fortune, Howie had finally resurfaced. He invited me to come sailing with him for the first three weeks in August, and my mother consented.

Deer Creek, high up in the Shoshone Valley, was a working ranch of 1,000 acres belonging to the former actress Hope Williams—more ranch-ranch than dude ranch. Life at Deer Creek was distinctly Western in character. It was modest and utterly satisfying. Two girls there were also from the east: Daphne Ryan, two years younger than me and an excellent rider, with whom I spent most of my days, and Bocarra Legendre, a year or so older, exotically southern with a sensuous, husky voice and a fully developed figure. (At just twelve, I still had the body of a board with an unattractive bulge at the stomach – the result of trying to gain weight by eating an excess of chocolate pudding). Bo was there with her English governess, Miss Evans, and was obsessed with boys. She was the most fun in the evening, when we compared crushes on the wranglers.

Daphne and I rode freely and unsupervised throughout the day, returning only for a quick lunch. Then we unwrapped our reins from the hitching post and were off again, crisscrossing the Shoshone River, and—thanks to Daphne's familiarity with the riverbed—always avoiding the quicksand. We rode high into the mountains along narrow precipices and galloped home through fields of tumbleweed.

There was quite a social life for adults in that valley and occasionally my mother rode out to a nearby ranch in the valley for drinks and dinner. One night she was late to come home. Even though I didn't yet know about the potential perils of drink, I was worried; I had no idea where she could be or how she could be so late. She finally appeared, soaking and disheveled, although the moonlit night was clear. She had wanted to cross the river at what she thought was the usual ford, and she believed she could see her way in the moonlight. Silver, her horse, kept balking, but she rode well and so coaxed him on into the river against his better instinct. Suddenly his haunches dropped below the surface of the water and into a bed of quicksand. She knew not to dismount or she would go down as well. She had to act fast, so she threw herself high onto his neck—his forelegs were on sound ground—and spurred him on to pull them both out of the river. She didn't go out at night after that. In fact, claiming some need to go yet again to Europe on business, my mother cut a deal with Bo's Miss Evans to look after both Bo and me and to get me on the train to Chicago to meet Howie at the end of the month. This time I didn't mind her taking off.

Part I: Brearley Girl

CHICAGO — AUGUST 1952

I was beside myself with excitement getting off the train from Denver. Howie's brother, my Uncle Sinc, met me and took me home to his apartment on Delaware Place, where I was greeted warmly by my Aunt Lis and my four younger first cousins, two of whom I had never met. Howie soon arrived and wrapped me in a big bear hug, as though we'd never been apart. The next morning, he collected me and drove us in his latest convertible to the marina where he kept his brand new yawl, *Stone Horse Light*. There we were joined by Howie's psychiatrist Jules Masserman, Jules's wife Christine, and Cissie McLeod, another of Jules' patients. Cissie was a glitzy divorcée who was just finishing her residency in psychiatry and whom Jules hoped Howie might help in some way. We soon set sail heading north on Lake Michigan, through the Straits of Mackinaw and into Lake Huron. Neither the Massermans nor Cissie had children, but each was lovely to me, and Howie was even more warm and embracing than I had remembered. Underway I met Bear Bear Armstrong Bear, the first and most important of Howie's stuffed bears, which my mother had apparently given to Howie in my name years before.

Howie was anxious to teach me the rudiments of sailing and navigation, and I was excited to learn. He named me his First Mate. The skies were cerulean blue, the breezes light and the clear fresh water sparkled in the sun. I took instantly to life on the water. Sailing in and around the barely populated pine-clad islands of Lake Huron's North Channel, and exploring little towns like Little Current was magical. I was hooked.

We made plans to sail again the following summer. Howie, then just forty, made me feel funny, smart and feminine - despite my still having the body of a boy. For the first time I felt kin to someone and treasured in a way my mother never managed to convey, however much she tried. Even to my twelve-year-old mind it seemed unfair that for the past five years she had done all the work of taking care of me and keeping a roof over our heads, and then, when it suited him, Howie appeared and stole the show.

NEW YORK — SEPTEMBER 1952

My mother returned from her time in Europe with yet another load of gorgeous clothes. While I was proud of her being so well dressed, I didn't understand why we were too poor for me to have ballet lessons or a piano to practice on, but we could have a special seamstress, Florence, come in on alternating Saturdays to take care of her clothes. My mother told me they were an investment and she needed Florence to maintain and protect the investment. In fairness to my mother, she did manage to sell some of her dresses to finance newer replacements. Then almost a decade later, when going twice yearly to the collections in Paris was no longer required as American couture was coming into its own, she donated much of her inventory to the costume collections of the Brooklyn Museum and the Metropolitan, where they were gratefully accepted.

While I hated my mother's trips abroad and the painful anxiety I felt in her absence, I adored the clothes themselves, and I especially loved helping my mother dress to go out in the evening. The fabrics were soft and sensuous. There were linings and inner linings, each with its own set of fastening devices. All the layers were perfectly stitched, hemmed, and seamed and invisibly connected to one another. The clothes were constructed with the assumption that the wearer would have a maid to hook and snap her in at the start of the evening and presumably someone to unhook and unsnap her on her return. Maybe this was a man's job. I was generally asleep when my mother came home from these affairs, so I am not sure how she managed. As far as I knew, she had had no serious admirer since she showed MR the door in the spring of 1948.

In seventh grade, Marilla and I were reunited in the same homeroom and in the same section after four years of separation. Once again I was in her thrall. Marilla, jock that she was, was also a bully. I was simply a cut-up. But the combination was lethal. We (and others) were particularly cruel to a new and very green young history teacher, Miss Sheila Biddle, who had come to teach at Brearley on graduating from Vassar. Miss Biddle would be going on about Caesar and the glory of Rome, or Hannibal and the elephants crossing the Alps, and we'd start humming and then launching wads of paper using tiny slingshots made of bent paper clips and rubber bands. I was lucky enough to meet Miss Biddle decades later, and like a recovering alcoholic seeking to make amends to those damaged by his or her actions while under the influence, literally took to my knees and begged her to accept my apologies for my appalling behavior. She did so with grace.

Each spring, the seventh graders put on a drastically cut version of a Gilbert and Sullivan operetta. Our year it was to be *Iolanthe*. Miss Gladys Bowen, another of Brearley's androgynous teachers, was in charge. I was to be the Lord Chancellor. I couldn't believe I had been cast in a major role! It was my first Brearley success and the beginning of my long attraction to the theatre. Best of all, my mother came to the performance and was on time!

I was no longer one of the smallest in the class, though I was still small for a Lord Chancellor. I had cleared five feet and was at last close to average height. Although my body showed no sign of impending womanhood, thanks to the growth spurt and my theatrical success, I felt less pathetic physically. Too bad there was no comparable scholastic growth.

That spring, my mother asked me if I would like to go to Europe in August. What kind of question was that? My mother felt it important that my first voyage to Europe should be by ship so I would appreciate the vastness of the ocean that lay between our two continents. She booked us a first-class cabin on the *Andrea Doria* departing New York, August 18, 1953, and arriving in Genoa nine days later, with stops in the Azores and in Naples. My mother never travelled less than first-class, although our cozy New York living accommodations were closer to steerage.

At the beginning of the summer I flew to Chicago to participate briefly in Howie's life on land and to meet his new girlfriend, Barbara Durbin, and her son John, one year my junior; after that we were to go sailing. While Howie was at work, Barbara invited me to spend a few days at their house in Wayne, Illinois, just west of Chicago. There, with Barbara and Johnny, living the rhythm of their semi-rural life, I felt at ease and at home in a way I never had in New York. When the weekend arrived, after a tearful goodbye to Barbara and Johnny, Howie and I drove north through Wisconsin to Sturgeon Bay, where he was keeping *Stone Horse*. He hadn't yet settled on a destination for the summer's cruise. But on the drive north, Howie went on about his distaste for the Great Lakes—its fresh water, dreary coast lines, and choppy seas.

The next morning, our first on board, he said, "Well, Poochwoman," (I never knew from whence this nickname came), "what about you and I sail to Edgartown this summer? What do you think?"

That spring, he had had an operation on a slipped disk, prior to which Barbara told me that he had lived on masses of aspirin to kill the pain. His back was still weak, he was not in great shape, and I was a wimpy undeveloped girl of thirteen. As the crow flies, Edgartown was 1,000 miles away, on Martha's Vineyard, off the coast Massachusetts.

"Sure, let's go," I replied without hesitation.

To get there on schedule, we had to make approximately fifty miles a day. Mostly we motored. Thirteen tons of steel is a lot to push through the water. However, for the most part, the seas were quiet, the daily run was tranquil and the harbors in which we moored or anchored were picturesque. In the evenings we cooked on the Primus stove. I loved learning to cook, because it was something my mother couldn't do. We ate well and cranked up Howie's portable record player. Bach was king. Howie reveled in the artistry of Wanda Landowska playing the *Well-Tempered Clavier* and practiced the fingering for the same preludes and fugues on the silent keyboard, which he slipped into leather straps affixed to the underside of the folding table in the main cabin. Bach's *Mass in B Minor* and *St. Matthew Passion* came next, followed by Brahms' *A German Requiem*, Beethoven's *Missa Solemnis* and *Symphonies 3, 5 and 9*, Mozart's *Requiem* and *Coronation Mass*, Schubert's *Mass in E-minor*, Prokofiev's *Classical Symphony* and more. There were only so many record albums you could fit on a small sailboat. I would tell him about listening to Bartok, Poulenc, Ravel, and Hindemith with my mother. He wasn't so interested in French anything.

"What about Tchaikovsky and Rachmaninoff?" I asked.

"Kid's stuff," Howie replied. Okay. I was a kid and would have to listen to those composers on my own at home, which I did.

We stopped in Buffalo and had our masts hauled out and lashed to sawhorses on the deck, in preparation for the very low bridges of the Erie Canal. As we headed under power out of Buffalo and north along the east branch of the Niagara River, Howie was below fixing breakfast and I was at the helm, chart in hand, expecting some huge green interstate road sign to mark the entrance to the Erie Canal. Howie, looking out through the hatch into the cockpit, noticed a shift in the direction of the sun. We had been moving northeast at first, and then the river turned and we were moving north northwest. He hauled himself up the ladder in the companionway and took a look at the shore, which was going by much faster than it had been. "Jesus Christ, we are really moving. Are you sure we haven't passed the entrance?"

"No, no," I said, referring to the chart, "It looks like—"

He grabbed the chart and yelled, "I don't give a flying fart what it looks like! Turn this fucking boat around, before we sail straight over Niagara Falls!" I jammed the big oak tiller to port and swung her bow around to starboard. Only by gunning the engine to full throttle were we able to make way against the current. Very slowly, we inched back against the western shore of Grand Island. Back eddies of current swirled around us. According to the chart, the entrance to the canal should have been just south of Tonawanda Island on the east side of the river. And there it was. There was no sign because the west end of the Erie Canal is a natural waterway called Tonawanda Creek. Who knew?

We arrived safely in Edgartown in mid-August of 1953. I used the phone at my grandfather's cabin high on a bluff on the Chappaquiddick side of Edgartown Harbor to connect with another school friend, Lucinda (Cindy) Childs, whose family summered in Edgartown and with whom I had become friendly over the winter. They invited us to dinner, and there my father met Cindy's father, also an MD but older (and more conservative) than Howie, and Cindy's stunning mother, Lucinda, Sr. We took Cindy and Lucinda out for a day sail. Cindy loved the boat and agreed to come with us for a longer sail the following summer. My father couldn't take his eyes off Lucinda. She was tall, literate, and articulate. And she was

Part I: Brearley Girl

trim enough to wear a two-piece bathing suit, which was unheard of in those days. She had a shock of wavy, prematurely white hair on top of a round face, with high cheekbones and a wall-to-wall smile. Lucinda clearly took to Howie as well. If anything happened between them, it was not for Cindy or me to know.

I left Howie and the boat in Edgartown and returned to New York in the midst of a typical high summer heat wave. I had the last of the shots that were required for re-entry from Europe: three typhoid shots, one typhus, one tetanus, and one smallpox vaccination in total. I packed and we boarded the *Andrea Doria*, as scheduled, on August 18, 1953.

Thereupon began my love affair with Italy and all things Italian.

The *Andrea Doria* was still sparkling with newness after her maiden voyage in January of that year. She and her sister ship, the *Cristoforo Colombo*, had been commissioned in the early 1950s by the Italian Line to show the world not only that Italy and its economy had recovered from World War II, but also that Italy was poised to take the lead in luxury transoceanic travel and in contemporary interior and industrial design. Her interiors were by the Milanese architect, Giulio Minoletti, with finishes, fabrics, lighting, and furniture hot off the press. She was relatively small, not especially fast, and had a high crew-to-passenger ratio. Like the *Titanic*, she had a double hull and had been designed for maximum safety.

I knew none of this when we boarded in the summer heat, but I saw that the *Andrea Doria* was long and sleek, and soon discovered that each lounge, bar, restaurant, staircase, passageway, and stateroom was more stunning than the one before. Hers was the most elegant interior environment that I had ever experienced, not that at age thirteen I had had much to compare it with. But I knew, even then, that if making something like this ship could be the work of an architect, that's what I wanted to be. Steaming out of New York Harbor past Miss Liberty and through the Narrows to the open sea was fully as dramatic as my mother had promised. The ship wasn't full because it was the end of summer. No one minded my exploring her every quarter in all three classes.

Everything about the passage was beyond expectation, not just the spectacular modernity of the design, but the sun, sea air, three swimming pools, our particular cabin, food, a full dress dinner with the captain, and the first sight of the Azores on the horizon, followed a day later by passing under the shadow of the giant Rock of Gibraltar as we entered the Mediterranean. The ship was to stop for a full day in Naples before heading north to her home port, Genoa, where we were to disembark.

My mother had an Italian friend in New York whom I knew as Hedy Clark. Just under five feet tall, even in platform heels, she was a showy dresser and had a big head of short curls in the color of the day. Her eyes twinkled behind sequined harlequin glasses, and her grin seemed to take up most of her face. Her accent was more Polish than Italian and she was never too clear about where she hailed from. Hedy had a huge heart and massive chutzpah. Though married to writer Delbert Clark, Hedy persuaded her first husband, Count Goffredo Giusti, to meet my mother and me when we landed in Naples, and to take us to lunch and a tour of the city, which, God knows why, he did.

Two days later we landed in Genoa and travelled by taxi to Rapallo, where we were met by another Italian man, a thin wiry lawyer, who had also been assigned by Hedy to take us to lunch and show us around. The lunch was in a simple restaurant. I was bored by the conversation: two lawyers being deeply courteous to one another comparing their respective practices in a stilted mix of English and French. But the main course was very thin sheets of white pasta, slightly larger than squares of American cheese, with a thin coating of oil and chopped herbs: simple, delicate, and delicious. I thought it was called lasagna. For years and years, I would order lasagna in Italian restaurants and out would come a massive plate of thick pasta, layered with meat sauce and ricotta cheese, all smothered in tomato sauce. No, that is not it, I would insist. Some fifteen years later, I prepared a pasta from a new cookbook to serve to friends and had a Proustian moment when I tasted the first bite of pesto alla Genovese, whose thin lasagna was the vehicle for the taste I had craved for so long.

When the lunch in Rapallo finally came to an end, my mother and I piled into another taxi with our luggage and headed for Santa Margherita Ligure, just down the coast from Rapallo. She apologized for failing to get us into a hotel in Portofino at the end of the point. Santa Margherita apparently was slightly tackier than Portofino, but I loved tacky. There was nothing about Santa Margherita that I didn't love: the hotel, the cafes (even Coca Cola without ice, with just a slice of lemon), the little shops with beaded curtains at the entrance, to provide shade from the blazing sun, the espadrilles, the wooden clogs with Cuban heels and leather straps, the scruffy pebbled beach across the road. Even the deafening noise of the Vespas weaving through the traffic and careening around the corners day and night was a joy. I loved the sound and sense of the language and took pride in learning new words every day. This Italian thing, I wanted to make it mine.

After far too few days we boarded a train from Genoa to Venice, disembarked and took a gondola to the Hotel Gritti, where we met up with Jane Carey, another of my mother's friends from New York, and Jane's black mid-sized poodle, Carino. I should have felt blessed to stay at the Gritti Palace and should have been enthralled by Venice, but I wasn't because the Gritti was old and musty (sort of like Jane), the water was dirty, and there was too much Jane and not enough of my mother.

My mother, with her passion for fine clothes, had developed a fixation about buying me my first "important dress." It was to be Fortuny silk, a specialty of Venice. As far as I could understand, a Fortuny silk dress was a large piece of very soft silk, somehow permanently pressed into tiny quarter-inch pleats, then sewn into a one-size-fits-all, sack-like shape, and stored all twisted up on itself like a skein of wool. With the help of a few cords or sashes, you adjusted the folds and were instantly transformed into a Greco-Roman goddess. My mother enlisted Jane's help to find a store with antique Fortuny dresses, one of which she hoped to procure to adorn my curveless body. We spent half a day going by boat to an ancient warehouse in one of the outer islands of the lagoon in search of this treasure. When we got there, a withered, toothless woman clad in black pulled out an ancient trunk covered in dust, opened it and there they were: wrapped in sheets of disintegrating waxed tissue, ten or twelve of these Fortuny dresses in various earthen colors dating from the 1920s—just what a flat-chested thirteen-year-old would want to wear to impress her friends at her class dance! They were even more costly than my mother had imagined and even she had to admit that they failed to transform me into a goddess.

We drove with Jane Carey and Carino from Venice to Rome, stopping en route to see the sights of Umbria and Tuscany. In Rome, my mother met Jane's dear friends, the Count and Countess Bonmartini. Had I been a different kid, this drive through the center of Italy with someone as knowledgeable and conversant in Italian as Jane would have been wondrous. But to me, it was yet another trip with my mother and a friend up front chatting away and me alone in back with the dog and feeling carsick.

Part I: Brearley Girl

From Rome, we flew to England to visit Shirley (my mother's third cousin) and Vernon Simmonds, to whom we were related through my mother's Grannie, Helen Naomi Salomon. The Simmonds lived in the New Forest, between Southampton and Bournemouth. Within the New Forest ponies, cattle, and some pigs run free across the moors and through the woods. They stand along the roadsides because there the odor of the asphalt protects them from the flies. Shirley and Vernon had a dairy farm in the village of Burley. At the mouth of the driveway into their farm, as at the entrance to all houses, village shops, and pubs in the New Forest, there are cattle grates to protect the perfectly manicured lawns and resplendent gardens, however tiny, from the insatiable appetite of the animals.

My brief stay at Manor Farm was almost like coming home. I was warmly embraced by Shirley, Vernon, their daughter Anthia, Shirley's old nanny Vera (who still worked for the family), and even by the dairyman's wife, Mrs. Baker. I got to ride across those moors and through those woods with my cousin Anthia, five years my junior but an accomplished rider. For me, at thirteen, it was heaven, but it was not so glorious for my mother. She was never much of an Anglophile and was soon bored by the rural provinciality and Vernon and Shirley's ultra-conservative politics, of which I was then unaware. It all ended too soon for me.

My mother was staying on in Europe for a few more weeks for "business," so I had to fly back to New York and start school on my own. Transatlantic flying was more of a production then than it is now. On the flight back from London, we got almost halfway across the leg from Iceland to Gander when one of the four engines conked out and we had to return to Iceland for repairs. Finally, we took off again. After landing in Gander hours later, we waited many more hours for a plane that could take us to New York. By the time we landed at Idlewild, I felt very small, anxious, and alone—yet again.

Part 2.
Sexed

4. SEXED

SEPTEMBER 1953

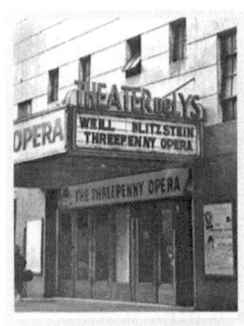
Theater de Lys on Christopher Street, Greenwich Village, 1955.

"Girls don't think about sex as much as boys." If that were true, then I was an anomaly even before reaching puberty. Starting at age ten, I had one crush after another on various boys. For a whole year of weekends, when I was about twelve, Tracy Coudert and I would crawl into his bed in the morning. We would wrap our arms around each other and we would gently and silently rub against one another, fully clothed, for close to an hour. There was no climax. It just felt warm and cozy. After we felt rubbed out, without a word, I would return to my room, which opened onto his, and shut the door. We would dress for the day and meet again downstairs for breakfast without the slightest acknowledgment of our earlier meeting.

In seventh grade, Camilla Cahill brought in an erotic poem, "This is My Beloved," which she had filched from the bedroom of her sexy twenty-five-year-old half-brother. Although explicit and titillating, the poem was tender and lyrical—a sweet introduction to the joys of romantic love and sex, which were years away.

Marilla and I more than once acted out what we imagined to be the preliminaries to having sex. But I don't remember either of us finding excitement or satisfaction in these efforts, although her parents got plenty worked up when they retrieved from their local drugstore a packet of photos developed from film we had taken of our flat and hairless bodies in ill-fitting bras stuffed with tissue and white cotton briefs rolled down to pass for G-strings.

Like most preteens and young teenagers (and many adults), I had no idea what to do with the waves of feelings that rolled over me nor how to process them. Although my mother had described the sex act to me (and it had sounded revolting at the time), and we'd had the requisite sex-ed class in sixth grade, sex still seemed remote even as we boys and girls danced cheek to cheek and hip to groin at the Christmas and spring dances that we all attended.

My academic performance at Brearley remained substandard. I recall agonizing over another "creative" writing assignment and going to my mother in despair. I couldn't bear the prospect of writing another composition and seeing another "Fair"—accompanied by scathing comments in red describing my ineptitude—at the top of the page. Brearley didn't give out As, Bs, and Cs. We had Very Good, Good, Fair, Passing, and Failing. I lived in the Land of Fair. My mother, encouraging me, cited the old chestnut, "Write about what you know."

"Like what? Everything I know is so boring."

"What about describing our neighborhood? Elliot Paul wrote charming stories about the *quartier*..." my mother loved dropping French words into ordinary speech—"where he lived in Paris. They were just descriptions, but they were little jewels."

"You think I could do the same thing about where we live?"

"Why not? Give it a try," she said. So I haltingly ground out "62nd and Lex. (with apologies to Elliot Paul)," in which I described what went on in the shops at the four corners of 62nd Street and Lexington Avenue. I got my first "Good." (Good equaled B. Very Goods were rare at Brearley.) More than half a century later, although the area is now a posh suburb of Bloomingdale's, no high-rises have replaced the original buildings on those four corners. "62nd and Lex." lives on.

By eighth grade, Marilla was gone. The van Beurens had decided that she was too old to have a governess, but were unprepared to deal with her themselves. So they sent Marilla off to boarding school and sent Miss Schill back to Switzerland. Losing Miss Schill broke Marilla. She developed a massive eating disorder—a combination of anorexia and bulimia—which was to mar the rest of her life. The boarding school wanted no further responsibility for her and sent her home mid-year into the inept and pickled arms of her parents on Park Avenue, and she was tutored privately. She recovered—at least from the breakdown—and returned to Brearley for the last three years of high school. But we weren't close again until after we had both grown up.

My remaining classmates seemed way ahead of me in all aspects of development. They were smarter, more motivated, and more accomplished academically. They were all better at making friends, better at sports, and beginning at least to look like young women. I was sure something was wrong with me. Was I going to be like my Aunt Elizabeth Armstrong and not go through puberty? Would I have to have massive shots of hormones and then grow giant breasts and a beard? Or was I really a boy in some cruel disguise? I didn't want to be a boy, and much as I loved Aunt Elizabeth, I didn't want to be her either.

Part 2: SEXED

My budding friendship with Linda Livingston, whose parents were becoming friends with my mother, made eighth grade feel better. Linda was the youngest of three very tall sisters. Big Lorna, their mother, stood over six feet in her Capezio flats. Big Lorna had a warm face and a husky laugh (thanks to cigarettes and booze), but she could be pretty volatile. My mother told me that, like my dreaded grandfather, Lorna had had a colostomy. But she didn't wear a bag. She had a patch over a hole in her stomach and flushed herself out from time to time. To me, this made Big Lorna all the more fascinating.

The Livingstons had a big sprawling apartment on East End Avenue overlooking the river, just a few blocks from school, and an even bigger, more sprawling Shingle Style house surrounded by potato fields in Wainscot, a once-sleepy village just west of East Hampton, where I spent several cozy winter weekends and a wonderful Easter devoid of religion but full of Easter eggs, chocolate bunnies, and jelly beans.

In early May of eighth grade, my mother left again for Europe and the Middle East, and I was once more bereft. Soon after my fourteenth birthday, a tell-tale spot of dark red appeared on my underpants. I was female after all.

Shortly after school ended in mid-June of 1954, I took another wretched transatlantic flight on my own to meet my mother in Rome. When I finally arrived, she whisked us off to the home of her new friends, Count and Countess Bonmartini, whom she had met through Jane Carey, her friend with the poodle. The apartment, which seemed to be a portion of a palazzo, was shrouded in the shadows of the fading twilight. A servant led us through the public rooms, which were lined with tapestries and large paintings of indeterminate subject matter. Heavy gilded furniture hugged the perimeter. We reached a row of high French doors covered with sheer curtains billowing in the soft evening breeze, and were shown onto an enormous terrace seemingly cantilevered out over the brilliantly illuminated Roman Forum. At the center of this terrace was a cluster of the Bonmartinis' friends and family who were gathered to meet and welcome my mother and her weary daughter. Among them was Francesco Bonmartini, their oldest son, who was somewhere between my mother and me in age and working in New York. I had met him on several occasions, as he was quite taken with my mother despite the difference in their ages. I was glad to see a familiar face in this unfamiliar but dazzling setting.

We didn't go to any museums in Rome. Instead, we spent our days visiting contemporary art galleries along the Via Sistina and Via Gregoriana, while my mother bought several small paintings of mournful-looking clowns and nuns on horseback that I admired for their irreverence. At the bottom of the Spanish Steps and slightly to the left, if you were looking up, was the house of the Italian couturier Mingolini Guggenheim. The very elegant, effeminate, and obsequious Carlo Guggenheim was a client of my mother's and wanted to pay her fees in clothes, not cash. Although my mother had accepted a tailored skirt by the American couturier Charles James as payment in kind for legal services, my mother would rarely wear anything that wasn't French, so she brought me in to Mingolini Guggenheim to see if there was anything by way of formal evening dresses in their collection that might suit me and my barely-feminine body.

The lines and fabrics of Mingolini Guggenheim's clothes were original, luxurious, and in keeping with the design standards I had acquired, thanks to my familiarity with my mother's clothes. My classmates and I were starting to go to formal dances. I could easily see the advantages of not wearing the kind of flouncy multilayered strapless tulle "formal" that made most of us look like potatoes on end. So I was excited about possibly having my own Mingolini Guggenheim evening dress, a definite step up from the Fortuny number that I had escaped the year before.

Signor Guggenheim decided that *il modello* best suited to my youth and figure was a two-part construction with a very full heavy, white faille, ballet-length skirt topped with a ruched (gathered) deep shocking pink chiffon bodice that was strapless on one side and went over the other shoulder. Having these materials draped over me and pinned in place was almost erotic. I was no longer a board on sticks with a bulge at the belly. I was Ava Gardner, dark and exotic, seductive and seducible.

Over the next four years, Mingolini Guggenheim churned out another four dresses for me, in payment of fees owed to my mother, each of which was more original and elegant than the last. My favorite was an almost Elizabethan cocktail dress in a heavy forest green satin with elbow length sleeves, a low scooped neck front and back, and a full skirt, trimmed with bands of two-inch-wide black velvet ribbon edged in tiny black jet beads. My next favorite was a basic black sleeveless cocktail dress in black crepe, with a boat neck in front that dipped to a V in the back, gathered front and back just below the bustline in vertical pleats to just below the waist and then released to fall into a "harem" balloon skirt ending just below the knee. My mother always talked about the importance of having a "little black dress." This was mine.

These dresses didn't make me feel that I fit in with my classmates any better than I had before, but by then, that was no longer my goal.

After Rome, we went to Paris. I finally got to stay at the Hotel Plaza Athenée and have drinks and dinner with my mother's Parisian friends at the Art Deco Relais on the corner. Better still, we met up with Linda Livingston and her mother, Big Lorna, for lunch on the Bateau Mouche. It was a welcome change to have a friend my own age to spend time with abroad. One afternoon, out on our own, at a kiosk near the Étoile, Linda and I bought a small portfolio of photos of nude women. We thought this was very hot stuff and spent hours in my mother's and my hotel room while my mother was elsewhere, poring over our new treasures in hopes that eventually we would also be so sexy and desirable.

One sunny morning in Paris, my mother's underwear lady came at the appointed hour to the door of our hotel room with suitcases containing soft velveteen cases of silk, satin, and crepe undergarments in an array of pastel colors, navy and black, and muted tones of taupe. All were trimmed with what had to be the life's work of an entire battalion of lacemaking nuns in Belgium. There were full slips, half slips, garter belts, brassieres with and without underwires, panties constructed like short tennis skirts, nightgowns, negligees, peignoirs, and possibly even corsets—but my mother wasn't into foundation garments. She was slender and didn't need them.

"Oui, Madam, of course we can do this canary yellow slip with the ivory lace that you admired on the black slip *là-bas ... et bien sur*, Madam, we can make the culottes and brassiere to match. ... *Et puis*, the usual also in the black and pale rose? ... *Certainement*."

Ka-ching, ka-ching!

Later that day, after lunch at the Relais with my mother's friend Odile Raymond, we went across the street to Maison Dior to take in the fall collection. Mlle. Suzanne, my mother's *vendeuse* (saleswoman), was waiting for us at the door wearing a hungry look. After the collection was shown, I sat with my mother and Mlle. Suzanne while they decided what my mother would order—which day dresses, suits, coat and/or evening dresses, and in what fabric, weight, texture, and color.

Part 2: SEXED

"And would there be any particular modifications required to suit Madam's specific requirements? ... *Je suis d'accord*, a leather belt would be better than a fabric belt for the country ... and of course, Madam always prefers a side zipper where possible... *Bien sur, Madam, je comprends tous tres bien.*" Then came the discussion of the bill, and the special discount because Madam was such a good customer of Dior.

Deep pocket ka-ching, ka-ching.

I had trouble reconciling all this expenditure with the modesty of our life in New York and my mother's constant complaints about not earning enough despite how hard she worked. Of course I knew about the Paris clothes, the fancy undergarments, the Dior and Delman shoes, and the Hermes handbags. But before this trip to Paris, I hadn't given much thought to how these items found their way to our fourth floor walk-up. Now I knew. On the one hand, I was confused, jealous, even angry. On the other, I marveled at it all and was proud of my mother for her smarts (which cost us nothing), for her elegance (which cost a lot), and for her setting both our sights so high.

We sailed home at the end of July on the *Ile de France*. However stately and grand, the boat had none of the allure of the *Andrea Doria*, at least not for me. I recognized a girl from the class below me at Brearley, amongst the passengers. Thanks to us, her father and my mother occasionally dined together and she and I became good friends, at least for the length of the passage—good enough that I felt comfortable showing her my Paris photos of nude women in exchange for which she not only showed me but gave me for safekeeping her contraband copy of *Fanny Hill,* which either she or her father had procured in Paris. In the still puritanical '50s, *Fanny Hill* was outlawed in the U.S. For all my lustiness, because the book was new and forbidden stuff, I was afraid to cut the pages. So when my mother found it amongst my books a year later, and asked how I had come by it, I had to confess that I had never even opened it.

Back in New York, after my third chunk of summer cruising with my father, and after having survived Hurricane Carol, I was getting serious about classical music. I went almost every day after school to a small record shop in a basement storefront on Lexington Avenue between 64th and 65th, owned and named for Mr. Marconi, an elegant and slightly older man with a trim handlebar moustache. His younger employees knew I was hooked on classical music. They would routinely tempt me with a new LP, a new composer, a new work. I would take the LP to one of their listening booths, fall in love with it, and want to take it home. But they were also cognizant of my financial limitations and would steer me towards iterations on unknown labels, conducted and/or performed by equally unknown musicians. So I began to build up a substantial record collection of fourth- and fifth-rate recordings. I knew and loved them all. Thanks to Marconi Records, I got through all the symphonies and piano concerti of Tchaikovsky, Rachmaninoff, and Grieg without my father or mother's criticism, and soon moved on.

In the fall of ninth grade, my mother got us tickets to a new production of Kurt Weill's *The Threepenny Opera*, starring Weill's widow, Lotte Lenya, in the role of Jenny at the Theatre de Lys in Greenwich Village. Over one of our Sunday suppers of cold meat and salad on the living room floor, my mother told me that *The Threepenny Opera*, written in the late '20s, was based on an eighteenth-century play, *The Beggar's Opera*. Bertholdt Brecht's text had been newly translated by the composer and librettist, Marc Blitzstein. She insisted that I would love it. I insisted I would not.
Wrong.

I was instantly hooked on the depravity of the setting, the rawness of the text, and the dissonance of the music. I memorized every word of every song and felt the cast members were my intimate friends. With her lyric soprano, Jo Sullivan (Loesser) was the personification of innocence wronged, in contrast to the powerful Beatrice Arthur, who delivered a throaty version of "Barbara Song." Scott Merrill was a handsome, smarmy Mack the Knife, as was Jerry Ohrbach in the same role in a later revival. Lotte Lenya, with her carrot-red hair, high-pitched metallic vibrato, and not-so-pretty face, was my heroine. Her husband Kurt Weill had died five years earlier, but now, in her mid-fifties, dressed as a hooker in a pink satin bodice trimmed in black jet, a skirt slit up the side, and fishnet stockings, here she was, belting out his raunchy songs and keeping his spirit alive. I went twice more on my own to the original production at the Theatre de Lys and to every revival I could find thereafter. I bought records of Lotte Lenya singing Weill's songs in German and memorized them as well.

Du hast kein Herz, Johnny	*You have no heart, Johnny*
Du bist ein Schuft, Johnny	*You are a heel, Johnny.*
Du gehst jetzt weg, Johnny,	*You are leaving now, Johnny.*
Sag mir den Grund.	*Tell me why.*
Ich liebe dich doch, Johnny	*I love you so, Johnny.*
Wie am ersten Tag, Johnny	*Like on that first day, Johnny.*
Nimm die Pfeife aus dem Maul,	*Take that pipe out of your face,*
du Hund.	*you dog.*

This verse from "Surabaya Johnny," remains my only German.

The Threepenny Opera was not standard fare for a Brearley ninth-grade theatre-goer, but I didn't care. It was mine. While my report cards continued to say that I was not living up to my potential, I was becoming seriously interested in the world beyond my own, an interest fed by the music I listened to and the many foreign movies my mother insisted we attend. The film that really hit home was *Domani e Troppo Tardi* (*Tomorrow is Too Late*) directed by Leonide Moguy and starring Anna Maria Pierangeli, later known as just Pier Angeli. It was about Franco and Mirella, students at a strict boarding school. Neither could go home for the summer holidays, and so they stayed on at the school for the summer recess, and bit by bit, fell in love. They were off somewhere on their own when a storm struck, and they repaired, soaking wet, to a cave for shelter. Franco managed to make a fire and slowly, gently persuaded Mirella to take off her soaking wet shirt and dry it over the fire. They kissed and eventually fell asleep in each other's arms until the storm passed, fully clothed but for the absent shirt. I am not sure how or by whom they were found, but all hell broke loose and it was assumed by the authorities that Franco had taken advantage of Mirella and her reputation, and thus her life was ruined. Mirella tried to commit suicide by throwing herself into a nearby lake, and Franco valiantly rescued both her and her reputation in the end. But the end didn't matter, at least not to me. What moved me was the gentleness of his persuading her to take off her shirt, the tenderness of their kiss, and the sweetness of their love. This was the way I wanted it to be for me. Night after night and year after year, I played that scene over and over in my mind before I fell asleep.

My mother's romantic life was a puzzle to me. Given how intelligent and attractive—almost beautiful—she was, and how she was cherished by her many friends, I didn't understand why she didn't have any serious suitors. A lineup of regulars—attractive and intelligent "bachelors" like Harmon Goldstone, as well as overtly gay men—took my mother to dinner and the theatre, but I was unaware of there being anyone important to her. Given her mix of cutting wit, style, and physical (read: sexual) shyness—which even I, as a teenager, could perceive—I despaired that she'd be forever single and unloved.

However, it seems my mother may have not been quite as shy as I had thought. In the spring of 1954, she fell for a French wine importer from Bordeaux whom she met on one of her myriad trips abroad. Unfortunately, there was a Mme. Vintner, from whom M. Vintner was separated but not divorced. Between the looming presence of Mme. Vintner and the width of the Atlantic, this relationship soon fizzled out, but the experience must have opened some window in the wall she seemed to have erected around a psyche that had been battered both by her father and mine.

In the fall of 1954, my mother received a call from an old friend from her Boston days, Hans Zinsser. Hans's father, the bacteriologist and author of the same name, had been my father's mentor in Boston, and, in his final year at Harvard Medical School, Hans the younger had been my father's student. My mother and Hans hadn't seen one another for twelve or more years. By now, Hans the younger had become a urologist on the Medical Faculty at Cal Tech, and he was in town for a conference. My mother invited him to the apartment for drinks before dinner.

She returned in an altered state. In just a few hours, she had fallen head over heels in love. I had to admit Hans was attractive, plus he had been very nice to me. He was six feet two and very thin, with chiseled Aryan features, pale blue twinkling eyes, and thick stick-straight "pus-colored" (his description) hair parted on the right side. Over dinner, he told my mother he had loved her since they had first met in Boston. At the time, she had been pregnant with me and he was engaged to his future wife, Nancy Drinker, who was very busy flirting with Howie. Hans and Nancy had married soon thereafter, done their respective residencies at Columbia Presbyterian Hospital in New York (hers was in psychiatry), moved to Pasadena, had two children, and set up their respective medical practices. But now they were separated. Seeing my mother again and meeting me (!) had at once rekindled and confirmed his love for my mother and his desire to spend the rest of his life with her. He told my mother he would be in touch with her shortly about his plan for both the short and the long term. And off he went into the night.

Their meeting was a genuine *coup de foudre.*

Hans was already in the process of getting divorced and was seeking full custody of his daughters since their mother had abandoned them to pursue an unorthodox approach to psychotherapy, for which she had lost her medical license. Going forward was going to be tough on both Hans and my mother because he couldn't risk the courts' knowing my mother was in the picture. He had to appear and act the perfect father. So their meetings would have to be infrequent, clandestine, and chaste. Suddenly, my role as the difficult daughter morphed into the difficult daughter-confidante.

Christmas vacation meant it was time for the Christmas dances. Of these, "the Holidays" ("the Hols") were the most exclusive. You had to be recommended and have letters to get in; it was almost like a club. Parents took care of all this. I feigned contempt for a process so snooty and selective, but I went because I liked to dance and there was no other way to meet boys in New York. The next most prestigious dances were "the Get Togethers" ("the Gets"), followed by "the Merry Makers," which had a somewhat broader population base—in other words, Jewish kids attended. I bathed and shaved everywhere, did the best I could to mold my fine, semi-wavy, mouse-brown hair into a pageboy, attached my stockings to

Part 2: Sexed

my garter belt, and slithered my non-Ava-Gardner body into the bipartite Mingolini Guggenheim evening dress, with its full white silk skirt and gathered shocking-pink chiffon top, and zipped it up the side. I did my best to apply eyeshadow and mascara, put on my glasses and my creamy white satin pumps dyed to match the skirt, slipped into a black satin evening coat and long white kid gloves (both borrowed from my mother), and took off with Tracy Coudert for the Merry Makers event in the ballroom of the nearby Hotel Sherry Netherland. As soon as Tracy and I went through the reception line, I was on my own. Tracy wouldn't even be walking me home because I was spending the night with Emily Manheim.

The evening began disastrously. There I was, glasses and all, in my gorgeous Italian dress like no one else's, one shoulder covered and one bare, amid a roomful of contemporaries clad in acres of layered tulle. No one came near me. Midway through the evening I went to the ladies' room and had a serious cry. Much as I wanted to, I couldn't go home. I had to wait for the dance to be over to go home with Emily. When I tired of feeling sorry for myself, I cleaned up my smudged mascara, put my glasses back on, and set out again into the crowd. On my way to my spot against the wall, a boy asked me to dance. I mumbled "Sure," somewhat incredulously and without even looking at him. I figured if I did he might disappear.

"What is your name?" he asked, as we began to dance.

"Leslie Armstrong, but I am called Layo at school and Lale at home. What's yours?"

"Bob Johnston. I am called Johnst. And I will call you Lale."

"Where do you go to school?"

"Andover. And you?"

"Brearley."

That was the drill and it was enough talk for both of us. Johnst was an acceptable dancer, and I couldn't afford to be picky. At least

I was dancing. He had dark curly hair, olive skin, wore glasses even thicker than mine, and was just enough taller than I was to be comfortable. I took off my glasses and held them folded in my left hand, which was just behind his right shoulder. Almost imperceptibly, we drew closer together until we were very, very close. When the music stopped, we disengaged, but continued to hold hands. We looked straight ahead without saying a word, and then, when the music started up again we reengaged and continued to dance just as closely as we possibly could. And so it went for the balance of the evening. We danced with no one else and no one cut in on us or suggested we do otherwise. When the evening was over, we could barely speak to say good night much less make conversation about another meeting. I went off with Emily in a dream state. I had no idea what had happened to me. Once we got to her new apartment on Fifth Avenue, I started babbling to her and her brother, Tony.

"I met this incredible boy, I danced with him and only him for the second half of the evening. I know nothing about him. He knows nothing about me. How will I ever find him and see him again? How can he find me?"

"Relax, Layo. Calm down. It can't be that hard. What was his name?"

"Bob Johnston. He goes to Andover, that's all I know"

Tony chuckled. "Think, Layo, where do I go to school?"

"Cut out the games, Tony, this is serious."

"Andover."

"Andover?"

"Yes, Andover. And Bob Johnston is in my class. Apart from being a bit of a bookworm, he's a nice guy. I think he lives somewhere on Park Avenue, in the 80s."

And so Tony Manheim called Johnst the next morning and told him where and how to call me. Quite soon after, and in the cold grey light of a raw winter afternoon, Johnst and I went for a long walk in Central Park. I was soon freezing except for my left hand, which was warmly enfolded in his. Johnst talked to me of his banker father Oswald, his older bookish brother Oswald, Jr., majoring in English at Yale, and the loss of their Chilean mother who died giving birth to him. He talked about how much he liked to draw and paint, and about e.e. cummings (of whom I had never heard), and I told him of my love of the sea and sailing, and of Brahms and Kurt Weill.

At the end of our walk, we didn't kiss goodbye, but he promised to write from school. Every day after school I would check the mailbox. Finally, there it was, a letter from Andover. My mother had picked up the mail that morning on her way to work and taken it with her as far as the entrance to the subway at 60th Street and Lex. When she saw the envelope from Andover, she walked the two-plus blocks back to the house and left it in the mailbox for me to find when I got home from school. My mother did have her moments.

Johnst promised we would see each other on his next weekend home, which we did. We kissed then, but lightly. That was enough.

He wrote beautiful, poetic letters, and I tried to reciprocate. He gave me two watercolors that he had painted and had framed for my fifteenth birthday, which was only twelve days after his eighteenth. In late May, he sent me a letter in which he said that he loved me. I reread that letter so many times it turned to dust.

There were three other highlights to ninth grade at Brearley. The first was that I had my first article published in *The Beaver*, Brearley's literary magazine. It was my spontaneous response to hearing Ursula Oppens, a seventh-grader, play a particular movement from a Beethoven piano sonata at a school assembly. Ursula was brilliant (and is now a well-known concert pianist), and I was thrilled to see my words and name in print. The second highlight was that we had a new English teacher, Mr. Robert Manson Myers. Mr. Myers was Southern, effeminate, and spoke with a light British accent. He wore natty tweed jackets with elbow patches, and tasteful ties, and carried his books in a green cloth bag as was done at Harvard, where, he let us know, he had been teaching. He wore his strawberry blond hair parted on the side with long bangs *a l'Anglaise* and was constantly flipping his head to keep the hair out of his pale blue eyes. We were reading Chaucer, and he took pains to point out just how sexy *The Nun's Tale* was, and as an aside, he told us about the function of the corncobs in Faulkner's *Sanctuary*, which he recommended as auxiliary reading. Mr. Myers was the proud author of a humorous treatise on English literature, *From Beowulf to Virginia Woolf*, which we were sure was both witty and off-color, although none of us had read it. In fact, some of us had little interest in reading anything other than our first piece of pornographic literature—exposure to which was the final highlight of the year.

Town Bull was brought to school in a paper bag by Ruth Wyler, one of our more brilliant classmates. She found it on the bookshelves of her parents' library. We believed it to be a Victorian work by Bob Stirling (though "Bob" doesn't sound very Victorian). It featured Belle, a madam, and her number one stud, Town Bull, whom she called in when one of her patrons or she herself was especially in need of fulfillment. The book described in lusty detail all aspects of Town Bull's ginormous member and every variation on heterosexual sex imaginable, including "water play." It treated in detail the frequent need for women to be warmed up by the tongues of prepubescent girls (in training) before succumbing to the thrill of penetration by Town Bull himself. The excitement of this book did not turn me into a porno addict. On the contrary, it was so complete

Part 2: SEXED

and explicit that nothing I have had occasion to read since comes anywhere near the titillation and tingle of reading those scenes at that age. Passing *Town Bull* around during English class, while Mr. Myers fluttered about in front of the blackboard, may explain why many of us remember little of what he said, only his delivery.

Sadly, Mr. Myers's time at Brearley was short. In February, Brearley held its annual Open Day for the parents to visit the children's classes. While my mother had many gay friends and found Mr. Myers's approach refreshing and invigorating, many other parents, most especially the Wall Street fathers, were offended by his manner and saw to it that Robert Manson Myers would not return for a second year. Mr. Myers died in January of 2014 after a distinguished career teaching literature in short stints, first at Yale, then at William & Mary, then at Tulane, and finally at the University of Maryland at College Park, where, according to his obituary, "his students praised him for his inspiring revelations about English literature." Brearley's loss.

5. Wicked Step

Monroe Street Marina, Chicago.

FEBRUARY 1955

The phone rang. I answered.

"Hello, Sweetheart! It's Uncle George. How are you doing?" Uncle George was Howie's uncle. In our first years back in New York, George Armstrong and his sister, Elizabeth, had been our only family.

"Fine, Uncle George. Ma's out. When are you coming to see us so I can practice my martini making?"

"I am calling to ask how you feel about Howie's remarriage. Do you know his new wife?"

"What? What remarriage?" I said in disbelief. "What new wife?"

"You don't know? Howie didn't tell you?"

"No, I ... I ... he never said anything when I spoke to him a few weeks ago."

"I am so sorry, honey, I shouldn't be the one to tell you. I only called because I thought you might be feeling drafty or upset."

Drafty or upset?! What about ignored and hurt!

"No," I mumbled, "I know nothing."

Part 2: Sexed

Visions of Howie's lady friends appeared before my eyes: It couldn't be this one because .... It couldn't be that one because ... It couldn't be Barbara Durbin from Chicago and Wayne, because I want it to be Barbara, which is reason enough for it not to be Barbara. And it surely couldn't be Cissie, the aspiring psychiatrist, because however sexy she thought she was, and however clever it had been for her to commission the construction of her sloop, *Flying Cloud*, and become Queen of the Seas so Howie could sail out of Chicago between summers on the Atlantic. Howie told me he thought she was dumb as dirt, so surely he wouldn't fall for that ploy.

"Who did Howie marry?" I could barely speak.

"A woman called Cissie McLeod. After her divorce she went to medical school and did her residency in psychiatry. She was a student of your father's..."

"I know Cissie McLeod, Uncle George," I interrupted. "She was on our first cruise together when I was twelve, then I met her again a bunch of times when I was out visiting Howie in Chicago. She was all over him."

"Really?"

"Yes, really. She even commissioned the construction of a steel hulled-sloop, similar to *Stone Horse* but smaller, so Howie would have a boat to sail in Chicago now that *Stone Horse* is on the East Coast."

"No kidding!"

"Last summer Howie said he couldn't stand her or her butterball mother, who is loaded and owns the largest bank in Peoria. He also said that he couldn't deal with Cissie having money. After my mother, he said he never wanted to be with anyone with money again. And he couldn't stand Cissie chasing him."

"She must have done quite a good job of whatever she did, kid, because it worked," said Uncle George. "Maybe he was too embarrassed to tell you."

"Yeah, maybe."

"I'm coming into town on the weekend. Let me take you to lunch and we can talk about it some more. I am so sorry this is how you had to find out."

"Me, too," I said, sniveling. "See you Saturday, then."

Howie might have felt embarrassed?

I bet he did.

MID-AUGUST, 1955

I unpacked from my mother's and my third trip to Europe, repacked for my first post-wedding cruise with Howie and Cissie, and the next day boarded the train for Marblehead, Massachusetts. My Brearley friend Lucinda ("Cindy") Childs would arrive the next day, and we would head directly east ("down east") and back to Maine.

My new stepmother had a high-pitched voice, giggled incessantly though she lacked a sense of humor, and was attractive in a baby-doll way: She was kittenish and worshipped Howie. The pet names with which they addressed one another were hard for a teenaged daughter to endure. "Big Tug" and "Little Tug," with various toots for different moods and meanings. Also, Cissie kept adding to the stuffed bear collection, which originally numbered four, goading my father on to give them all names, personalities, and narratives.

And this woman was a practicing psychiatrist?

She called herself my "Wicked Step."

As the summer evolved, her shortcomings became more and more evident. Cissie wasn't much of a sailor, even though she now had her own boat in Chicago. She could neither cook nor hold her liquor at parties. On matters literary and intellectual, it was clear even to me at fifteen that she wasn't in Howie's league.

Over time, Howie grew disenchanted with her and turned his attention toward molding me into a perfect sailor. When I failed to achieve certain undeclared goals, or just did something stupid—like smoking a cigarette near an open gas tank or allowing an expensive searchlight to fall into the drink from a pitching float in a forty-mile gale—he wouldn't speak to me for days, so deep was his anger and disappointment.

Fortunately, I had developed interests outside the boat and was not as dependent on the intimacy I had once shared with Howie. My friend Cindy's company on *Stone Horse* was a gift and a relief. We were both aspiring artists, she an actress, I an architect, we were serious about life and the world of ideas as only arty teenagers can be, and we both loved the sailing, the sea, and the scenery. Cindy sailed with us in and around Penobscot Bay and to Mt. Desert for ten days that summer before returning to Edgartown. Emily Manheim flew up to Southwest Harbor to join us on the next leg of our cruise. We headed out into the open sea and further east along the coast, passed Frenchman's Bay to Roque Island, passed Campobello Island to Eastport and Lubec, the easternmost town in the contiguous United States, where eighteen-foot tides run fiercely. Despite the beauty and emptiness of the coastline and the harbors in which we anchored, Emily didn't cotton to the sea as Cindy had. Nor did she take to our buying lobsters from lobster boats we passed, boiling them live in a huge kettle, cracking the shells and eating the meat with melted butter. Emily found the process of picking out the meat, and the meat itself, repulsive. So, without telling anyone, she took her lobster and its shells and flushed it all down *Stone Horse*'s head.

Flushing anything down a marine head (manual or otherwise)

other than human waste accompanied by three or four squares of airmail-weight toilet paper is an invitation to trouble. After dinner, the head was completely jammed. Emily denied flushing anything unauthorized down, but when Howie was obliged to take the head apart to clear the blockage, there were the lobster shells. More denials. The rest of the week on board passed with no more lobster and little conversation—not easy in a space only thirty-seven feet long and seven feet wide. Finally, the week was over. Emily and I left for New York, and Big Tug and Little Tug went back to Chicago. A few days later, Howie got a call from Joe White (son of legendary *New Yorker* writer E. B. White), who owned the boatyard in Centre Harbor where *Stone Horse* was to be laid up for the winter. *Stone Horse* had sunk at her mooring. Only the tops of her masts were visible above the water.

When she was hauled up from the bottom, everything inside and out, including the engine, was caked in mud, kelp, and salt. Lobster shells were found stuck in the waste outlet just below the water line. The petcock, which is normally turned shut, could not close around the shells. The movement of the water had dislodged them, leaving the petcock partially open. In the darkness of the Maine night, the steel hull filled with water and she sank to the harbor floor.

When Howie was offered the job as chief of medicine at Cook County Hospital, he gave up his apartment on Chicago's North Side and insisted that he and Cissie move into one of the residence halls on the hospital grounds in what was then a very unsavory neighborhood. Little Tug went along with anything Big Tug wanted, and Howie wanted to be close to his patients, his residents, his interns, and his students. He basked in the role of dedicated/impoverished doctor/teacher.

Part 2: SEXED

The following spring, when I was visiting them in Chicago, all Howie wanted to do was to take me sailing on Cissie's sloop, *Flying Cloud,* for more work on my nautical development. I was just sixteen, and all I wanted was a drivers' license. You had to be eighteen in New York City, but only sixteen in Illinois. To Cissie's credit, it was she who took me for my driver's test in her dark blue convertible Dyna Flow Buick complete with automatic transmission. When I blew through a stop sign and thus flunked the test (and wouldn't be allowed to take it again at that location before I'd have to return to New York, thus incurring yet another blast of Howie's wrath and ensuing silence), Cissie drove me to Evanston just north of Chicago, where, thank God and thank Cissie, I passed.

Despite Howie's slow-growing paranoia, his diminishing respect for Cissie, and my own general indifference to her, for four straight summers I loved the life we led on the boat: the winds, the tides, the navigation, setting jib and jigger in a stiff head wind, riding the bowsprit on a broad reach, and rowing in to shore to explore the unpeopled islands and the little towns and communities that we sailed by. I reveled in the richness and variety of classical music Howie played when we were at anchor, and in the meals he and I cooked together on board. Howie taught me to drink (straight gin for all menstrual and gastro-intestinal problems, otherwise bourbon) and to curse. He was proud that I took to both with enthusiasm. Although Howie was full of contradictions, I loved and admired him and basked in his warmth and humor.

Come the fifth summer of sailing with Howie and Cissie, the winds would change.

6. Foggy Bottom

NEW YORK — SPRING 1955

242 East 62nd Street — the bottom two floors were ours.

My mother wanted us to move to a larger apartment, but where was the money for that? Dior dresses and Delman shoes were one thing, but a proper apartment? Besides, that wasn't really her goal: an entire brownstone is what she wanted. Because she had re-met Hans, who was respectable and had honorable intentions, she had the courage to reconnect with her father and Mrs. Fitzpatrick. Gaffer liked young Hans and had admired his father. Closing the multi-year breech between Gaffer and my mother loosened the purse strings and permitted my mother access to the remaining money left to her by her grandmother, Helen Naomi Salomon.

She soon found a narrow but deep brownstone on 62nd Street east of Third Avenue. When I was a little girl, one or another of my sitters and I would ride the El all the way down to the Bowery and back. I would stand at the front of the front car, mesmerized by the way the tracks converged at a point in the distance while the tops of the buildings lining Third Avenue and further downtown along the Bowery flew by. Over the years I became very attached to the Third Avenue El, but street life beneath the El remained forbidding, with the same drunks falling out of dingy Irish bars, the same bums hunkered in the filthy doorways of tenements, the same pawn shops, and the same store windows full of hernia belts and artificial limbs that had terrified me as a little girl. The El was slated to be taken down that spring. Its last run was to be in May 1955. I wanted to ride it down to the end of Manhattan and back on the last day of its operational existence, but I had a dentist appointment, so I settled for taking my final run the day before. My mother was certain that the new house, though it was literally on the other side of the tracks, would be a perfect home for us and a fine investment.

It was sixteen feet wide. There was a duplex apartment on the bottom that had been built to the full depth of the lot, with an open patio in the middle, a glazed corridor along one side, and three small floor-through apartments above. The duplex was accessed from an areaway at the front of the house, and the rental apartments were accessed from the stoop.

The bottom floor of the duplex had a small room with a tiny WC under the stoop, and a kitchen between the front room and the dining room at the back of the main section of the house, which faced the little patio. The narrow corridor flanking the patio led to a paneled library at the back. On the second floor, my room would be in front, the living room in the middle, and my mother's room and bath would be in the back, over the library. The apartments above would give my mother rental income to help pay the mortgage and carrying costs of the house.

Enter d'Argout Fergusson, a gay couple in business together as decorators: Pierre d'Argout, who claimed once to have been an actor with La Comedie Française, and Neil Fergusson, who had been trained as an architect but preferred interior design and decorating; or maybe he just preferred Pierre. My mother wanted to scrap everything from our little apartment and start again *a la française*— as close to the style of Louis XVI as she could afford. It was to be her version of her Grannie's house on the Avenue Hoche. No more old, English hand-me-downs, and certainly nothing modern.

I was mortified. I loved our little apartment and its mix of styles. It was comfortable, familiar, and clever. I didn't want everything I held dear replaced with gilt chairs with bowed legs and oval backs, chests of drawers with curved fronts and marble tops, however elaborate the intaglio marble or the carved legs and bases. I was a modernist. If we were going to have change, it should be a change towards the new. Further, what was to be my room in the new house was way smaller than my room in the apartment. So what was in this move for me?

My mother begged me to trust her. Edward Wormley, her client and friend, was a little guy with a short neck, a round head topped by closely-clipped greying hair, a squeaky voice tinged with a Southern accent, and a gimp leg. Wormley was a furniture and interior designer. My mother made the same deal with Wormley as she had with Carlo Guggenheim. In exchange for legal services, Edward Wormley was going to make magic for me in that little room.

Are you kidding? With a name like that?

"What about Hans and his daughters?" I asked. "Where will they fit in if you get married? There will only be two bedrooms!"

"We cannot count on anything happening with Hans," she said stoically.

My mother's courtship was not progressing as swiftly as she had hoped, but she was not surprised. It was hard enough for a man to obtain full custody of his children in those days, but in the State of California it was almost unheard of.

Against Hans's wishes, my mother pressed on with her plans to go abroad again for a long stretch over the summer. Again, she took me with her for the first part of her trip. We crossed on the *Andrea Doria*'s sister ship, the *Cristoforo Colombo*. It wasn't half as much fun: no retired diplomat to amuse my mother and no Cubans for me, just a bunch of young people too grown up to want me in their company. We disembarked in Naples this time and took a smaller boat straight to Capri.

Capri was almost as wonderful as Santa Margherita had been two years before: the main square, situated in the saddle between the two mini volcanic mountains that rise from the sea to comprise Capri, was lined with boutiques full of sparkling gold jewelry, stunningly simple beach clothes, and an array of minimal leather sandals. Cafes full of bronzed tourists of all nationalities spilled into the center of the piazza. Ana Capri, hidden high up on one of the mini mountains, was mysterious. Gracie Fields' resort hotel—by the cerulean blue water on the side of the island, opposite the ferry landing—was noisy and enticing. The shimmering rocks just below the clear water's surface, punctuated by clusters of pitch black sea urchins, beckoned.

I got my first bikini and two pairs of the minimal sandals, yet I was antsy and peevish.

My mother was driving me nuts. On the one hand, she behaved like a teenager needing assurance that she was attractive and loved (by Hans and by me), and that everything would work out as she wanted it to. I wasn't sure how to respond to her girlish anxieties, being just on the cusp of womanhood myself. On the other hand, she was mortified by my burgeoning sexuality. My lips were too thick and sensual, and my skin was too dark. I was forbidden to wear red. Red was for prostitutes. The way I talked and moved was provocative and would be "misunderstood." I was sick of being treated like a child even though, at barely fifteen, that's what I was.

Sitting around Gracie Fields' swimming pool, I got into conversation with Hillary, a young, exotic blonde Englishwoman who called herself Ilaria. I would go on long walks with Hillary, and even have lunch with her, leaving my mother on her own. My mother was convinced Hillary was a lesbian and was after my young body, but she was too uptight to tell me the nature of her qualms until long after. The day following my last long walk and lunch with Hillary, I donned my tiny bikini and dove into the water off Gracie Field's concrete sun deck and started to swim way out to where the big yachts were anchored. I was a pretty good swimmer (thanks to all those days at camp in the icy waters of Round Lake) and was reveling in my aquatic freedom and the feel of the warm salt water over so much of my bare skin. Most of the boats were far grander than Howie's chunky steel yawl. Many had hulls of glistening mahogany, and most had big sun awnings over the cockpit and afterdeck, where paid crew members swabbed the decks or served cappuccinos and biscotti to barely-clad passengers stretched out in the sun. An older man (probably no more than forty) semi-trim, semi-balding, in a marginally adequate swim suit, called down to me in the water from a particularly striking ketch, "*Buon giorno, signorina.* You have swum a long way out from the shore." I guess he knew I was either English or American, because neither French nor Italian girls spent much time actually swimming.

"I love sail boats and there are so many beautiful boats in the harbor," I called back, "I wanted to see them all. Yours is *bellissima!*"

"Would you like to come aboard and see her for yourself, *signorina?*"

"Oh yes, I'd love to," I said, treading water as gracefully as I could.

A swimming ladder was lowered over the side and secured by a crew member, and I climbed up and was offered a towel. As I dried my hair and shoulders, I continued carrying on about the teak decks, the perfect bright work (mahogany trim), the sparkling chrome winches, the beautifully furled sails and their sail covers, the unusual self-furling hardware on the Genoa jib (this was new then), and otherwise flaunting my appreciation of things nautical. My genial and welcoming host asked me if I'd like to see the interior of the cabins below decks.

"Of course, that would be lovely. Thank you so much!" I replied.

And down the companionway, all eager, I scrambled after my host, smack into his open arms. He wheeled me around ninety degrees, pinned me against the side of the cabin, pressing his body against me, and went for my mouth with his tongue.

Oh, no.

This was not going to happen.

There were only four small cloth triangles plus his minimal swimsuit separating my body from his. Fortunately, his grip was loose because he was so focused on where his tongue was going. Because I was still slightly wet, I was able to feint left to avoid the tongue and with a downward twist of my almost-naked torso, slither out of his arms. He seemed momentarily stunned by the rejection, which gave me the time I needed to say something idiotic like, "I have to go now," and race up the ship's ladder, over the cockpit combing, onto the deck, and dive into the sea.

I swam so fast that I felt ill with exhaustion and disgust, and the shore was still in the distance. I had gone way too far in every sense. Yachts back then flushed their toilets directly into the harbor and a large Kielbasa-sized turd floated by as if to remind me in just what dangerous waters I had been.

Spending further time with Hillary subsequently lost its appeal.

My mother was a trustee of Robert College of Istanbul—a coeducational middle school, lycée, and two-year college founded in 1863 for students from Turkey and the adjacent Arab world, not for foreigners. She was also a trustee of the American Farm School in Salonika in Greece. The Farm School was less exalted intellectually, but equally important to the community it serves. Its mission was to teach the children of Greek farmers the latest American farming methods and technology. The Farm School's annual board meeting was generally held in mid- or late June, and we were to go to this year's board meeting together.

After Capri, we stayed briefly at the Grand Bretagne in Athens, paid a visit to the Parthenon—where I learned of entasis (a slight outward curve in the shaft of a column or a horizontal plinth, developed by the Greeks to correct the optical illusion of concavity generated by a completely straight line). We then took an endless hot and dusty drive up to the Oracle of Delphi and back. I was sweating it out alone in the back seat, with not even a poodle for company, while my mother jabbered up front to Dimitri Zanos, the latest addition to her string of European legal colleagues and a fellow trustee of the Farm School. After Athens, we were to fly to Salonika and stay in the austere dormitories at the school—not exactly my mother's type of accommodations, but she had to show she was a team player. Then, together with Zanos and his wife, we would board a caïque, a beamy, old-fashioned Greek fishing boat converted to a pleasure boat, and sail further east along the coast and around Mt. Athos. On the way, we would spend a night with Elinor Hope Reed, an old friend of the Farm School who lived in the ruin of a tower at the throat of the causeway that gives access

Part 2: SEXED

to the peninsula of Mt. Athos, the autonomous home of numerous ancient monasteries.

It was yet another junket to which I was not looking forward.

Despite the wakeup call that the long swim in Capri had provided, I was becoming increasingly impatient with the long lunches and dinners with my mother's foreign friends and business acquaintances. Despite the windows and doors of experience my mother continued to open for me, I found the Greek food and folk dancing at the Farm School barely tolerable, and said so. While I had been excited about sailing on the Mediterranean, I found our caïque annoying, and I said so. It was as broad as it was long, and had sails that were never raised and a giant tiller that I was not allowed to touch. The stench of the diesel fumes made me nauseous, and I said so. Dimitri Zanos and his wife were young, attractive, and very good to me. They played backgammon with me endlessly (I was good but they were better), and taught me to whistle piercingly using my fingers, lips, and teeth altogether. But I wouldn't admit I liked them. And I didn't care for Mrs. Reed either.

Mrs. Reed lived in a snug little house at the base of her ancient tower. We, her guests, had rooms in the tower itself, which was indeed a ruin: great chunks of exterior wall had fallen to the beach below, thanks to a combination of earthquakes and the ravages of time. No repairs had been made. Only a board here and there was in place to protect you from falling to your death as you climbed the spiral stone stairs up, up, up to your assigned chamber. There was a bare electric light bulb in each room and a ceramic pitcher and wash bowl, but no water unless you brought it up yourself. Some rooms had windows that actually closed. Most, including mine, had ill-fitting casements and broken glass, sagging metal beds, scratchy sheets, and blankets. No plumbing. But there was an outhouse: a partially-covered wooden structure tacked onto the side of the tower sixty feet above the shore below. To get to it, you had to climb through a glassless window onto a narrow, open wood catwalk precariously affixed to the side of the tower. There was nothing but air between the seat on which you sat and the rocky beach below.

Dinner was the usual grilled fish, pilaf, feta cheese, and salad of cucumbers and tomatoes. Thanks to the flow of ouzo and retsina, the adults became increasingly vocal about the myriad good works of Mrs. Reed and her late husband, but I was aware of a commensurate increase in the whistling of the wind and the rattling of windows and doors in their frames. A serious storm had kicked up, with almost no rain, just wind; typical, apparently, for that area and that time of year. The captain of our caïque stuck his grizzled head in the dining room and said in Greek to Dimitri Zanos that because of the gathering storm and the currents around the peninsula, in order to sail past Mt. Athos, to view the monasteries from the boat and reach our destination by the next evening, we would have to be on board by 5:00 a.m. and weigh anchor at 5:30 a.m.. That broke up the party fast.

We said our thanks and good nights to Mrs. Reed and headed across the sand to the tower, as we would not be seeing her in the morning. By then the wind was fierce and the flying sand stung like tiny hornets. We hung onto the rope railing on the stairs for balance as we headed to our rooms while the wind swirled around us. The few bulbs that lit our way and our rooms flickered on and off. Doors and casements shook in their frames. I was definitely scared. High winds always scare me. My mother saw me to my room to be sure I had light and could shut my door, then bid me goodnight. With all that wind alternately screeching and roaring, my little room with its sagging iron bed, its pitcher and wash basin, was no safe haven. There was the matter of going to the bathroom before going to bed, and there was no chamber pot. That meant the outhouse. I crept back down to my mother's room. What to do? No one could be fool enough to spend five minutes in that outhouse, much less walk across the open catwalk in this gale. But there was no choice other than to pee on the floor. The trip across the catwalk as it trembled in the wind was not unlike creeping forward along the companionway of *Stone Horse* during Hurricane Carol. The outhouse provided some shelter but the fear of the little shed coming loose and plummeting down onto the rocks and into the churning sea sixty feet below far outweighed the benefit of its shelter.

Of course I made it there and back. If the tower is still standing, that little outhouse and the catwalk are also probably still affixed high on its south face. When a grey dawn broke the next morning, we boarded the caïque. The captain cranked up her powerful diesel engine and nosed her out of the little harbor into a mild following sea. As the tower receded into the distance over our stern, the smell of the diesel exhaust wafting across the cabin trunk was almost welcome. I slept soundly on deck, only occasionally waking to the extraordinary sight of the huge monasteries clinging to the steep cliffs of Mt. Athos's southern shore.

Our next stop was Austria: first Salzburg, and then on to Vienna. The first piece of music I had ever adored was the overture to *Die Fledermaus*. The first piece I played on the piano was a kiddie version of the *Blue Danube*. I had come to love the zither as played in *The Third Man* and as I'd heard it played in Kitzbuhl the year before. I was excited to visit the city of my dreams.

After World War II, Austria and Vienna were divided into four zones administered by the United States, the Soviet Union, the U.K., and France, until spring of 1955, when because of a thaw in the Cold War and in exchange for the promise of perpetual neutrality, Austria was granted its independence. My mother and I arrived in Vienna a month later. The city was still reeling from the years of occupation. The Ringstrasse's grand palaces and high Baroque churches were dirty and derelict. The broad streets and boulevards were barren of trade and traffic. Worst of all, the Blue Danube was a polluted yellow.

My mother had seemed particularly edgy when we landed at the airport in Vienna, looking around and over her shoulder every few minutes.

"I know it sounds strange, but I think we are being followed," she said.

"Why would that be?" I asked.

"I don't know, but it's ... there... that guy ... over there in the raincoat."

I turned my head but too late. The guy had vanished. Kind of exciting, I thought.

Once we were in the taxi, she calmed down, or seemed to. Maybe I was too preoccupied with my disappointment in Vienna's sorry appearance to notice. Our taxi drove along the Ringstrasse, then turned in along the side of the Vienna Opera House to the Hotel Sacher. We checked in and gave up our passports. My mother collected her mail, which included a letter from Hans, and we were shown to our room. We unpacked and then went downstairs in search of the Café Mozart, where we were seated in delicate gilded chairs at a tiny round marble table. My mother ordered a black coffee for herself (as always) and *Kaffee mit Schlag über* and a piece of the famous Sacher-torte for me. I would have preferred something else, as I was not keen on chocolate. But because she was always dieting, she ordered for me any dessert she wanted, and then ate sparingly off my plate.

I knew she was upset when she didn't touch the Sacher-torte.

"What's the matter?" I asked.

Part 2: SEXED

"I'm not sure," she replied.

"How was the letter from Hans?"

"He is angry at me for continuing to travel around Europe on my own and with you. He wants me to come back to New York immediately."

"That doesn't seem fair," I said. "He's still stuck in California. Why shouldn't you do want you want and go where you want 'til he is free? I can see why you're upset." Although she still wouldn't touch the Sacher-torte, she was slightly less agitated.

When we returned to our room, she started looking through the wardrobe and drawers, convinced that our bags, clothes, and accoutrements had been searched. While my mother was protective of her belongings and carried them in heavy hard-framed suitcases that she almost always kept locked, this sort of paranoia was out of character. It was late afternoon, the time we usually napped or read. Reading was an endless source of pleasure for her. Once she opened her book she seemed to settle down a bit. I was never a great reader, much to her and my own disappointment, so I opted to explore the area around the hotel, and she gave her reluctant permission. The previous summer, when I walked around our hotel in Barcelona, I happened on the Casa Mila, the last civic work of Anton Gaudi before he dedicated himself to the still-unfinished Sagrada Familia Cathedral. I had never heard of Gaudi. All I knew was that the sensuous three-dimensionality and organic symmetry of the façade, the encrusted wrought iron railings of the balconies, and the phantasmagorical spirals and waffle patterns of the chimneys that soared above the undulating cornices were completely new, unexpected, and exhilarating to my young eyes. How did this building happen? Was it a mistake or intended? Was it medieval or modern? Who did it? After snapping countless photographs with my Brownie, I tore back to our hotel in search of further understanding. That had been my introduction to Gaudi. Now, as I explored the streets of Vienna, I found that its opulent grandeur, which may have been the best the Baroque and Rococo periods had to offer, was not to my taste, and the city was still covered with the grime of post war Europe.

The next morning we took a taxi out to Schönbrunn, formerly the summer residence of the Hapsburg imperial family until its downfall in 1918. The monumental scale of the palace itself, the triumphal arches of the Gloriette, and the acres of flat French gardens and miles of abandoned gravel pathways laid out with strict geometric precision, with inoperative fountains at key intersections, were frightening because of their size and emptiness. After lunch we visited the Belvedere, whose upper and lower palaces were separated from one another by more French gardens, fully as formal but smaller than those of Schönbrunn, The Belvedere seemed almost cozy by comparison.

Back to the Sacher for a read and a nap. Then time for drinks: the usual vodka martini(s) for my mother and warm Coke for me. Ice cubes were hard to come by. Dinner in a nearby restaurant. Back to the Sacher again, undress, read in bed for a bit.

"Good night, Bunny dear," my mother said with greater warmth and poignancy than usual, as she came to hug and kiss me goodnight. Then she slipped off her satin dressing gown, slid into her bed and turned out her light. It had been a long day. We were soon fast asleep.

Or so I thought.

As dawn was breaking, I awoke to see her standing by my bed, fully dressed, glasses on, hair disheveled, face dirty, and clasping, no, *wringing* her hands, staring down at me.

"What's the matter, Ma?" I asked, "Why are you staring at me? Are you okay?"

"Yes. I am here, Bunny," she said haltingly. "I am back. I made it. But I am never, ever doing it again. Hans is right. It is over. It has to be."

"Doing what? What is over? What are you talking about?" I switched on the light as she sat on my bed, the blood drained from her pale face and hands, and told me what had happened.

"After I was sure you were asleep, I went into the bathroom, got dressed and slipped out of our room. I went to the lobby and took a taxi to the Vienna Bahnhof. I had an appointment to meet a locomotive engineer there. I had been given some papers that had to be delivered to someone on the other side of the Iron Curtain. But I didn't want to give them to the engineer. I wanted to deliver them myself. I claimed Gaffer's experience as a railroad engineer as my own so the engineer would take me across the border in the cabin of his locomotive. Then I asked him to arrange for the engineer on the train going back across the border from East to West to bring me back to Vienna where I would get a taxi back to the Sacher, ascend to our room and get into the bed as though nothing had happened. Mission accomplished.

"That was the idea, except on one or the other side of the Iron Curtain someone got wind that something funny was going down. After I had delivered the papers to the guy who was supposed to receive them, I got on the next train heading west, but on the Vienna side of the border, I was taken to the police for questioning,"

"Jesus, Ma!"

"It wasn't just questioning. They put electrodes under my fingernails and gave me electric shock treatment to confirm that I was telling the truth about the extent of my mission. When they were convinced that I had nothing further to tell, they released me and allowed me to return to you."

"Have you ever done anything like this before?" I asked.

"Yes, but I never involved you or endangered you as I did tonight."

"Endanger me?" I squawked. "What about you, Ma? No wonder Hans is climbing the walls. Does he know what you've been up to?"

"Yes, he knows. He's the only one who knew until now, and he begged me to stop. Now you know, but you must not discuss this with anyone."

"You wouldn't stop?"

"No. But I promised Hans this would be my last run."

"Why did you ... why do you do this?" I wailed.

"For my country, our country," she said.

"What does that mean?"

"You know how proud I am to be an American and..."

"Aw, come on, Ma, you spend every minute you can in any country but America. You live and breathe for everything European."

"That's the point. Have you heard of the CIA, the Central Intelligence Agency?"

"Yes, of course. I'm not an idiot."

"Do you remember Ting Sheldon and Jack Kellogg?" These were friends of hers from Washington whom she had met through Howie's Aunt Elizabeth when I was much younger. "Aunt Elizabeth worked for the State Department and they recruited me to work for the Agency."

"Why you? I thought you were a lawyer."

"That's why I was an ideal candidate. Because I am a woman, upper class, well educated, well dressed, and I speak fluent French and have an excellent memory," she said, without modesty. "As a lawyer with international clients, I have the opportunity to visit places and meet people that the average American tourist or business person doesn't. I can and have collected valuable information for the Agency, and I have served as a courier from time to time."

"How long have you been doing this?"

"For years."

"How many years?"

"About five or six."

"Is this what you do when you park me in camp and go on junkets to eat yogurt and caviar on the shores of the Caspian Sea with the big wigs of ARAMCO? Is this what you do when you carry on in Beirut with prominent merchant families like the Kettanehs, and in the Atlas Mountains with the Pasha of Marrakesh and Berber tribal chiefs, and in Monaco with Prince Rainier and in Cairo with whom? King Farouk? "

"More or less, although I never met King Farouk."

"No? Too bad," I said with no small tinge of sarcasm. "So you're telling me you are a spy?"

"Not exactly."

"*Not exactly?*" I said with a mix of anger, incredulity and pride. My mother, a spy?

"I don't get paid."

"You don't get paid?" I all but yelled. "That makes no sense. You risk your life and you don't get *paid*?"

"I told you, I do it for our country. But it's over. That was it. No more. We will not discuss this again, ever. It's over," she said a second time.

There ended the inquisition and the confession.

Then my mother said, "Actually, it isn't quite over. Remember the guy at the airport?"

"Yes," I said.

"He's still around, and I think he's still on my tail, so get yourself packed as fast as you can, and let's you and I get the hell out of here." My mother rarely cursed.

We stopped in Paris overnight and were taken by her Coudert

Frères chums to dinner at the famous five-star restaurant Laserre. The food and service were beyond anything I'd experienced. The flaming crepe suzettes were like fireworks, and when the restaurant's entire ceiling slid open to the stars, I thought I was being catapulted to the heavens.

We'd made it to safety. We were in Paris.

"How would you like your martini, Mme. Armstrong?"

"Rocks and a twist. Stirred but not shaken."

True to her word, she never discussed this with me again, and I never dared bring it up. Still, I was impressed. My mother was a spy!

Postscript: It wasn't as glamorous as I had thought. And maybe this one time in Vienna was the only time it was dangerous. Many decades later, I learned that the OSS, the Office of Strategic Services, was set up as an ad hoc information gathering service by FDR during World War II, and continued on during the post-war era and out of it grew the CIA. For many insiders, OSS stood for "Oh So Social." In those early Cold War years, everyone in the right social circles who could was "spying" for the OSS and the CIA. To many critics of the Eisenhower presidency, Ike's greatest mistake was the appointment of the Dulles Brothers to positions of power: John Foster Dulles as Secretary of State, and Allen Dulles as head of the CIA. Apparently, Allen bedded everyone he could and then encouraged his bedmates to travel far and wide and report back on everything they saw and heard. I doubt my mother had ever met, much less slept with, Allen Dulles. But I am sure she enjoyed being part of that elite circle and applied herself to the job willingly. I reckon that being as bright and ambitious as she was, she took the task of information-gathering for God and Country farther and wider than most—and did it better as well.

7. Step II

Entrance to Fallingwater, Bear Run, PA.

SEPTEMBER 1955

My mother moved us into the new house even before it was ready. Least ready was my room, where the design miracle was supposed to happen. For the first month of school, I slept in a tiny room off the kitchen. It was fitted with a single bed with a Toile de Jouy spread and back cushions to make it look like a sofa, a little French Provincial handpainted bureau, and a small table desk which Dagmar and I shared during the day. But the design miracle was worth the wait. Edward Wormley was some designer. In a room nine feet wide, eleven feet deep, and almost ten feet high, he found space for all this: two narrow single beds, stacked on top of one another, wall-to-wall bookshelves above the beds, a tall narrow bureau with drawers of graduated heights, a built-in desk with a bank of drawers to one side, a built-in record player and space for my records, and a concealed bin for storing bedding for the second bed. The design was so clean and tight that there was visual as well as actual space for an array of movable furniture which included a small (Dunbar) easy chair—Wormley was Dunbar Furniture's top designer—plus an armless (Bertoia) desk chair on casters, a twenty-four-inch round (Dunbar) occasional table with a travertine top, along with the black lacquer mini-piano (two octaves short) and its bench, that my mother had finally procured for me during the last year we were at the apartment.

An oversized, almost spherical paper lantern by Isamu Noguchi hung in the middle of the room to provide light and lower the visual height of the ceiling. The walls were grass cloth. The wood was honey blonde, maybe birch. A shiny black Formica counter edged in the same blonde wood stretched across the windows, which faced the street, and served as the desktop. The fabrics and upholstery were in a wheat color with accents in chrome yellow, rich ochers and oranges, some smooth and silky and others a coarser, open weave. The raw linen curtains with their black-out linings fell from the ceiling to just past the desk counter. And the wall between the window and the door to the tenant's hall was covered with a grid of small cylindrical stainless-steel pins about ten inches on center that enabled the hanging of art of any size in any configuration. It was magic.

Although I had more homework in tenth grade than previously, school was getting interesting, though I still couldn't write a decent essay. Algebra and trig were still anathema to me. I kept fouling up the order of the numbers in the long equations and extrapolations, and dropping decimal places. We did it all by hand, including square roots. No slide rules and no calculators. French was better, in part because I had been using my French in my travels with my mother, and also because we had a very stern young teacher, Mme. (Edith) Arndt, whom I thought gorgeous and brilliant. Latin, although still deadly, was somewhat familiar by now, and it had to

Part 2: SEXED

be done. Our teacher, Signora Bona di Panizza Koska, was a short, fierce woman from Trieste with an almost impenetrable Italian accent. She taught like a drill sergeant and took no prisoners. But I forgave her because she was Italian.

Hans's plan to divorce, move east with his kids, and drag my mother (and me) into his personal cave was barely progressing. To supplement her earnings in trusts and estates, small business, and international law, my mother was becoming a specialist in matrimonial law. But that didn't make things easier. Letters flew back and forth and transcontinental phone lines buzzed. Hans's and my mother's limited times together were intense. Their talk of books, poetry, and their past lives, lubricated by snifters of vodka and cognac, lasted long into the night. When Hans would return to Pasadena, my mother would be undone, weeping and frustrated, and I was called upon to be the calming friend and confidante. Usually I played my role with enthusiasm and affection. But sometimes I was vile, even though Hans was a wonderful guy, both in his own right and for my mother and me.

In the meantime, Johnst was becoming more assertive sexually. When he tried to French-kiss me, I was repelled. For all my fanaticizing about sex with boys, I was unprepared for the reality. But having a boyfriend so brilliant and sensitive, and who had just begun his first year at Harvard, was hard to beat. Johnst invited me to homecoming weekend, which was a little weird as neither of us was interested in team sports, and I was excited.

I showed my mother his invitation and the envelope with the Kirkland Hall return address. She looked it over and handed it back.

"I am afraid that isn't going to be possible, Bunny."

"Not possible? You gotta be kidding, Ma."

"We've been invited away for that weekend," she responded firmly.

"What do you mean away for 'that weekend'? "

"You know my friend, Edgar Kaufmann, the man who has an apartment next to Ed Wormley's apartment on East 52nd Street?" (They had adjacent apartments three levels below the street, opening onto a noisy garden adjacent to the FDR Drive. Greta Garbo lived upstairs.)

"I remember he came to the party you gave at our old apartment last spring. What about him?"

"He's asked me to represent him."

"Represent him doing what?"

"To be his lawyer."

"Great. So what does this have to do with my going to Harvard with Johnst?

"He has invited us to his country house that weekend and we are going."

"No! I am not going!"

"Yes, you are."

"Why? You can go, but why do I have to go?"

"Because his country house is the most famous house in America, designed for Edgar's parents by Frank Lloyd Wright. I told Edgar that you wanted to be an architect, so he has invited you to come as well."

"Who is Frank Lloyd Wright? And why do I have to go?" I sputtered.

"I thought you wanted to be an architect?"

"I do. But who is Frank Lloyd Wright, and what's so great about this house?"

"You'll see."

My mother was rightly irritated, but she held her ground and I lost mine. So I declined Johnst's invitation, explaining I had to fly to Pittsburgh and then drive hours to some house in the middle of nowhere, built out over a waterfall, in order to make nice-nice to my mother's latest hotshot client.

Part 2: SEXED

On a Friday afternoon in October, Edgar Kaufmann, my mother, and I were met at the Pittsburgh airport by a black driver who beckoned us into a large black sedan and drove what seemed like four hours through heavily wooded territory to Bear Run. Edgar sat up front with the driver. My mother and I were in back, barely speaking. We arrived at Fallingwater in the dead of night. At the entrance, there was a glow of light from a single overhead source bouncing off thin slices of rough stone adjacent to a solid door. The door was opened from the inside by a reticent young man, Paul Mayèn, a fellow guest, who had arrived ahead of us. We entered a cramped vestibule with a very low ceiling where introductions were made. Then we ascended a short flight of stairs that opened onto the most amazing space I had ever seen.

Directly ahead of us were enormous rounded boulders that seemed to push their way up through the stone paving. At the end of the short allée of boulders was a tall fireplace that went from floor to the bottom of an ornamental band at the ceiling and was set within the side walls of the sliced stone, complete with crackling log fire. To the right, in a cozy niche, was a dining table set for our supper. To the left of the fireplace was an oval drinks tray and a commodious sitting area with low built-in sofas covered with rich earth-colored fabrics, fur and flat, woven throws, a long, low coffee table and several square ottomans, the center sections of which were upholstered with bright fabrics of different solid colors. Here we were to have drinks: for Edgar and Paul, Campari and soda; for my mother, her vodka martini; I chose dry sherry, which I had begun to drink at home. A corner defined by a black ribbon of windows giving onto the dark night contained more seating and a pair of doors to an outside terrace. Continuing around counterclockwise were glass doors that opened onto a set of suspended exterior stairs leading down to a manmade pool carved from the stream at the top of the falls. Here, Edgar swam daily in the freezing waters of Bear Run, except in midwinter. This was the huge living space that everyone has seen cantilevered over the falls in photographs. After drinks, we were called to supper in the niche by the fireplace, which was served by our driver. I said my good nights, repaired to my room on the top floor, and fell into an enchanted sleep.

In the morning, I awoke to the sound of the cascading water and looked out from my bed, through a strip of floor-to-ceiling glass, over the woods and down onto the pool below the falls. Without my having to move, it was all there to see. My room was at the top of the vertical row of small red-framed windows that one sees in photographs of the house from the bottom of the falls. The experience of that small room—the cork floors underfoot, the fabrics on the bed, the handcrafted desk and chair, and the whiter-than-white bathroom fixtures and towels against the warm woods, cork, and stone—was sensuous and unforgettable.

After breakfast, my mother and Edgar repaired to his study to discuss business, and Edgar's friend Paul gave me a tour of the house and the adjacent guest house across and uphill from the main house's diminutive entrance. I was particularly impressed by the guest house's own forest-green mini swimming pool nestled into its terrace, which melded perfectly with the surrounding architecture and woods. Paul, an industrial designer (meaning a designer of furniture and millwork), seemed younger, more limber and less formal than Edgar, and certainly better-looking, with his darkly exotic hair and complexion. Though Edgar was not a looker, he was more than presentable. He had fair freckled skin already susceptible to skin cancers, a warm smile, and laughing eyes. He wore his thick, almost kinky, mouse-brown hair slicked straight back off his high forehead and into wavy obedience by some sort of gel. Although Edgar's voice and eyes were gentle, his mind and his use of language inspired respect if not actual fear. Paul, when out of Edgar's radius, became spontaneous, almost impish. I cherished my time with Paul and remember to this day the grace and patience with which he answered my myriad questions about the house and his work as an industrial designer. And so began a close friendship between us that was uninterrupted until Paul's death in 2000.

Nothing had prepared me for the experience of Fallingwater. Yes, I wanted to be an architect, but I knew there was no way I would ever be capable of this level of achievement. This did not diminish my enjoyment of our two days under Edgar's roof nor my determination to pursue a career in architecture. But I saw that the slope of the uphill battle would be steeper than I had reckoned.

For my mother, the weekend was also a success. She secured Edgar as client. While Edgar did not have a job in the traditional sense and had not yet begun to teach, he was immensely well off, and both his life and his affairs were complex. In addition to amassing a priceless collection of modern paintings and sculpture and artifacts from antiquity, he was involved in his family-owned department stores and in the running of Fallingwater, which was no small task. As his attorney, my mother would have plenty to do.

During that autumn, my mother also started to work in earnest for a Russian émigré, Richard Davis, who aspired to importing foreign films and distributing them in the United States. Mr. Davis was a small, rotund man of middle age, with thinning, dyed dark brown hair. His face had been badly burned and scarred as a child. He reminded me of a well-fed mole. He had a thick Russian accent and a wife who (he claimed) had once been a famous ballerina but was now chronically ill, and so never appeared socially.

My mother and I were always going to foreign films. If a movie was French, we saw it: *Fanfan La Tulipe* (Gerard Philipe was my first serious movie star crush), Jacques Tati's *M. Hulot's Holiday,* Yves Montand in *Wages of Fear.* My mother was thrilled to be representing Mr. Davis in his new venture. He had either just bought or built the Fine Arts Theatre on 58th Street between Park and Lexington. He wanted his to be the first movie theatre in New York to be devoted entirely to showing independent foreign films. Monday, November 21, 1955 was to be the Grand Opening. The film was to be Henri-Georges Clouzot's *Diabolique,* starring his wife Vera Clouzot and Simone Signoret, with M. Clouzot in the lead male role as the hated school head.

The night of the opening l wore my first all-black dress: plain black velvet (real velvet, not velveteen, like so many of our dancing school dresses), black heels, borrowed pearls. l hoped l looked very grownup. From the moment the projector started to roll, l was paralyzed with fear; as the action progressed, l did not move. l walked home stunned, took off my coat and found a shiny impression of my right hand on the right side of my skirt thanks to the sweat exuded as l gripped my own right thigh in terror. The handprint was like a beacon and served as a source of comic relief to many others who had been similarly terrified.

Diablolique was a huge success, as was *Le Rififi* and the many films that followed. By way of thanks, Mr. Davis gave my mother two large sterling silver cigarette boxes with the *Diabolique*'s logo engraved on the lids, which she displayed on her coffee table long after she had to give up smoking.

When l wasn't drawing floor plans or stretched out on my narrow bed talking on my own phone—the new house had two telephone lines and a hold button so you could go from one to another—l listened to music coming from my hidden record player. And

Part 2: SEXED

I was beginning to read authors to whom my mother steered me—among them Evelyn Waugh, Elizabeth Bowen, and Saki.

My group of Brearley friends was also expanding. From dancing school there was Lynn Gilmore, who went to Miss Hewitt's (now the Hewitt School). Lynn's parents were always away on weekends, so our weekend parties were generally at her house, complete with booze and boys. The boys were from Buckley, Collegiate, and St. Ignatius Loyola. Though cigarettes and alcohol (rum and coke, bourbon or gin and ginger ale) were staples at these teen gatherings, sex was confined to close dancing, necking, and some modest petting.

Cindy Childs and I were growing closer. Her family had moved from West End Avenue to a cavernous duplex apartment on 66th Street and Lexington with a double-height living room opening onto a dark courtyard. Over a third of this troglodytic space, the third nearest the tall windows, was devoted to Lucinda Sr.'s sewing and costume-making for theatre productions in which she also starred at the nearby Cosmopolitan Club (a bastion for New York ladies of literary and intellectual inclination). Cindy was the star actress of our class and had the undivided attention of Miss Bowen, our drama teacher. Our play that year was Ferber and Kaufman's *Stage Door*, on which the 1937 film of the same name was based. Cindy played Terry Randall, the Katharine Hepburn lead. I wanted to play one of the aspiring showgirls. However, Miss Bowen was hell-bent on casting me in male roles. Despite finally going through puberty and my mother's concern that I had the looks of a prostitute-in-training, I still had reservations about my femininity. Was I really a girl, or was I a fake? Miss Bowen wasn't helping. She cast me as the Hollywood producer, Adolphe Menjou, for which I received a standing ovation, some small compensation for my sexual identity angst.

Step II

Saturday nights I often had dinner with the Childs. There was usually a standing rib roast, very unlike the tough, tasteless, fatless, rolled roasts that my mother had Dagmar buy in the interests of maintaining her girlish figure. Dr. Childs would carve and then be seated while vegetables were served and wine was poured. Throughout the meal, he would make snide remarks to and about his wife and daughters regarding their theatrical and operatic aspirations. His son Eddy and I escaped his derision. Although Dr. Childs wasn't very nice to his women, I was attracted by the kind of family setting I desired: mother, father, and children, all handsome, all smart, gathered around a monster piece of beef, with roast potatoes and gravy, using silver forks and knives with silver handles and carbon steel blades that had to be especially cleaned after the meal with moistened corks and dry Comet or Ajax to keep the rust at bay.

Newer to me than Cindy and the others was Claire Carrié, short, trim, fast on her feet, with an infectious laugh. Her stern French father was a professor of European History at Barnard College, and her less stern but still formidable mother was American, but had been educated in England and had a slight English lilt to her speech. They had a sprawling apartment on Claremont Avenue, adjacent to Barnard. Going to Claire's for dinner was like going to Europe for a meal. Mrs. Carrié served up ingredients and tastes that were new and different to me, accompanied with crusty French bread. My first taste of sweet breads chez Carrié was a gastronomic eye-opener, especially as I couldn't abide the liver and kidneys that my mother adored and Dagmar cooked regularly. Even the Carriés' table was set differently, with a well-used tablecloth, slightly tattered heavy cloth napkins, and little crystal racks at each place for the knives to rest between courses.

Claire was smarter and better at school than I. She was bilingual and had a smattering of Italian. Because of my passion for Italy and things Italian, I had a few words as well. We called each other "Bambina." At school we greeted each other with *"Ciao, bambina!"* and carried on about the latest French or Italian film we had seen. Claire was a talented pianist and played Schumann and Brahms almost as well as Clara. Claire played the guitar and already had a sizeable repertoire of folk music under her belt. She didn't live the life of lunch at Schrafft's and shopping with friends after school that some of us pursued downtown, and there were no horseback riding sessions and formal dances during vacations for Claire. Her friends were public school kids, boys as well as girls, from the poorer families of upper Broadway and environs. I envied Claire, her friends, her family, her talent and her way of life. After midyear exams, Claire organized eight of us to take the subway uptown to the George Washington Bridge, walk across to New Jersey in the bitter cold of winter with a bottle of red wine for sustenance, hike north along the Palisades, then turn around and walk back. We did this after midyear exams until we graduated.

Then there was Camilla Cahill, a big-boned girl with thick, silky, reddish-brown hair to her shoulders and a slash of bangs across her freckled forehead. She, her parents, an older half brother, two sisters, and a younger brother, plus several household staff, inhabited a large limestone townhouse at 15 East 72nd Street, between Madison and Fifth Avenues. Mr. (John T.) Cahill was the son of an Irish cop. He had attended Columbia and Harvard, become a lawyer, and eventually served as U.S. attorney for the Southern District in New York. His law firm, Cahill Gordon Jenkins and Reindel, remains famous for its innovative corporate practices and litigative successes. When I visited Camilla's house Mr. Cahill was rarely in evidence, and when he was, the decibel level in the house lowered to a whisper. Mrs. Cahill was diminutive and pretty but also somewhat brittle and unapproachable. She had been a Southern belle, possibly even an actress of some note.

She had been married before and had an older son, Dickie Pickens, who had provided us with the erotic poetry that we pored over in seventh grade. Camilla and her mother were both first-rate pianists and raced through Chopin's *Minute Waltz* and other complex showpieces. Camilla was also somewhat mysterious and silent. She read a great deal and wrote, but she kept her writings to herself. While she was bigger and stronger than I was, and did better at school (who didn't?), there was something fragile about her. Although playful and witty, she kept a certain distance, which I respected. In eleventh grade she went off to boarding school. But before she left we vowed that wherever we lived, and whatever else we were doing, we would meet in the year 2000 at the front door of her house on 72nd Street on the first of January at noon to celebrate the millennium and pick up where we had left off. We would be sixty years old.

It was a date she could not keep. In her adult life, Camilla succumbed to incurable schizophrenia, and hanged herself in the institution where she had been incarcerated for well over a decade. At noon on the first of January 2000, I went alone to East 72nd Street, stopping briefly across the street from what had been her house to remember her and to grieve for her.

I took classical piano lessons, first at Brearley and then at the Mannes College of Music. I got into Mannes because I was so admiring of Tracy Coudert's playing Beethoven that I memorized the opening measures of the *Pathétique Sonata*, stopping in the middle of page two just when the going got rough. But it became clear that I did not have the patience required to meet Mannes's level of expectation, and I wasn't interested in downsizing my ambition to "Für Elise" or catchy little tunes by Copeland and Thomson. Whatever I did had to happen faster, the way Eo and Tracy were learning to play popular music and show tunes by ear from their teacher, Mr.

Part 2: SEXED

(Jerry) Kruger. I can't imagine why, but my mother bought into my wishes, and Mr. Kruger soon came to our house to teach me as well. Mr. Kruger taught me chord structure, harmony, and the beginnings of music theory. He taught me how to accompany melodies picked out by the right hand with harmonies and chord patterns using the left hand. They sounded like foxtrots, tangos, or beguines. This I loved. I no longer had to feel quite so inadequate next to Claire and Camilla. I had my own thing.

In the middle of eighth grade, I started filling little diaries that had been given to my mother at Christmas by her friend, Leonard Lee, a short, squat but trim Englishman, rather like a grownup Little Lord Fauntleroy. Mr. Lee came complete with the requisite wavy hair, tweed suits with double-vented jackets, regimental ties, a pronounced upper-crust accent, and a wife to whom he was supposedly devoted but who never made an appearance. My mother credited Mr. Lee with the invention of the first British forklift truck, which, together with Godiva fire pumps and various marine diesel engines, were manufactured by his family business, Coventry Climax, in Coventry, England. Though there was little exciting about Mr. Lee, I thought Coventry Climax (and the off-color innuendo suggested by the company name) quite glamorous because the company developed and manufactured the "featherweight" engines (with a high ratio of horse power to weight) that dominated British Formula I racing in the late '50s and early '60s, especially when installed inside a Lotus Elite body.

The Featherweight diaries were covered in stamped leather, generally navy blue. On the front lower-right corner, the year was embossed in gold. Such diaries were given as corporate gifts by many company CEOs to recipients like my mother. Other companies, such as Gucci in Italy, and Hermès and Lanvin in Paris, made comparable diaries and datebooks. Since my mother considered things French better than things English, the Coventry Climax diaries were passed to me. I used them to record a bare outline of what I was to do or had done on a given day, with whom and where. Sometimes I entered homework assignments and exam grades, which is why I know for certain that at this point I had not broken out of the land of "Fair."

I don't remember much about the spring of tenth grade, but the diary for that time indicates that one problem was my handwriting. We received no handwriting instruction at Brearley. We were left to our own devices, and most girls printed with big rounded letters. My mother had learned calligraphy as a child, and became very good at it. When I was younger she had tried to impart this skill to me. She taught me to set up the page, tape it squarely to an inclined board, rule out the lines with light pencil for the body of the letters and for the ascenders and descenders, which could be the same height as the body or less, depending on the alphabet you were lettering. You had to grind the ink, sharpen the nibs, and hold your hand and the nib straight up and down as you worked, not at an angle. No splotches or you'd have to start again. No dragging your hand across the wet ink. No spelling mistakes.

I had no patience for this, but I did get a feel for what a flat nib could do for handwriting. I was determined not to print like my classmates but rather to write with joined letters, so I developed an illegible script that I wrote with a series of Esterbrook fountain pens with interchangeable nibs. It remains a nightmare to decipher, but those many Featherweight diaries have awakened my memory of the details of those years.

In the spring of tenth grade, I developed a friendship with Lois Kahn, who was my age but a class ahead of me. Lois was shortish, dark, smart, and curt. What I had to offer to her I don't know, but we got along well and she folded me into her set, which included a whole gang of very bright boys from Trinity School. Trinity was on the West Side and, like Collegiate and Brearley, went through to the twelfth grade. The group included Jack Davies, Mike Janeway and his younger brother Bill (sons of economist Elliott Janeway and author Elizabeth Janeway), Hank Resnick and his older brother Mike (sons of playwright Muriel Resnick, whose family lived in the garden duplex of a brownstone on East 74th Street where the choreographer, Jerome Robbins—"Jerry"—lived above). We palled around together intermittently for the next two and a half years. I was particularly partial to Mike Janeway, a medium-height, skinny guy who was very well read and verbally facile, and I liked his mother too. Partial to me was Hank Resnick, who was short and chunky and less appealing, although I came to know and like Hank's quick-witted, diminutive mother even better than Mrs. Janeway. I remember a bunch of us driving around the city in Jane Fonda's convertible. Jane and her brother Peter lived across the street from the Resnicks. Mike Janeway took the lead for these events, He was into Hemingway, and we played that we were off to Pamplona to run before the bulls. Although I hadn't yet read Hemingway (but kept quiet about it), I qualified as Lady Brett Ashley as I'd actually been to Pamplona. Mike was Jake... or was he Robert Cohn?

"Bulls have no balls!" Mike would shout to passersby. We thought we were so damned funny and so damned smart.

Things were finally moving ahead with Hans's divorce. My mother figured that sometime during the summer he might be free to move east with full custody of his two daughters. He had managed to secure a position on the faculty of Columbia College of Physicians and Surgeons (P & S), where he had done his residency in urology years before, and somehow was taken into someone's practice. In the meantime, in order to accommodate his daughters, schools had to be found, uniforms ordered, bus transport arranged, dancing classes arranged for—the works. And some serious changes had to be made to the living arrangements at 242 East 62nd Street.

My mother wanted to take over the apartment immediately above our duplex and install an interior stair so we'd all be connected, but the tenant refused to move out. He had been in residence before my mother bought the house and had a long lease on the two-bedroom apartment, which included the roof of the back of our duplex. So my mother asked the tenant immediately above him to move so we three kids could live up there, until Tenant One's lease expired and my mother could kick him out. My beautiful room-as-work-of-art was to become Hans's study. I wasn't a bit pleased about giving up my room, but I was happy that Hans and my mother were getting married and by the prospect of no longer being an only child.

I was to spend July and part of August with Cindy and her family in Edgartown while the upstairs apartment was being redecorated as bedrooms—the back room for Katherine, known as Pago, age five, and the front "bedsit" to be shared by Judy, just thirteen, and me, sixteen.

A summer in Edgartown with the Childses was a dream come true: my best friend and favorite family (after the Couderts) in a real summer resort that I knew and loved, where I, too, had roots and where we would swim and body surf on South Beach, play tennis, go to yacht club dances, and otherwise do what I thought the young were supposed to do. Dr. Childs had just bought Cindy an expensive toy—this was unusual, as he didn't part easily with money. It was an International 110 racing sailboat, which he wanted Cindy, and, eventually, her younger brother Eddy, to race, perhaps in the hopes that this diversion might take her mind off her determination to become an actress. The 110, designed in 1939, is twenty-four feet long and four feet wide. It has a double-ended hull with a flat bottom and rides low to the water. It looks like a floating cigar with a mast as high as the hull is long. It sports a mainsail, jib, and spinnaker. Its stability comes from a three-foot-deep, 300-pound bulb keel bolted to the flat underside of its Fiberglass hull.

Cindy's and my job was to do our best in the twice-weekly races organized by the Edgarton Yacht Club (EYC). There was little I had learned from cruising that could be applied to small boat racing, nor was Cindy an experienced skipper. However well we may have crossed the starting line or fetched the first buoy, the spinnaker run did us in. A spinnaker is a large and tricky sail on any boat. The 110's spinnaker pole was hard to handle in a stiff wind, and if the wind isn't stiff, the sail is hard to fill. Our spinnaker spent a lot of time in the water as we tried to set it. The dousing of the spinnaker was generally repeated if the wind direction and course required us to jibe. We never quite got it right. Sixth place was our best showing. But at the end of July we got second place for being the cleanest and tidiest boat in the fleet.

I am not sure either of us enjoyed the racing, but it had to be done. In contrast, swimming and sunbathing at South Beach in the late morning was sublime, as was taking our bikes across the little ferry to Chappaquiddick and riding out to East Beach for a late afternoon swim in those calm waters. Dinners were lively, especially when Dr. Childs had to remain in New York for work. Together with Lucinda Sr., we each had a glass of Tio Pepe sherry beforehand, ate well, talked lots, and listened to Bach and Mozart on the record player while we did the dishes.

And we read. I read *War and Peace* in two weeks, remembering precious little, and *The Fountainhead* in the next two weeks. The latter knocked my socks off, as it related to my chosen profession. I admired Howard Rouark for sticking to his guns, but I found him a bit of a pig and thought I might have preferred to be Dominique Francon, his long-legged and equally strong-minded girlfriend.

While I cherished Cindy's and my friendship, our endless talks and the things we did together, I was also jealous of her. Of course she was better at school and a better athlete than I was. But she was also better liked, certainly by the boys who were around that summer, and certainly by the one I particularly fancied—Mike Janeway. Mike's parents took rooms at the Harborview Inn, a large old-fashioned, Shingle Style hulk of a hotel at the north end of North Water Street, right by the shore, adjacent to the Edgartown Lighthouse. I was so glad Mike would be coming because I would have a friend of my own in Edgartown. But as soon as he clapped eyes on Cindy, he would barely speak to me. While Cindy seemed indifferent to Mike and to the attention of other boys, my envy smoldered. What was it that she had that I had not? Why couldn't I also be indifferent and aloof? Why was I craving attention when she did not?

The fact is, I thought Cindy *was* better than me. Her drive to be an actress came from deep within, and she had already proven to be good at it. Although she appreciated support, Cindy didn't need the attention of others to validate her ambition or her commitment to the theatre. In contrast, my drive to be an architect was totally superficial. My fascination with floor plans and my experience of Frank Lloyd Wright's Fallingwater and Gaudi's Casa Milá notwithstanding, I knew nothing about architecture, what it stood for, how it was conceived, and to what benefit or harm to whom. Beyond reading *The Fountainhead*, I was making no effort to learn. I couldn't draw. Nor would I try. I only wanted to be an architect to call attention to myself.

I spent many hours that summer smoking Marlboros and moping on the roof of Cindy's garage, or, alternatively, skipping stones

Part 2: SEXED

furiously from the shore of Edgartown's Outer Harbor, sobbing because Mike or some other boy on whom I fixated wouldn't give me the time of day.

JULY 25, 1956 — NEWSFLASH FROM CHANEL 11 TV:
"On the last night of an Atlantic voyage, only hours from safe harbor in New York, the *Andrea Doria*, the 29,000-ton luxury liner and pride of the Italian fleet, was broadsided by the eastbound 13,000-ton *Stockholm* of the Swedish American line, in an accident that killed forty-six and imperiled more than 1,700 passengers and crew.

"The efficiency of the crew and the rapid response of other ships averted a disaster similar in scale to that of *Titanic* in 1912. One thousand and six hundred and sixty passengers and crew were rescued and survived...

"Because of the sophisticated design of her double hull, the *Andrea Doria* was able to stay afloat for eleven hours after the ramming. With the world watching in horror during one of the first televised tragedies, the *Andrea Doria* sank, sparking a ferocious debate over fault that has never been resolved and ending the era of luxury cruise liners."

No, no. This cannot be true.
And so close by.
No, please no, please no.
More smoking Marlboros on the roof of Cindy's garage. More tears of sorrow. More skipping of stones atop the shallow waves of Edgartown's Outer Harbor.
At the end of July, still grieving for the world's and my loss, I returned to New York for a first meeting with my new-sister-to-be, Judith Phaigre Zinsser, whom I liked immediately. Judy, Hans, my mother, and I all had dinner at our house on 62nd Street, and then

Step II

Hans and Judy went elsewhere for the night. That was the first day Judy had ever seen the house in which she would soon be living full time. It was probably just one day after she had met the woman who was to take her mother's place in her father's life, and just two days after she had learned that she would no longer be living in Pasadena, no longer seeing her best friends at the end of summer, and not entering Pasadena High School as a ninth grader. How could any kid come to terms with so much change in so short a time?

The next day, Monday, August 6, 1956, Hans and my mother were finally married.

8. Hans's Haus

SEPTEMBER 1956

Ruby Zinsser's Studio/Garden Apartment on East 72nd St.

Hans Handforth Zinsser, my new stepfather, was skinny, quirky, funny, iconoclastic, super bright, romantic, loving, kind, and politically and socially conservative—a diehard Republican, in sharp contrast to my mother, who was committed to all things liberal and Democratic. He was a highly skilled, humane surgeon who did innovative research, creating new software for the very earliest mainframe computers to analyze matrices that he developed to organize and isolate the various components and symptoms of kidney disease. By so doing, he discovered different and heretofore unidentified strains that would respond to different treatments.

As expected, my mother's and Mssrs. d'Argout Fergusson's transformation of the house to accommodate Hans and his girls was efficient and effective. However, The Parents (as we soon came to call them) and we kids weren't even living in the same apartment. If five-year-old Pago wanted her Dada, she had to ask either Judy or me to get our keys, unlock the door to our apartment, descend two flights of public stairs, use another set of keys to get into the bottom duplex through my old room, now Hans's study, cross the upstairs living room to the double doors that led to the corridor that went around the patio and to The Parents' room at the back, then go through another door at the entrance to that room. My mother kept both sets of doors locked when The Parents were in their room. No amount of whining on the living room side of those doors would disturb their privacy until they were ready to emerge.

In late September I began eleventh grade at Brearley and Judy began ninth grade, a new girl complete with new blue gym tunic, blue buttoned overskirt to below the knees (a required add-on from sixth grade up), blue bloomers, and new maroon blazer. I was so proud to have my very own sister to show off and look out for. Pago was to go to Chapin, Brearley's rival school and only two blocks away, because Hans's sister's girls were there and Chapin was thought to be a gentler and possibly more nurturing environment, preferable for someone so small and vulnerable as Pago.

After the first week, during which The Parents took Pago to school, we three girls journeyed to school together. Judy and I would get ourselves and Pago dressed. The Chapin uniform was a pale green, square-necked, knee-length tunic with green bloomers, white blouse, and green blazer. Hair combed, teeth brushed, we took out the keys and down we went through the tenant stairs and to the kitchen for breakfast on the fly. Then to First Avenue to get the bus uptown. We'd drop Pago off at Chapin at 84th Street and East End before heading East on 83d Street in time for the morning bell at 8:40.

Hans's (and his sister Gretel's) formidable mother, known as Mingii, picked up a good deal of the slack for child care, especially with regard to Pago (whose nickname derived from the letters A

Part 2: SEXED

and G standing for Act of God, as her mother thought she couldn't have a second child). Pago went to Mingii's house on East 72nd Street almost every afternoon, and she and Judy spent time with Mingii and Antonia, Gretel's daughter, on the weekends.

Mingii was the daughter of mineralogist George Frederick Kunz, who is still revered for his classification of gems and the work he did for Tiffany's, including the discovery of Morganite (named for J.P. Morgan) and Kunzite (named for himself). Mingii and her sister Bessie were both artists, but Bessie had died in a carriage accident in the 1920s. This I know because someone endowed an art prize at Brearley in Bessie's memory, a prize of which I was a recipient.

For a lady pushing eighty, Mingii looked terrific. She had fine aquiline features and pale blue eyes, which she enhanced with smudges of blue eye shadow and the application of a standard HB Mogol pencil to line her eyes and darken her brows. She lived alone on the garden floor of her brownstone on East 72nd Street between Second and Third Avenues. The entryway, which was set back from the street, was dim and cluttered, then opened up to a large sunny double-height living room-cum-studio chock full of nineteenth-century furniture: a huge canopied bed, a sofa, settees, arm chairs, tables, Oriental carpets, and bookcases of various heights stuffed with books, albums, and priceless artifacts from the Wiener Werkstatte. There were sculpting stands with clay heads in various stages of completion and easels with at least one painting underway. The high walls of Mingii's studio/living room were plastered with midsize and small paintings—portraits and landscapes, mostly hers—and multiple gold-framed mirrors with the glass criss-crossed with yellowing Scotch Tape. The upper windows looking onto the garden were also taped. The tape was a residue from World War II, when people in New York were instructed to tape their windows and mirrors to control the shattering of glass should New York be bombed. Although the war had been over for more than a decade, Mingii never removed the tape, nor had she stopped sending daily weather reports to Washington, as she and many other conscientious citizens had done throughout the war.

When The Parents were home for dinner, one or the other would call us on the intercom to tell us to come down for cocktails. Out would come the keys and down we would go. Drinks for The Parents were one two-ounce vodka martini each, plus one "divvy" each of almost the same size. Then we'd go downstairs to the dining room for dinner at the five-legged, five-sided, quasi-Louis XVI painted wood table (which d'Argout Fergusson had found and bought for my mother before Hans's family was combined with ours). Dinner was cooked and served by Dagmar, just as it had been when only my mother and I were there. Throughout the meal, my mother would recount the details of her day at the office. Hans spoke barely a word but poured the wine copiously and listened adoringly. We children rarely spoke and were usually excused before coffee. Out came the keys and back upstairs we'd go. It was for Judy and me to see that Pago bathed, changed into her PJs, and brushed her teeth. Judy was used to this responsibility, as their mother had been absent for some time, but looking after a five-year-old was new to me. Later, Hans would come up to talk and play with us a little, maybe tell Pago a story and kiss us all good night. Maybe my mother came up too, but I can't remember.

Pago, ever adorable and game, would go to sleep with the door ajar, and Judy and I would press on with homework, listen to albums of show tunes, or talk. I wanted to open everything in my world to my new sister in hopes of easing whatever unhappiness or pain the transition from Pasadena to New York was causing. I could not imagine how she could process all this change, not to mention the loss of a totally different and more casual way of life. While my mother may have had the best intentions for us all and may have been an excellent administrator of this new family group, she was not experienced with small or even midsized children. Unsurprisingly, given her own lonely childhood, what heart and love she had to give was focused on Hans. But Judy never complained. She threw herself into her new life and situation with vigor and fortitude. If she suffered or found fault either with my mother, me, or her new situation, she kept it to herself. She almost seemed to be studying my mother as a model for her own eventual success—first as a fellow Brearley girl, then as a Bryn Mawr graduate, and ultimately as an inspired teacher of history and women's studies, and a distinguished author and scholar.

Once during that fall, Howie came to the house to visit me and the newlyweds. I was so pleased about my mother's marriage to Hans and having his daughters as my sisters that I thought I, too, would take the name Zinsser so I could be like everyone else in our house. Hans treated me then and always as one of his own. But when Howie visited, I realized I couldn't do that to him. However unfatherly he was, and however financially irresponsible he was regarding my support, he was still my father in a way Hans could never be.

Howie's visit was going well. He seemed genuinely fond of Hans, and happy for him and my mother. I am not sure how Hans felt. I didn't know then that Hans was both jealous and possessive of my mother, and that Howie had flirted with Hans's then-fiancée, Nancy Drinker, back in Boston just before I was born. But that evening they were all the beneficiaries of the healing powers of drink. I asked Howie: Could I take him on a tour of the rest of the house, including our digs on the fourth floor? Yes.

As we climbed the stairs to our flat and I got out my keys, he told me that he had always cared for Nancy and wanted to know what her children were like, or at least looked like. I widened the opening of the door to Pago's darkened room so the hall light would be enough for him to get a proper glimpse of her. He approached her bedside and looked upon her small round face and sleeping body with more tenderness and affection than I can remember him ever bestowing on any thing or person, much less one so little. Then he bent over and gently placed his short furry paw on her forehead and pushed aside a wisp of her amber hair, and then, after a moment or two, withdrew it.

The social tenor of life in Hans's Haus ratcheted up a notch. There were dinner parties and benefits for The Parents to attend, and dinners to host. The house was larger than before, with more of us to look after, so my mother looked for a chambermaid to assist Dagmar. Suzanne Morvan, the very young wife of Henri Soule's newest waiter-in-training at Le Pavilion, was the first hire. Short and stocky, with dark, close-cropped, curly hair and the strength of a small ox, she was no glamour-puss. Her duties were to clean the house, look after my mother's clothes, and serve at table. Dealing with Dagmar couldn't have been easy, but she succeeded somehow. My mother loved speaking French to Suzanne, and Judy and I loved to wrestle with her, though we always lost.

Gone were most of my mother's quasi-Bohemian friends as well as most of her gay friends. In addition to the Couderts, there was a new crowd of Mr. and Mrs. This and That with Park and Fifth Avenue addresses, some of whom were part of Hans's extended family. Hans wore his velvet smoking jacket to these dinners and my mother wore commensurately elegant long skirts or dresses. Hans filled giant Baccarat tumblers to the brim with whisky or gin or vodka for guests having before-dinner drinks. After dinner, the

Part 2: SEXED

ladies would stagger to the living room upstairs. The men would repair to the library to smoke cigars. When the men and women reconvened upstairs, liberal dosages of Courvoisier or Cointreau or Poire William were poured into snifters as conversation became louder and less cogent.

Suzanne handled all this very well but soon became pregnant, so she wasn't with us for long. She was followed by Elsa, a squat, middle-aged, humorless German woman who seemed close to useless but looked good in the black uniform with the starched white apron, collar, and cuffs. Both The Parents seemed to revel in the pomp of it all. My guess is that Hans took it less seriously than my mother, but he liked the role of host and wanted nothing more than her happiness. Thanks to him, she was at last the somebody she had always wanted to be: Mrs. Hans H. Zinsser. Years later, well into her marriage and with her career well established, she was interviewed for a magazine article on women working in the professions. When she was asked how she managed having a career, a husband, and children, she replied: "I have money and can afford help." No women's liberation for my mother.

Despite the bifurcated living arrangements, we did feel like and act as a family. Meals for the five of us at the five-sided table held us together, as did all manner of jokes and conversation. After dinner on the weekends when there were no guests, The Parents played ballroom dance music on the record player in the library, which was piped into the dining room, and we would all dance: my mother and Hans, Hans with each of us, and Pago and Judy and I together. The glazed passage along the side of the patio was great for practicing the Viennese waltz. It was very narrow and you had to get the turns just right to make it from one end to the other without hitting the mirror on one side or the big plate glass window on the other. We rarely succeeded, given the amount of wine we were drinking.

At Christmastime the residents of the houses on 61st and 62nd Streets between Second and Third Avenues (once known as Treadwell Farms), walked around the block singing Christmas carols to the residents remaining indoors and to the patrons of the Irish bars on Second and Third Avenues. This was our second Christmas there and our first Christmas block party. I remet Geoffrey Hellman, the New Yorker writer, whom I used to see at the Brearley bus stop with his young daughter Daisy. They lived at 228 East 61st Street. They were there with Daisy's glamorous mother, Daphne, and Daphne's son by a prior marriage, Sandy Bull. Daphne Hellman was a professional jazz harpist with a sylphlike figure, long blonde tresses, slanted almond eyes, and a Lauren Bacall smile. She and her trio played regularly at Julius Monk's Upstairs at the Downstairs. Her son Sandy—tall, soft-spoken, and willowy—shared his mother's blonde good looks and her musical talent, but not her gregariousness. He played the five-string banjo and was a protegé of Pete Seeger. Even though Sandy was a year younger than me, we hit it off immediately, although we didn't see that much of each other at first, as he was a boarding student at the Woodstock Country School in Vermont. But soon after Christmas, he and my folksinging friend Claire Carrié unknowingly inspired me to visit a pawnshop around the corner on Third Avenue and buy my first steel-string guitar. I had no clue how to play it. But I soon figured how to transpose basic chords from the piano to the guitar thanks to my lessons with Mr. Kruger. At a Christmas dance shortly after I got the guitar, I fell into a swoon over a boy called Roderick Franzius (whom I never saw again). In a few days, with the fingertips of my left hand raw from pressing the steel strings down on the steel frets, I composed "Rodrigues," a lament which declared my undying love:

Rodrigues, for someone or other this girl will surely cry,
Rodrigues, you are the lover for whom this girl will die.
(bridge):
You filled my heart with sorrow
When you said you'd return on the morrow.
But when that day was done,
I found you'd gone with the rising sun.

Powerful stuff!

The guys at Marconi Records had already introduced me to classical guitar music, and I was soon attempting to transpose the likes of "Jesu, Joy of Man's Desiring" to the guitar. In February of 1956, I bought a ticket to a solo concert at Town Hall performed by Andres Segovia and was transported by his artistry. Later in the week, I wrote a long letter recording my response to the Segovia concert to an old friend from dancing school who had gone off to board at Hebron Academy in Maine and with whom I corresponded regularly. My friend passed my effusive letter on to his friend and classmate, Gordon Dennis Bok, known then as Denny, who played classical guitar as well as sang and played folk songs. Denny wrote me back about Segovia, I wrote back to him, and he again to me. Thus began the great romance of my teenage years.

Denny had remarkable handwriting: small clearly rendered upper- and lower-case letters with long ascenders and descenders and generous distance between lines, to give shape and form to the negative space created by the long stems. He wrote like a poet, maybe more like a minstrel. He was from Camden, Maine, and in summers he crewed on the windjammers that operated out of Camden. I knew about those; I wrote him that I had been sailing in Penobscot Bay with my father and rattled off the little harbors I knew so well: Dark Harbor, North Haven, Brooklin, Centre Harbor, Blue Hill, Northeast and Southwest Harbors.

"Bok?" I wrote. His last name seemed strange; why wasn't it spelled Bach?

"Dutch," he explained.

"Oh, okay."

We met a month later when Denny and his guitar came to New York to visit a friend over spring break. He was tall, thickly set without an ounce of fat. His eyes were a soft blue and his skin more gold than pink. His mane of thick blond hair was cut short, and parted on the side, and his long bangs fell across his eyes when he leaned lovingly over his guitar and his large hands caressed its strings and frets. His smile was broad and his deep voice soft and mellow. I was ready to fall at his feet based on our correspondence, but the sight of him was almost more than I could bear. Denny responded positively to me but kept his distance (due to shyness, perhaps), and soon after we met, he returned to Hebron Academy. He came back to New York for a brief visit in April. I could sense he was uncomfortable in the city. Its energy and abrasiveness weren't to his taste. But we continued to write to one another regularly. He sent me poems and the lyrics of songs and shanties that he loved. He wrote a little about his parents, a mother to whom he was close and a reclusive father to whom he was not. He wrote of his grandmother, Nona, who lived in Southwest Harbor. I wrote to him about my parents and the bifurcated life I lived given their separation—one foot in Europe and the other in Penobscot Bay—and about whatever artistic stuff I could think up that might endear me to him: new songs I was learning from Claire or Sandy Bull, and poetry that

Part 2: SEXED

I was starting to read on my own. In downtimes during class, on the way to and from school, and especially at night before sleep, I yearned for the weeks to pass until I would be sailing again and Denny and I might meet up in Camden and get to know each other better, maybe even become close.

Would Denny be there the same few days that I would be there? Howie didn't like to stay put in any one harbor for too long.

Would Denny be off on a windjammer, and would we miss each other?

Would Denny touch me? Of course he would.

How and where? In a car, by the sea? On a boat? On his parents' porch?

Would Denny kiss me? Of course he would.

How and where?

I went through myriad variations of this scenario (though nothing more sexually advanced or intimate, strangely enough) until sleep would rescue me from my madness.

I wrote to Howie about Denny to prepare him for my wanting to spend some serious time in Camden in order to meet up with a boy of modest origins that I had recently met. I apologized that his name was not spelled B-a-c-h. Howie said B-o-k was just fine and seemed to know considerably more about Denny's family background than I did.

"Poochwoman, you ever heard of Curtis Island?" he asked in one of our long-distance phone calls.

"Yes," I replied, "It's the island at the mouth of Camden Harbor."

"That's it. And what about the *Saturday Evening Post*? You've heard of that?"

"Yep."

"Well, the *Saturday Evening Post* is published by the Curtis Publishing Company."

"So?"

"And they own the island, and they founded the Curtis School of Music in Philadelphia, while we're at it."

"So?"

"The Curtises and Boks are intermarried. Get it? They probably own all of Camden and a good hunk of Philadelphia too."

"Oh."

Yes, I was surprised. Hardly the impression Denny had given. But I was also sort of pleased. I knew what a snob Howie was and was relieved that the object of my obsession was intimately connected with a famous conservatory of music and a publishing house. That Denny was an accomplished sailor, and could play Scarlatti and Soler as well as Hank Williams and Leadbelly on his honey-colored guitar, augured well for a successful summer meeting.

Under the aegis of Brearley's innovative art teacher, Mrs. (Mary) Carpenter and her sidekick, Mr. (Armin) Landeck, an artist of note in his own right, I was starting to paint in earnest both in class and on my own. At home, in the room I shared with Judy, though I had never seen or heard of Joseph Albers, I painted strange geometric forms rendered in heavy oil paint with Albersesque iterations in differently colored bands radiating from the source object. I moved on to render surrealistic buildings that had holes cut out of the center, with little command of perspective. That's just how Mrs. Carpenter wanted it to be. She wanted her students to express themselves freely without the inhibition of knowing what had been done before. Mrs. Carpenter's and Mr. Landeck's encouragement inspired my artistic awakening. At school, I began a painting of a giant sea serpent, looping in and out of a turbulent, roughly textured sea. Tiny clipper ships clustered around the various places where his huge length broke the surface of the troubled waters.

Part 2: SEXED

His skin was patterned in harlequin-colored diamonds outlined in black. His head was proud and his eyes fierce. Flames spewed from his mouth. His name was Sire Gregoire. It was a goofy painting, but I was having great fun with the contrasting colors and textures.

The art studio was down the hall from the office of Miss Basinger, the head of the middle school, who had told my mother years before that my plentitude of petty crimes in earlier years were her and the school's problems, not my mother's. One afternoon, when I was working hard to get the saturated colors of Sire Gregoire's diamond skin just right, Miss Basinger strode into the studio for a look-see and stopped short in front of Sire Gregoire.

"That's wonderful, Leslie!" she said, studying Sire Gregoire and the churning sea around him. "Just wonderful."

"Thank you, Miss Basinger."

"When you are done with your serpent, I would like to hang him in my office—that is, if you wouldn't mind parting with him. He really is wonderful. Would that be all right?"

My painting in your office?

I saw my very first "Very Good" that year in art. Art didn't count as an academic grade at Brearley, but it counted for me. Big time. Sire Gregoire lived in Miss Basinger's office until long after I graduated.

As a result of my passion for the songs of Kurt Weill, I had wanted to take German in eleventh grade, but only Cindy and I were interested, and the minimum for a class was four, so I was suckered into a fourth year of Latin in part by the promise of reading Virgil. Latin required huge amounts of memorization. Memorization was very difficult for me then (and now); likewise, understanding the subtleties of grammar and syntax (even in English). I didn't quite get Virgil but liked the poems of Ovid and elected to translate one for extra credit, but I did such an appalling job that my teacher, Mrs.

Tully, kindly agreed not to diminish my grade but rather to write the whole thing off.

At Eastertime, Mrs. Tully told us about the speaking of Latin during the Dark and Middle Ages and thought we might be interested in a text of vulgar Latin recently set to music by the German composer Carl Orff. She played *Carmina Burana* for us during class and required us to translate the text. Now *that* was my kind of Latin!

The college application process did not begin in earnest until the start of senior year, but in eleventh grade we began mulling it over. We had taken the Preliminary Scholastic Aptitude Test (PSAT) in tenth grade. I had done badly, but my teachers hoped this was an aberration. These were aptitude tests and I was supposedly smart, so how come I couldn't eke out a decent score? My teachers thought I was bright enough, but didn't apply myself.

"No matter, Leslie, these won't count," my tenth grade homeroom teacher told me. "You'll take the SAT next year and again in your senior year and those will be the scores you'll use to get into college."

My SAT scores in eleventh grade were no better than they were in tenth grade. Nor were my scores on the ACT tests. The multiple choice format totally threw me.

"No matter, Leslie, these won't count," my eleventh grade homeroom teacher said. "You'll take them again next year, you will do better and those will be the scores you'll use for your college applications."

"If you say so." But I sensed I was in some kind of trouble that I didn't know how to fix.

Where to apply? My mother's and my first thought had been that I should go afar to "broaden my horizons." Stanford, perhaps. But then she decided Palo Alto was too far. People often settle where they go to college, she said, and she didn't want to lose me to California. Flattering, I suppose. But I also thought California to be far more foreign than Europe and thus more foreign than I was ready for.

Bryn Mawr wasn't even in the running. I wasn't going to compete with my mother, plus any women-only college was out; eleven years at all-girl Brearley were enough.

Secretly, I thought I was a natural for Radcliffe, but there were my grades to consider. Radcliffe was tops. I was not. Also I knew I had a long haul ahead: four years of college plus four years of architectural school before I could even begin to be an architect. Was there any way to speed things up? No, Harmon Goldstone had been clear: in order to succeed as a female entering the field, I would have to have more education and be better qualified than my fellow males if I wished to be hired by a decent firm.

No shortcuts. But maybe a jumpstart?

Early in the spring, I announced to The Parents that I wanted to work that summer. I wanted a real job in the city. My mother had never allowed me to earn extra money babysitting. She thought that babysitting was lower-class, being a Girl Scout was middle-class, and learning to type was demeaning. I wanted to do it all. But she approved of my having a real job, and leaned on her friends in fashion. Sarah Tomerlin Lee, who had risen fast in the combined world of fashion and interior design to be the editor of *Vogue,* came up with my big break. I was to be a clerk and gofer for Mrs. Dorothy Waddington, the executive director of the Fashion Group, an organization of and for women in executive positions in the fashion industry.

Starting Monday, June 10, 1957, every weekday morning for two months, I donned an actual dress, heels, makeup, and white cotton gloves and set out for the Lexington Avenue bus downtown. I got off at 51st Street, then walked west to 30 Rockefeller Center, stopping en route at Hamburger Heaven for a sticky bun and a thick mug of coffee at the counter. I felt so independent, so smart, so grown up at last. That Mrs. Waddington was nasty and impatient, especially with me, didn't matter. My three co-workers seemed to enjoy showing me how to answer the phone and take messages, how to file correspondence and invoices, how to keep track of the membership and what to send to whom when dues were unpaid. I learned to order and set up lunches for committee meetings held in the office (and to clean up afterwards). During my forty-five minute lunch break, I explored the fast-food eateries around Rockefeller Center and found my way to West 48th Street, a music mecca then, home to numerous brownstone storefronts that sold better guitars than mine (as well as violins, cellos, horns, clarinets, saxophones, cymbals, and drum sets) which kindled my lust for a guitar with nylon strings, maybe a Martin. But my thirty-three-dollars-per-week paycheck wasn't going to buy me a Martin, given the cost of the sticky buns and lunch.

By the end of June, most of my friends were away, as were Judy and Pago. But Sandy Bull was very much around, and we spent a lot of time together. I would listen to him play. He'd listen to me talk. On Saturdays, if I didn't take the train out to Jones Beach with Sandy to fry my olive skin to a crisp, I explored secondhand bookstores like Argosy Books on East 59th Street or went to the movies in the afternoon with The Parents and joined them for the usual cold meat and salad supper. Then I would paint through the night. On Sundays, at first led by Sandy and then on my own, I would sling the fancy ribbon that served as a strap for "Rodrigues," my two-bit, steel-string guitar, over my shoulder and head for the Lexington Avenue subway and down to Washington Square, where many

Part 2: SEXED

kids and adults who loved folk music gathered around the fountain in the middle of the park to play and sing and talk and meet like-minded folk. The Parents were mortified by my heading to the Village, clad in a perky cotton sundress and minimal Italian sandals, hair flying, guitar not even in a case, exposing myself to the world.

And singing?

Folk music?

In public?

With people I didn't know and hadn't been introduced to?

I don't know about Hans, but my mother rarely traveled south of 59th Street unless it was to Wall Street or to one of the city or state courthouses, in which case she'd take the subway. She had little first-hand, street-level experience of the territory in between the southern tip of Manhattan and the snug, smug security of the Upper East Side. Although she had taken me to the Theatre de Lys on Christopher Street to see *The Threepenny Opera* for the first time, that had proved to be a one-off urban safari, not to be repeated. Greenwich Village, the epicenter of artistic life and Bohemian behavior, with all its dubious connotations, was strictly off limits.

For her, but not for me.

I was now a working girl and could go where I wanted. And I did.

Those Sundays were fantastic: the hours spent at Israel Young's cluttered dusty shop, the Folklore Center, on the east side of MacDougal Street, poring over old vinyl records by famous folk singers and reading sheet music of songs to be learned; the first taste of American espresso and cappuccino at Figaro's and its nearby spinoffs; singing and playing in the cool shade of Washington Square's enormous plane trees; meeting new people who knew nothing about who I was or from whence I had come, and didn't judge me except for my music—which wasn't great. But I could hold my own.

Hans's Haus

The best part of working at the Fashion Group was planning the fashion shows that we sponsored regularly. Some were small and focused largely on one particular aspect of fashion: evening wear, sportswear, millinery, each featuring attendant lines of shoes, handbags, and costume jewelry. But each season there would also be a blockbuster show that included everything. My contributions were various: helping to track and coordinate deliveries of clothes and accessories to the various hotels and ballrooms where these events were held; ensuring these items were later returned to the manufacturers or designers who supplied them; being certain that the models hired for the show would show up; helping the models assemble the planned outfits and accessories so each tallied with what was written in the program; helping the models dress for their short prance down the runway, and then undressing and redressing them for the next prance. It wasn't Maison Dior. The costume jewelry was just that, often flashy and vulgar. The clothes weren't works of architecture but just clothes: prêt a porter/ready-to-wear suits, day dresses, cocktail and evening dresses, made with fabrics that were often synthetic.

There were no hushed silences as the models slinked down the runway apron, as there had been in Paris. The Fashion Group shows were full of energy and excitement. The models would come into the dressing rooms without makeup and with street clothes hanging off their scrawny bodies and in a few harried minutes transform themselves into perfectly coiffed, slender goddesses. They bobbed silently and solemnly down the catwalk, slinging their long legs out from the hip, knees straight, one high-heeled foot crossing in front of the other, spinning on their back foot—all these movements meant to show all sides of their outfit to the viewers. Once off the runway and out of sight, they would race to the dressing

Part 2: SEXED

room, drop what they were wearing to the floor, and with our help, scramble into the next outfit; clip on new earrings; slide on bracelets; slip into heels; grab a boa, a faux-fur stole, or a handbag; and set off down the catwalk yet again. The models worked like mules, and were often treated less well than mules. I understood why they were so well paid.

My favorite model was Brenda, a playful redhead who actually smiled genuinely and deigned to converse with her dressers. She said that I should consider modeling, I had the facial planes and the build if not the height—I'd only have to lose a few pounds, and she and I were more or less equally tall. Eileen Ford, the premier agency of the time, would love me. Could she help? No, no, thank you. But I was flattered. Mrs. Waddington was right. I was lousy at doing what I was told to do, especially if I didn't see the sense of it. And I would have to give up all those sticky buns.

My last day at the Fashion Group was at the beginning of August, and that very Friday after work I took the train north to meet up with Howie and Cissie at Charlecote, my Armstrong grandparents' brick house in Washington, Connecticut. We had a stuffy and unpleasant dinner at the Mayflower Inn. A memory of my grandmother stuffing an enema tube into my clenched, five-year-old anus had dissipated any warm feelings I might have had for her. My grandfather seemed unable to think or act independently in her presence. The next day Howie, Cissie, and I took off in their convertible, stopping first in Marblehead to catch up with a few old friends from what Howie termed the "Boston gin belt," and then heading north and east to Centre Harbor, Maine, where *Stone Horse* had spent the winter. My nerves and heart were in a state, because I so hoped I would soon be meeting up with Denny Bok.

Over the next two weeks, sailing in and around Camden and Penobscot Bay, and in and around Mount Desert Island, I saw a lot of Denny, almost more than I had expected. Somehow the windjammer he was crewing on would turn up where we were going, or I would persuade Howie to drop our hook where the windjammer was scheduled to anchor next. Howie seemed to like Denny, which was a relief. And Denny's mother, whom I only met once, and his grandmother, whom I met several times, were tolerant of me.

Did Denny touch me? Yes. Did we kiss? Yes, long kisses, at the end of many long evenings, in many diverse and picturesque settings. Neither of us wanted or expected more. We seemed at ease talking to each other when he wasn't singing or playing, and he seemed to enjoy our intimacy although he never spoke of it. It was clear he wasn't looking for any sort of involvement. I think he would have been as happy at the wheel of a windjammer or playing his guitar on a spit of rock looking into the sunset. Denny was a loner.

In mid-August we sailed *Stone Horse* out of the populated waters around Mount Desert and headed east—just Howie, Cissie, and me, from Cape Split to Cutler to Campobello. Campobello, a vacation home of FDR's and officially in New Brunswick, wasn't like other parts of the Maine coast. Its shore wasn't just evergreens on low-lying rocks, but lush, deciduous trees and rolling meadows. After a one-night stop in Campobello for a party at someone's boathouse, we headed north into Passamaquoddy Bay to St. Andrews, where we stayed several days. Cissie and Howie played golf on the Algonquin course, and I happily stayed on board, knitting, reading, and occasionally plugging quarters into the phone box on the dock to report my whereabouts to Denny. Then we set out to sea again into the Bay of Fundy and further east to St. John, the capital of New Brunswick, at the mouth of the St. John River.

There the difference between high tide and low tide is the largest in the world—over twenty-nine feet. The river cuts its way to the Bay of Fundy through a deep submerged gorge with hairpin-type turns worthy of the French Riviera's Grande Corniche. Every six hours, the sea level drops to fourteen feet below the level of the river, and water churns and boils through the gorge into the bay. Six hours later, the bay is fifteen feet higher than the river and the direction of the falls and rapids reverses, pushing the river waters as far north as Fredericton, eighty miles up-river. Access to and from the river can be had only during slack tide when the level of the river and the Bay of Fundy are more or less the same. This lasts barely an hour. No boat or ship, however large or small, is allowed to go through without a pilot.

Traversing the falls at slack tide made our many trips through Woods Hole and our one trip through Hell's Gate, in New York, look like walks in the park. We went through toward the end of slack tide, and the water was moving with us. The passage was narrower than it looked on the charts. One, or possibly two, boats could pass through in each direction at a time. We could see the angry waters roiling and churning beneath the surface. Howie was at the helm, with the pilot by his side. The big oak tiller fought him as he followed the pilot's instructions to steer a clear center course around the hairpin turns. We seemed to be flying. Little whirlpools began to spin around us everywhere, getting bigger by the minute. Then all of a sudden, we were out the other side and into the river's wide delta, where open water moved rapidly though no longer angrily. A skiff came out to pick up our pilot, whom we thanked and whose number we took for the return trip. Kennebecasis Island was up ahead to starboard. The burgee of the Royal Kennebecasis Yacht Club beckoned. We gladly accepted a mooring and spent the rest of the day exploring St. John on foot and by taxi before heading upriver.

The trip upriver to Fredericton and back was a dream. The sun was hot, the air was soft, the water smooth, so unlike the nastiness of the weather in the Bay of Fundy. Farmland dotted with heads of cattle stretched out on either side of the river, punctuated by little villages with tall white church steeples reaching up toward the occasional cloud, scuttling by overhead. We had the wind behind us and were able to sail on our way north. On the way back to St. John, we traveled the outgoing tides. We moored again at the Royal Kennebacasis Yacht Club and met our pilot the next day. The return trip through the Reversing Falls was less dramatic, because this time it really was slack tide. We came out into St John's harbor and headed straight into a low-lying cloud bank hovering over the open sea. The prevailing southwest wind was at first moderate, but then, as we headed southwest, following the coastline, it really began to blow. We were determined to make it to Roque Island in one shot.

The journey was an endless slog upwind and "up west." For most of that long night, I was alone on deck at the helm, with screaming headwinds tearing at my ears, lashing rain drenching my face, head, and hands, and waves breaking over the bows and coating my glasses with so much salt that I could hardly make out the compass bearing on the dimly lit binnacle. But I held fast and drove *Stone Horse*, bucking and pitching forward, through the oncoming seas, the big oak tiller wedged between my right arm and my right side, legs splayed and boots jammed up against the sides of the cockpit for bracing. It was hard work, but I was good at it—or so I thought until I spotted the flash from Swallow Tail Light on Grand Manan Island. We were going backwards. Only when the tide began to ebb in the direction of our travel did we make way against the shore. But sailing into Roque Island's crablike embrace as the rising sun dispersed the clouds and spread its fingers over the calming seas was ample reward for the long night's struggle.

9. Hamlet and Henchard

SEPTEMBER 1957

The '21' Club on West 52nd Street.

Miss Joycelynn Gibson, super British Oxford graduate, head of the English Department and most formidable of all faculty members, took the senior class—all four sections. Her dark oak desk by the window presented its side to us as we entered. Miss Gibson looked out over six rows of wooden tablet/arm chairs, each row with eight chairs. Here we sat for morning roll call, announcements, and any classes assigned to our room. But mostly we gathered in the airy sun-drenched corner at the back of the room, where we were permitted to lounge on a faded sofa or one of several easy chairs and pile our belongings on a large surface passing for a coffee table. The north wall was lined with wooden cubbies where we kept our books. The window sills were deep and high, with shabby cushions that were good for sitting as well. So were the locker tops. This living room setup was one of many privileges that we enjoyed as seniors. We could also come and go from the school after the last academic classes were over without permission slips. And we could smoke during lunch hour (forty minutes, not a real hour), but only in the cafeteria down on Deck B.

I finally had some very good friends, particularly Claire Carrié, Vicky Etnier, and Cindy Childs. At lunch every day, we sat together at a little table for four in the cafeteria adjacent to the famous table for four occupied for many consecutive years by Miss Mitchell, Miss Gibson, Miss Carling (head of the gym department), and Mrs. Licht (head of the Latin Department and also, like Miss Carling, from my mother's day). Of those four, only Mrs. Licht seemed comfortable with her biological gender, but they were good friends, laughed a lot, and smoked incessantly during the short lunch period. So did we, all but Vicky, who was studying voice. We four thought we were hot stuff as budding artists and musicians. In addition, I had assumed several pretentious affectations: I had started to use a stick pen with a metal nib for notetaking, which required me to carry a bottle of ink in my uniform pocket. And, taking after my mother, I sprinkled only ground pepper on my food, necessitating the presence of a small pepper mill next to the ink bottle. Occasionally, I also sported a cigarette holder.

I was finally elected class prefect for a month term because I was the only member of the class who had never been elected to any class office. I worked briefly on a new school paper and was elected to the writing team for the Senior Show, which was to be performed close to graduation. I ran the school spelling bee but made a mistake in the spelling of "picnicking," insisting it had two k's not one, and put out one student after another until Miss Gibson shouted out from the balcony of the auditorium in her piercing British accent,

"And how do *you* think picnicking is spelled, Leslie?"

Life at Hans's Haus rolled on. Now that our parents were

married, they talked about having a child. My mother was just forty-two and Hans was thirty-nine. It didn't happen, so they decided to get a dog—not just any dog, but a Chow Chow, and not just any color Chow, but a black Chow, because that's what my mother had grown up with. Chows were reputed to be mean and strictly one-man dogs, so maybe this wasn't the best choice. But I liked Chows, despite their reputation. I loved their chunky size and strength, their thick fur, and their dignity. A flurry of research turned up a local breeder with a litter soon due. In early October, The Parents rented a car and drove to Metuchen, New Jersey, to collect our very own ball of black fluff, complete with blue tongue. Gaffer's Chows had always had Chinese names, as Chows were originally Chinese guard dogs. My mother's favorite had been Ling. Hans had a simple Chinese dictionary, which indicated that Ling meant "sweet." After much deliberation, we named our black fluff ball Chiu Mo Ling, meaning Wine Ink Sweet. Soon she was known just as Mo.

Mo was adorable. She was the perfect surrogate child for The Parents: reserved but never mean, loving but not too much so. They enjoyed being attentive to her grooming and the adjustments to her diet. They took her to dog training classes, but soon forgot what she and they learned and did little to provide her the exercise she needed, but she didn't complain. She did her business on the patio in the morning and during the day. Neither we kids nor Dagmar nor Elsa were assigned to specific dog-walking duties, and by late evening The Parents were generally way too "tired" to take her for a walk. But I often took her out after school and sometimes in the late evening as an excuse to get out of the house and go round the corner to visit Sandy Bull when he was home from school in Vermont.

Visiting Sandy could mean hanging out with his glamorous mother, Daphne, and her coterie of famous and exotic friends. It could also mean listening to Daphne and her jazz harp trio rehearse in the Hellmans' sprawling living room. Or it could mean listening to Sandy play his latest instrument or piece, with or without his wild-assed, ether-sniffing musician friends. But almost always, it ended up with Sandy and me making out well into the night in his room, which was on the left as you entered the house from the top of the stoop. Sandy had a girlfriend at school, but she lived near Chicago. I didn't like being second best. On the other hand, I was still obsessed by Denny Bok, and he wasn't around either. I liked Sandy's looks and found his moodiness appealing. I admired his musicianship and adored his mother and her scene, so the unstated arrangement suited us both. There was no question of our doing anything more advanced than making out. Kids our age didn't seem to do more back then. But we went at making out with dedicated enthusiasm. Mo was more than tolerant as she dozed on the floor by Sandy's bed, awaiting the short walk home.

On my own, long after Judy and Pago had gone to bed, I continued to listen to music and paint on the floor of our upstairs apartment. During the day, I struggled on with my move up and out of the Land of Fair. If I were actually moving at all, it was imperceptible. But if it didn't happen somehow, there was no way I would get into a decent college, and I certainly wasn't going to settle for some girlie-girlie finishing school-type institution. Our courses were math again, introductory set theory, and pre-calculus with Miss Cook, a mild milk-toasty type in whose class I had been sassy and rude the year before, but who somehow got through to me despite my behavior and was thus largely responsible for turning me around in math. Physics was with a teacher I hardly knew, but surprisingly I found the subject fascinating. I took French again, this year with Mme. Giachine, head of the French Department, who threw chalk at students she didn't favor (I was repeatedly the unhappy target).

Part 2: SEXED

For American history, I had Miss Bartlett, whom I'd had in eighth grade and admired although I hadn't done well in her class. English was with the formidable Miss Gibson, whom I'd never had and who struck terror in my heart. Last but not least, our class had a weekly meeting and discussion of ethics with the equally formidable but surprisingly gentle, soft-spoken Jean Fair Mitchell, our headmistress.

We had college counseling with Miss Mitchell and her dogged, downtrodden assistant Miss Mary Ward, a sexless clone of Olive Oyl, Popeye's emaciated but devoted inamorata. With all the girls' colleges out of the running, likewise anything proximate to New York City, I narrowed my choices down to three: Radcliffe, Pembroke, and the University of Wisconsin.

I already knew I was the Radcliffe type but wasn't sure I wanted to go there, and Miss Ward assured me that, given my academic record, the chance of my being admitted was slim. Pembroke was the women's division of Brown University, but unlike Radcliffe (or Barnard), it did not have its own faculty, nor did it confer its own degree. It was little more than a cluster of dormitories, an eating hall, a library, a gym and phys-ed department, and administrative offices. Everything else came under the Brown University umbrella. But Pembroke did have its own Admissions Department. While Brown was then at the rock bottom of the Ivy League in terms of cachet and was thus a repository for those rejected by its more exalted brethren (Yale, Harvard, Princeton, Dartmouth, Cornell, and Columbia), Pembroke attracted smarter applicants from the best public high schools around the country. I am not sure why, but very few Brearley girls applied or went there. One deterrent was Brown's stringent distribution program; all students were required to take at least one year of math and one year of a hard science (geology, botany, zoology, and psychology didn't count). To get into architecture school, I knew I would have to take calculus, and go further in physics, so this requirement was fine by me. Best of all, Brown students were permitted to take classes at the Rhode Island School of Design. Therein lay a possible shortcut! Maybe I could take two years of all the hard stuff at Brown and then transfer to an undergraduate architectural school. My backup choice was the University of Wisconsin, far from New York, but in somewhat familiar terrain, given its proximity to Chicago and the parts of Wisconsin in which I had sailed in my first summers with Howie.

Early in the fall of my senior year, I took the Scholastic Aptitude Test for the last time. The results were as bad as in the previous years. I don't recall the exact scores but they were in the range of 500 out of 800 for English and a little higher in math. There'd been no substantive improvement over the year before, and there was no third chance. Even if I might do better on the Achievement tests that were given later in the year, I was still going to have to do something dramatic to prove to the colleges of my choice that I wasn't a bottom-of-the-barrel type. But what and how? With this hanging over my head, I took the train to Providence to visit Brown and have an interview with Pembroke's Department of Admissions.

Back then, Providence was a backwater, and Brown's collection of late-eighteenth-century and nineteenth-century disparate building types did not convey the gravitas of Harvard, Yale or Princeton's grand architectural homogeneity. But to my eyes, there was something funky and appealing about the mix of building styles and the lawns and quadrants that they defined. The more I walked around, the more I liked it. I even cottoned to the big old Victorian houses surrounding the campus, although I had never before liked anything Victorian.

I was interviewed by the assistant director of admissions, a personable, youngish woman, who did her best to draw me out and put me at my ease. But I was nervous, not just because my SATs were bad (and my grades were barely average), but because I really wanted to go to Brown, and I had a gift for shooting myself in the foot when I really wanted something. I nattered on about my interest in music and art, my determination to become an architect, and how I looked forward to getting to know my grandfather's first cousin, Sinclair Wallace Armstrong, who was on the history faculty at Brown, but whom I'd never met. At the end of the interview, which I thought had gone reasonably well, I said to my interviewer,

"Do you think I will fit in here at Brown and Pembroke?"

She looked at me for a minute and said, "No, actually, I don't think this will be a good fit for you …" She said something else by way of closing the interview, but I didn't hear her. My heart was in my shoes, my stomach flipped.

"But, but this is really where I want to go," I sputtered. "Can we talk about it some more, please? Can I tell you why I want to be here, what I like about your course requirements, about your mix of students, about the campus, about all the buildings I've seen? Can I try to persuade you that I would be a good fit?" The tone of the interview shifted. I quit being New York City slick. I talked from the heart and she listened. Then she talked and I listened. We ended on an entirely different note.

On my way out the door, she shook my hand warmly and said, "I think you might fit in very well after all. I will put in a good word for you when the time comes."

Nothing guaranteed, but maybe, if I could get out of the Land of Fair, I had a chance.

In English class we were reading *Hamlet* with Miss Gibson. I found Shakespearean English almost incomprehensible (no surprise, given my English aptitude scores), and Hamlet himself a wimpy and unsympathetic type. Although Miss Gibson's readings from the text were inspiring, I found her references and cross-references completely alien. Where did this sort of thinking come from? Yes, it was interesting that Shakespeare generally mentioned something important twice in case someone like me or a snoozing theatre-goer missed it the first time, likewise his use of prose for the speech of common folk and verse for the principal characters, but then what? It was all flying over my head.

One day, after a particularly opaque English class, I waited until Miss Gibson had gone home and went up to her big wooden desk. Among a row of books between two bookends at the back of her blotter was her copy of *Hamlet*. I opened it and found notations on almost every page. A goldmine! Much too much to take in in one sitting. I snuck her *Hamlet* into my book bag, took it home and spent the better part of the night copying every single note and marking from her book into mine. For the first time ever, I was in school early the following morning, to get the book back in its place before she arrived.

Studying her notes was mind-blowing. What she'd been teaching us began to make sense. But how did she figure all this out? And how was I going to convey to her that I could figure it out as well without revealing my source? We had a big paper to write about *Hamlet*. In past years, I had not done well on these papers, although we had been well trained in our history classes to do research, to record information on three-by-five-inch index cards, to footnote our sources with appropriate *ibids* and *op. cits*, and to cite our sources in a bibliography at the end. I had been lazy, or so I and my teachers thought, and I hadn't taken the process seriously before. But now that I had all this inside information, I would have to figure how to document it—assuming I could find it elsewhere. For the first time ever, I went to our local branch library—not the school library, because I didn't want anyone to know about my private goldmine, how I obtained it, and how I had to make it mine—and read everything I could find about *Hamlet* in hopes that some of Miss Gibson's insights would be corroborated. Surprise, surprise, I was able to source almost every notation and come up with some of my own! I found the process fascinating. I spent many long hours on my paper, working harder than I'd ever worked before, carefully organizing it thematically and documenting the source of every observation or analysis made. I made a clean longhand copy and handed it in. On time, too. For the first time ever, I got a "Very Good"—Brearley's equivalent of an A—in something other than art.

My mother had been climbing the social ladder for as long as I could remember. She had her heart set on my making a proper debut at one of the big Christmas dances. Now that she was no longer a single mother, but respectably remarried into a prominent family, this seemed a possibility. But I would have none of it. I was no bride, saw no need to wear white, and had no use for the ladies to whom I was to be presented, nor would they have had any use for me if they knew anything about me. If the purpose of coming out was for a young woman to be introduced as a fledging adult into the society of her parents (with the unspoken hope of finding a suitable match amongst their sons), fine. I liked my mother's Bohemian and bluestocking friends. I liked that many of her older friends were Jewish and as many were gay. I even liked a few from Park Avenue. And I liked some of their children. If I were to "come out," it was going to be a la Henry James: at home at an afternoon tea (with drinks served in the background), and the guests were to be the children of her friends, people with whom I grew up. I was adamant. She capitulated but not without calling the *New York Times* in hopes of having my archaic home debut announced on the society page. The date was to be the Saturday afternoon of Thanksgiving weekend.

The *New York Times* apparently thought this to be a super-exclusive event, and wanted to send a reporter to interview and photograph me in the morning. My mother was ecstatic. And I reveled in the unexpected attention.

The Parents were out when the reporter and photographer arrived. Pago and I received them. I was partially made up, to the extent I knew how to apply makeup, and wearing rolled-up jeans; one of Hans's old white shirts, with a slightly frayed collar and tails out; and my favorite beaten-up Capezio flats. This sort of attire may be the norm now, but it wasn't then. The reporter, after taking me in from head to foot, began to ask a series of questions about where the supper would be served, and where the dancing would be, and how many pieces in the orchestra.

"What supper? What dancing? What orchestra?" I replied, "This is an old-fashioned coming-out party. I am to be presented to my parents' circle of friends at a tea here at home at four o'clock this afternoon. That's the way it used to be done. And that's how we are doing it."

Silence. Then finally, the reporter asked,

"What will you wear this evening? May we see your dress?"

"Sure." I said," I'll go get it."

"We want to photograph you in the dress you're going to wear."

The photographer perked up, thinking he might have something to do after all. I perked up, too, because he was gorgeous, like a young Franz Liszt—thin, hollow cheeks below high cheekbones, sallow skin, longish hair, mournful eyes.

"Certainly," I said. "I'll get changed at once. May I offer you some tea or coffee while you wait? Please sit here. This is where the tea will be served, at this table." And I showed them to chairs at the five-sided dining table.

Part 2: SEXED

"Thank you, just some water, please," said the not-so-handsome reporter.

I came back with glasses, ice, and a pitcher of tap water that Pago poured for them. Out came the keys, and Pago and I ripped upstairs to our apartment. I jumped into my dark green satin Mingolini Guggenheim cocktail dress, the one with the long sleeves, scoop neck, broad bands of black velvet ribbon edged with tiny black jet beads running horizontally in parallel around the sleeves, the back of the bodice and its full skirt. The whole dress felt Elizabethan although it was very simple. It was empowering to wear. Pago zipped up the back. I jammed on my black satin heels, sans stockings, threw on some lipstick and tore back down to the dining room. As I turned the corner into the room I removed my glasses, shook out my fine shoulder-length brown hair and said "This is it!"

"That's it?" said the reporter. "That's what you are wearing?"

"Yes."

"It's not white."

"No, sir, it is not white. I am being presented to my parents' friends as a young adult. I am not getting married." The reporter was disconsolate. But Mr. Liszt beamed. Out came the Nikon, the extra lenses, and the flash attachment. He began to shoot casual head shots, then me in the whole dress, which he declared exquisite, then me at the five-sided table where the tea would be served.

"I find your features fascinating," he said in heavily accented English. He took several posed close-ups that showed me exactly as I had always wanted to look: dark, moody, exotic, and intense. The photo session was an exhilarating start to what turned into a wonderful party and a wonderful day. The next day, Sunday, there was the photo of me looking dark, moody, exotic, and intense in the *New York Times*, together with a short article about Dr. and Mrs. Hans H. Zinsser presenting their daughter, Leslie Armstrong, to society from their home on East 62nd Street, the text just as my mother had wanted and the photo just as I had wanted. Thank you, Franz.

My last shot at the college boards was scheduled for a Saturday in January. These were the Achievement tests for which we had to study and for which I did study—lots. The compulsory subjects were English and math. French was my elective. At that time, very few students took Advanced Placement tests, possibly only three girls in our class. Given my scores and grades, Advanced Placement wasn't for me. I was not looking forward to taking the Achievement tests. I had already sat through two sets of what seemed like endless two- and three-hour exams in one or another unfamiliar gym at one or another of New York's public high schools, staring at page after page of multiple-choice questions to which I should have known at least eighty percent of the answers, but did not. A bit before 8:00 a.m. that Saturday, I turned up in yet another unfamiliar gym in another unfamiliar school and waited as the exam booklets for the first of the three subjects were handed out. Once again, a semi-opaque scrim descended between my brain and the exam booklet, blending the specifics of one question with the rules or facts or formulae that obtained to the next. As instructed, I set about first answering those questions to which the answers seemed obvious. But there were so few. The wording of the questions that remained blended into unintelligible sequences as I pawed through the viscous fluid that contained the body of knowledge I had brought into the exam in search of the bit of grammar or math I needed to determine which of two alternatives was true or false, or which of four was correct.

Brain, why hast thou forsaken me?

The bell rang. I turned in my incomplete answer sheet, took a bathroom break and munched on some crackers before resuming my seat for the second exam. The same thing happened again, although the subject was math and not English. There were those word problems: If you start with twenty-four cherries weighing two ounces each and twelve apples weighing six ounces each, how far apart from one another would each be on the ground if you were in a car going at forty miles per hour for five minutes and alternately threw a cherry and an apple straight out the driver's seat window every thirty seconds? Such problems drove me to tears in school and to such despair during the exam that I lost what little confidence I had in those few answers I did know. Another bathroom break and a banana. The last test was in French. I looked at the questions and thought of Mme. Giachine hurling chalk at me and figured I just plain didn't give a damn. I ripped through the questions, filling in those little ovals on the answer sheet with my number-two pencil while fighting the descent of scrim that would soon fog my brain if I let it fall into place. I left the strange gym in the strange school soon after noon, feeling ill. I knew that something was very wrong with me. I knew my fellow students and friends didn't have this sort of trouble with these exams. My parents had never had any academic problems. They were always the brightest and best. Why me? Why was I shooting myself in the foot yet again?

On the Friday after the Achievement tests, I took my second legal cut day and went by train to Cambridge for a tour of Radcliffe and an interview. A frosty wind was blowing off the Charles River. It was cold and raw. Radcliffe didn't look as exciting as I had expected. When I arrived at the admissions office, I was ushered into the office of Miss Constance Ballou, Radcliffe's dean of admissions. She was shortish and attractive, with straw-colored hair cut in a bob, glasses on her nose, and dressed in business attire that matched her business-like manner. I had no idea why the dean of admissions was bothering with me as a candidate.

"Good afternoon, Miss Armstrong," she said as she showed me to a seat opposite her and riffled through the file on her desk.

"Good afternoon, Miss Ballou," I replied.

"The reason we have granted you an interview is that we could not believe anyone would have the nerve to apply to Radcliffe with College Board scores and grades such as yours. We had to see who you were."

And they hadn't yet seen the lousy scores that were soon to come in from the Achievement tests!

Miss Ballou pressed on, "What can you tell us about yourself that might make us even consider accepting you?"

I don't remember what or how I replied. But the interview was over almost before it began. I found my way to the street, to a pay phone, and called Tracy Coudert, who by then was a freshman at Harvard. We went to a bar and got loaded while I wept. He put me on the Merchants' Limited back to New York. Once I was home from Penn Station, I took to my bed, hungover and sick with self-disgust.

French was the only subject in which I got over 600. Math was well below. And English, again, way below math. Even Brearley didn't know what to say or do. I asked Miss Mitchell if she would consider writing to the colleges to which I was applying to request that their admissions people not consider the College Board scores an accurate reflection of my aptitude or ability. As a bargaining tool, I had had the Very Good on the *Hamlet* paper. She agreed but was by no means sure that it would be effective. We wouldn't know until mid-May.

In spite of these setbacks, I went with family and friends to the movies, the theatre, and even the opera, for which I hadn't yet developed much enthusiasm. I even snuck off to the Museum of

Modern Art from time to time, but only when no one was looking. I continued to paint furiously, and to sing and play the guitar to anyone who would listen. I pined for Denny Bok, worked on the script for the Senior Show, and studied hard, increasingly grateful to Miss Gibson for opening my eyes and my brain.

In the spring we read Thomas Hardy's *The Mayor of Casterbridge*. I loved this book and its structure, setting, and characters. I loved that Hardy had been an architect. Another critical paper was assigned. But this time I knew the drill: pinch Miss Gibson's copy, transcribe all her notes into my copy, go off to the library for several days in succession to read every critical evaluation of Hardy I could find, establish a hypothesis, make an outline, flesh the outline into text, develop a reasonable and readable conclusion, polish the draft, copy it over in longhand (none of us typed then, and few of us even knew how) and hand it in (on time). Done.

On May 5, 1958, I got a fat envelope from the University of Wisconsin informing me of my acceptance, times and dates for freshman orientation. It included nformation about residences for freshman men, and an invitation to become acquainted with the various fraternity houses I might rush. I figured I'd let that slide until I heard from Radcliffe and Brown, and would only set Wisconsin straight as to my gender and loathing of anything relating to fraternity (or sorority) life if I planned to go there. But it was a relief to know I had gotten in somewhere.

The next week I got a skinny envelope from Radcliffe (expected), and a fat one from Pembroke/Brown (hoped and prayed for, but not expected). Thank you, Jean Fair Mitchell. Your letter must have worked.

Just before my eighteenth birthday, I went out on a grownup dinner date with Francesco Bonmartini, the son of my mother's

Italian friends from Rome. Francesco was midway in age between my mother and me, meaning he was over thirty. He was single and living in Elizabeth, New Jersey, where he worked for Standard Oil as an engineer. My mother figured his parents were putting the screws on him to get married and to produce an heir. So far no one had yet measured up to his standards. Sadly, I didn't find him attractive. His kinky hair, bottle-bottom glasses, and sad-sack demeanor didn't advance his cause. But he was very bright, sarcastic, and irreverent. I was flattered by his attention, although over time it became a somewhat cloying infatuation. But that evening at dinner at Orsini's, it was all new and sparkly.

I noticed that Francesco wore a gold signet ring, so I told him how pleased I was that my grandfather Armstrong was giving me a signet ring for my eighteenth birthday. I was to pick out the ring at Tiffany's, research the crest and coat of arms of the LeBoutelliers, my grandmother's Huguenot family, and order it, and my grandfather would foot the bill. He'd never done anything like that for me before. I told Francesco that I had just been to Tiffany's Heraldry Department. I had found the crest (the image on top of the shield)—a clenched fist rising vertically from a twisted bar signifying the sea, and clutching an olive branch. Centuries earlier, one of the LeBoutelliers rescued King George III from drowning off the coast of Jersey, and the olive branch in the family's crest was his reward. I went on proudly to tell Francesco that the LeBoutellier shield was full of piles, bend dexters and sinisters, chevrons, goves and gussets, dovetailed, engrailed and otherwise invected, and topped with both Tudor roses and Fleurs de Lys. As I was describing this riot of shapes and colors, Francesco looked at me sadly through his thick lenses, then took my hand gently.

"Lale," Francesco began in his lightly accented English, "The older and more noble the family, the simpler the shield and coat of

Part 2: SEXED

arms. One chevron, or maybe a bar or two. One or two colors. That does it. Only the newer families aspiring to royal favor or high position need all that other nonsense to show who favored or thanked whom for what favors."

"Oh," I said. He then sketched out on a cocktail napkin the Bonmartini coat of arms: one red chevron on a white field. That was it.

"I get it," I said. Although I was disappointed to learn that the LeBoutellier coat of arms was *nouveau riche* trash, I found Francesco interesting on many subjects, not just heraldry. On the way from Orsini's to El Morocco's—where we finished off the evening dancing and listening to jazz—Francesco explained that like his father, he, too, was a count. (No primogeniture in Italy.) He reached into his billfold and pulled out one of several stiff, oversized calling cards which had engraved on the face below a golden coronet his first and last name (his ten or so additional saints' names were not included). To all who needed to know, the coronet indicated his noble birth. As people of my parents' vintage would cross out the Mr. or Mrs. or Dr. when they handed a social calling card to a friend or would-be acquaintance, Francesco explained that he just crossed out the coronet.

Later in May, our class yearbook came out. In those days, students did not participate in selecting the content or determining the design for their yearbook page. It was strictly formulaic: a big, glossy white page, your full name in caps with nicknames in italics below, a formal black-and-white head shot, and a quote selected by the Yearbook Editorial Board, which was comprised of classmates and a faculty advisor. Below the quotation were some hard facts about when you entered school and extracurricular activities, with a single line caricature to one side. Below that was a series of attributes or references relating particularly to you and your closest friends, family, interests, and/or eccentricities. Finally, at the bottom, would be a list of whatever athletic awards you might have received. Ruth Wyler, one of our class' most stellar students (along with Sally Woodman and Kassie Abramovitz), was editor of the yearbook. I couldn't wait to see what she and her buddies had written about me.

My quote was:

"Rugged Individualism."
— Herbert Hoover.

That's a quote?

The drawing was of me in the school uniform holding a set of blueprints. Fine.

My string of attributes was acceptable.

At the front of the book after the photos of faculty members and key administrative personnel, there were two solid facing pages of text written by our editorial board. The first was called "Back Issues" and dealt imaginatively and metaphorically with our class's collective progress through our years at Brearley. The second was called "Coming Events." Here, the hypothesis was that we would all reconvene at some future date at the offices of the *New Yorker*, of which, by then, our stellar classmate, Sally Woodman, would be editor-in-chief. In this context, the author/editor took a small group of us on a tour of the magazine and at each department picked up news on where others were, what each was doing and how, or if we were continuing to pursue interests or even fetishes that we had nursed in our years at school. As soon as I got my copy and checked out my own page, I headed to the cleverly conceived "Coming Events" to see what they all thought I might be up to five or twenty-five

Part 2: SEXED

years hence. Nothing. The tour was over and everyone had been mentioned but me. However, the penultimate paragraph read as follows:

> While we waited for the elevator *Miss Woodman* excused herself and opened a letter she had just received from the Circulation Department. She sighed and passed it to us. *Miss Leslie Armstrong*, it seemed, had written denouncing the whole publication, putting forth a neat list of complaints, and promising to sue the magazine for three times its assessed value, which is, after all, only $4.00.

Ouch!

On Thursday, June 5, our class, each of us in our non-matching white dresses, convened at Ruth Wyler's apartment for breakfast, and then made our way to 610 East 83rd Street and down to Deck C for Commencement. The usual processionals were played as the lower classes and faculty filled the hall while we seniors waited outside, lined up in order of the number of years we'd been in school. Those who had entered in kindergarten were first. Those who didn't enter until eleventh grade brought up the rear. The first chords of "Pomp and Circumstance" from the piano were our cue to enter the assembly hall and take our places on the stage.

Brearley commencements were relatively informal events, despite Elgar's processional. It was, after all, a beginning, not an ending. No outside speakers, no handing out of diplomas. (We received these afterwards.) Miss Mitchell and Miss Gibson must have addressed us. Some prayers must have been offered. Some hymns like "Jerusalem" were sung. And prizes were announced. I won the Bessie M. Kunz art prize as I had done the year before. But we all knew art didn't count for much. Still, I was glad to have it twice in a row. I came forward to collect my prize and returned to my seat to daydream while other prizes were announced, when out of a soft fog I heard Miss Gibson's piercing voice:

"And the Julia Whiton prize for English essay writing is split this year between Leslie Armstrong and Sally Woodman." *I had split the English prize with Sally Woodman?*

Back in our homeroom, we received our diplomas and collected the last of our belongings. In the evening, we reconvened as a class at Jack and Charlie's '21' Club. Jack and Charlie, the father and uncle of our classmate, Karen Kriendler, owned '21,' and that is where we seniors had our graduation dinner, courtesy of the Kriendlers.

What I remember most of that evening was that I, with under 500 in the final English Achievement Test, had shared the English prize with Sally Woodman, who probably hadn't seen an SAT score under 790!

Hot damn!

NUCLEAR FAMILY

My father, Howie, at the helm of his first sailboat, Debonair.

My mother, Barby—her favorite picture of herself.

The gate to the alley leading to One Primus Avenue, on the backside of Beacon Hill.

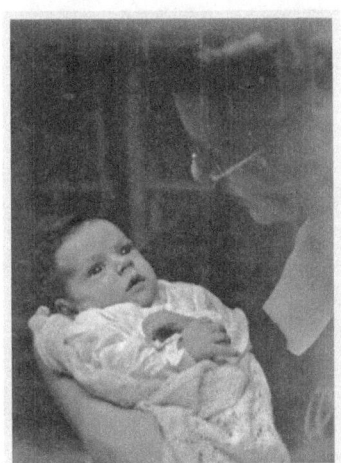

My mother holding me as a baby.

The alley to One Primus Avenue.

ARMSTRONGS

From right to left, my grandfather, Sinclair Howard Armstrong and his brothers, George Alexander Armstrong and William Campbell Armstrong, as boys.

My grandfather's younger sister Elizabeth Howard Armstrong (my great Aunt Elizabeth), as a young woman.

My grandmother's father, Charles Le Boutellier, and her mother, Sarah Graydon Martin, at the front door to Charlecote.

My grandfather, my cousin Stephen Armstrong, and my grandmother at my cousin Kittrin Armstrong's wedding, 1969.

Uncle George Armstrong with Howie as a baby.

Top Masthead, one of two cabins my grandfather owned on the Chappaquiddick bluff opposite Edgartown, MA.

Manhattan House, 200 East 66th Street, designed by Gordon Bunschaft of Skidmore Owings and Merrill and built in 1950 and 1951. My grandparents moved into apartment 14E soon after it opened.

Sunset from the deck at Top Masthead.

Charlecote, the Armstrong house in Washington, CT, built in 1908 by Grandpop Le Boutellier.

Charlecote, south façade.

Helen Naomi Salomon, my mother's Grannie.

William Jones Salomon, Grannie's second husband, known as Uncle Willie.

My grandfather, Clarence McKenzie Lewis, known as Gaffer, and Mrs. Louise Fitzpatrick, known to me as Granny Pat, on the terrace at Skylands, mid '40s.

Gaffer showing Howie how to handle a rifle.

1000 Park Avenue where my mother and her brother, Mac, were raised. Their apartment was on the corner of the 9th floor.

Skylands, the Lewis country house in northern New Jersey, designed by John Russell Pope and completed in 1928.

Skylands, rear façade.

My mother and her mother, Annah Churchill Ripley Lewis.

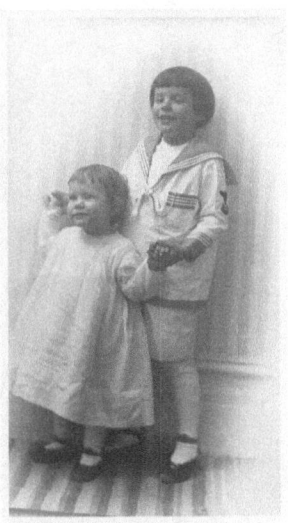

My mother and her brother Mac.

TEENAGE YEARS

Bareback on my favorite quarter horse at Deer Creek Ranch, Cody, WY, 1952.

Sharing Stone Horse Light's bowsprit with Howie.

My eventual stepmother, Cissie, with Bear Bear Armstrong Bear.

Howie and me in Stone Horse's cockpit.

The captain of the SS Cristoforo Colombo, with my mother and me, 1955.

ZINSSERS

My stepfather, Hans Handforth Zinsser.

Hans's mother, Ruby Handforth Zinsser, known as Mingii, well into her 80s.

Hans's older daughter, Judith, known as Judy.

Hans's younger daughter, Katherine, still known by some as Pago.

Hans's beloved 1956 Mark II Lincoln Continental, known as Çok Güzel.

Photos taken by the New York Times to announce my "debut" in November 1957.

161

BREARLEY SENIOR YEAR

Claire Albrecht-Carrié

Lucinda Childs

Emily Manheim

Cecile Miller

Marilla van Beuren

Class XII yearbook photo. Claire and I are in the back row, and Cindy is one in from the left in the row below. Marilla is front and center one row above our class president, Kassie Abramovitz. Emily is absent.

Part 3.
Howard's End

10. Harrods

The Club of the Three Wise Monkeys, Pont Street, Cadogan Square, London. My room was above the entry on the left.

LONDON — JUNE 1958

Like my mother, I believed anything European was better than anything American. Unlike my mother, I believed anything English was better still. I prevailed upon my mother to call in her social and business chips and find me a summer job in England, much as she had found my Fashion Group gig the summer before. Unbeknownst to me, England was still staggering from the effects of World War II: food rationing had only just been eliminated, unemployment was way up, and the economy was way down. Finding me a summer job there couldn't have been easy, but she did it. I was to spend the summer of 1958 as a sales assistant in the model suits department at Harrods Department Store.

I would reside at the Club of the Three Wise Monkeys, a finishing school for girls in a lugubrious Victorian terrace house on Pont Street, opposite the Cadogan Hotel. Its dingy, soiled interiors were quite a change from the glittering Art Deco of Claridge's, where I

Part 3: Howard's End

had stayed with The Parents when we first arrived. The Monkey Club was owned and managed by the Honorable Miss Joynson-Hicks, an English spinster who came to supper with us girls every evening, wearing a stained, brown lace dress and ropes of pearls cascading over her pendulous bosom. She was always accompanied by her friend and companion, who was called simply "Matron." Matron bore the hands-on responsibility for our well-being. In the summer, academic activities at the Monkey Club were suspended and the Hon. Miss J-H and Matron took in foreign girls like me who needed a "nice" place to stay with a modicum of supervision.

My sponsor and boss at Harrods was Mrs. Laurie Newton Sharp. She was a friend of Whitney Straight (who, originally American, had married an earl's daughter and was an executive at BOAC), the friend my mother had prevailed upon to get me my summer job. Mrs. Newton Sharp (no hyphen, although she would have liked one) was a tall, slender, severe blonde with zero personal warmth or humor. But she took pleasure in taking on the odd, unpolished American debutante and honing her into a refined English equivalent.

I had heard Harrods was the biggest department store in the world, even bigger than Macy's. It occupies a huge, irregularly-shaped block in Knightsbridge, with various back-office functions spilling into adjacent buildings across the narrow streets. Its block-long, terra cotta-encrusted façade remains an imposing presence. I had been told that a Maharajah in India could order an elephant from Harrods, if he wished, and Harrods would have it delivered to his palace. Harrods had the first food halls in the U.K., which were devoted to the sale of fresh and prepackaged gourmet food. The food halls were—and remain—magnificent due to their design as well as their content, especially at a time when decent food of any sort was hard to find in the U.K. The departments on the ground floor, especially those devoted to menswear, had dark wooden, illuminated display cases, and library-type cabinets. But above the ground floor, things were bare-boned. The lighting was harsh and the displays were unimaginative. On the other hand, this was not Bergdorf Goodman or Henri Bendel. It was postwar London, and by the U.K. standards of the time, Harrods was as good as it got.

My first day there was spent in training, and that was my only day in training. We punched in on one of several huge, brass time clocks, and learned to navigate the subterranean tunnels from the staff entrance into the store itself without fear of the army of rats for whom the tunnels were home. As some of the English seemed as confused as we foreigners by the monetary system, we were given lessons in counting money and making change (twelve pence to the shilling, twenty shillings to the pound, twenty-one shillings to the guinea), and in using the pneumatic tube system for shuttling money and related paperwork around the store. We were taught the importance not just of courtesy but of subservience, and were instructed in our sartorial requirements. Ladies could wear only navy blue or black dresses. I had brought neither from the States and had to spend well over my first week's salary of five guineas (the equivalent of about fifteen dollars before taxes) fulfilling this requirement before returning to work the second morning.

I proved an immediate disaster in the model suit department, not just because subservience didn't come naturally to me, but also because at that time, the only customers who bought model or tailored suits off the rack in England were Americans. (An Englishwoman would have her suits made by her family tailor.) And no American from New York, Chicago, or Nebraska wanted to travel all the way to London and shop at Harrods only to be waited on by a (very young and inexperienced) American. I lasted two days and then was mercifully delivered from the floor by Mrs. Newton

Sharp, who installed me in her editorial news office as her personal lackey.

There I met two young women who gave me a crash course in which of the daily and weekly papers Harrods sought editorial coverage from and why, as well as who were the most accessible editors and why. They spared me our boss's wrath by coaching me in spelling á l'anglaise: e.g. cheque, colour, programme, jewellery, etc. (Clearly, I wasn't losing my Americanness fast enough for Mrs. NS.) And they occasionally folded me into their after-work activities. Gill took me to Wimbledon, and Barbara Gorham-Holmes (who was convinced that Mrs. NS was jealous because Barbara's surname was truly hyphenated and not a do-it-yourself number, as was hers) from time to time asked me to join her for drinks and dinner with her longtime fiancé, a shaggy, ill-humored man somewhat older than she whom she had met when she was living at home in Cambridge and he was an undergraduate. Barbara was ten years my senior. We weren't quite on the same wavelength, but I was grateful for her friendship, which lasted many years beyond that summer.

Most weekends I spent at Manor Farm in the New Forest with my Aunt Shirley and Uncle Vernon Simmonds and their daughter Anthia. While Shirley was my third cousin once removed, she soon became my "second mum." Although far from a successful mother to her own child, she had all the warmth and fondness for me (and I for her) that I missed at home. During the day, Anthia, five years my junior, and I rode out onto the open moors and through the dense woods that still surround the village of Burley. Evenings at Manor Farm were spent sipping sherry and eating delicious sweet and savory pies prepared either by Shirley or by shrill Vera, Aunt Shirley's old nanny, or else by Mrs. Baker, the dairyman's wife. Conversation, led generally by my uncle, centered on his career as a fighter pilot in the Battle of Britain, farming, the protection of land usage and values in the village, or the virtues of the Roman Catholic Church. But sometimes Shirley would get on a spiritual bent and talk about her visions and the recent success of one of her healing episodes, which were taken as fact by both Shirley and Vernon, and which I began to believe as well.

Twice that summer I had a different sort of English weekend experience. I was invited to Ramsbury, the way-over-the-top Georgian Manor House in Wiltshire that belonged to Annie Rootes, who had recently married the self-made motor car tycoon, Lord (William) Rootes. Annie had insisted on keeping her mews house, off Upper Brook Street in Mayfair, despite Billy's desire for a grander presence in town, so when Ramsbury came on the market, Billy snatched it up, parked a herd of Black Angus in the front field, and told Annie to do it up so he could entertain with pride and comfort the dignitaries and friends that went with his work and his recently-awarded peerage. Annie loved life at the top, entertaining and spending money on clothes and houses. She had no trouble doing Billy's bidding.

The first weekend I was invited to Ramsbury, I assembled the last of my dresses from Mingolini Guggenheim in Rome (the basic black with the Harem skirt), two pairs of stockings, black heels, pajamas, comb, brush, toothbrush, etc., plus some Frank Sinatra records for Annie (she was a sucker for American popular music and for Miller High Life beer), and threw them all into my only suitcase, which was much too big for weekend travel. But it was all I had. In a wad of Kleenex, I wrapped the double strand of pearls I had been given for my eighteenth birthday and a round gold pin shaped like a daisy—it had a turquoise center surrounded by a few almost invisible diamonds and white cloisonné on the petals—and tucked these in the suitcase's side pocket. I was sure both my hair and the dress flopping around in the empty suitcase would be a mess when I arrived, thanks to the walk to the train station in the rain, but my mother had assured me that I could get my dress pressed before dinner.

When I arrived, I was greeted by a woman who was clearly not a maid because she was in civilian clothes. Wrong. She was a personal maid. The status of personal maids was so elevated that they did not wear uniforms. Furthermore, she was to be *my* maid.

I was eighteen years old and had a personal maid for the weekend?

This lady told me that Annie was napping and would see me shortly in her rooms for tea. In the meantime, she would show me my room and where I might freshen up. She took my bag, led me up the glorious Regency stairs and down the hall to my room. While I was freshening up as instructed, she unpacked my bag and said,

"Excuse me, madam, but where is madam's evening underwear?" Evening underwear?

I replied, "Madam's evening underwear is on her."

At tea with Annie, I was put at ease. I had known Annie since I was little. She had been around even in my father's time and had briefly been the girlfriend of one of his best friends. She was still unspeakably beautiful, well dressed and coiffed. I was only slightly disappointed that her taste in music ran to Frank Sinatra (whom I did not yet appreciate), whereas I thought she ought to be tuned into Mable Mercer or wallowing in Mahler. She told me Billy wouldn't be down for the weekend (she didn't seem too upset about that) and that she'd invited some young people for dinner whom she hoped would interest me. She apologized for giving me the number two guestroom.

"The bathroom for the number one guestroom is being redone for Anthony Eden's visit next weekend, but I would love your help in selecting a marble for the skirting around the bath," she said.

"Absolutely," I replied.

There was no fire in my room, which was a shame. Despite its being midsummer, it was raining, the house was cold, and I was freezing. I thought I might take comfort under the down quilt and have a snooze before dinner, but there was a knock on the door.

"Come in," I said. Ah, my maid again, with my dress freshly pressed.

"Shall I draw madam's evening bath?" she inquired.

"No, thank you," I answered. "I am fine," I said, peeking out from under the quilt. I wasn't fine at all, but I was damned if I was going to risk getting colder still, stepping into two or three inches of tepid water.

I remember little about the evening other than I was underdressed and underjeweled, but *tant pis*. I had a wonderful time. The public rooms were stunning even to my untrained eye and filled with the scent of fresh-cut flowers. The food was sumptuous and the drink plentiful. The people Annie had invited were fun, and we all stayed up well into the night drinking liqueurs and dancing to records in a smaller sitting room. I knew I'd have a crushing hangover in the morning and couldn't wait to sleep in.

7:45 a.m. Sunday. Tap, tap on the door. "Come in," I mumbled. It took two exchanges before she heard me.

"Shall I draw madam's morning bath?" she inquired.

"No, thank you," I answered, "I am fine as it is." Once again, I wasn't fine at all. The predicted hangover had settled in, and all I wanted was sleep.

"But madam didn't have her bath last night...."

Nailed.

Apart from that first weekend at Ramsbury and riding around the New Forest with my younger cousin Anthia, I had very little contact with people my own age. My work in the Harrods news

Part 3: Howard's End

office was often dull and demeaning, thanks to Mrs. Newton Sharp's evident disdain for me. Although Gill and Barbara included me in their lives from time to time, evenings at the Monkey Club were lackluster and lonely. The only other residents were a group of feisty, flirty Italian girls, thin and fair-haired, who were noisy but kept very much to themselves and went out as soon as dinner was over. I was never asked to join them, and so I returned to my dimly lit, narrow bedroom on the second floor, and parked myself at the small writing table under the window, where I filled reams of thin, blue airmail paper with my impressions of London and working at Harrods—neither of which was as magical or exciting as I had anticipated. Amongst the letters I received in return were a series of quasi-love letters from my Italian admirer, Francesco Bonmartini. In these letters, he bemoaned the impossibility of our eventual union (quite correctly, which nonetheless made me feel guilty), followed by running commentary on the unpleasant process of looking for alternative candidates for marriage, and descriptions of whomever was then being interviewed for the job. Did I really need to know this?

And so it went, evening after midsummer evening, until a girl whom I had met at Camp Treetops arrived in London, and her mother decided to host a party at the American Embassy to introduce suitable American and British "young" who were in London for the summer to one another. Mrs. Newton Sharp also seemed to know my friend's mother and excused me from work early on the given day so I could have time to get ready for the party.

I was more than ready.

Not far from Harrods, living in a flat on Basil Street, was Andrew Bullmore, age nineteen, discharged from the Royal Navy after six weeks' service (having broken his back playing rugby), who was discussing his invitation to the same party, which his grandmother had procured through her friend Laurie Newton Sharp. He did not want to go. He had been in a plaster body cast for over a year and felt embarrassed and awkward. Mrs. Bullmore was more mother than grandmother to Andrew. She had looked after him when his parents were stationed in Malaya during and after the war. She had overseen his education and his introduction to music and art; she had taken him to hear Maria Callas and Tito Gobbi at Covent Garden. She assured Andrew that an invitation that came via Mrs. Newton Sharp was not one to be cast aside and insisted that he go. Thus it was in mid-July of 1958 at a sort of cocktail party/tea dance in Grosvenor Square, to the music of Tommy Kingsman's orchestra, that I met Andrew Bullmore.

Andrew was very tall, solidly built, more awkward than handsome, with blue eyes and the requisite long wave of strawberry blonde hair descending from a high forehead. He explained about the broken back and the plaster cast and the pity of it all. Andrew had wanted a career in the navy, just as his forebears on both sides had pursued for thirty generations. Instead, he had had to accept his medical discharge and was doing a summer job in London until September, when he would be going to Cambridge. After this introductory conversation, in which I also gave him my details in brief, I scanned the room. Andrew was clearly the best act around. However, I was not taken by the format of the party. It reminded me too much of the stuffy pre-debutante dances that I'd scorned in New York. Moreover, the International Horse Show was on at White City that week. As I was a big fan of International Jumping in general and the Irish Army team in particular, I asked Andrew if he liked horses and wanted to cut out of the party and come with me. He said yes to both, and so we began, Andrew and I.

After work, we'd meet for coffee and go for walks from time to time during the summer. Although I wasn't attracted to Andrew, I loved his conversation, his sensitivity, his self-effacing humor, and I was flattered by his interest in me.

Meanwhile, Mrs. Newton Sharp was getting me down. Between bouts of scathing criticism for what I did do, I often had nothing to do at all. I had more or less mastered English spelling and spoke with a Mid-Atlantic accent that was more English than American. (I did try to hang onto my New York accent just to piss off Mrs. NS, but it was fast slipping away.) Five guineas seemed inadequate compensation for five and a half days a week of being alternately bored or demeaned. In early August, Howie wrote that he and Cissie would be starting their annual cruise in mid-August and I would be welcome to join them if I were back from London. When I asked my mother if I could cut my time at Harrods short by two weeks to return to go sailing, she was disgusted and rightfully called me a quitter. She had every reason to be furious and disappointed, given the trouble she'd taken to get me the job. But she changed my ticket anyway, I am not sure why. When I made my early departure, Mrs. Newton Sharp didn't seem a bit sorry to see me go.

Just before I was to leave for New York, Andrew bought tickets to *Duel of the Angels* with Claire Bloom and Vivienne Leigh. Seeing them on stage in person was extraordinary. I still have the program(me). Then Andrew took me to dinner at an Italian bistro in Soho. I was quite overwhelmed. It was such a grownup thing to do, on a par with dinner at Delmonico's, but better, because I knew this was a big deal for Andrew, whereas for Francesco, Delmonico's had been just another night out on the town. After that evening, I felt even more awkward about not being attracted to him, but things went more slowly in those days.

Soon after, I bid sad goodbyes to Barbara and Gill, Annie Rootes, Andrew, and my New Forest cousins, packed my single suitcase and took leave of the Monkey Club without suggesting to the Hon. Miss

Joynson-Hicks that she might want to have the brown lace dress dry-cleaned before the next academic year began. I took the bus to the airport, and flew home and then flew to Maine for my sailing fix. I was unhappy about letting my mother down, but at least I had my newly acquired English accent as a souvenir of my aborted summer employment.

11. Sin

PROVIDENCE — SEPTEMBER 1958

Van Wickle Gates, Brown University, Providence, RI.

We were due at Pembroke College, Brown University, at 1:00 p.m. on Sunday, September 7, for freshman orientation. At 10:00 a.m., The Parents and I loaded my trunk and other baggage into Hans's dream car, a brand-new secondhand Lincoln Mark II—an enormous white floater, vintage 1956 with power brakes, power steering, white leather bucket seats, electrically-controlled windows, and the hint of the spare tire pushing through the lid of the trunk. The Parents thought the Mark II was the automotive cat's meow, despite its being white not black, which they would have preferred, and despite its having two rather than four doors, which we kids would have preferred because we had to crawl into the back. They named the car Çok Güzel, which means "very beautiful" in Turkish—one of the few Turkish phrases my mother picked up in her forty years of service to Robert College in Istanbul. They pronounced Çok Güzel "Chock Goozle" which slightly diminished the car's magnificence.

Hans had no idea how long the drive would take, but figured three hours would do it. The car was fast and he was faster. Thanks to a flat tire outside of New Haven, and starter problems once the spare was in place, we limped into Providence at 5:00 p.m. and crawled up the Hill (Brown and all of Providence's more elegant residences are on "the Hill") to one of several large wood-frame houses north of the campus which served as freshman dorms for incoming Pembrokers. We were barely speaking—I because we were so late, they because they had sacrificed a whole Sunday for me and all they had received in return was car trouble, insolence, and ingratitude. I unloaded my belongings as fast as I could, and The Parents took off for the return to New York as soon as the trunk was closed.

The ratio of incoming men to women was four to one—1,000 Brown men and 250 of us. The women's freshman houses, which were of varying size, style, and appearance, were to give us girls, many away from home for the first time, a sense of community and belonging, which they largely did. Allinson House was a few blocks north of Pembroke's main dormitories and dining hall and housed some thirty of us on three floors in double rooms.

I was assigned to share a room up under the eaves with Honoré Clark, from near Philadelphia. She had been called Mary by her family and friends at home, but now she was Honoré. Good move. I had been called Leslie at Brearley by my teachers, Layo by my friends, but always Lale at home. I hated Leslie except for signing it as my real name, and Layo had originated as a corruption of Lale. So following Honore's example, I would henceforth be Lale to one and all.

Beyond that, Honoré and I had little in common. Tall and skinny, fair-skinned, with dark sunken eyes and equally dark straight hair trained into the mandatory pageboy, she was fond of Peter Pan collars, circle pins, pleated plaid skirts, bobby sox, and saddle shoes.

Part 3: Howard's End

Like many of our classmates, she had come to college mainly to find a husband. Was I any better, with my long, stringy hair pulled into a George Washington ponytail at the nape of my neck and my long-haired music, black stockings, Capezio flats, quill pens, ink bottles, portable pepper mill, cigarette holder, imported cigarettes (while they lasted), and phony English accent?

We spent freshman orientation week finding the dining hall (no meal plan nor menu choices), finding places to eat other than the dining hall; finding the libraries and other places to study, the post office, the dean's office, the girls' gym, the boys' gym, the swimming pool, the theatre, places to shop; and figuring out how to get downtown and where to go once there. The Biltmore was the only downtown hotel and boasted the only acceptable restaurant other than some of the older Italian restaurants on Allen Street. Orientation included sessions on dress code: skirts to be worn to all classes, in all libraries, and to all meals except breakfast and Saturday lunch and dinner; parietal rules: no boys in the dorm rooms, only in the lounges, and all occupants had to have at least one foot on the floor at all times; curfew hours: girls had to sign out of and back into the dorms every evening, even to go to the library. If we had parental permission and no Saturday classes, we were permitted to go away on weekends, which meant more signing in and out. No booze anywhere. The legal age for drinking in New York was eighteen, but in Rhode Island it was twenty-one. Smoking was okay. Most of us smoked and could smoke anywhere on campus. Marijuana was not even discussed. It was used only by musicians and really arty types, and if you got caught smoking or possessing it, jail time was the likely outcome.

We had been assigned to read *The Organization Man* by William H. Whyte over the summer, so we participated in workshops on the subject during Freshman Week. For all the ennui I had experienced during the long midsummer evenings at the Monkey Club, I had never once cracked this book. I wanted nothing to do with the Organization Man, with corporate America, or with what I thought the men in grey flannel suits stood for. I was sloughing off, protesting, rebelling before I even arrived on campus.

Then came the placement exams. We all had to take an English aptitude test to determine our placement in the first semester compulsory English class. I opened the exam book. Déjà vu: the English SATs all over again. I knew I did miserably, the Julia Whitton essay prize notwithstanding.

We were assigned advisors who asked what our majors might be. I wanted to design a pre-architecture course of study and figured this would best be done with a major in art history. My advisor told me that I had scored 485 out of 800 on the English Aptitude test. I was to study English grammar and writing with the entering science geeks and football players. No arguing. The scores spoke the truth. My other courses were to be introductory art history, a seminar on eighteenth- and nineteenth-century political science, and the math was introductory probability theory. Nothing too advanced, I hoped. Still I would have to work hard. I was at Brown now, to which I had barely gained admission, and I was coming from a high school in which I had rarely achieved a grader higher than the equivalent of a C.

The first days of classes were mind boggling. Boys in the classroom. Professors who addressed us as Miss and Mr. It was truly a new beginning. My reputation at Brearley did not follow me to Brown. I learned soon to speak of Brearley as high school and to lie low about how I had been raised, by whom and where. I was taken for who I was, as I presented myself on the spot: quill pen, phony English accent and all. The worlds of art, philosophy, political science, and probability were unfolding before me. I was terrified that I didn't have the discipline or smarts to keep up. I spent long evenings in the vast reading room at the Hay Library, researching, notetaking, and analyzing as I had done for Miss Gibson's papers on *Hamlet* and on the noble *Mayor of Casterbridge*. And I kept getting As. It was a thrilling turn of events that I had experienced only under Miss Gibson's aegis: being exposed to information and ideas, absorbing or digesting same, reiterating or regurgitating same, and being rewarded for doing it well. Intoxicating!

Possibly most amazing of all was my English class. A graduate student assistant taught my lower-than-low level of freshman English. He gave us a short essay as our first assignment, and after the next class he asked me to stay.

"I don't know what you are doing in this class, Miss Armstrong," he said. "Do you?"

"I got 485 out of 800 on the aptitude test," I replied. "I had the same problem with the SATs and the Achievement tests in high school, especially in English. I did better both in math and French."

"You obviously don't belong here, but you're stuck here until the end of the semester. I will do my best not to waste your time. But this will be between you and me. Is that understood?"

"Yes, sir," I said. I had no idea what he was talking about.

From then on, after he handed out the next assignment at the end of each class, I would stop at his desk to receive a special assignment: to write a critical essay with a different focus from what he assigned to the others, or on a totally different topic, or to write a short story, or a fictitious newspaper article. Because of his consideration, I never cut his classes (although I did knit through most of them—knitting was, surprisingly, permitted) and did my best to participate as constructively as I could.

In contrast, my social life was bleak. With all my affectations, I was a lousy fit. Though I could hold my liquor as well as any incoming freshman, the fraternity scene, which many of my male peers were rushing, was not up my alley. When, at the beginning of the semester, the Pembroke administration spoke of freshman hazing for us girls, even though sororities had been banished from Pembroke some years before, I went berserk and vehemently declared that no one was going to haze me, ever. I made such a stink about the indignity and sadistic cruelty of hazing that my stance caught fire and all the girls in my house joined in. Soon the other freshman houses followed, and hazing was toast. But I was no social leader. I was just protecting my own ass.

Sinclair Wallace Armstrong was my Armstrong grandfather's first cousin, but I had never met him. I asked around about him and learned that he was a retired professor of European History who had been widowed that spring when his wife Mary died of leukemia. Both he and Mary were much loved by students and faculty alike. I found his phone number and called to introduce myself and ask if we could meet. Yes, he knew I had come to Brown, but had been waiting until I settled in to get in touch.

It was a blustery late September afternoon when I arrived at the door of his modest white frame house on the south side of Power Street, two doors down from President and Mrs. Barnaby Keeney's appropriately presidential mansion. Power Street was at the opposite end of the Brown campus from Pembroke and even farther from Allinson House. It was a long walk. I knocked and the door was opened by a tall Ichabod Crane-type gentleman in his late sixties or early seventies with stick-straight, steel-grey hair parted on the side, a chiseled face, and smiling eyes.

"You must be Leslie," he said.

"Yes, I am, but please call me Lale."

"And I am Sinclair," he answered as he ushered me into the narrow hallway and took my jacket.

"Would you like some tea?"

"Yes, sir, that would be lovely." I followed him through a door that led into an old fashioned eat-in kitchen where he had prepared a simple tea tray with two mugs, a bowl of sugar, a small pitcher of milk, and a plate of cookies. We made small talk while we waited for the water to come to a boil. Then he carried the tray into the adjacent neat but cozy living room with bookcases lining the walls, and beckoned me to sit in the smaller of two comfortable arm chairs gathered around a low table. He sat in the large easy chair that was obviously his accustomed place.

"Please help yourself," he said, gesturing to the mugs of tea on the tray.

"Thank you, I will."

"Lale. That's an interesting name. You must tell me about it. How do you spell it?"

"L-A-L-E, like male or Yale," I said. "My parents called me Laley when I was little, and it was shortened to Lale as I grew up."

"And where did Laley come from?" he asked.

"I'm not sure. I've heard two explanations. One is that my mother used to speak to me in French when I was very little, and Leslie with a French accent comes out as Lay-lee because the 's' doesn't sound. The other is that my mother's grandmother, whom she adored, had a close friend whose nickname was Laley, after whom I was nicknamed. I have no idea if either is true, but I like the second explanation, and I love the name. I've never liked Leslie."

"Lale it will be then, and please, you call me Sin. That's what my friends and family call me."

Sin, my newfound first-cousin-twice-removed, was so different from his first cousin, my well-intentioned but dreary, distant, and elderly grandfather. Sin was elegant in a New England sort of way yet seemingly accessible.

"How are you finding your first weeks at Pembroke?" he asked.

"I am so glad that Pembroke is just a name and we are all students at Brown."

"Don't be so quick to reduce Pembroke to nonexistence. Pembroke's Dean Tonks is a good friend of mine."

"I'm sorry, I didn't mean to be rude."

"You weren't. You were just speaking your mind. What classes are you taking?"

I rattled off my four classes, glossing over my having been placed at the lowest level of freshman English. Sin knew and thought highly of both Allen McConnell, who taught the political science seminar, and Bill Loerke, who taught the Art History 101 blockbuster. He didn't know David Buchsbaum, the modern algebrist who taught probability theory, but said that wasn't surprising, as math and the sciences were not his strengths.

At the end of this exchange he fixed a stern eye on me and said, "About a week ago I received a letter from your mother thanking me for my part in getting you into Pembroke. I want to be very clear to you, and I will be equally clear to her when I reply: I had nothing to do with your getting into Brown or Pembroke. I had been told I had a relative who was applying, but I couldn't possibly have put in a good word for you, as we did not know one another. You were admitted to this university entirely on your own merits. Do you understand?"

"Yes, sir. I understand. Thank you for telling me. I had no idea my mother had written to you." How very strange. Clearly, my mother had little faith in me. Sin sensed my discomfort and rose to make us another round of tea, then hesitated and asked,

"Would you rather have a drink?"

"Yes, please, that would be great."

"What is your pleasure?"

"Do you have any dry sherry?"

He pulled out a bottle of Tio Pepe and poured me a glass, then poured a scotch on the rocks with a splash for himself. We returned to our two chairs in the living room.

"That's where my late wife Mary used to sit," he said, gesturing to my chair. "She died last spring. Leukemia. I miss her very much."

"I am so sorry. I have heard she was wonderful. Did you have children?"

"No, we didn't." After a brief pause, he continued: "We used to spend almost all our weekends at our farmhouse in Middletown, Rhode Island. We named it the Rock Pasture, because the fields around the house are dotted with very large boulders that look like cattle grazing. I don't get down there as much these days." I thought to mention knowing Middletown from having stayed at Grey Craig with the van Beurens, then thought it best not to, at least not at that moment.

We talked on about his family background and mine until I realized how late it was, and I would soon be missing dinner at Pembroke. I made my apologies and took my leave, asking if I could please return soon.

"Of course," said Sin. "And next time stay to dinner."

"I certainly will," I replied, and reached up to kiss him on the cheek. I raced northwards across the Brown campus, across the streets separating Brown from Pembroke, across the Pembroke campus and into the dining hall in the basement of Andrews. My breath was short but my heart was jubilant.

Brown had a real chorus that I wanted to join, as I loved choral music. I tried out, admitting that despite my piano lessons I could barely read music, but my ear was good. My voice was low, and they were short on tenors. I got in. Also accepted to the tenor section was an unusually slender and handsome blond (male), Ray Rhinehart from Washington, DC. Ray could read music and had a lovely voice, so I made sure to sit next to him so as to follow his lead. I soon learned he had as quick a tongue as I and was just as irreverent, but because he looked so angelic, it was less apparent. Ray seemed to be fitting into the fraternity scene at Brown with about the same ease that I was fitting into the pageboy-and-circle-pin set on the Pembroke campus. We looked forward to seeing each other at our two nights a week of rehearsals. Plus, I developed a mini-crush on Eddie Roberts, a senior who was the associate conductor and barely knew I was alive.

Just after Thanksgiving break, Pembroke freshman houses traditionally competed for the job of doing the decorations for Pembroke's Christmas Dance, which was held in the dining hall in the basement of Andrews Hall. The year before, at the Museum of Modern Art, I had seen the sculptures of the Russian Constructivist brothers Antoine Pevsner and Naum Gabo, and was mesmerized by the precision and beauty of their work and the simplicity of the basic idea: straight lines of wire creating sensuous, warped planes. I proposed to take this idea and use it to reframe the entry to the hall in which the Christmas dance was to take place, along with other openings to this large, low-ceilinged space. Then I suggested that we decorate the obligatory Christmas tree and any swagged garlands with nothing but red and white crepe paper roses tied with silver ribbon, and trimmed with the same silver string we would use to make the super-sized Constructivist shapes at the entrance. Allinson House won the competition for the decorations.

At our next chorus rehearsal, I asked Ray if he would accompany me to the dance. I was sure he was gay. But I didn't care. He said he'd loved to come. At the end of the rehearsal, our chorus master announced the date of our Christmas performance of Thomas Tallis's "Lamentations of Jeremiah" at Saint Thomas's Church in New York. The concert was to be part of the vespers service on the same Saturday as the dance. There was no way to do both. But I had to. I was committed to do the decorations and committed to sing in the chorus. So I rallied my housemates to get all the roses made well in advance of that weekend. The day before the dance, we put up the framework around the doors to the hall and threaded the miles of silver string over and around the framework to reshape the experience of entering the room. That Saturday morning, my housemates completed decorating the hall according to plan while Ray and I boarded the Brown University Chorus bus for New York, he in his tuxedo and I in a long, full black taffeta skirt and white silk blouse borrowed from my mother in hopes that this ensemble might pass as dance attire, should we manage to return to Providence before the dance was over. The concert was a success and we raced onto the bus back to Providence and from the bus to Andrews. As we entered the hall, the shimmering strands of silver defined zaftig curves and paper roses glowed everywhere. We had made it back for the very last dance.

When we returned to Providence in January, we took our final exams for the first semester. I got four As. I had never before seen one A in an academic subject, much less four. Brearley had done me proud. Maybe a dismal social life had some benefits after all.

I had been writing to Howie about Sin and how much I wanted Howie to meet him. Howie had a conference to attend in Boston and arranged to stop in Providence the Friday beforehand to meet Sin, have dinner at his house, and stay the night. Howie and I would then drive together to Cambridge the next day, where we would spend the rest of the weekend with his favorite first cousin, Mary

Armstrong Eustis (daughter of my Uncle George Armstrong) and Mary's family: her husband Bill and four kids, ages nine to thirteen. I had no experience with little kids other than Pago. But anything with Howie was fun, especially if he was on his own. The Eustis's shabby grey frame house on Lakeview Avenue was chaos: kids and kids' clutter everywhere. Mary and Bill were each very tall, very thin, and very welcoming, not just to Howie but also to me, even though they had never before met me. The gin flowed, and Mary was glad I had learned from her father how to make a martini at a young age—a much-appreciated skill in the Eustis household. The kids ate while we had cocktails. When they were finished eating they wandered in and out, the elder girls looking after the younger twins, everyone filling up on potato chips (never seen in our house) while the grownups scarfed down cheese and crackers to sop up the gin. Dinner was simple, delicious, and served with an abundance of cheap red wine. Once the kids were in bed, it was highball time. Eventually, when I could barely stand from the quantity of booze I had ingested, I was shown to a messy bed somewhere in an upstairs room, where I promptly curled up and fell fast asleep. Howie and Mary talked long into the night. In a very short time, the Eustises became my second family on our side of the Atlantic.

Later in the winter, Denny Bok blew into town, and Sin invited him for dinner and to stay as well. I was floored. My parents would never allow me to have a boy stay overnight in their house. What would people say? But Sin took it all in stride, which allowed me some cherished time alone with Denny as well as together with Sin.

From time to time, Uncle George—Mary Eustis' father and Sin's first cousin—would come stay with Sin. They were both elegant men, but physical opposites of one another. George was short and bald, with the beginning of a paunch, and he seemed to skate fast

Part 3: Howard's End

and skillfully along the surface of ideas and sentiments, while Sin was slow and thoughtful. But they were clearly close. Uncle George began to visit Sin more frequently and stay for longer and longer periods of time. This delighted me, though I didn't understand why, as he had a perfectly good home of his own in New Jersey. George offered no explanation. Life was lively at Sin's. President Barnaby Keeney and his wife Barbara came and went regularly, as did Professor Pat Kenny and his wife. Pat was a jolly about-to-retire professor of English who lived across the street. The Kennys had been particularly close to Sin and Mary, and were now close to Uncle George. President Keeney told Sin that he was convinced that I had to have cheated to get four As at the end of my first semester. My grades were probably brought to Keeney's attention because people in the administration knew that Sin and I were related, and no one could figure how, with the grades and college board scores I'd had coming into Brown, I could pick up four As without cheating. Sin knew my story, and stood up for me, thus clearing my name.

As Uncle George spent increasingly more time under Sin's roof, I visited less and less frequently because, in addition to studying hard, I was working in a half-hearted way on *Brownbrokers*, a revue written, presented, and performed by the students at the end of the academic year, like Princeton's famous *Triangle Show*. So I hardly noticed that I hadn't been to Sin's for tea or dinner for several weeks. When it dawned on me, I called and was told by Uncle George that Sin had been ill. Nothing to worry about, but best not to come by for the moment. I called again in a week's time.

"Hi, Uncle George. What news of Sin? How he's doing?"

"Not so well, Honey. Sin's in the hospital."

"With what?" I asked.

"With leukemia, same as his wife Mary had," Uncle George replied.

"How come? How long has he had it?"
"For quite a while now."
"How come I never knew?"
"Sin didn't want anyone to know. He didn't want people to worry."
My heart was on the floor.
"May I come to see him?"
"No, honey, not 'til he comes home."
"Will he be coming home?"
"I think so."
"Will you tell me when he does?"
"Sure, Honey."

I called a few days later and got no answer, so I found Pat Kenny's number and called him. The prognosis was bad. Sin was too sick for visitors.

Two days later, on Thursday, March, 19, 1959, I, dressed all in black for some inexplicable reason: a black letter sweater I'd just bought, and a black skirt. Only my sneakers and socks were white. As I was heading out to the dining hall for breakfast, there was a call for me.

"Lale, it's Pat, Pat Kenny. Sin died early this morning. George wanted to tell you himself but is beside himself with grief, so I said I would let you know. I am so sorry."

"Me too. I just got to know him. It's not fair," I whispered.
"I know, Lale."
"And it's even more terrible for you. You were such close friends."
"Yeah, we were. Very close." Pat paused, then continued, "By the way, there isn't going to be a funeral. But there will be a memorial service later in the spring."
"No funeral? That's it? That's the end?"
"Yeah," said Pat. "That's it for now. Take care, kid."
"Yeah.... I will.... Thanks for telling me.... Bye."

I thought I would be sick all day and the next and for several thereafter.

I never said goodbye to this gentle man whom I had known for so short a time. But on one of those cozy winter evenings in front of his fire, I had promised him that I would name a child after him, as he had none of his own.

I kept that promise.

12. My Funny Valentine

Emmanuel College, Cambridge University, designed by Sir Christopher Wren, 1668–74.

Every six weeks or so, my dim personal life was illuminated by the arrival of a thin, pale blue airmail letter from Andrew Bullmore, addressed in his typical English quasi-Chancery hand. The year before, when Andrew applied to Cambridge, he had wanted to study Classics from the outset, but there was a glitch. The dean of the college at which Andrew had interviewed had liked Andrew immensely. No surprise, given that the dean was in plaster from the waist down, having broken both legs in a car accident, and Andrew was in plaster from the hips up. The dean said Andrew was just the sort of person that his college was looking for, a perfect fit. However, there were no more places for the coming fall in classics. Would Andrew be willing to read Far Eastern languages? Andrew, being no fool, decided to avail himself of this easy entrée to Cambridge, and said fine.

Andrew reported that when he arrived at his college in Cambridge that fall the head porter consulted his list and checked him in: "Ah, Mr. Bullmore, you'll be reading Far Eastern languages." To which

Part 3: HOWARD'S END

Andrew replied, "Oh, no sir, there's been a mistake, I am to read classics and archeology." The porter shook his head, glanced again at Andrew, then took out his pencil, made the change to his roster, and Andrew spent the next three years reading classics and archeology!

Sometime during that winter, Andrew wrote to invite me to a May Ball at Clare College (not his college; his was Emmanuel, from which John Harvard received a BA in 1632 and an MA in 1635 before emigrating to the Bay Colonies), probably thinking I would never accept. But going to a May Ball on Andrew's arm was appealing. The May Balls, held in early June at Cambridge and Oxford, were the big social events of the academic year. I liked Andrew, and he liked me. As The Parents were taking my two sisters and me to Europe on a short family holiday in June of 1959, my mother felt the cost of getting me from the Continent to Cambridge and back for a weekend was manageable.

However, in early April, shortly after Sin's death and between the time I accepted Andrew's invitation and the time of the May Ball, I met and became infatuated with Alvin Curran, a promising young musician and composition student two years ahead of me. Al was the exact opposite of Andrew. He was scruffy and short, with appalling posture and a bowl of black hair surrounding a finely defined, almost patrician face. He was bright, funny, talented, and deservedly cocky. Al was a "townie," a native of Providence, and lived with his family in a frame house on Overhill Road, about a mile north of the campus. He was Jewish and his parents were observant. Al's father Marty played in the Providence orchestra. His mother Pearl worked hard at an office job. They were openly disgusted that their talented middle child, Alvin, had fallen for a skinny *shiksa* when there were so many nice Jewish girls at what they called "Brown's College." Al's older brother, Joel, had done the right thing. He was a doctor and had already married a nice Jewish girl. Al's little sister, Reeba, was still in high school and hadn't done much of anything. But she was a girl and little was expected of her.

I couldn't imagine what Al saw in me, but he was clearly intrigued. He thought all the little English affectations I'd managed to perpetuate were endearing. He reveled in my sense of humor, my love of things foreign (especially Italian), my love of music (his music in particular), and presumably my body as well. However, although I was madly in love, I was not ready for total immersion. I was genuinely afraid that if I gave in to my delight in physical intimacy with someone for whom I cared, I would become a sex addict, a card-carrying nymphomaniac, unable to think about anything else but the next opportunity for copulation.

Al was patient.

We had a perfect spring, meeting for lunch with like-minded, long-haired Bohemians at the Blue Room in Faunce House and talking deep talk, laughing. In the library we passed each other notes in stream-of-consciousness prose about what we were reading or studying and how funny and exciting it was to have our minds pried open by this experience called college. We met at the theatre at night where Al's music was being rehearsed and I was painting sets, and we stopped repeatedly to kiss in the shadows of flowering shrubs and bushes as he walked me back to Allinson House on those warm spring nights before he took the Hope Street bus back to Overhill Road.

Falling so completely for Al made me feel even more awkward about going to the May Ball with Andrew, but then I had never been physically attracted to Andrew, so acting accordingly would not represent any behavioral change. Andrew's letters indicated a great deal of planning: collecting me at the airport, having me stay with his granny in London, finding lodgings for me in Cambridge,

Part 3: Howard's End

planning visits to his digs, dinner with his friends, and the ball itself. It was too late to back out.

At the end of the semester, my grades came in: art history A, and political science A—both continuations from the previous semester. I got a B+ in whatever English course I was now allowed to take. But I failed the final in Introductory Calculus.

Failed? I'd never failed anything before, other than multiple choice exams. I was called into Dean Gretchen Tonk's office. She was Pembroke's associate dean and a good friend of Sin's. She was known to be tough but fair.

"What happened?" asked Miss Tonks.

"I ... ah ...well ..." Oh hell, why not tell the truth? "I met this guy, Al Curran, and I fell in love. All of a sudden I had places to be other than the library every evening."

Miss Tonks' cracked a smile, a real smile, no snarkiness. "Good for you, but what are you going to do about the math?"

"Because I did better than I'd expected in probability theory, I thought I could coast a bit through beginning calculus. But it got way ahead of me," I said. "I have to get through calculus if I am going to study architecture. I have to understand it well enough to pass. I actually want to understand it, but it doesn't come easily to me."

"Okay," she said. "I'll see if I can get you a D for this course instead of an F, and then you can go on in the calculus sequence, but you will really have to apply yourself next year to make up for what happened this semester. It isn't going to be easy."

"I am sure it won't. But I'll make it happen. And thank you so much."

Reprieved, but barely. Two As, a B+, and a D. Not quite the same as four As. But I was still in the game.

Campus Dance marked the end of the academic year. Al and I were facing the summer apart. Al wasn't much of a dancer but Campus Dance is one of Brown's great traditions. A huge dance floor composed of many flat wooden platforms leveled on jacks is set out under the elms in the center of the campus. There's a full orchestra playing, with Japanese lanterns glowing, and people of all ages, including faculty and visiting alumni, dancing under the stars. Even proto-hippies like us couldn't resist its appeal. The next day I finished packing up and set off for New York. Al was going to join me in a few days. For some perverse reason, I wanted Al to meet my parents, though I couldn't imagine how they would respond to this peculiar young man of dubious background and heritage who had captured my heart. There was no thought of asking The Parents if he could stay with us (God forbid!). He had college friends in New York with whom he could crash. Al showed up for dinner with a fresh bowl haircut, walking at his customary forty-five-degree angle to the ground. But thanks to his jacket (though ill-fitting) and tie (though narrow), he passed the first hurdle (unlike Denny Bok, who had refused to wear either on his first visit).

Next hurdle:

"What will you have to drink?" asked Hans.

"Scotch, please," Al replied.

Hans poured a ginormous quantity of scotch into an equally ginormous and very heavy Baccarat crystal glass with three lone ice cubes floating around the rim. This was Hans's way of testing the mettle of Judy's and my suitors. If they staggered about after drinking all that brown liquid, they were non-contenders. Al held his own with the scotch and in conversation with my parents too. He joked with my sisters and won his way into my family's heart in the course of a single evening.

Soon after his social triumph, Al headed off to the Borscht Belt in the Catskills, where he had a summer gig playing piano at one of the big hotels. (Think: Grossinger's. Think: *Dirty Dancing*). And we all took off for Italy. Al and I wrote back and forth furiously.

Part 3: Howard's End

Ischia was beautiful, larger than Capri, but less dramatic. It had real beaches, not just rocks like on the Ligurian coast. I loved the sun and stayed on the beach for hours, roasting my olive skin to raisin brown. One day, Hans decided he, Judy, and I should all go water-skiing. I had never managed to get up onto the skis from the water when I tried in Newport with Marilla, and I was constantly losing parts of my suit in the process. I couldn't afford to fail in Ischia. All I had on was an itsy-bitsy bikini held to my body with strings. I had to make it up onto the skis. And so I did. It was thrilling, criss-crossing the boat's wake with Vesuvius in the background. That evening, after another delicious dinner at the hotel, I leaned out the window of Judy's and my room listening to the band below playing "My Funny Valentine." It was the sort of band Al played in at home to earn his tuition. I missed him all the more.

I was not prepared for Cambridge. Not one bit. I don't remember much about the weekend other than punting on the Cam and fragments from the night and early morning of the ball itself. I do recall the endless daylight that morphed into white night during which I alternated between eating piles of strawberries and clotted cream and furiously dancing the Charleston in order to avoid any slow dancing, which might have required some close physical contact. I felt badly that I didn't want to be intimate with Andrew, but he seemed to take my behavior in stride. Maybe it was enough to have as his date a girl who had come from New York, and whom he may have had on some kind of pedestal. Mercifully, four days later I flew back to Naples and took the boat back to Ischia, embraced my family, basked in the warmth of the Italian language and the sun, and once again leaned out the hotel window to pick up the strains of "My Funny Valentine."

After Ischia, we returned with The Parents to England. I had persuaded them that I needed a car when I returned to school in the fall, both to get around Providence and to travel to and from New York. Thanks to the family friendship with Lord Rootes, husband of Annie Rootes, I acquired a new Hillman Minx saloon (sedan) with left-hand drive for use in the U.S. I named the car El Al (Lale spelled backwards) in hopes of currying favor with Al Curran's anti-goy parents. (Unsuccessful). El Al needed to be "run in" before being shipped to the States, so Judy and I spent two giddy weeks driving all over England, Wales, and Scotland.

Much to my relief, when we returned to England, Andrew had already departed on an archeological expedition to dig up half of Leptis Magna, the ruins of a Roman settlement on the edge of the Sahara. During the rest of the summer and over the next several years, Andrew continued to be a superb correspondent. He wrote long letters on thin blue airmail paper peppered with little drawings and diagrams of archeological relics, to which I replied in my still-illegible script and at great length, managing to say close to nothing.

Ours had the promise of being a lifetime friendship.

It almost was.

13. Sacrificial Anode

WASHINGTON, CONNECTICUT — JULY 1959

The Edgartown Yacht Club, Edgartown, MA.

Howie and Cissie were to drive from Chicago to Charlecote in their latest gas-guzzling convertible, and I was to come up from New York with Howie's younger brother, Sinc. I hardly knew Sinc because my mother and father both thought he was a lightweight intellectually—however well liked he was (very), however well he played tennis (very), and however successful a career he'd had, first as a lawyer in Chicago, then as head of the SEC, then as Assistant Under Secretary of the Navy. Sinc had four kids, whom I barely knew; they were younger than me and grew up in Washington, DC, where Sinc and his wife, my aunt Lis, had moved when he was appointed by Eisenhower to head the Securities Exchange Commission. Lis had recently made the mistake of having a baby sired by someone other than Sinc. For the sake of propriety, Sinc assumed patrimony and financial responsibility for his new daughter, but this embarrassing development cost him his job with the Navy and his social reputation in Washington. So Sinc divorced Lis and moved back to New

York to start anew. He was being groomed to be CEO of the U.S. Trust Co., and had a new and improved wife, Joan Miller Gilchrist.

When Sinc and I rolled up Charlecote's crunchy driveway, Grandmother and Grandfather were waiting for us outside. Grandfather's rumpled, slightly soiled, three-piece, pinstriped suit hung loosely on his diminished frame. Grandmother's ratty camel hair polo coat had mismatched buttons, and one or two were missing. Her midcalf-length skirt hung unevenly below the hem of the coat. Her beige lisle stockings bagged at the ankles, and her scuffed leather pumps with straps over the insteps had seen better decades. Her dark hair, peppered with grey, was piled in a disorderly heap on top of her long, narrow, wrinkled face. We said our hellos. I kissed the Admiral and was genuinely glad to see him. Grandmother treated me to her usual icy glare.

"Hello, Grandmother. It is good to see you. You are looking well," I said. "I love your polo coat." I approached tentatively to kiss her bony check. The rancid smell of age was toxic.

"Abercrombie & Fitch, 1932," she responded curtly. "Made to last."

Sinc and I ascended the narrow creaky stairs to the small apartment above the garage, where he and Joan, plus his four older kids and her two by a previous marriage were all living in close quarters. It was known as Starfield, as if a name alone could add cubic footage and dignity to what were clearly third-class accommodations. I laid claim to the only horizontal surface remaining for me to sleep on that night, the rest of them having been taken up by other children. Howie and Cissie arrived soon after and were assigned Starfield's second bedroom. Although rivals in sports, intellectual capabilities, and achievements (and in the pursuit of women), Sinc and Howie were generally cordial to one another, especially after a few drinks. They each downed a quick one, then we all reconvened at the big house on one of the three brick patios under one of the three

Part 3: Howard's End

Palladian porticos for tea, which my grandmother poured from a tea service much in need of a good scrubbing—never mind polishing—and meted out cookies the size of postage stamps. My grandparents begged yet again for Howie to give up his practice and his teaching in Chicago and return to his home in Washington, Connecticut—the likelihood of which was nil. Howie openly professed his dislike of his mother and barely tolerated his father. Nonetheless, some years before, the Admiral had bought a grand Federal-style house with its own columned portico on Washington's village green, and he was holding it for Howie and Cissie in the event they might actually return to Washington—while Sinc and Joan, with six kids coming and going, remained stuffed into Starfield.

Howie had that kind of hold over people, even those he actively disliked.

The previous September, Howie and Cissie sailed *Stone Horse* back from Maine to a yard in New Bedford, where she was hauled and spent the winter. Howie had agreed to give the gentler waters around Massachusetts another try. Much as I loved Maine and savored my times with Denny Bok in the many small harbors and towns where we would meet up, Denny's hold over my heart had been released by My Funny Valentine. I had missed the warmer waters, the gentler tides and winds, and the soft sandy bottoms of Massachusetts, and I looked forward to seeing and sailing with friends I had made on Martha's Vineyard and the Cape during the summer I'd stayed with Cindy Childs and her family.

When in mid-July we rolled into the yard in New Bedford and found *Stone Horse*'s decks still encrusted with rust from the previous summer, Howie was furious. Rust is a big problem on boats with steel hulls and decks, especially in salt water. By building *Stone Horse*'s hull in steel, Howie had hoped to bypass all the waterproofing problems of wooden hulls. With steel, he thought he would have more usable interior space for comparable displacement, stronger cladding material, and less overall maintenance. Even though the iron in steel does oxidize in fresh water, the corrosive process results in a thin protective coating over the steel, which actually slows the rate of oxidation. *Stone Horse* looked pretty good while she remained in the Great Lakes, but once the salt of the Atlantic met with her undersides, she was like a kid hitting puberty: there was acne everywhere. While *Stone Horse* was still in Maine, Howie had installed what are known as sacrificial anodes below her water line on either side of her bow and stern. Here's how they work: In the electrolytic table of metals, if two different metals are put in contact with one another, the lower and more active or volatile metal, known as the anode, will corrode, whereas the higher, less active, more stable material, known as the cathode, will not corrode because the anode is doing the corroding for both materials. (Hence "sacrificial.") This form of remediation had been in use for decades to protect the hulls and decks of large commercial vessels. It should have worked for *Stone Horse*, but it didn't seem to. I don't know why.

The first thing we did in New Bedford was unpack the convertible. Out came a new working jib, then dozens of duffle and ditty bags monogrammed with initials and/or the burgees of the Edgartown and Eastern Yacht Clubs. These contained not only Howie and Cissie's maritime wardrobe—Howie liked his women well turned out—but their whole society of stuffed bears. There was the hardcore group from prior years: Bear Bear Armstrong Bear (known simply as Bear), then Colonel Whitehead Bear, whom we had picked up while in the Great Lakes, and his bride Lady Whitehead Bear. (The Colonel and his wife were both of darker hue than Bear, and of a lesser, more matted faux fur, which made them the subject of endless politically incorrect jibes from the other bears.) Then came Super Bear, who, although slightly darker than Bear, was not as dark as the Colonel. Super Bear was smarter than the Colonel but less intellectual than Bear. But Super Bear gave Bear a run for his money and smarts because of his outspoken arrogance. Super Bear was accompanied by Blue Bear, an orsine femme fatale complete with aluminum foil bling wrapped around her massive arm. Her vulgarity was redeemed by her apparent appreciation of light classical music, particularly operetta. In addition, a panoply of new and mostly smaller stuffed bears, purchased over the previous years by Cissie for Howie's amusement, spilled out of the duffle. Each had a name and personality of its own. Howie would animate them while Cissie giggled and urged him on.

Just Big Tug and Little Tug having fun.

Three days later, we left New Bedford and headed to Edgartown. I was hoping these would be a letter from My Funny Valentine awaiting me at the Yacht Club. There was.

In the 1930s, the Chappaquiddick shore opposite Edgartown, with its Yacht Club and the Reading Room and the charming array of houses that once belonged to whaling captains, was virtually uninhabited. There was one small house right on the water, and there were two one-room cabins at some distance from one another, high up on the bluff. All three were shingled, and the cabins each had rubble-stone chimneys standing proud of their low-slung roofs. During Prohibition, the gentlemen from Edgartown would row over to the dock projecting into the harbor from the house, tie up their dinghies, climb the rickety steps up the bluff and go to the cabins to drink and play cards. Sometime in the 1940s, my grandfather bought both cabins and the land between them. The one looking out over the harbor he named Top Masthead. The one further to the south overlooking Katama Bay he named Bold

Water. Both had sensational views in three directions. He had wells dug and septic systems installed in both locations, then claimed Top Masthead for himself and rented out Bold Water. He built a small addition to the north side of Top Masthead that served as a tiny bedroom, like a ship's cabin, and in a corresponding addition to the south, he installed a small bathroom and a galley. He had the carpenter make two crudely painted narrow wooden cots and procured horsehair mattresses so these could double as spare beds and settees. He bought six painted wooden chairs and an old table so he could sleep and eat there when he came to the Vineyard without my grandmother.

In the 1950s, Sinc wanted his kids to have the same experience of the Vineyard that he and Howie had had when Howie was a boy. So the Admiral, who never parted easily with money except to pay his club dues, commissioned the construction of a shoebox cabin behind and at an angle to the main cabin. This was comprised of two bedrooms flanking a central bathroom and utility room. Like the main cabin, the new cabin was Spartan: no insulation, no interior finishes, no frills. The Admiral provided boats for the kids to sail and to row across the harbor into town. At the bottom of the hill was the Chappaquiddick Beach Club (featured in the movie *Jaws*), with its red-and-white-striped cabanas and blue-haired ladies sipping gin and tonics while their grandchildren frolicked at the water's edge under the watchful eyes of mothers and au pairs. The Chappy ferry was within walking distance of the two cabins, and the Yacht Club, the tennis courts, and the grocery and liquor stores were within walking distance of the other side of the ferry. Food was basic but sufficient. Drink was plentiful. Sunsets viewed from the deck of Top Masthead were and remain as spectacular as any, anywhere.

Top Masthead was heaven to all of us except Howie, who always preferred being on the water to being on land and wanted little or no association with anything belonging to his parents.

We spent the next few days in Edgartown being entertained by Lucinda Childs Sr., plus Cindy's sister, Eleanor, and brother, Eddy. Howie's mood seemed unusually dark, despite his affection for Lucinda Sr. He was drinking even more than usual. Cissie seemed oblivious. I called my mother just to check in and told her I was alarmed. She knew all about Howie's drinking. She had told me that once, when they were still married, after an evening of drinking Howie had attacked and almost killed her, thinking she was his mother. Not exactly comforting. During our phone call, she reminded me that Hans's birthday was coming up and to be sure to call him. Of course.

I figured maybe if I went to work on the rust on the decks while we were at anchor, it might help. I started at the bow on the port side, first with a mallet and coal chisel to knock off the big blisters. Then, with a rotary brush on the end of a electric drill, I eliminated more rust. Next, I sanded each spot with two grades of sandpaper, and applied two coats of Cordobond, a heavy duty, rust-colored anti-corrosive epoxy. The Cordobond looked even worse than the rust.

Howie's dark spirit alarmed me. I thought it might be a respite for me and a surprise for Hans if I turned up in New York for his birthday. That evening when we were working on our first drink, I said to Howie, "Would it be all right if I went back to New York this weekend, just for a few days, to celebrate Hans's birthday? It's this Sunday, August 3rd. The Parents are having a party and I'd like to be there."

"What?" he asked, incredulous.

"It's Hans's birthday on Sunday and I'd like to be there," I repeated. "I could leave from Woods Hole and take the bus to the city, and then

I'll come back to wherever you are on the day after. That would be Tuesday the fourth. I'd be gone only three or at most four days."

Even though I had never left the boat during a cruise, not even for an overnight, I figured this idea would fly because I was no longer a child and because Howie and my mother were getting along reasonably well; both were remarried; Hans had been his good friend many years ago, and I knew they were still in communication over matters medical.

"Leave the boat?" he sputtered, "Leave in the middle of a cruise?" His already tawny skin darkened further as his face flushed and rage twisted his features.

"When you sign on for a cruise, you sign on for the duration," he exploded. "You don't just hop on and off at will. Sailing is not a joke. It is a way of life. You are in for the duration." He paused, took a big slug of his drink, emptied the cup and handed it to Cissie for a refill.

"No. Absolutely not. You may not go."

I was stunned. I looked to Cissie for a sign, for help. She looked away.

I don't know how we got through the rest of drinks and dinner. Probably Howie cooked, as he generally did, and Cissie and I cleaned up. He put some music on the record player and he and Cissie sat at the bunk on the forward side of the table in the main cabin, sipping high balls from the bamboo glasses we used on board. The collection of bears sat on the bunk opposite them, while I settled sheepishly into my narrow bunk on the starboard side and tried to read. The record came to an end, Howie took out his soundless practice keyboard from its sling under the table and began to pound out Preludes II and III from Book I of Bach's "Well Tempered Clavier" in quick succession. The clicking of the keys was fast and furious. He came to a tricky spot, went over the fingering again and again, couldn't seem to get it right, then slammed the lid

Part 3: Howard's End

shut and stood up in the narrow companionway. He turned round and looked daggers at me as I lay in my bunk, pretending to read.

"You want to leave this boat to go to Hans Zinsser's birthday party? That's just swell, isn't it?" He glowered, drink in hand, "I am going to have fucking Hans Zinsser disbarred and have his fucking license to practice medicine ripped from its frame on the wall of his Park Avenue office. Do you have any idea what that cocksucker has done to me?"

"No, sir, I don't know," I whispered. Though Howie's foul language wasn't new to me—after all, I had learned to curse from him—I had never heard him apply these terms to anyone I knew and cared for.

"Have you ever heard of Kevin Owen?" he spat out.

"No, sir. I haven't."

"Your mother's new husband, whose fucking birthday you want to celebrate, sent me a resident named Kevin Owen. He told me Owen was brilliant and I took him on. And guess what? Guess what, Smart One Who Wants to Go to New York to celebrate his birthday," he hurled at me, "Kevin Owen is shit, pure shit. Owen doesn't know his asshole from his left nostril. He has less diagnostic ability than Blue Bear. Kevin Owen has fucked up everything he has touched since he came on my rotation." And on and on he went, up and down the nine-foot length of the narrow companionway, cursing and ranting against Kevin Owen and Hans, while I lay supine on my bunk, trembling.

Cissie, as usual, said and did nothing.

The next morning, Howie's rage had subsided. The only difference was that I was no longer allowed to leave the boat without explaining my purpose and getting formal permission. We sailed to Edgartown, and some of Howie and Cissie's friends came on board for dinner. I asked if after dinner I could row into the dock and go up to Top Masthead to phone my mother to say I would not be coming for the weekend. I dared not mention Hans's name. I was given forty minutes for the round trip. When I got to the cabin, the Admiral was there, but I had to get through to my mother because I was terrified of Howie and didn't know how to respond; so I risked having the Admiral overhear my telling her of the previous night's events. She was mortified on my behalf and said she would get in touch with her former shrink, Herbert Spiegel, to see if he could offer any concrete suggestions.

Tuesday, August 4, the day I would have been returning from New York had things gone differently, we set out under power for Nantucket, then raised our sails and shut off the engine. I had never been to Nantucket. For the most part, landlubbers who go to the Vineyard do not go to Nantucket, and vice versa. Only sailors and real tourists experience both. It's a long sail and the winds were light, so Howie told me to turn on the kicker.

"She won't turn over," I said, pressing the starter button repeatedly.

"What do you mean?"

"Just that, she won't start. You try."

Howie tried. No go.

He grabbed a flashlight and went below to the engine, which was lodged below the quarter berth at the stern of the boat below the cockpit. After a few minutes, he emerged in the companionway, his face expressionless. He began in measured tones:

"After your dim-witted school friend sank the boat, Joe White at the yard in Maine put in a new exhaust pipe and welded it to the remains of the existing exhaust pipe. The connection has corroded, allowing salt water into the engine."

"I don't understand."

"No, you wouldn't." He glowered at me accusingly. "Engines operate on diesel fuel, not salt water," he said with disgust.

Part 3: Howard's End

"Could you please explain further?" I asked meekly.

"Jesus Holy Christ." He took a deep breath "The existing exhaust pipe was galvanized metal and the new extension is monel, which is a stable, non-corrosive, and very expensive metal. Joe thought he was doing us a fucking service using monel for the extension. Instead, he's created a disaster, all thanks to that lying Jewess you invited to sail with us."

Jewess? I hadn't heard that before and I felt sick, but I was beginning to get it.

This latest disaster was my fault.

After my friend Emily Manheim had flushed lobster shells down the head (and lied about it) two summers before, and *Stone Horse* sank at her mooring in Brooklin, Maine, Joe White, the mechanic, thinking he was installing a tail pipe of the best possible (read: most inactive) of all metals, either did not know about or forgot about the electrolytic action between two metals in different positions on the Electrolytic Table. The lower metal of the pipe, which connected directly to the engine, was the sacrificial anode. Over the intervening two years, it had corroded where the two metals were joined and salt water had entered the engine.

The next morning, at 6:00 a.m., we crept out of Nantucket under sail, catching the early morning tide to get through Pollock Rip and over Stone Horse shoal—after whose long-gone light ship our vessel was named. Both were under the elbow of Cape Cod. Then we headed north for Marblehead where Howie knew there was a reliable mechanic. There was no wind. It was a very long sail. Howie reiterated his position: The salt in the engine was my problem and my obligation to put right.

"So what are you planning to do about this mess you've created?" he demanded.

"I don't know. What can I do? If I could fix it myself, I would. You know I would."

He kept at me throughout the day, and I kept asking "What can I do? I don't have money of my own to contribute." He was silent.

"But listen," I pleaded, "once we get to Marblehead, let me call the yard and organize the time for the mechanic to come to the boat. I'll stay on board while the mechanic works so you and Cissie can visit your friends and play golf, and I'll go back to removing the rust from the deck and the cabin trunk as soon as we get to port while the repairs are being made. I'll do nothing else."

No response.

"And for now, I'll stay at the helm for as long as it takes to sail to Marblehead, so you and Cissie don't have to be bothered."

Through the afternoon and early evening, we ghosted north, parallel to the eastern coast of Cape Cod. From the galley, Howie handed me the occasional cracker and soft drink as I stood at the helm, but otherwise he didn't speak to me. Towards evening, with the tide turned against us and not a breath of wind, we drifted backwards against the shore with limply hanging sails. When, after midnight, the tide changed again, we slipped slowly and noiselessly through the warm summer night, passed the rotating beacon of the Race Point Lighthouse in Provincetown, and slid into the glassy waters of the Bay of Massachusetts, which was saturated in moonlight. Cissie and Howie had gone below, maybe to sleep, maybe not. Very early the next morning we turned west into Marblehead's outer harbor. The pale dawn revealed no hint of the devastation wreaked by Hurricane Carol five years previously. Howie appeared at the hatch. Without a word or gesture, he took the helm as we glided towards the Eastern Yacht Club fleet. He brought us alongside a mooring buoy. I went forward with the boat hook, picked it up, hauled it aboard and secured the heavy line to which it was attached. Without speaking, we furled and stopped the sails and went below to sleep. It was Sunday morning. Nothing could be done about the engine until Monday at the earliest.

Time to kill.

If you are a member of an established yacht club and come into port on a boat, you have privileges at any of the yacht clubs in that port. The big clubs all used to have at least one and sometimes several launches that scurried around the fleet, collecting yachtsmen and their crews from their boats and bringing them into the clubhouse and back. In addition, the launches would take kids out to their smaller-class boats for day sailing and racing, and take little kids out to the floats where the even smaller sailboats used for teaching would be tied up. When you were ready to go ashore, you'd get out a long narrow conical brass horn and aim the horn in the direction of the nearest launch, blow three short blasts and wait to be picked up. An almost greater luxury than the passenger launches were the garbage boats that the bigger clubs would send around the fleet very early every weekday morning to collect plastic and paper bags of garbage, which yachtsmen were entitled to leave at their sterns. In some harbors, the garbage boats would replace the garbage with the *Daily Bleat*—Howie's name for the local daily newspaper.

The Sunday morning, after our windless sail from Nantucket to Marblehead, we caught up on sleep and rose close to noon. Howie was having spasms in his back. Movement was painful and he remained engulfed in gloom. I broke the silence and tried to draw him out about his work back in Chicago: what was he up to, what aspect of his research and his teaching excited him? What about his buddies, Karl Meyer, Steven Schwartz, and other luminaries of the Chicago's mid-century medical scene? What about his protégé

Dan Kushner? What was Dan working on? What about the research in hematology and renal disease that he had been doing at the Hektoen Institute? What about his Public Health program?

Nothing excited him. He said that no one understood what he was trying to achieve at Hektoen except possibly Dan Kushner. Dan was good. No one else appreciated his vision for an effective Public Health system. No one understood what he brought to the practice of medicine as a diagnostician and a clinician—least of all, surgeons.

"Surgeons are fools, assholes, mechanics, plumbers, bloodletters." He was ranting again. (Hans was a urologist. Urologists are surgeons.) "Surgeons make no diagnoses. They don't know shit from Shinola about disease. They take no responsibility for patient care. But they get all the kudos for prolonging lives, worse, for saving lives. They should all go fuck themselves!" With his rage temporarily spent, Howie returned to the dark cave of his unhappiness. He was only forty-five years old. Where else could he go but down, feeling so underappreciated and misunderstood?

I asked permission to go into the yacht club to see what might be there by way of entertainment. Permission was granted. I got out the brass horn, blew my three blasts into the windless air and was soon on the launch into the clubhouse. On the way to the desk in hopes of collecting another letter from Al, I saw, sitting at the bar, large brown drink in hand, my mother's friend Seth Milliken, whom I had always liked. Seth was a real bachelor (i.e., heterosexual), a rarity in her circle. He was handsome in a shaggy, boozy sort of way, wry, full of half-smiles, and allegedly an excellent sailor. He was the owner of an eight-meter sailboat called *Lara*.

"What a surprise! What are you doing here in Marblehead, Lale?"

"I'm here on my father's boat, *Stone Horse Light*. We just sailed in from Nantucket early this morning."

"I had forgotten that you spend summers sailing with your father.

Part 3: Howard's End

How long will you be around?" asked Seth, head cocked to one side, dark sandy bangs falling over the lower eyebrow.

"I'm not sure. We've had some engine difficulties and will try to get a mechanic to have a look tomorrow."

"Then, we'll be seeing some more of you, I hope," he said with cheer I couldn't match. "I am waiting for my friend Carol Perrera to come up from New York."

Did Seth actually have a girlfriend? I would have to report this to my mother.

"Okay, then, Seth. See you around." And I pecked him on the cheek as he reclaimed his barstool and wrapped his large paw lovingly around the frosty glass. I headed towards the main desk, where there was another letter from Al, full of anecdotes from his summer of piano playing in the Borscht Belt and sympathetic noises about Howie's anti-Hans rant, which I had described to him in some detail.

The next morning, Monday, was warm, clear and bright. Howie's back was a bit better but the cloud of gloom remained. Between Howie and me, it was all business. My job was to get coffee made (no sign of Cissie), to get the five-horsepower Evinrude outboard motor out of the lazerette and affix it to the stern of the dinghy, and to accompany Howie to the shipyard at the western end of Marblehead Harbor, where the wonder mechanic worked. We set off just after 8:00 a.m., in hopes of engaging him before he was assigned to another job. Fifteen minutes later, we disembarked and went to the yard's office.

Howie began turning on his charm. "We got an engine problem. The junction of the monel tail pipe and the galvanized exhaust pipe leading from the engine has rusted through. We got salt water in the engine."

"I'm sorry to hear that," the man behind the counter said. "That's a bad one."

"I've heard you have a great mechanic here and we'd like him to come out to our boat, take a look at what has to be done, give us a price, and then get started."

"We can help you, but not this minute, sir. Robin, our mechanic, is tied up for the morning. but he can probably get to you in the afternoon, and depending on what he finds, we can get you an estimate, and he can probably fix you up in a couple of days."

"That would be great. My name is Howard Armstrong, and I'll settle with you when we're done. But this is my daughter's problem. You'll be dealing with her," said Howie, gesturing in my direction. I looked up and nodded affirmatively. "She'll be in charge of getting this fixed. We're a grey yawl, *Stone Horse Light*, moored off the Eastern Yacht Club. She will be on board waiting for Robin and will supply him with any information or additional tools that he needs."

"Okay, sir. Robin will see you this afternoon." We left the office and in silence untied our dinghy, cranked up the Evinrude, and went back to the boat. Cissie was up and dressed. She had made a second round of coffee. After breakfast, they hailed the launch and went off for a day with their friends.

The morning sun was blazing. I stripped down to a pair of shorts and a skimpy top to maximize my exposure to the sun, and set to work chipping, grinding, sanding and polishing. It was hard but satisfying work. In the early afternoon, Robin, a gruff middle-aged man of few words and many tools, came and went. He seemed to know exactly what had to be done and did it well and efficiently over the next day and a half.

On the second afternoon, after Robin had successfully completed his work but before I completed mine, Seth came by in the

Part 3: Howard's End

Lara's dinghy, which had a much fancier outboard engine than our Evinrude.

"Hi, Lale! What are you up to?" he said as he slowed his dinghy to a stop, shut off the engine and stood to grab hold of our port rail.

"I'm trying to clean up this rust bucket boat of ours."

"What?"

"She's steel hull, steel decks, steel everything. There are blisters of rust everywhere. Some patches are left from last season too. I told Howie I'd spend some time trying to get rid of it."

"You shouldn't be doing that with those hand tools," Seth said, "They pay people at boatyards to do that sort of work and give them electric brushes and sanders to work with."

"Yeah, maybe, but I said I'd give it a try. By the way, if you wanted to talk to Cissie or Howie, they are playing golf and should be back to change before dinner."

"No, I actually came to talk to you. I wanted to ask if you would like to come sailing for a few days with me and my friend, Carol Pererra, on the *Lara*. We could use another pair of hands, and it doesn't seem as though you are getting in much sailing here in Marblehead."

"I would love to, Seth. Oh my God, what a wonderful idea! Oh, yes, I would. But I will have to get permission from Howie."

"That shouldn't be a problem. If you'd like to come, I'm happy to speak to your father myself."

"That would be great. When are you leaving?"

"Tomorrow morning around 9:30 or 10:00. We'll head up towards Gloucester, spend the night in Annisquam, and then head East towards Maine. We'll see how far we get, and we can leave you off anywhere on the way."

"I am sure we'll be at the club for dinner. Maybe you can talk to Howie then?"

"I'll do that, and I'll count on picking you up on the yacht club dock at 9:00 tomorrow, or better still, just take the launch with your gear out to us on the *Lara*."

"Okay, Seth, it sounds wonderful. See you this evening to confirm." And Seth let go of the rail, pulled the starter chord on his outboard and was off.

How to sell this to Howie?

How to persuade him this was not another instance of mutiny?

Lara. An eight-meter. I had sailed on no boat other than *Stone Horse* for any length of time. If I were to become the sailor that Howie wanted me to be, I needed to have experience on other boats as well, didn't I? Accepting Seth's invitation to sail a class boat like *Lara* would be a logical step in continuing my maritime education.

We went to dinner at the yacht club. Seth sauntered casually over to our table—sauntering casually was his customary gait—greeted Howie and Cissie, and introduced Mrs. Pererra to all three of us. Then he said to Howie, "I stopped by your boat this afternoon and invited Lale to join us for few days to a week of sailing on the *Lara*, if you can spare her."

"You did?" said Howie.

"Yes, she was working on the rust on the decks when I came by—and doing a damned good job, too, despite having only hand tools. Wish I could get labor like that!" He chuckled and then pressed on. "Lale said she would like to come but needed your consent. We're a bit shorthanded, as Carol hasn't done much sailing, and I know Lale is very experienced, thanks to all her summers with you. Carol and I both hope she will join us."

Silence from Howie.

"We're off around 9:30 or 10:00 tomorrow morning," Seth continued, then turned to me and said, "Looking forward to seeing you tomorrow, Lale." And he took Carol Perrera by the elbow and steered her over to his usual place at the bar.

Howie was speechless. I made my pitch about having known Seth since I was little, about wanting and needing further experience on different boats to further my sailing skills, and I added that I'd be back in a few days' time and would get myself to wherever they might be to rejoin them.

He seemed to accept that my acceptance was a fait accompli.

I excused myself from the table to telephone my mother to tell her the change in plan and express my immense relief that my incarceration was soon to come to an end, all thanks to lovely, funny, boozy Seth's invitation. No, I didn't know where we were going beyond Annisquam nor how long I'd be on their boat. No, I didn't know anything about Mrs. Pererra. Yes, I would keep in touch.

Cissie, Howie and I returned to the boat in silence. In silence I began to pack my things for the morning departure. Howie fixed highballs for himself and Cissie, and without a word they retired to the forward cabin. I finished my packing and stowed my duffle in the quarter berth to make for an early and soundless departure. I had no desire to say goodbye. I got my pillow and my Hudson Bay blankets from the locker, made up my bunk, crawled between the blankets and switched off the light over my head. My mind was spinning.

On the one hand, I was afraid Howie would burst out of the forward cabin and do me bodily harm. What had happened to him? How had he morphed from warm, loving father/musician/teacher/philosopher into paranoid Captain Queeg? On the other hand, where was I going and with whom? Would Seth and Mrs. Perrera also be crazy? Would they have designs on me, like the guy on the mahogany boat in Capri? And how and when would I get back home? Around and around these questions swirled until I succumbed to Morpheus.

I awoke with a jerk. The light was dim. It had to be very early in the morning. Someone was rapping on the steel hull right near my head.

"Ahoy, *Stone Hawse Light*," I heard someone shout. I climbed up the ship's ladder to the cockpit and there was the guy running the garbage boat making a hell of a racket. He had his bumpers snug up against our starboard side.

"I am looking for a Leslie Ahmstroang," he said with a strong New England accent.

"That's me," I said rubbing sleep from my eyes.

"I come to tell ya Dawktah and Missus Zinza are on the dawk waiting for you. They told me not to come back widdout cha."

"Who?" I asked?

"Dowktah and Missus Zinza. Dey sez dey ah your parents and dey've come to take you home. Step abowad, please."

"I gotta get dressed and get my stuff."

"Okay, but make it quick. I gawt the whole fleet to take care of. And I just stahted out."

I returned below, threw on my clothes and was about to grab my duffle when Howie emerged from the forward cabin, clutching Super Bear.

"And what do you have to say for yourself?" he asked.

"I am leaving," I replied.

"More important," he continued, holding Super Bear so his face was angled toward me accusingly, "What do you have to say to Super Bear to whom you swore that you would never desert ship?"

I turned and hoisted my duffle up the ship's ladder to the cockpit, then looked back at this man who was my father, holding the

Part 3: Howard's End

stuffed bear whose temperament and character flaws resembled his own.

"Tell Super Bear that l have had to break my promise ... even if it means l can't come back."

l climbed the ship's ladder, tears welling in my eyes, jumped over the cockpit coaming, and down over the side into the garbage boat. We took off for shore.

My parents had gone to bed after l called about moving from *Stone Horse* to *Lara*, but the same thoughts seemed to have gone through their minds that had gone through mine. At 2:00 a.m., they got out of bed, grabbed some Nescafe, which they made from the hot water tap in their bathroom, dressed, got the Mark II Lincoln from the garage on 63rd Street and Third Avenue, and took off into the night, arriving at the Eastern Yacht Club well before l would be taking off on the *Lara*.

Never were my sorry eyes happier to see any two people.

Never had Çok Güzel looked so "Very Beautiful."

14. The Andrews Sisters

Andrews Hall, Pembroke Campus, Brown University, Providence, RI.

PROVIDENCE — FALL 1959

Academically, it was going to be rough. I had a whole year of calculus and a lot of catching up to do, a semester of Newtonian physics followed by a semester introducing the basic principles of modern particle physics—all of which was fascinating but none of which came easily to me. Plus I had a semester of the history of nineteenth- and twentieth-century American architecture, taught by Brown's already legendary architectural historian, William Jordy, and a year of applied art under Brown's best known painter, Walter Feldman.

The calculus, the analysis and quantification of change, a branch of mathematics my now-estranged father had taught himself just for the fun of it, was my nemesis. Yes, it was more than interesting, but it was also very abstract, without much there for a mind like mine to hang onto. I couldn't just memorize it, because my memory had never been very good. I had to understand it, feel it, make it part of me. Physics seemed more tangible and accessible, perhaps because of the charismatic delivery of Robert Morse, our physics professor, who, in addition to giving lectures that brought all aspects of physics to life, seriously snowed some of us by driving around campus in a brand-new 1959 forest-green convertible Mercedes, top down.

Applied Art should have been right up my alley, but I'd lost my nerve as an artist. I remained stunned that my own prior work had been fraudulent. I was envious of my fellow students, who were able to let loose and experiment with line, color, and form. By comparison, my work looked as though it had been squeezed out of a tube of stale toothpaste.

Meanwhile, Al and I were still going strong. He was working on composing his senior thesis, an opera. We met almost every day for lunch. Friday evenings we often had dinner with Al's parents (more about my being such a skinny *shiksa*), and then we would all but copulate in front of the television while his parents went to temple. Some Saturday mornings Al and I would get on a bus and go wherever Brown was playing football, not because we were fans, or because Brown had such a hot team (we were close to the bottom of the Ivy League), but because the Brown band was made up of students so unskilled that the music professor responsible for the band insisted that Al march in the front row playing trombone to keep the band together. There would be Al, with his pre-Beatle haircut, a foot shorter than everyone else, marching in an ill-fitting uniform on the far left of the front row. While all the other guys stood up tall, with their trombones out in front dead level, each like a direct descendant of John Philip Souza, Al stooped, holding his trombone almost vertically, and blew straight down into the ground in front of him. But no one squawked because Al held the band together. Often on Saturday nights, he would have a gig playing piano on his own, or in his buddy Billy Vogel's band at one of the frat houses, and then we'd head for whatever party was being hosted by one of our crowd.

At least one weekend a month, I drove to New York, sometimes with friends, always with laundry. One November weekend, Al came down with me and stayed with a friend who lived on Central Park West. Our friend's parents were away and we all had dinner there and lots of wine. Our host repaired to one bedroom with his girlfriend, and Al and I went to another, but I knew I would have to be home by midnight. For all their liberal talk, The Parents were very conventional when it came to Judy's and my actual behavior—especially mine, as I was the oldest and deemed wild. At the end of the summer, when Al returned from Vegas and Judy and I were back from Maine, Hans caught us almost entirely naked on the narrow bunk in what had been my room and was now his study. I was sent upstairs to our "apartment" immediately, and Al was sent away and knew not to return in the near future. I knew not to rock the boat again, and getting home before midnight on that November evening was a must.

For all the pleasure both Al and I derived from the physical side of our relationship, I was holding onto my virginity. Why? Was I worried about my reputation? Given that our friends had repaired together to a bedroom, surely they thought Al and I were doing the same for the same reason. So if I had a reputation, it was already shot. Was I saving myself for my eventual husband? That was nonsense. I had read everything in the book on "free love" and was totally committed to the concept. But I continued to be afraid that once I experienced the complete act of intercourse, stark naked in a beautiful bed with clean white sheets and my lover's body entwined with mine, I would become a sex addict.

For my sophomore year, I shared a triple in Andrews Hall with

Honoré Clark, my freshman roommate, and Deena Rosen, another girl from Allinson House. When I got back to school, after the evening on Central Park West, there was a lot of tittering going on. Apparently both my roommates had given up their "cherries," one that very weekend, and the other a few weeks before.

"How was it?" I asked.

I don't remember either of them describing anything particularly pleasurable, maybe because they were both shy and unused to putting words to such an event or feeling. Or maybe because it seemed to each of them an inevitability but little more. Each had been going with the same guy since freshman year and was "pinned." Each was on the marriage track. While they knew they were supposed to wait until they were married, girls nowadays were more progressive. Maybe girls always did more than they said. More tittering, but no talk.

Well, well.

If Deena and Honoré, who were much more conventional than I, could succumb, so, certainly, could I.

I indicated to Al that I was ready. He borrowed a friend's off-campus apartment for the next Saturday night. We had dinner and plenty of Chianti at Smith's, our favorite Italian restaurant on Allen Street (Smith's was unconcerned that the drinking age in Rhode Island was twenty-one), then drove to our friend's apartment. The bed was freshly made and within minutes we were totally naked and between clean white sheets. I wish I could find words to convey the romantic and physical pleasure of my deflowering. Much later in life I learned of a writer who specializes in ghostwriting the juicy sex scenes that are an essential feature of many best-selling novels. Suffice it to say that Al's entry to my body was everything I had hoped for and more. I felt my insides to be lined in soft velvet, every fiber standing straight up, as if electrified, as wave after wave of pleasure engulfed me.

I had been right to fear addiction.

Our first-semester exams were held at the end of January, which gave us time over Christmas vacation to study. I had been assigned to the calculus section taught by David Buchsbaum, whose probability theory class I'd taken in my freshman year and whom I liked and admired. Mr. Buchsbaum finished the coursework before the Christmas break and his pre-Christmas treat for us was to prove, algebraically, the existence of the positive integers—in other words, how to get from integer 1 to integer 2 to integer 3 using algebraic processes. It was fascinating, the way some very complex music like Mahler is fascinating. You don't have to understand how Mahler composed the music to find it pleasurable or even awe-inspiring. My friend Sandy Walcott, a class below me (and the daughter of a friend and colleague of Hans), seemed to have no trouble following these proofs. But I followed Mr. Buchsbaum halfway through the trip from integer 1 to the creation of 2, then I got lost and remained in a state of dumb admiration for the remaining two classes required to complete the proofs. What did Sandy Walcott have that I didn't have?

I pulled a forty-four in the calculus exam. Not good.

I went to Mr. Buchsbaum in despair. I told him of my need to pass his course to continue on in architecture. I also told him I loved mathematics, but more as an enthusiastic spectator than as a participant, and that I found grasping the basic concepts of calculus extremely difficult. I told him how I felt about the proofs of the positive integers and made the analogy to music appreciation. He listened kindly and with empathy. He said if I could manage a better understanding of the material and pull off a better grade at the end of the year, that would be the grade on my record for both semesters. Then he suggested that, as much as he would regret losing me, I should transfer to the "other" section of Calculus 22, which was being taught in a slightly more conventional manner (thus implying that the instructor might be an unimaginative plodder), whose teaching methods might be better tailored to my needs. He also suggested I get in touch with Joanne Rapf, a very talented math major in the class ahead of me, who might be willing to help me on the side.

Joanne willingly took me on, free of charge. Night after night, I would trudge up one flight, knock on her door, and sheepishly announce that I was stuck again. Joanne never turned me down. She would put aside her own work and help me through. As often as not, her roommate, Jan, who had lost her leg as a child, would be hopping around their room, and her prosthetic leg, straps and all, would be standing in the corner. This took some getting used to, given my fear of the prostheses in the windows on Third Avenue when I was a child, but eventually I didn't even notice.

The second semester was not unlike the first, except for seasonal differences and my umbilical attachment to Joanne. Calculus was now with Mr. Small (yes, that was his name) and, with Joanne's help, almost manageable. The introduction to nuclear physics class was riveting. Professor Morse's lectures were to be topped only by those Richard Feynman delivered to incoming freshman at Cal Tech several years later in the 1960s (and which I heard decades later). But Walter Feldman's painting studio, a creative outlet for others, for me continued to be painful and discouraging.

We all had to take a Phys Ed class each semester for two years. So I signed up for an 8:00 a.m. squash class at Brown's Marvel Gym, which was located along Hope Street, partway between campus and Al's house on Overhill Road. Twice a week I'd get up at the crack of dawn, scrape the ice off El Al's windshield, drive to Marvel Gym, and attempt to learn the appropriate wrist action required to fire rocklike balls around the glaring white squash court. At nine, I was back in El Al and on my way to Al's. The absence of his parents' car indicated that they had already left for work and he had left the front door open for me, so I could go straight upstairs to his bedroom, strip, crawl into his bed, and enjoy the highs of my new addiction.

Despite the pleasure of those early morning trysts, Al and I were beginning to argue. Theme One was his obsession with his talent in general (which was indisputable), plus his plans for graduate school and, more specifically, with the creation and performance of his opera, *The Damask Drum*. Theme Two was my feeling that I was required to be his personal acolyte. But we pressed on. *The Damask Drum* opened on the night of St. Patrick's Day of 1959. It was a huge success, and Al was rightly celebrated. Afterwards, a party was held at the house of Arlen Coolidge, the Music Department Chairman, and his wife Sylvia. Their son, Clark, Al's best friend from Classical High School, was there as well.

Clark had dropped out of college and was writing poetry and playing drums on his own. He was still living at home. There was something appealing about Clark. He was as tall and hefty as Al was not, but seemed sort of lost, whereas Al had definitely been found. Clark was as quiet as Al was not, but if he had something to say, out it came, softly but clearly. He had a big mop of dark, straight hair, with long bangs that fell over his fair-skinned face when he played the drums, which he did very well. I found myself drawn to Clark, maybe just because he was hard to find and harder to talk to, and maybe just because he was Al's opposite.

Spring. Daffodils dotted the campus lawns, the hanging branches of the willows were turning yellow-green, and the magnolia blossoms were starting to erupt. In what little spare time I had, I returned to the theatre, this time as second-string theatre critic for the *Brown Daily Herald,* and so became acquainted with four remarkable girls, all a class ahead of me, all involved in some aspect of the theatre.

Joyce Reed was a slight, hauntingly beautiful and brilliant English major and aspiring actress from Toronto. Without affectation, Joyce looked and acted the perfect lady, as though to the manor born. However, she hadn't two nickels to rub together, had earned a named scholarship, and worked various on-campus jobs. Joyce was the star actress of Brown theatre and a favorite of Richard Foreman, the star playwright of our campus years and of the New York avant-garde for decades thereafter.

Elizabeth Diggs, Joyce's roommate, the oldest of five kids from a Tulsa, Oklahoma, family, was an ebullient and very pretty girl with a hint of a drawl, an iron will, a huge smile that revealed perfect teeth, and a passion for dance, literature, musical theatre, and the finer things of life, which she was able to afford since her father was doing well as a lawyer in an oil-rich town.

Emily Arnold was from Great Neck, Long Island. Her parents, like mine, had been divorced, and like mine, were intimately acquainted with the ramifications of drink. Emily was slight and wiry, with a gentle demeanor that belied her huge intelligence and inner strength. She had a tremendous talent for illustration and a gift for singing, acting, and writing for the theatre. She, too, worked additional jobs on campus to make ends meet.

Susie Ross had been Emily's roommate from their freshman year. They had been stuck in Bates House, a freshman dorm for scholarship students. They cooked their own meals and cleaned their own rooms, which meant that they ate almost nothing and were isolated from the rest of campus life. Susie, who came from Albany, was dark, funny, not quite the intellectual or the student that the others were, but hugely personable—and could she sing and dance! Like Joyce and Emily, Susie waited on tables. She also typed people's papers for extra spending money.

As I became less in awe of these four girls and got to know them better, I spent more and more time in their rooms. They took to me as much as I had taken to them and encouraged me to apply for a single room near those they were hoping for on the fourth floor of Andrews, Pembroke's largest residence hall, for the next year.

That spring my mother had started nagging me about getting a summer job. I loved working and was looking forward to having a job in the city. Liz Diggs, Liz's ballet-dancing sister Bev, and Emily Arnold had sublet an apartment on 60th Street, just west of Second Avenue, two blocks south of our house on 62nd Street. Liz and Bev were to devote the summer to studying ballet. Emily and her boyfriend, George McCully, who had sublet an apartment on 114th Street, had secured jobs working at Freedomland, then a brand-new quasi-cultural theme park built on 205 acres of marshland in the Bronx. (It would be demolished just five years later.) I was envious of Emily and George's employment, but my mother wouldn't have allowed me to take such a job. Like babysitting, it would do nothing to enhance my resume. I'd had a couple of interviews over the spring but had come up with nothing. My mother said I wasn't trying hard enough. But if childcare or working as a temporary salesgirl in a local shop or somewhere like Freedomland were out, then what?

We took our finals. I got a B in calculus for both semesters thanks to Joanne and to Mr. Small, As in physics for both semesters, As in art history for both semesters, and Bs in Feldman's Applied Art, thanks to turning in a series of small panels influenced by Chinese screen painting that represented the seven days of Creation, which Feldman found acceptable.

Al and I finished the year at Campus Dance, followed by his graduation, the only Brown graduation I ever attended. It wasn't the same as the year before. Al and I were running out of steam. His ego was growing beyond my endurance. He was off to wherever to earn money during the summer and then to Yale for graduate school in the fall. I was soon to return to New York to partake of a weeklong family vacation to Bermuda, job or no job.

Bermuda was picturesque, with its clear skies, coral beaches, exotic tropical vegetation, bicycles, mopeds, and sparkling white houses with stepped rooflines that trapped the rain water. Bermuda would have been a lot more enjoyable if Pago hadn't caught a horrific cough midway through our stay. As a result, we spent much of our time in our pink hotel in downtown Hamilton rather than exploring and living the beach life. As soon as we returned, my mother resumed harping at me about getting a summer job, but by mid-June it was too late to get anything worthy of parental approval. My mother was disgusted with me.

However, in The Parents' view, summer employment was more about self-improvement than cash earnings, so I figured maybe the time had come for me to follow in the footsteps of Liz and her sister Bev and take ballet. The problem was twofold. First, when Cindy Childs and I had been allowed to take modern dance classes outside of Brearley with Anita Zahn, a disciple of Isadora Duncan, I had proved to be stiff, almost arrhythmic, and inhibited, whereas for Cindy, dance was liberating and the start of her distinguished career as dancer and choreographer. Second, I picked up a milder but more tenacious version of the nasty cough Pago got in Bermuda, and while I wasn't laid up, I couldn't shake it, and exercise sent me into bouts of debilitating hacking and coughing. So ballet was out.

My next idea was to study Italian. I made an appointment to visit my mother's old friend, Hedy Giusti-Lanham, who, after the death of her second husband had to reinvent herself quickly or face the shame and inconvenience of poverty. She married a Texas oilman and become executive director of the America Italy Society, with offices on East 60th Street. To give credence to the total picture, she attached the name of her first husband, Goffredo Giusti, to her new married name. Hedy Giusti-Lanham became a one-lady lobby for the Italian language and Italian culture at a time when things Italian were not as fashionable as they have since become. Hedy recommended that I study with Signora Delle Donne, who lived uptown at 508 West 139th Street. Appointments were set up for twice-weekly lessons.

Hedy was less interested in improving my language skills than in fixing me up with her latest protégé, Sven Lukin, a young Latvian-born painter. She was so sure I would want to go to bed with him the moment I laid eyes on him that I had to tell her I probably wouldn't, however attractive he might be, as I was very inexperienced and had no protection. She declared that there was no excuse for a woman of my age not to enjoy the pleasures of sex without concern. Even though in the late Fifties no self-respecting gynecologist would prescribe birth control for an unwed woman, Hedy's gynecologist was of a different ilk and culture. She made an appointment for me to see him on the spot and promised not to tell my mother.

Dr. Hans Lehfeldt certainly was of a different ilk. He was probably only just sixty at the time of our first appointment, but I was barely twenty, so he seemed very old. Rather than the white coats that the doctors in my family wore, he preferred a short-sleeved,

Part 3: Howard's End

high-collared dentist's jacket with buttons along one shoulder that exposed his long, furry, liver-spotted arms. He had a thick Prussian accent, which conveyed formidable authority, but he soon put me at my ease, speaking warmly of Hedy and of his fervent belief in birth control for women of all ages and marital states. He went about the examination (my first of that sort) and diaphragm-fitting with gentleness and skill. He made me practice inserting and removing it until he was satisfied that I knew what I was doing. Then, with military fervor, he made it clear that the diaphragm was useless without the contraceptive ointment that formed the seal with the vaginal wall. He counseled me to anticipate when I might be having sex and to insert the diaphragm several hours before so it could settle into place. I felt blessed to have met this man and very comfortable with the direction I was taking.

In mid-July I met Sven Lukin at one of Hedy's gatherings. He was slim, smart, cocky, and gorgeous, with honey-colored skin, tartar eyes, and a forelock of straight blond hair that he constantly flicked aside. We met more than once thereafter for drinks, but never for dinner. He was an artist. He didn't buy food. One evening I drove downtown and we met at a cheap bar on the Lower East Side. We drank a good deal and then climbed the rickety stairs to his studio-cum-apartment at 168½ Delancey Street. With neither fore-talk nor foreplay, he drunkenly began unbuttoning my shirt. I was still young and idealistic. This wasn't the way love was supposed to happen. I stopped him.

"Just a minute. Do you know who I am?"

"Yeah, sure," he mumbled.

"No, stop. Do you remember my name?" He looked quite alarmed.

"No," he said. "I don't." He rolled onto his back, almond eyes half closed, looking smug and sexy in the light from the flashing neon sign outside the window.

"What does it matter?"

I buttoned up my shirt, zipped up my skirt, found my shoes and the keys to El Al, and took off into the night.

The rest of the summer was downhill from there. I'd blown it with Sven, and Al and I had fizzled out. The muscles around my rib cage ached from constant coughing. I could hardly turn the steering wheel of my car to get into a parking place. I barely made it to my Italian lessons. Some evenings I hung around with Sandy Bull and his musician friends. One of them was playing bass for Ornette Coleman, and we'd go downtown to hear them play. But I was not a jazz fan, and however brilliant Coleman may have been, I hated that kind of music.

Also, Sandy and his friends were into a level of drug "experimentation" that scared the hell out of me. One of them, Charlie Haden, also a bass player, had taken up with a girl from my class at Brearley. They came round with Sandy one evening when The Parents were out. I was glad to see her. Charlie, whom I'd met before, was another silent type and barely said hello. He went straight into Hans's study (my old bedroom) and for some time we heard doors and drawers opening and closing. He came back into the living room.

"Where's your father's medical bag?" he asked.

"I don't know. Why?"

"He's gotta have some stuff in it. I am coming down."

"I don't think he has any narcotics, if that's what you're looking for."

"All doctors carry opium derivatives for treating pain. Surely he's got some belladonna somewhere, even crystals. We could melt those down."

"I don't know, and it's not for me to look for or find. You've gotta get what you need somewhere else." To my immense relief, the three of them disappeared as fast as they had come in. Sandy, or

Part 3: Howard's End

maybe even Daphne, probably had something at home that would settle Charlie down. And Sandy's house was around the corner.

My ribs were shot and I seemed to be losing weight, but I wasn't sick enough to stay home. Sven, whom I still met from time to time for drinks, introduced me to the Cedar Tavern, on University Place a few blocks east of Greenwich Village, then a very sleazy area peppered with SROs (Single Room Occupancy buildings populated by people near the bottom of the economic ladder). In the mid-Fifties the Cedar Tavern had been the number-one watering hole for abstract expressionist painters like Motherwell, de Kooning, Pollock, and Franz Kline—all heavy drinkers. Even in 1960, it retained some of that cachet. Unbeknownst to my parents, I started going there on my own, far preferring its seedy vitality to the screeching jazz saxophone of Ornette Coleman, and hoping for a glimpse of Sven. One evening at the bar, sipping a cheap gin martini on the rocks, I met a Frenchman named Michel. Michel was an artist, or so he said, but like me, he lived on the Upper East Side rather than in the Village. He took quite a shine to me, and I might have been interested were it not for his odorous breath. At the end of the evening, he looked me over and up and down, and in his very thick French accent said:

"I would take you home to bed with me, but we are both so thin our bones would crunch."

Jesus! Was it that bad?

Hans continued to insist the cough was nothing. At the end of the summer, he invited his old friend Agnes Wilson to dinner. Dr. Wilson had been the Brearley School doctor after Dr. Spock retired. (Before my time at Brearley, Dr. Benjamin Spock was the man who checked the throats of every little girl coming back to school after being sick.) We sat down to drinks as we always did, and I had a coughing fit.

"Leslie, how long have you been coughing like that?" Dr. Wilson asked.

"Most of the summer, Dr, Wilson."

"Hans, listen to her!" she exclaimed. "She's got whooping cough! You can hear it. Listen to the end of each cough."

Neither parent begged forgiveness, nor did they even apologize.

There is no cure for whooping cough. You just have to get through it.

PROVIDENCE — FALL 1960

Following in my mother's footsteps, Judy went off to Bryn Mawr for orientation in early September. And I returned to Providence in mid-September and carted my stuff up to the fourth floor of Andrews. I had been assigned Room No. 457, a single next to Emily Arnold. Susie Ross, Liz Diggs, and Joyce Reed all had singles across the hall. By then, each of them had a significant love interest and was seriously considering marriage immediately after graduation. I had no such plan and felt left out. With Al safely in graduate school at Yale, I decided to track down Clark Coolidge and see what sort of trouble I could raise. Clark was still writing poetry, playing the drums, and living at home with his parents. This was not my finest hour. My need to have someone—anyone—in my life, someone to be attached to, to care for, even if he might be ill-equipped to care for me, has never been my best attribute. But the need was strong. So I wormed my way into Clark's life. I had dinners with his parents during which they watched television nonstop. (A department head of a major university watching TV during dinner?) I listened to Clark play drums, slept with him on the rare occasions that his

Part 3: Howard's End

parents went out, and even talked myself and Clark into thinking that we might marry, so much did I want to be like Emily, Joyce, Liz, and Susie.

Luckily, my courses were more interesting than my love life, and finally I was able to cash in on the alleged reciprocity between Brown and the Rhode Island School of Design. RISD required that all incoming first-year students, regardless of their eventual field of study, take Freshman Foundation, which included, among other subjects, life drawing, mechanical drawing, two-dimensional design, three-dimensional design, and calligraphy. In order to take any advanced courses at RISD, Brown students also had to complete the Freshman Foundation. One academic course credit at Brown equaled three Freshman Foundation components, one of which had to be Life Drawing. My friend Sandy Walcott signed up for Life Drawing, 2D Design, and 3D Design. I signed up for Life Drawing, Mechanical Drawing (drafting), and Calligraphy. I had had enough of the creative stuff the previous year with Walter Feldman. I needed to learn mechanical drawing for architecture, and I loved the idea of learning calligraphy, an art I had always admired and a skill at which my mother had excelled when she was young and had unsuccessfully tried to impart to me.

Taking classes at RISD wasn't easy. I had only ten minutes between classes to walk down the hill to the RISD campus carrying art supplies, and another ten minutes to walk back up. I was coughing less, but moving so fast up and down that steep hill was hard on my lungs and my ribs. My first shot at Life Drawing was a disaster. Of course, Sandy Walcott got the hang of it immediately, as she had with calculus. I looked from the model to the efforts of the other kids around me, including Sandy. They varied, but they at least seemed to bear some resemblance to the naked body before us, whereas the marks on my sheet of newsprint had almost none. The complexity of the human figure daunted me. Its proportions relative to one another and to the surrounding space seemed impossible to capture. I saw light and shadow everywhere, but I couldn't figure how to use either to define form on paper. It was as if I were trying to draw blindfolded. I made only chicken scratches that attempted but failed miserably to represent the outline of the figure. Class after class went by until our instructor, Mr. Macomber, a short, stout elderly man stood behind me and said in his broad Providence accent, "Miss Ahmstrong. You draw like Two Tank Aman."

The reference to Tutankhamen might have been encouraging had Mr. Macomber not been implying that my markings looked not like rendered form but like hieroglyphs. Eventually, Mr. Macomber got me to look at—more accurately, to *see*—the anatomy of the figure and use it as a path to capturing the basics of the human form, rather than focusing on the simple outline. And so I got by. Just.

By contrast, in Mechanical Drawing I felt on my way, finally, to learning something that would serve me as an architect. I loved the geometry of the projections; the sharp, hard pencils; the T-square and the clear plastic triangles; the straight lines, the perfect curves of the circles and ellipses; the ability to represent space and objects in space accurately on a two-dimensional surface.

And I adored calligraphy. We worked from a hardcover textbook called *The Elements of Lettering* by John Howard Benson and Arthur Graham Carey, originally published in 1940, the year I was born. We started with a piece of bamboo and fashioned our own pens from scratch, inserting a segment of a watch spring inside the nib to hold the ink. We learned the importance of a sharp bevel. We learned to cut quills. We learned to work on an inclined surface so as to regulate the flow of ink. We learned the practical and decorative

Part 3: Howard's End

function of serifs, triangular heads, variants, and ligatures. We constructed Roman capitals and copied alphabet after alphabet: rustic capitals; early Roman and insular half uncials; Lombardic, Carolingian, and Humanist miniscule; Northern and Southern blackletter; and finally, Chancery Italic, the style that evolved into the cursive writing that we use today. I soon developed my own italic hand, a skill that has served me ever since.

Close to Christmas of 1960, I used Clark's and my tepid thoughts about getting married as an excuse to write to Howie, to tell him about Clark and to see if I could do something to restore our relationship. However painful had been the circumstances leading to my departure from *Stone Horse Light*, I missed having my brilliant, crazy, funny father in my life. My mother had said that in the event of a breach in the relationship between parent and child, it is the child who generally has to take the first step towards reconciliation. It was she who had initiated the restoration of her relationship with her father. So if things were to improve with Howie, it would be up to me to make the first move. Howie wrote me back almost as though nothing had happened between us, and with sufficient warmth asked if I was looking forward to coming out to Chicago later in the spring. But I did little about it. The window was beginning to open. That was enough for the time being.

On the other side of my Andrews single was another senior, Gael McManus, with whom I was less close than my four "Andrews Sisters" but whom I liked very much. Gael was no scholar and had no interest in the theatre, but she was a serious party drinker and a good soul. She had grown up in New York and we had several friends in common, among them Sandy Bull, who had graduated from the Woodstock School two years after Gael. In mid-February there was to be some sort of reunion at Woodstock, and Gael asked if I wanted to come.

Sure. Why not?

On a snowy Friday afternoon in February, Gael and I put chains on El Al and headed north, arriving in Woodstock, Vermont, in time for a Pete Seeger concert that evening. We skied the next day. (Woodstock boasts of having the very first ski lift in the United States, installed in 1934.) In the evening we went to a less formal but more magical concert, where Pete Seeger and Sandy Bull played together, then repaired to the bar at the Woodstock Inn for a long night of talking and drinking with a gaggle of people our age. Those days in Woodstock were the best I had had all year and they helped me acknowledge that my relationship with Clark was not happening. Lately Clark was taciturn at best, morose at worst. He had taken to hanging out with an unpleasant bearded buddy, and smoking, sniffing, and otherwise ingesting whatever marijuana or other stuff was available. Drugs of any sort petrified me. During the weeks following our return from Woodstock, I did my best to persuade Clark that he was no longer in love with me.

My Andrews Sisters were all engaged to be married and I was not. I would have to live with that reality.

At least I wouldn't be bored to death.

15. Howard's End

Mies van der Rohe's Lake Shore Drive Apartments, Chicago, 1955.

PROVIDENCE — MARCH 1961

The phone rang in our corridor in Andrews Hall. I was in the shower. Joyce took a message. It was Harriet Welling, an old and close friend of Howie's in Chicago. Why would she be calling me? Something must be very wrong. I went downstairs to the switchboard and called her back collect.

"Hello, Harriet. Sorry to call collect. What's going on?"

I could hear Harriet taking a deep breath. "Lale, Howie is dying. I think you should come out as soon as you can."

"What do you mean, *dying*? Dying of what?"

"Dying of hepatitis."

"Hepatitis?" My mother had had hepatitis two years before, and she'd been pretty sick but still managed to down a split of champagne every evening even though booze was off limits. Obviously, one didn't die of hepatitis.

"Do you not know that Howie has been sick?"

"No. I haven't spoken to Howie or Cissie for a year and a half."

"Really?" she said. "You didn't know about his operation this winter?"

"No. What operation, for what?"

"Duodenal ulcers. You really don't know about any of this? Hasn't anyone else in the family called you?"

"No."

"Not Sinc? Not Howard?" Howard, my grandfather, had been a Princeton classmate of Harriet's late husband, Paul.

"No, Harriet. I know nothing."

"Well, this isn't the time or place to go into the details," said Harriet. "Howie has been in decline for some time and yesterday went into a coma. Dan Kushner, his associate, says there's next to no hope of his coming out of it. I'll speak to Sinc and get him to book you a flight and get you a ticket. I will tell you whatever else I know when you get here. It's best you stay here at the house with me and M.P." M.P. was Harriet's older married daughter, Mary Paul, slightly younger than Howie and Sinc, and Harriet's favorite person on this earth.

"Okay, Harriet, I'll get there as soon as I can."

"Do that, Lale."

"I will, and thanks for letting me know."

I felt as though my ribcage had been kicked in.

I would have called The Parents, but they were abroad. Hans was delivering a paper on fertility in Kabul. They took pride in never spending a night apart, and so my mother was by his side. That was probably a good thing. This had nothing to do with them.

Sinc, to whom I hadn't spoken since my ignominious departure from *Stone Horse*, booked me a flight from Providence to Chicago for the next day. I called Clark to tell him I was leaving and why, but

Part 3: HOWARD'S END

got his mother instead, who took the occasion to chew me out for breaking the heart of her "beautiful boy."

The next day Susie Ross and her fiancé drove me to the airport, and M.P. collected me from O'Hare in the early afternoon. We drove to Harriet's large house on North Astor Street, where I met up with Sinc. We exchanged somber hellos and I transferred to Sinc's rental car for the long drive across Chicago to the residence hall at Cook County Hospital, where Howie had insisted that he and Cissie live in order to be close to both his patients and his students.

I couldn't get it through my head that Howie might be dying and that no one had thought to tell me. The forty-minute drive across Chicago seemed endless. I would have liked to talk to Sinc, first about Howie's condition and then about what had led to my leaving *Stone Horse*, but he wasn't making any effort to talk to me. Neither he nor any other Armstrong told me why, nor asked for my version of what had led to my departure.

So I thought about Harriet and my debt to her for having contacted me and arranging for me to come to Chicago. Harriet, like my mother, was a bluestocking Bryn Mawr graduate. In 1912 and 1913, in her early twenties, she marched on behalf of Women's suffrage and was a charter member of the League of Women Voters. She was the young wife of John Paul Welling, my grandfather's classmate (Princeton '03), which is how the Wellings came into Howie's life. Paul had a stroke and lived the last twenty years of his life in a wheelchair with Harriet by his side, pushing him here and there, interpreting the strange sounds that he used to communicate, spoon-feeding him his meals, and seeing to the staff that took care of him. I remembered them both from earlier trips to Chicago. Paul was like a specter, but Harriet was active, attractive, and sharp. The Wellings's large house on North Astor Street was the Chicago base for their good friend Adlai Stevenson while he was Governor of Illinois and made his failed bid for the presidency in the 1952. In the late '50s, Paul died and set Harriet free. Howie adored Harriet because she was as smart as he was, and honest to a fault.

It was late on a typically windy Chicago afternoon when Sinc parked outside the Cook County residence hall on Harrison Avenue, and we went up the elevator to Howie and Cissie's floor. Although Howie was comatose, Sinc told me they had decided not to move him from his apartment to a regular hospital room. Instead, his team of medical associates and protégés, led by Dr. Daniel Kushner, set up a hospital bed and all the related life-support equipment he needed in what had been the dining area of his and Cissie's large living room. Nursing staff and physicians could as easily tend to him there as in a room down the hall or in the next building, and it would be easier for Cissie and visitors to have him at home. Sinc rang the doorbell. It was opened by Dan Kushner, who wrapped his arms around me as he wiped the tears from his eyes.

"Where is he?" I asked.

"Over there." Dan gestured to the right. He took my hand and led me to the bedside. Howie, unconscious, was lying on his back, bloated, with yellowed skin stretched across his formerly handsome elongated, face. His breathing was shallow. He looked so diminished, so distant, already in Charon's care, already halfway across the Styx. I wanted to puke, to scream, to lash out at someone, anyone—anyone other than Dan Kushner, whose pain and grief I felt as I felt my own.

"*Why didn't anyone tell me? Why? WHY?*" I wanted to shout. But I knew I could say nothing. Even before I spoke to Cissie, who hadn't come to greet me, I knew I was not welcome in that apartment. I was no longer part of her and Howie's life. Sinc's relative indifference to me indicated that I might not be part of the larger Armstrong context either.

"*Well, guys, tough shit!*" I thought. "*That swollen residue of a man in that bed over there is still my father, and I am his daughter, his only offspring, and I am staying in this apartment, by his bedside, as much or as little as I like, until he departs this world, whether you like it or not.*

"*Fuck you all!*"

After a bit, Cissie deigned to appear, and she flew into a fit of theatrical sobbing about having had only five years with Howie, the love of her life, and asking how could this terrible thing be happening to her? Dan Kushner decided I'd had enough and took me to his office on a lower floor in the same building. We sat side by side on the visitor's side of his cluttered desk as he recounted the story of Howie's illness.

Howie had had problems with his back for a long time. I remember his being unable to do much heavy lifting the summer when we sailed from Wisconsin to Martha's Vineyard because he had had surgery the prior spring to address his slipped discs. The surgery helped but didn't totally ameliorate the pain. So, according to Dan, Howie started popping huge quantities of aspirin, and over the years it ate through the wall of his duodenum, resulting in internal hemorrhaging. As far back as I could remember, Howie had been popping aspirin for one reason or another. No wonder he had almost bled to death.

Immediate surgery, a gastrectomy, was the only answer. But Howie hated surgeons, and the duodenum was within his area of expertise. He was a crack internist, and no plumbers or bloodletters were going to play on his turf unless he was in full command. So, according to Dan, Howie arranged to have the gastrectomy done under local anaesthesia so that he could supervise the entire procedure. What should have been a simple operation took forever. Howie bled so much during the course of it that he had to have twenty-three blood transfusions before he was sewn up. In those days, there was no way to screen blood for hepatitis. With twenty-three transfusions, chances were very good that Howie was going to contract hepatitis, and if that happened, he would need to have a very strong liver to deal with it.

A very strong liver is something that Howie did not have. I asked Dan whether Howie had cirrhosis. I assumed everyone knew how much Howie drank, and everybody must have asked the same question. Dan didn't want to say. His reluctance gave me all the answer I needed.

I had met Dan and his wife, Gail, on earlier trips to Chicago. Dan was mid-height, medium build, olive skinned. There were patches of grey in his dark, buzz-cut hair. His appeal lay in his character; his kindness and his honesty drew you in. The same was true of Gail, who was slender and pretty, with shoulder-length hair, a sincere smile, and a no-nonsense way of making things happen. I knew about their house in North Chicago, their four kids, and how fond of Dan Howie had always been. But I didn't really know Dan, nor did I realize how important Howie was to Dan until we spoke. Howie was Dan's teacher, his mentor, his hero. Howie was grooming Dan to succeed him. Dan clearly loved Howie as much as I had loved him. I couldn't believe that in that hotbed of emotional hostility I had found a kindred spirit.

Dan said Howie's recovery from the surgery was pretty normal until serum homologous hepatitis set in. He said that Cissie then decided to take Howie to Florida to get him away from the hospital and the teaching in hopes that he would relax, sit in the sun, and maybe play a little golf until he got his strength back. Howie had told me many times in past years that he loathed the state of Florida for no other reason than that his parents had a bungalow in Delray Beach where they spent the winters, and anywhere his

Part 3: Howard's End

mother resided was where he did not want to be. I couldn't imagine a trip to Florida being any sort of palliative for Howie.

Dan had taken his family down to Florida to spend some time with them. Much to Dan's surprise, instead of encouraging Howie to rest, Cissie ran him around like crazy: parties here, shopping there. Howie was much worse on his return from Florida than when they set out. Dan as much as suggested that it was Cissie who was responsible for his approaching demise, that Howie had long lost the will to resist and otherwise deal with her. He had basically thrown in the towel—a mindset I had seen hints of during that last summer with Howie and Cissie on *Stone Horse*.

On the way back up to Howie's apartment, Dan said I shouldn't stay there alone with Cissie. He offered to drive me back to Harriet's on his way home. I could come back first thing in the morning. Howie would still be there.

Death Watch, Day Two. When I returned the next morning, Howie was indeed still there, in the same position, yellow and swollen, breathing lightly. I kissed him good morning and sat by his bedside for a while, holding his puffy hand. Cissie was in somewhat better shape and casually asked me to pick up some prescription medicine she wanted at the local pharmacy, as though I had been living next door, or even in the next room, all along. When I returned, Cissie took the drugs and repaired to her and Howie's bedroom. She closed the door behind her. In her absence I used the phone to make dinner arrangements with Mort and Hortense Neimark, other close friends of Howie who had been wonderful to me in the past. The Neimarks had two sons, one of whom I especially liked.

Then I took in my surroundings. Cissie's uniformed black maid, Ada, puttered around in the kitchen and emerged from time to time to take a pass at dusting the large combined living room and dining area, which was unimaginatively furnished but bright, thanks to a row of double-hung windows facing the street. On the floor, under the windows directly across from the entry, I saw, as if for the first time, the lineup of the stuffed bears. They were situated so that Howie could have seen them easily were he conscious. There must have been at least twenty. Bear Bear Armstrong Bear was at the center, flanked by Super Bear and Colonel Whitehead Bear, each of whom were flanked by their ladies—Blue Bear, with her aluminum foil bling, and Lady Whitehead Bear. On either side of these were several more bears of different types and colors, ranked in size, whose names and personalities I didn't know and didn't want to know.

People came in and out to check on Howie. Cissie came and went, hardly acknowledging me. Dan stopped by at lunchtime to take me to the cafeteria for something to eat. But for most of the day, I was alone with Howie. When I was not by his side, I curled up in a more comfortable chair by the window, diagonally across from him, and tried to sink my teeth into the next reading assignment for my English class. Sartre, *No Exit*. It seemed appropriate.

In the evening, I went directly from Howie's to the Neimarks' apartment at 860 Lake Shore Drive, one of the two steel-and-glass apartment towers designed by Mies van der Rohe and completed in 1951. Mort, a successful dentist, and his not-quite-concert-pianist wife, Hortense, were among the first to buy into the towers, whose gridded facades set the gold standard for steel-and-glass office and residential towers worldwide. The Neimarks' three-bedroom apartment was as glistening and modern (and sterile) as Harriet's wonderful house on North Astor was fusty and lugubrious (and cozy). The ceilings were low, and a ribbon of windows from floor to ceiling brought Lake Michigan smack into the open plan living room. In those days, all the windows in the curtain wall, large and small, were operable. There was central heating but no air conditioning, so in the summer, inside really was like outside. Everything in the Neimarks' apartment was white and chrome except for the shining ebony Steinway D concert grand and the mandatory grey curtains, which Mies had insisted every apartment have so the façade would appear uniform from the outside.

Mort was a lovely guy but had his hands full dealing with his prima donna wife. Philip, their younger son and my friend, had little good to say about his mother's maternal instincts and track record. Howie held most dentists in low esteem, but because Mort was such a mensch, and because Hortense played the piano like an angel, he overlooked his usual prejudices and they had become fast friends. I was basking in their warm welcome, enjoying good food and drink and good talk about Howie's horrific situation, their contempt for Cissie, and their affection for Dan Kushner—sentiments which I shared—when the phone rang. It was Sinc, I should return to Cook County immediately. Howie had taken a turn for the worse.

When I arrived, Howie was clearly in some sort of deep internal distress. His groaning, audible from as far away as the elevator, was ghostly and terrifying. Cissie was sobbing by his bedside. Sinc, Dan, and a colleague were standing out of the way by the windows, quietly discussing what action to take. I stopped by the bedside to take a look. Howie was alternately twitching and thrashing. I flashed Dan a questioning look. Neither he nor his buddy quite knew what was happening—only that it wasn't good. I repaired to my chair in the far corner by the window. The others found places to sit, and together, in a silent vigil, we waited out the night. By morning, Howie had settled down. The crisis had passed.

Death Watch, Day Three. In the morning I went back to Harriet's, slept a little and tidied up. Being with Harriet recharged my internal battery. She gave me strength as well as compassion. I returned in the afternoon. There was some discussion of hooking Howie up to an artificial kidney. Something was very wrong, either with his processing or voiding urine. I wanted to stay all night but Sinc insisted I return to Harriet's.

Death Watch, Day Four. Much the same routine. In the evening, as Howie seemed stable, I went again to the Neimarks'. After dinner, I called in and was told the end was near. Mort and Hortense drove me back to Cook County. Cissie met me at the door and unloaded a heap of venom on me about Dan Kushner.

"You like Dan, don't you?" she hissed.

"Yes, I do. Why wouldn't I? Howie loved him too."

"Dan Kushner is why my husband of only five years is dying."

"How is that?" I asked.

"You don't know anything, do you?"

"I guess not."

"A week ago your Dan Kushner had a terrible cold and, instead of withdrawing from caring for Howie until he was no longer infectious, Dan insisted on staying involved, examining Howie several times a day, and breathing all over Howie, who was too weak to resist infection. Howie is lying there in a coma because of Dan. And when he dies, it will be because of Dan. Dan will have killed him!"

More hysterical sobbing. More anti-Dan propaganda related to his quest for power and prestige, for Howie's teaching and administrative positions. Then she went to work on Sinc, by which time I couldn't process anymore. I curled up in my chair by the window and let her rant.

Death Watch, Day Five. My grandparents arrived at the apartment in the morning, accompanied by Sinc, their less favorite son. They had come on the train from New York. (Neither of them flew anywhere.) The Admiral acknowledged me with his usual formality. Grandmother looked straight through me. Despite or possibly

Part 3: Howard's End

because of her demeanor, I had the first inkling of how horrific it must be to lose a child, even a grownup child, that losing a child must be far harder to process and bear than losing a parent or a spouse or a lover. For once I didn't mind her looking through me. I felt her pain.

Howie's heart was starting to fail. They had arrived just in time but soon left to check into their hotel. Dan was there with his team, keeping at a respectful distance as Howie's breathing became increasingly faint. I was holding Howie's puffy hand when he breathed his last early in the afternoon. Cissie was painting her nails in her bedroom. When she heard Howie had died, she tore in from her bedroom, hands and wet nails aloft, elbowed me out of the way and began to administer obscene caresses to Howie's dead body until the orderlies came to take what remained of him away.

Dan put his arms around my shoulders and held me through it all. His strength was my strength. With Howie gone, he had to leave to attend to paperwork, but he said he'd be back for me shortly. As soon as the gurney bearing Howie's body was rolled out the front door, Cissie grabbed her mink coat, stepped into her high heels, and sashayed out into the hall and into the elevator, leaving me with her maid, Ada, and a hospital bed full of rumpled sheets, blankets, and bandages stained with blood, puss, and urine. Ada took one look at the bed and the soiled linens and all but shrieked, "I ain't sittin' around with that stuff still in the apartment." She wailed, "I've had enough of death and dyin'. I'm gong home, now! Someone else can clean that stuff up." She flung her coat over her uniform, and without even a nod in my direction, was out the door, hard on Cissie's heels.

I don't know how long I was there alone with the empty bed, the soiled bedding and the line-up of bears. Eventually, Dan returned with his wife, Gail, who held me closely and encouraged me to cry, except I couldn't. She felt as Dan did about Cissie. "Lale," she said, "if there's anything you want in this apartment to remember Howie by, you'd better take it now because I have the feeling that this may be the last you ever see of anything that belonged to Howie."

I found that hard to believe. Surely Howie would leave me something, at the very least the use of *Stone Horse* from time to time. On the other hand, much of what was happening was hard to believe, so I looked around quickly and saw an antique nautical mahogany telescope that Howie had had on *Stone Horse* when I first sailed with him in 1952. It was very handsome, clad in mahogany with brass fittings.

"I think I'd like to take the telescope over there on the desk. Howie had it on *Stone Horse* above the chart table. I always loved it, though I could never hold it still enough when it was extended to focus on anything at a distance. Maybe if I had it, I might learn."

"Let's get you and it out of here. C'mon Danny." She called to her husband, who seemed as numb and inert as I. Gail grabbed me with one hand and the telescope with the other, and she thrust the telescope under her coat as she pulled the door shut. Down we went, out into the cold blustery March afternoon and into their car.

The Neimarks were feeding us all, including the Kushners, yet again. Then it was back to Harriet's for a long sleep.

In the morning Harriet told me that my Uncle Mac, my mother's brother, who had been Howie's classmate at Princeton, had gotten in touch with her and was on his way to Chicago that very day to be with me. How did Mac know Howie was sick? They hadn't been in touch for decades. How could he have found out so fast that Howie had died? Howie hadn't been gone even twenty-four hours.

I met Mac for lunch in the Cape Cod Room at the Drake Hotel where he was staying. I asked him these same questions. Mac simply said that he had heard the news (maybe via the Princeton network?), and with my mother and Hans so far away and out of touch, he thought I might like some company. I was speechless. I hardly knew Mac. He and my mother were not close, and I barely knew his wife and his four boys, all younger than I. I figured he certainly couldn't know anything about the difficulties I had had with Howie and Cissie in the past. Or maybe he did. But there he was, quietly by my side, his presence lending some legitimacy to my claim to be part of Howie's family.

Mac and I spent the afternoon at the Art Institute, walking through an exhibit of Chinese painting, which interested us both. We returned to Harriet's for drinks and then joined the Armstrong family, including my great-uncle George Armstrong, who had flown in from New Jersey, for dinner at some hotel. My grandparents loved hotels and hotel dining. Despite their grief and their loss, they were in their element.

Late the next morning, M.P. took me to the Episcopal church where the funeral would be held in the early afternoon. Howie hated church—any church—and most especially the Episcopal Church, but he was no longer able to protest. M.P. and I arranged the flowers. When we were done, we were joined at the back of the church by Uncle Mac. People began to come in for the service. Most I'd never seen before, as they were staff from both Presbyterian and Cook County hospitals. People I knew said hello, and I proudly introduced them to my Uncle Mac, Howie's college roommate. Eventually, family members were ushered in: the Admiral and Grandmother, Sinc and his wife Joan, Uncle George, Cissie and her brother and her nephew. Each passed us by without a nod or a greeting. Not one of them stopped and asked me or us to sit at the front of the church with the family. The service began. Mac and I took two of the remaining seats in the back row.

Mac returned to Pittsburgh. I said goodbye to Harriet and M.P. and spent the night with Dan and Gail. The next morning, they drove me to the airport. We hugged and kissed goodbye, and Dan and I promised to write one another.

That was the first big mistake.

Howie's fatal illness, his demise and the events surrounding it comprised the ultimate rejection. The physical pain took weeks to recede. The damage to my psyche took far longer to repair. During those first weeks, I stayed up way too late every night, talking to whomever would talk to me, drinking with whomever would drink with me, and listening endlessly to music on my own while I fantasized about Dan Kushner.

Dan and I wrote to one another. Our correspondence became increasingly heated. I even went so far as to return to Chicago to visit Dan, Gail, and their children for a spring weekend. On Saturday night after dinner, Gail retired, and Dan and I stayed up late necking like teenagers on their sofa while we listened to the "Missa Solemnis" and mourned the loss of my father and his mentor and friend. Gail awoke to the music and came into the living room to find us fully clothed but totally entwined. Understandably, she went berserk, sent me straight to bed, and put me on the first plane to Providence the next day. That pathetic episode ended any further communication I had with the Kushners, the Neimarks, or with Harriet Welling and her family. It was shameful. I was shameful. I returned to Providence even more diminished, both by my humiliation and my failure as both daughter and friend.

Part 4.
La Vita Dolce-Amara

16. Post Mortem

NEW YORK — MARCH 1961

228 East 61st Street— home to Geoffrey and Daphne Hellman and Sandy Bull.

I was in bad shape when I returned to New York for spring break. My mother thought an interesting plan for the summer might help. She had hung two of my high school oil paintings in her office on 42nd Street. One was a sparse pattern of colored dots on a black field: city lights seen from an airplane at night. The other was the inside of a church, painted in a distorted perspective (not intentionally, but because I didn't know how perspective worked, and it had been against Mrs. Carpenter's principles to teach me). The paintings were simplistic, even naïve, but my mother liked them, and I was flattered that she had them on display.

My mother was representing Domenico Gnoli, an Italian artist who was having a show in New York. Gnoli asked about the two paintings and then about me. My mother told him I wanted to be an architect. Given the paintings, he thought I should consider set design.

Gnoli told her about a new theatre festival in Spoleto, Italy, called

Part 4: La Vita Dolce-Amara

Il Festivale dei Due Mondi. It had been started three years before by the Italian composer Gian Carlo Menotti, who wanted to bring together musical, theatrical, and operatic talent from Italy and America (the "two worlds"—*due mondi*), and at the same time bring life and economic prosperity to an almost abandoned Umbrian hill town. Spoleto is about two-thirds of the way between Rome and Perugia, but just far enough off the beaten track to have missed Italy's post-war economic resurgence. The old town is perched high on a hilltop where its full-sized nineteenth-century opera house and smaller eighteenth-century mini-opera house were crying for salvation.

Menotti gathered support from the local gentry as well as from movers and shakers who were committed to the arts in Italy and New York—most notably Egidio Ortona, then Ambassador from Italy to Washington; his wife, Donna Giulia; and the Anglo-American philanthropist Drew Heinz. Menotti knew everyone in the performing arts and had no trouble attracting the best actors, directors, musicians, singers, choreographers, and designers to his undertaking. The festival got off to a tremendous start. The Institute of International Education set up a program for students from Italy and America to work in all of the disciplines related to the performing arts. Gnoli decided I was an ideal candidate for set design.

The problem with his suggestion was I had never felt very good about anything I had made, designed, or painted, following the discovery that my painting was derivative at best. My academic success at the end of Brearley and at Brown was only in matters critical and analytical. My feeling of having zero creative worth had not been ameliorated by the fallout with Howie, his death, and its aftermath. I figured that however much I liked Gnoli's paintings (and they were sublime), and however charming Gnoli himself, he was just sucking up to my mother to be sure his art opening would be a critical and financial success. Therefore, despite his offer to write a recommendation for me, I refused even to look into the festival's scholarship program.

When I returned to college after spring break, two of my four Andrews Sisters were busy writing most of the music and lyrics for *Brownbrokers*, the annual student review. Other students were encouraged to submit skits and songs. I decided to write a torch song in French, with the help of another senior who had done a year in France and spoke excellent French.

Al Curran came through Providence one weekend to visit his family, and in a single sitting, he wrote music for our song, based on the opening of the third movement of Brahms' Third Symphony. The song was called "C'est le Complex d'Oedipus Rex." It was enthusiastically accepted for *Brownbrokers*.

Though I was not much of a singer and had long abandoned acting, like Lotte Lenya I looked good in fishnet stockings and a black slit skirt, and my flat, throaty voice was good for torch songs. The success of my performance was such a heady kick, after feeling so much emptiness for so long, that after the first night a bunch of us went out drinking. I downed four grasshoppers (equal parts crème de menthe, crème de cacao, and light cream) as though they were soda pop. I didn't feel drunk when we left the bar downtown, but as Walt, my ride for the evening, drove me up the hill, and to the back door of Andrews Hall, I became paralytic. We had missed the curfew. The Bowen Street entrance to Andrews was locked. Walt, also drunk, slammed his fist through the wire glass in the door to get at the handle from the inside, to no avail—except for the blood and glass shards everywhere. My Andrews Sisters, led by Joyce Reed, heard the ruckus and called down to Walt to bring me around to the side entrance of the adjacent dorm so they could come down and unlock the door from the inside, give him a towel for his hand, and take me upstairs. I remember nothing after Walt's fist went through the window. But somehow it all happened as they instructed, and I awoke the next morning in my bed, all cleaned up. No recriminations. No repercussions. Just blankets on my teeth and tongue and a horrific hangover.

We were almost done with classes. Liz, Joyce, and Emily were finalizing their plans to marry in Providence right after graduation, and Susie was working on her wedding, scheduled for early August in her hometown near Albany. I was finalizing my plans for what courses to take once they had abandoned me. The Art History Department was urging me to do a year-long honors thesis, but on what subject? We had studied a different period of European art in each semester, and when appropriate I wrote my term papers on the sacred architecture of that period and the metaphysical significance of the geometry used to develop the architectural language of that period. We were just completing the semester on Baroque art, which I didn't care for—too elaborate and emotive compared to the balance and serenity of Renaissance painting and architecture. But I admired Henry Millon, a visiting professor from MIT, who came to lecture on Baroque architecture. Millon conveyed a real feel for how architectural expression burst forth from the static geometry of the Neo-Platonic Renaissance and became the highly rigorous, dynamic formal vocabulary that characterizes the Baroque. I decided to do my thesis on Baroque architecture, if only because I didn't like it.

Great, said my advisor, but there was no one on the faculty who knew enough about Baroque architecture to guide me in this endeavor. A few days later, my advisor told me that Brown had made an arrangement with MIT, and Professor Millon had agreed to take me on.

My Andrews Sisters were devotees of Professor Juan Lopez-Morillas, a brilliant Spaniard whose class on comparative literature all except Susie and I had taken. I knew I had missed out. There was nothing L-M (as he was known) was teaching that I qualified for the following year, so I asked my advisor if I could read all of Proust under L-M's tutelage in a single semester and in French. Liz, Emily, and Joyce, his star students, put in a good word for me and L-M accepted me. I knew that otherwise I would never have the discipline to plough through those seven volumes that my mother and father had devoured during my early childhood.

I never was happy without a male in my life to whom I was connected or about whom I could obsess. So I fixed my sights on Eddie Roberts, on whom I'd had a crush in freshman year when he was assistant conductor of the now-defunct Brown University Chorus. Eddie was a year ahead of Al (now called Alvin) and three years ahead of me. He was also getting a masters in music at Yale, and was a close friend of all my Andrews Sisters. He was sharing an apartment with Alvin in New Haven, so I went down for a weekend as Eddie's date. Alvin didn't seem to mind. Alvin was always wrapped up with Alvin and never lacking for female attention. Eddie and I got to talking about summer plans. I had none other than attending the weddings of my friends.

"So, what's up for you this summer, Eddie?"

"I heard about this new festival in Italy. They have a scholarship program for kids in college and grad school. So I applied and just got accepted as a pianist."

"What festival in Italy?"

"The Festival of Two Worlds in Spoleto."

"You gotta be kidding."

"Not kidding. Not at all. As soon as Will and Liz get married, they are going as well. Will applied as an actor and just got his acceptance yesterday. He and Liz are going to Spoleto as their honeymoon."

"No!"

"Yes!" said Eddie, "It will be my first trip to Italy, and I can't wait!" So we all, including Alvin, cracked open several bottles of cheap raffia-wrapped Chianti, the kind we used for lamps and candle holders, and drank to Eddie's good fortune.

How was I going to jump onto this bandwagon and get myself into the student program at Spoleto at this late date? My motive was not so much that I had decided I was talented enough after all and would profit enormously from a summer assisting in set design at a festival in Italy, but that I was interested in Eddie and didn't want to be left behind.

This was not the night to consummate Eddie's and my new relationship. I was too busy scheming, and we were both too drunk. Instead, we stripped down to thin layers of sweaty undergarments, and with limbs comingled, we both passed out on his single bed.

I called my mother the next morning as soon as I could get to a phone. She made it clear that she had done her bit and could do no more. I was on my own. Fair enough.

First thing Monday morning, I called the Institute for International Education. The deadline for applications for scholarships with stipends was long closed. What if I wanted to come without a stipend? Would there be a place? My mother was so worried about my general mental state and so dreaded the prospect of my spending another summer at home that she agreed to front my expenses if I could secure a place. I was put in touch with William Crawford III, who was in charge of administering the American side of the festival, including the student program. I pleaded my case, inventing some lame excuse about why I had missed the deadline, but emphasized that I didn't need a stipend. I would pay my own way. Crawford wasn't enthusiastic. But I persisted. He finally agreed to set up a meeting for me with the young American director who was in charge of student applicants in the theatrical disciplines. Soon after I got to New York, I met him at a theatre downtown, where he was in the process of directing a play. He was so preoccupied with his own work that he spent close to no time talking to me and waved me through.

My mother was more than relieved that I was in, and now focused on my approaching birthday. I would be twenty-one on May 17th. Why was my lawyer mother so excited? Because she had prepared an accounting for all the money she had received from her father for my benefit and administered on my behalf during my minority. I was to review it in detail and then sign off on it if I found the accounting satisfactory. And she had prepared a Last Will and Testament for me to execute as well.

Why was I not excited? Because this money had been left to her by her grandmother, and would have gone to her outright had her father played fair and square. Instead she'd had to finagle it out of him, and I wanted nothing to do with it. I certainly enjoyed having nice clothes and my own little car and not worrying about who was paying for my education or summer expenses in Spoleto, but I didn't want to be thought of as a "poor little rich girl." I wanted to be poor and worthy like my Andrews Sisters. Hadn't Howie shown contempt both for my mother and Cissie because they had money? (Although he didn't seem to mind relieving them of said money.) To say that I was confused about money and had been since early childhood would be an understatement. But one thing was clear: I didn't want to waste a beautiful day in May in some stuffy lawyer's office going over a pile of papers the size of an old Manhattan telephone book, which I would be unable to evaluate or understand.

When I came down from Providence the day before my birthday,

Part 4: La Vita Dolce-Amara

Sandy Bull told me that his mother, Daphne Hellman, was throwing one of her famous parties and hoped I might stop by. After dinner at home, feeling almost pretty in a new princess-line linen dress with shoestring straps tied at the shoulder, I pulled on my sling-back heels and clip-clopped around the corner to 228 East 61st Street.

I had never seen so many New York "smart" celebrities packed into one room. Daphne crinkled her almond eyes into a welcoming smile, got me a drink, and immediately introduced me to the *New Yorker* artist Saul Steinberg, whose overall slightness and beady eyes reminded me of a creature born of a weasel and a large bird. I idolized his drawings and cartoons but found myself tongue-tied. He did little to put me at ease. I reconnected with Bernard Rudofsky, the Romanian architectural writer, and his soft-spoken Austrian wife, Bertha, whom I had known and loved as a child but hadn't seen for years, not since my mother had remarried. I saw Julius Monk, the director/impressario who had hired Daphne's jazz trio to play at Julius Monk's Upstairs at the Downstairs. Norman Mailer, whom I did not meet, was shouting at some guy in the far corner of the Hellmans's large living room and close to punching him out when, thankfully, someone intervened. In the meantime, Montgomery Clift, who lived two doors west of Daphne, was leaning against a distant door frame, his eyes glazed over. Daphne swept by again and introduced me to Charles Addams, a handsome, elegant hulk of a man, utterly unlike any of his cartoon characters. Addams looked me over, then literally swept me off my feet, and deposited me on his lap.

"And who are you?" he asked, looking down at my neatly crossed ankles.

Good question.

I had bought wedding presents for Joyce and Liz in New York, but I decided to make my present for Emily and George. (Susie wasn't getting married until later in the summer. Her present could wait.) George had written Emily a love poem. I snuck into Emily's room and copied out the poem, shut myself in my adjacent room and lettered it onto four pages of translucent rice paper. I made a boxlike frame of bass wood, installed a light socket in the middle, and glued the lettered pages to each side of the frame to create a lamp—a labor of love.

I was proud enough that I photographed it before giving it to them, just for the record.

Once exams and papers were in, I took the train back to New York, packed what I could in preparation for leaving for Spoleto, and then took the train back up to Providence for Matrimoniana: seeing three of my four Andrews Sisters married in two days.

17. Decisive Moments

Piazza del Duomo, Spoleto.

NEW YORK — JUNE 1961

In preparation for Spoleto, Hans plied me with large quantities of antibiotics, not for fear of the water quality or food poisoning but because he was convinced that all young men are determined to impregnate (not just sleep with, but impregnate!) all young women within their reach. Because of this relentless drive in man's base nature, I would surely fall victim and contract some previously incurable venereal disease. He described at length the symptoms of these diseases and inspected my luggage to be sure I hadn't left any of the pills behind.

We were having our usual Sunday lunch of cold cuts and salad on the patio between the dining room and the library when Hans decided, mid-mouthful, that I also urgently needed an introduction to the art of photography and a proper camera to record the experiences I was about to have. He excused himself and raced upstairs to retrieve what he described as "the perfect instrument for the job."

I was hoping for an old Leica like Cissie had—elegant, sleek and compact. But Hans returned carrying a worn (out) leather case with a broken strap, from which he extracted a large black metal box, about 3.5 by 3.5 by seven inches, with two big apertures on the front, one above the other, and a lot of cranks and dials on the sides.

"Here, Lale, this should do you fine." He passed it across the table to me. "It is the Contaflex TLR that I used to shoot in Iceland before I went to medical school."

"Contaflex TLR?"

"Yep, it's a beautiful little machine designed in the mid-1930s by Zeiss."

"That's great, Hans," I stammered, balking at the camera's obvious age and weight and daunted by its complexity, "but I've never used anything other than a Brownie. I have no idea how to …"

"This baby will do it all for you. It's the first camera ever to have a built-in light meter, so that's all taken care of. And it's a twin lens reflex, thus 'TLR,' meaning that when you look into the view finder from the top, you're seeing what the lens sees."

"Twin lens reflex?"

"All you need to learn now is the relationship between shutter speed and f-stop."

"F-stop?"

"The diameter of the opening of the lens. It will only take a minute." When Hans decided something was going to happen, such as me learning to use this monster box and taking it to Italy, it was going to happen. In the hour or so remaining before we left for the airport, I listened carefully, and watched him work the dials and cranks: the one on the left rewound the film, the one on the right wound the shutter and set the shutter speed. I learned to open and close the viewfinder, respond to the light meter indicator, and focus by adjusting the lever around the viewing lens. I took careful notes on the relationship between shutter speeds and f-stops, and thereby acquired a superficial understanding of the workings of this extraordinary object. On the way out the door, Hans pressed into my hands some rolls of black-and-white 35mm film while my mother and I piled into Çok Güzel, their now thoroughly dilapidated Mark II Lincoln Continental, (Hans wasn't big on maintenance.) On the way to the airport, Hans delivered a short lecture on ASA ratings and film speeds, thus completing my crash course in photography.

Eddie Roberts and I met at the gate for our Alitalia flight to Rome. In the weeks between the early spring weekend at Yale and our actual departure, I had lost all romantic interest in him. He had found a large starfish on a beach in Rhode Island and, knowing my love of all things oceanic, mailed it to me in New York as a present. The dead starfish was three weeks in the mail. When I opened the box, the stench and rot put the kiss of death on what remained of my feelings for Eddie. As we'd never consummated our relationship, and at this point neither of us was interested in doing so, we turned our attention to drinking all the free booze that Alitalia could provide during our overnight flight.

We landed in the morning, hungover and clutching our instructions from the New York office of the festival. We took the bus from the new Fiumicino Airport into Rome and camped out in the Piazza Navona at a café, sipping wine and people-watching until it was time to board the train to Spoleto. We fell asleep at once and awoke to the conductor announcing our arrival in Assisi, two stops beyond where we were meant to disembark. I shook Eddie awake and organized our luggage, and we got off the train just in time. Fortunately, it was not too long a wait until a train came along that would take us back to Spoleto.

The train station where we disembarked was at the base of the mountain on top of which Spoleto was firmly perched. We went to the head of the line of matchbox-sized taxis and mumbled, "*Spoleto, ufficio del festival?*" to the driver, who nodded, stuffed our bags in his boot and took our lives in his hands. Off we zoomed to the foot of the mountain, then up, up, up on a series of winding narrow streets with hairpin turns and almost no sidewalks, up and further up and into the Piazza della Libertà, where the vista opened and our taxi screeched to a halt.

"*Eccolo! L'ufficio del festival,*" said our driver, pointing to a row of windows on the second floor of a large building occupying the entire south side of the square. We tumbled out into the cold afternoon, gathered our belongings, identified a door that would lead to those second-floor windows, and agreed that Eddie would stay with the luggage while I went upstairs to find the festival office for further direction. There, a very efficient woman speaking perfect English and later identified as (Countess) Camilla Pecci-Blunt, head of the student program, greeted me, checked us off on a list (very reassuring), and assigned an Italian fellow student to help us with our bags and walk us to our respective digs farther up the hill, and then escort us into the heart of the town.

Several other students and I were to board with Signora Luna, who had a flat on the second floor of a building on the east side of the Piazza Mercato. Signora Luna, a short, square woman of stern countenance and greasy hair, and her husband and children, whom we rarely saw, had been squeezed into two rooms at the back of the flat so that six of us could be accommodated in double rooms along the square. We were instructed to appear that evening at the Teatro Nuovo, the larger of Spoleto's two main theatres, where Menotti would be rehearsing *Vanessa* (with his lyrics and Samuel Barber's music). Menotti would be directing. It would be the season's opening production.

It was as cold inside Signora Luna's as it was outside. I opened

Part 4: La Vita Dolce-Amara

my suitcase and put on as many layers of light summer clothes as I could, then set out into the dank chill of early evening in hopes up of meeting up with a familiar face on my way back down the hill. Whereas it had been warm and sunny in Rome, here on this Umbrian hilltop it was bitingly cold, damp, and grey.

The inside of the mid-nineteenth-century Teatro Nuovo was typical of its period. Five tiers of boxes were piled up in a typical horseshoe shape around a gently sloped orchestra level or *platea*. The tiers of boxes morphed elegantly into proscenium boxes at each end that defined the stage opening. The boxes were capped by a flat but richly decorated circular ceiling with frescoed medallions containing various figures and connected by floral motifs. The partitions between the boxes came right out to the fronts of them, so the grid was very pronounced. The faces of the boxes were slightly convex and encrusted with gold and white garlands and *putti*. The Teatro Nuovo had languished for many years before Menotti, and his benefactors had fully restored it some five years before.

Most of the people who showed up for this briefing were unfamiliar to me except Eddie, Liz, and Will, whom I spotted across the rows of deep red upholstered theatre seats. Once all were assembled, (Countess) Camilla Pecci-Blunt rose from her seat at the front of the orchestra, greeted us formally, and introduced other staff members from the festival office, including preppy Bill Crawford (whom I had met in New York and who was in charge of American productions), and Giulietta Franchi from the press office. Camilla spelled out a few general rules and regulations and then some specifics relating to perks of the festival that were unavailable to us students, none of which I chose to remember. Then Menotti himself welcomed us to the festival. Menotti was slim, with dark, wiry hair and a long patrician face complete with a Roman nose and a winning smile. He spoke perfect but heavily accented English. Charisma and creativity exuded from his every pore. He was surrounded by a bevy of young, beautiful people, mainly men but some women too, and a whole clique of drop-dead gorgeous Germans, whom I later learned were somehow bound to the German photographer, Herbert List, a regular at the festival, who had not yet arrived on the scene.

The next day, Camilla Pecci-Blunt came by Signora Luna's with the Italian scenic student Eddie and I had met when we first arrived. He and I were to collect picture frames from the house of a local priest. I wasn't sure why two people were required for this task, especially since one of the pair of us couldn't speak Italian, but I enjoyed learning my way around the town, and though the damp and cold persisted, Spoleto's architecture and its narrow streets and myriad piazzas were magical, with each vista like a stage set for *Romeo and Juliet.*

As it was still the pre-season there were only a few functioning restaurants, which helped the *stranieri* get to know each other. We all ate at the same Trattoria del Teatro for lunch and the more upscale Il Pentegramma for dinner. Once introduced, we stuck close to one another, and soon became acquainted with the beautiful Germans. As friends and disciples of the legendary Herbert List, most of them were aspiring photographers. One who was especially handsome, Roger Fritz (who pronounced his name Ro-*zhay* as though it were French), was taking pictures all over town. He had his Nikon and his light meter around his neck and was constantly consulting the light meter as he checked the settings on the camera. I had never seen a light meter in action and was glad my Contaflex had automated this function.

The Germans had a whole apartment to themselves uphill from where I lived. One night after dinner several of us repaired there for more wine and also (since it had a fireplace and firewood) some warmth. In the absence of Fritz's regular girlfriend, Crista, who would be arriving later with Herr List, I was invited to his bed, first for play and then for the first warm night of sleep since my arrival.

On day four, after a hasty breakfast of caffe latte and a piece of unsalted bread in Signora Luna's spare kitchen, Giada Franchi arrived in her Fiat Seicento to pick me up. A feisty young Italian girl/woman with wavy strawberry blonde hair and a profile any Greek goddess would kill for, she sported a simple dress, a heavy cardigan sweater, sensible Gucci loafers with medium heels, and a bulging leather shoulder bag with a silk scarf tied dashingly around the strap at the base. She was all business but chic as hell. I had seen her that first night at the Teatro Nuovo but she hadn't been introduced, and now she had come in her Fiat Seicento to take me down to the *scenografia*, a large mid-nineteenth-century warehouse on the side of the mountain, where the scenery for each production was made. Slightly older and slightly shorter than I was, she spoke flawless English, and had an axe to grind about how young Americans came to Italy but never made an effort to learn either the language or the way things were done there. Instead, she said, they stuck to their own smug ways and went home none the wiser.

That was not going to be me.

At the scenografia, Giada introduced me to Fiorella Mariani, a stunning young set designer with an androgynous figure and a beatific smile who also spoke almost perfect English. Fiorella, who was to be my boss, was the assistant to Lila de Nobili, who had designed the sets for a small dramatic work on the program and was seeing to their execution. A scenic and costume designer with many productions at *La Scala* under her belt, Lila was in the far distance, bending over as if to study something on the floor. Her posture, her concentration, the shape of her graying hair and the bend of her neck and shoulders brought to mind the images of

Wanda Landowska that I remembered from the album covers of my father's recordings of *The Well-Tempered Clavier*.

Fiorella said I was to assist in the painting of a backdrop designed by Lila and turned me over to Renato Marozzi, the head of the scene shop, a skinny, gruff, grizzle-haired guy who spoke no English and had little time for anyone who interrupted the routine of his work. There was a heated exchange in Italian with Marozzi shouting, Fiorella holding her own calmly but insistently, and a lot of large-scale hand gestures. Marozzi stomped off.

"It's going to be fine. Renato is a pussy cat. Wait and see," said Fiorella.

Marozzi returned with a cigarette in one hand (and another behind his ear) and a long stick with a paint brush at its end in the other hand. He gestured across the open floor to a sort of music stand with a colored sketch on it. Fiorella beckoned to me to walk to the music stand across a huge piece of canvas that had been laid out on the floor. A grid had been laid over the sketch and numbered in both directions.

"The grid on the *bozzetto* or sketch," she explained, "corresponds to the grid that you see drawn on the canvas that we are standing on." I realized that the canvas on the floor was the backdrop itself! Here, and maybe everywhere in Italy for all I knew, scenery was painted on the flat, not vertically from scaffolding as we had done it in college.

"Your job," Fiorella continued," is to paint what you see in each square of the sketch onto the corresponding square on the canvas. You try to work with one color at a time in each square. When you've done all you can with one color, wash your brush and start with another. You'll have to mix colors as you go. Clean up as you go. The paints are over there."

You've gotta be kidding, I thought. *Painting by numbers*. I

Part 4: La Vita Dolce-Amara

remembered doing something like that as a kid, but this wasn't the same. The scale was daunting.

"Let me show you. Work beside me. Take the brush Renato gave you and get started." And she herself grabbed a brush and began. We started at 9:00, broke for a short lunch of bread, salami, and cheese, which we had brought with us as there were no cafes in this part of town, and went on through the afternoon. It was tedious work, but I was good at detail and gave it my all. At the end of the day, Fiorella would drive me back up to my lodgings in the Piazza Mercato in her Fiat Seicento.

I was already picking up a bit of Italian from Signor Marozzi and the other Italian employees who worked for him. My schoolgirl French and the lessons with Signora Delle Donne helped, but more surprising was the huge payoff that came directly from the four miserable years of Latin, at which I had done so poorly at Brearley. Fiorella, Giada, and her sister Giulietta from the press office, who was taller and more regal than the feisty Giada, seemed pleased with my progress in Italian. We were becoming good enough friends that I asked them to call me Lale, not Leslie. Despite their excellent English, they found that Lale had too many Ls and too few vowels for Italian lingual comfort, so they nicknamed me Lulù, pronounced LooLOO, which at first appalled me, but which I soon came to like.

In the evenings, everyone, including the pre-season guests and visitors, congregated at the Teatro Nuovo to observe the progress of the rehearsals for *Vanessa*. My mother had taken me to *Vanessa* in 1958, shortly after it premiered at the Met. I didn't like opera then, and I certainly didn't like *Vanessa*. But in Spoleto it was different. Menotti had translated his own libretto into Italian, and somehow transformed *Vanessa* into a quasi-lyric opera. Hearing the same passages rehearsed night after night, my initial displeasure with dissonant harmonies and a dysfunctional and unsatisfactory narrative was replaced by the comfort of familiarity. In less than a week, I had become a fan.

Menotti and the members of his intimate entourage lived in an apartment in the Piazza del Duomo. But the festival rented grander quarters at the Palazzo Campello, nearer to the top of the town, for visiting dignitaries and larger functions. One evening after rehearsal, Menotti hosted a gathering for us students at the palazzo. My mother had told me that festivals like this were largely funded by private donors, many of whom were local gentry. She said to look out for these people and to be super polite and appreciative of them, rather than my usual smart-ass self. When we students arrived at the apartment in Campello, all the beautiful Germans, including Roger (*Roger* a la Française) Fritz and his newly arrived girlfriend Crista, were hovering around a large, probably once-handsome but now sinister and debauched-looking older man in a crumpled suit and loosened tie, who was wedged into the corner of a large plush sofa. His thinning hair was slicked back, and his eyebrows seemed permanently knitted together. A lit cigarette hung from the right corner of his narrow, downturned mouth. He could have been a member of the local gentry. The acolytes who weren't seated next to him leaned over the back of the sofa or sat on the floor at his feet, each attempting maximum proximity to his noble personage.

Roger, who was sitting next to him, waved to me and then returned to the activity on which they were all focused. They were playing a variation on the Marienbad game in which ten matchsticks are laid out in four rows with four, three, two, and one matchstick per row. Each player in turn takes as many sticks off each row as he wants. The loser is the one left with the last stick. Play was interrupted long enough for us students to be introduced. The noble personage seemed to be a viscount. (I had thought Italy had only counts and the odd prince.) When my turn came, I laid on my most obsequious smile, held out my hand, and did my stuff:

"I am very pleased to meet you, sir. We all want to thank you for all you are doing for the festival."

Without extending his hand towards mine, he knitted his brow into a straight line, threw me a scowl, then removed the dangling cigarette from his lips and, turning to Roger, said in accented English, "Who the hell is she? And what the fuck is she talking about?"

Lots of laughter all around. What had I said wrong?

"Come here," the viscount called to me, "you think you're so smart? Come play this game with us and see if you can win. Crista," he said to Roger's girlfriend, who was at the other end of the sofa, "get up so she"—he beckoned to me—"can sit here and play." And so, fortified by crude Spoletino wine, I sat at the other end of the sofa and played Marienbad with this strange group well into the night, never figuring out the combination of moves that would result in my not being left with the last matchstick. Once outside and on the way back down to my room at Signora Luna's, I asked Eddie Roberts, "Who was that guy?"

"Luchino Visconti."

"Who is Luchino Visconti?" I asked.

"Haven't you heard of *Rocco and his Brothers*?"

"Yeah, but ...." I had seen *Rocco and his Brothers* in New York and had been terrified by its violence.

"He was the director, *stupida*!" (We were all learning bits of Italian.) "He's a genius and he's here now to direct *Salome*, the opera after *Vanessa*. It should be amazing!"

Luchino Visconti, Count of Lonato Pozzolo, rich as Croesus and a registered Communist, I later discovered. What did I know from Italian nobility?

Decisive Moments

A few nights after the Visconti gaffe, I decided the time had come to bring out the Contaflex and try to take some pictures of the Teatro Nuovo's spectacular interior. I was enjoying looking into the twin-lens reflex viewfinder, setting the dials and knobs, running up and down the center aisle of the orchestra, snapping this and that, when my foot caught on the hem of a coat that was hanging off one of the aisle seats. I tripped, and in catching myself on the back of the chair ahead, I dropped the Contaflex onto the bare wooden floor.

The built-in light meter.

When I picked the camera up, pointed it towards the illuminated stage and looked into the viewfinder lens, the light meter indicator was stationary. I collapsed into the nearest aisle seat, put the camera between my legs and my head between my hands and groaned. How could I ever explain to Hans what I had done? How could I expect forgiveness for such clumsiness?

While yet again confronting my interminable inadequacy, I felt a gentle tap on my shoulder and turned around. Seated directly behind me was a slight, middle-aged man with short white hair, a high forehead defined by a receding hair line, a finely chiseled face, large, not quite circular wire-rimmed glasses set on a narrow nose, and a gentle smile that revealed slightly snaggled teeth.

"I saw you taking pictures, and wondered if you might have been using a Contaflex?" he asked in lightly accented English.

"Yes, it was my stepfather's. He used it when he was a photographer for *Look* magazine before the war, and now, the very first time I have tried to use it, I've broken it. It's finished." I almost sobbed.

"I am not sure it is broken," he said. "Would you let me see it?"

"Of course." And I handed it to him, still enclosed in its beaten-up leather case. He took it out of the case, turned it over, and fiddled with its various parts.

"This is a lovely camera. It is in excellent condition," he said.

"Yes, but I've broken it," I insisted.

"Yes, the light meter is broken and is probably irreparable. But the rest of the camera is fine. You can learn to take photographs without a light meter."

How can that be? Roger Fritz cannot move without consulting the light meter. He practically wears it to bed, I thought.

"I take a lot of pictures and I never use a light meter," he went on. "You will soon get the feel of it, and you will do it by instinct."

"Really?" I said.

He went on to tell me that some things must be absolutely precise to be valid. For example, his Javanese wife, a dancer, broke a finger on her right hand. When it healed, it had remained crooked, out of alignment. Because so much of Javanese dance is narrative and told through the very specific gestures and positions of the body, its limbs and their extremities, she had to give up her art because of her one crooked finger.

"But taking pictures isn't like that. It is not so precise," he continued. "The smallest thing can be a great subject. You should give yourself some time with that lovely camera. It will come to you."

"Thank you so much, sir," I said, "You have made me feel so much better."

"I am glad," he said, this time smiling broadly. "I hope we'll meet again."

"Oh yes, I hope so," I said and added, "I am a student here, in set design. My name is Leslie Armstrong." And once again, I held out my hand.

He shook it warmly and said, "And I am Henri Cartier-Bresson."

A few days later, Giada came down to the scenografia to tell me that I was being transferred to work as a gofer for Beni Montresor, the set designer for *Vanessa*. Beni was a short, very attractive, boyish-looking Italian whose entourage included his tall, handsome boyfriend Joe, an Italian-American from New York, and a blond Englishwoman at least ten years my senior who seemed to be in love with both Beni and Joe. Working with Beni, cute as he was, was all work and no play. Beni often wanted us in the theatre as early as 5:00 a.m. to have access to the sets before anyone else came to work, and we often left as late as 2:00 a.m. His English was poor and he mumbled his instructions incomprehensibly. Fortunately, my Italian was improving daily. Joe and I were also to assemble props for Beni. What we couldn't find in the shops in town, we had made in the theatre's property shop. Other days, we spent gluing faux gold leaf all over Beni's lavish sets.

In Italy, and thus also in Spoleto, the *prova generale*, the dress rehearsal takes place the night before the actual opening, and is the performance to which the critics come. The excitement was heightened by the fact that the sun finally made an appearance. Early that morning, the stones of the houses and palazzi slowly turned from monochromatic greys to rich tones of umber and burnt sienna as the moisture they had been harboring evaporated. Shutters were lifted, casements were thrown open, potted geraniums appeared on every window sill and in every portal. Laundry was hung out to dry above and across the narrow streets and alleys. Summer had arrived at last.

That evening, as I was standing in the wings chewing my nails because the Italian tenor playing Anatole had failed to make his entrance, I saw a tall balding man, clearly American, standing nearby in a corresponding state of dismay. It had to be Samuel Barber. We started to chat, at first about the production, about which he had mixed feelings, and then about our personal details. It turned out that he had an apartment in New York, at 61st Street

Part 4: La Vita Dolce-Amara

and Lexington, only two blocks from my parents' house. We even ordered our liquor from the same store. Sam seemed to take a shine to me, and I was totally starstruck. He asked me if I'd join him for dinner after the *prova generale*.

Yes.

By then I already knew something of Sam and Gian Carlo Menotti's story. They had met almost thirty years before when they were students at the Curtis Institute in Philadelphia. Sam was from a prominent professional family in Westchester, Pennsylvania. Gian Carlo was born in Northern Italy near Lago Maggiore. His father was a coffee merchant, and when he died, his mother moved the family to Colombia in an attempt to save the family business. That was when she enrolled her young son at Curtis. Gian Carlo and Sam fell in love and lived their love openly, which was unusual and courageous for those times. Sometime after graduation, they bought a house together in Mt. Kisco, an hour outside of New York City, and named it Capricorn. The house had separate studios and living quarters for each of them, connected by a large common living and dining room, library, and kitchen. This layout served them well over time, as their attraction to one another diminished and to younger men increased.

By the time I was pasting bits of gold on Beni's sets for *Vanessa*, Sam and Gian Carlo were no longer together, and they each could be quite cynical about the other's work, lifestyles, and lovers. But they still had a large body of work in common, and shared the house in Mt. Kisco and a chalet in Santa Cristina in the Dolomites. They did not share living quarters in Spoleto, however. The festival was Gian Carlo's thing, not Sam's—he was there as a guest artist, nothing more.

On opening night, the night following my dinner with Sam, there was to be a huge party. Camilla Pecci-Blunt made it clear that we students were not invited. I have never liked being left out, especially to be cut out of the celebration of something I worked hard to help make happen. Everyone with whom I had worked was going: Beni, Joe, the English third, Fiorella and Giada, and Giada's sister Giulietta, Roger Fritz, and their group. I had three separate invitations to the party, including one from Sam.

Pecci-Blunt said no.

I had no choice but to obey, but I couldn't stop myself from putting on the nicest dress I had, slipping into my new pair of Italian heels, fixing my hair, making up my eyes and inserting my painful hard contact lenses for the opening performance. It was thrilling to stand in the wings shoulder to shoulder with Samuel Barber, to watch the house fill with dignitaries and celebrities, and then see the performance proceed flawlessly. During the final applause Sam tapped my shoulder.

"I have to go up to Palazzo Campello now and talk to the press. I will see you there in a while. Yes?"

"No, Sam, I am not allowed to go. I am only a student. I thought I explained that last night at dinner. We students are strictly forbidden to attend. Camilla is adamant."

"That's ridiculous. I wrote this damned opera, and I can invite whomever I damn please to the opening night party."

"You can?"

"Yes, I can. I will expect to see you there. Do not disappoint me."

"Of course not, Sam. Wouldn't dream of it. See you later, Sam, and thank you, Sam!"

There was a considerable time gap between the end of the performance and the start of the party. Giada and Fiorella were also backstage. So, very slowly we collected our belongings (I got rid of my contacts) and headed up to Palazzo Campello in Giada's Fiat Seicento. On the way she said, "Lulù, you promised to sing us that

Part 4: La Vita Dolce-Amara

song you wrote when you were in college, you know, the one about Oedipus Rex. When are you going to keep your promise?"

"Anytime, I suppose, but I need an accompanist, my voice isn't good enough to sing it on my own." We parked near the palazzo and saw Eddie Roberts also heading for the party, even though as a student he wasn't allowed to go either. I caught up with him.

"Eddie, do you remember the song that Al wrote for me for *Brownbrokers*? The one in French?"

"I think so. It's based on Brahms's Third."

"That's it. Do you think you can play it so I can sing it for Giada and Fiorella?

"Sure, but we need a piano." Giada knew Palazzo Campello inside and out and soon found us a largish unoccupied room with an upright piano. Eddie, who was a whiz at musical theatre, sat down and fiddled with the 88s until he and I agreed that he had it right.

He looked at me and smiled. "Ready?"

Fiorella, Giada, and Giada's sister Giulietta, who had joined us, took their seats on a nearby sofa and armchair.

"Almost." I took off my jacket, put my glasses in the pocket, climbed up on the piano stool and sat down. I pulled my polished chintz skirt just above my knees, crossed my legs, and closed my eyes. "Ready."

They loved it. Eddie looked up at me said softly, "Keep going, they're eating from your hand. What else can you sing?"

"Kurt Weill," I whispered, "That's all I know by heart. *Threepenny Opera*—'Barbara Song' and maybe 'Pirate Jenny.'"

"Let's go!" said Eddie, and he gave me my intro. Eyes closed, off I went. When I was done, the applause was almost deafening. I opened my eyes. The room was packed. Everyone I knew was there, along with many whom I did not know. Standing room only. I was in shock.

"Sing the one in French again," someone shouted from the back. I did.

"And the Kurt Weill again." I did.

More applause.

Eddie handed me down from my seat on the piano. We took our bows and tried to disappear into the crowd. Camilla Pecci-Blunt came at us, guns a-blazing.

"I told you time and again that this party is off-limits to students."

"Samuel Barber invited me," I replied lamely. "So did several other people."

"You were told not to come. Gian Carlo is also furious. You will be punished for this."

"I understand."

The next day, *Corriera della Sera* , the Italian newspaper, ran the following headline to its article on the opening of the Festival:

"Lelie Armostron [sic], una Cantante Psicoanalistica apra Il Quarto Festival dei due Mondi." Loosely translated this says, "Leslie Armstrong, a psychoanalytical singer, opens the fourth Festival of Two Worlds." The reporter then spent the first two paragraphs of the piece describing me and my performance. Small wonder Camilla and Gian Carlo were pissed off.

The next day I hand delivered a letter of apology to Gian Carlo. Two days after, he invited me to sit with him during a rehearsal of *Foglie d'Album*, the revue for which I had been assisting Fiorella and Lila de Nobili on the sets. He asked if I would like to perform in *Foglie d'Album*. I declined. I could only assume I was forgiven.

With the festival launched and in full swing, cafes, restaurants, and shops opened all over town. Many of us went drinking after evening rehearsals and performances, often at the Festival Club, where Eddie and I were frequently begged to repeat our opening night act. And we did, to a variety of audiences. But my working routine did not change: long hours in the theatre, lots of work with and for very talented people. No complaints. As the festival progressed and production after production opened, there were fewer sets to build, paint, and prop, and I had a little more time during the day.

Among the most magical things about the Festival were the chamber music concerts held at noon every day in the Caio Melisso, the eighteenth-century mini opera house with four tiers of tiny boxes and ten rows of seats in the orchestra. It was and remains a jewel. The programming was varied and imaginative. Those of us working at the festival got in for free. Early in July, after one such concert, I spotted a young man in the crowd on the piazza outside the Caio Melisso who was as gorgeous a young man as I had ever seen. He was almost a head taller than everyone around him, slender but fit, with tousled, medium brown hair crowning a round, fair-skinned face, and he was wearing horn-rimmed glasses. I couldn't take my eyes off him. Where had he come from? To whom did he belong? How to find out?

Giada grabbed me and said we were going to lunch with some friends before going back to work. And there he was. He was introduced to me as Freddie, which seemed odd, as he was clearly Italian. It turned out that his siblings and Giada and Giulietta had grown up together, and because Giada and Giulietta had spent time in the U.S. when they were young, they had taken to calling him Freddie instead of Federico.

Federico Roccati was from Milan. He had come for the opening of *Salome* and to visit Giada and Giulietta, but especially Giulietta, with whom he'd been in love since childhood. It seemed that while Giulietta loved Freddie, she was not as in love with him as he may have been with her. It was hard to tell, as my command of Italian wasn't very nuanced. I had the next few days off, the first since I had arrived a month before. When I said I was going to Florence for a thirty-six-hour sightseeing trip, Freddie offered to drive me there on his way back to Milano. His English was on a par with my Italian, so our conversation was limited, but I learned that he was one of four children; his sister had died of bone cancer at sixteen; his father was half German and had been a Fascist during the war; and he, Freddie, was studying engineering, about which he wasn't enthusiastic. He was more inclined to the arts, but that was not in the cards for him. The more time I spent in his company, the more infatuated I became.

Thank God he went on to Milan and I returned to Spoleto. I would have thrown myself at his feet.

The festival had only another week to run. There was a backdrop to prepare for the outdoor performance of the Verdi "Requiem" in front of the façade of the Duomo, and then I would be done. The first time I had heard the Verdi "Requiem" was in Chicago with Howie when I was sixteen; Fritz Reiner was conducting the Chicago Symphony.

"Wait'll you hear this, Poochwoman," Howie had said on our way to Chicago's sumptuous Symphony Hall. Howie thought Brahms, Mozart, Bach, Beethoven, and even Schubert conveyed in their sacred music a deep connection to the Almighty, in whom Howie did not believe, but which he still appreciated. In contrast, he thought Verdi was a musical hack, writing for the nineteenth-century equivalent of Hollywood. Even I had to laugh when the opening chords of the "Dies Irae" made me jump from my seat.

The performance in Spoleto was worthy of a Hollywood spectacle. There was reserved seating in many rows of portable chairs in front of the Duomo. Behind these, the whole piazza and the long trapezoidal flight of shallow steps leading down to it were crammed with spectators. The members of the enormous chorus filed in and took their places on the risers behind the orchestra, against the backdrop we had painted. Maestro Schippers brought them to attention and the concert began. The unspeakable beauty of the setting, the respectful silence of the throngs of people, and then the music itself brought forth from me a depth of grief and sadness that I had been unable or unwilling to experience since my departure from *Stone Horse* and my father's subsequent death.

Who was this man who had been my father? Where was he now?

Why wasn't he here with me sharing the spectrum of emotion that music provided—music to which he had introduced me?

Why and how had it all gone so horribly wrong?

How could he have died before we could put wrong to right?

Why had he forsaken me?

18. Unhappy Returns

PROVIDENCE — SEPTEMBER 1961

The Colony Hotel, Delray Beach, FL.

Senior year. I was a mess. My Andrews Sisters were gone, and no one came near to replacing them. The excitement of Spoleto was over. Howie was truly gone and, thanks to my behavior right after his death, I was estranged from his friends and most of his family. Early in the fall, I initiated an affair with my medieval art history professor, who had caught my eye with his beaten-up, British racing-green convertible Jag. Henri Brunner (real name Heinrich, another Teuton, like Roger Fritz, who preferred French to German identity) was Swiss-German. He was both scholarly and sophisticated. He was tall, skinny, appropriately disheveled, with long straight graying mouse-brown-bangs that fell over a once-chiseled face. He was fourteen years my senior, a Raskolnikov look-alike, my kind of attractive. The soft accent, a mix of French and German, was icing on the cake. And he was married.

Early in October, while his wife was at work, we consummated our mutual attraction on the daybed in the study of his apartment

Part 4: La Vita Dolce-Amara

on Benefit Street. His wife had posted her temperature charts all over their apartment because she was trying, thus far unsuccessfully, to get pregnant. Henri spoke of his wife as though she inhabited some lower ring in the intellectual hierarchy of humanity. Over the course of successive encounters, Henri made it clear that although his wife was trying to get pregnant, he wanted out of the marriage and had no misgivings about his attraction to me. We would make a superb couple, and he was looking forward to taking me with him, as his new wife, to Princeton's Institute of Advanced Studies, where he had an academic appointment the following year, and where I would be ideally suited to running a salon celebrating his (and maybe also my?) vast knowledge of art and architecture.

How could I have bought into this? Not only did I, but I did it wholeheartedly.

Soon after our relationship got underway, my childhood friend Eo Coudert announced her intention to elope with her father's legal protégé, Edward Gottesman. Ed was charming but not from "the same block in the parish," as my mother was fond of saying. In fact, he wasn't from any parish. He was Jewish and from New Jersey. Neither her parents nor mine knew which was worse. However, Ed was well spoken, smarter than smart, and had graduated from the University of Chicago at seventeen or so and from law school at twenty. Eo was a junior at Vassar. She would complete her junior year, after which she planned to move to London, where Ed was to set up the London office of Coudert Frères, and she would somehow complete her degree. How could this have happened? Eo—the star student, the athlete, the all-around good person, good to her friends, good to her parents—was going so off track.

Was what I was doing any better?

Meanwhile, I had to create a social life for myself on campus. I had a few male friends from prior years. Most were preppy fraternity types. Some, like Rich Boardman, had a marginal interest in the arts, and others, like Ralph Watson, in the humanities. Ralph feigned academic disinterest and spent days and evenings drinking and playing backgammon with his fraternity brothers, then withdrew to his off-campus apartment and studied until dawn in hopes no one would find out he had a brain and was actually using it. I continued to visit Eddie and Alvin at Yale and went back and forth to New York to see my family, do laundry. and reconnect with as many of my Spoleto friends as I could find.

Reading Proust was far harder than I thought, and reading it in French was impossible. It took me over three hours to get through a page and a half, and I'm not sure I understood what I read because Proust's French is so idiomatic. But the weekly sessions with L-M were all that I had hoped for. My semester-end paper on Henri Bergson and Proust's concept of time was as hard to think through and to present as any ideas that I have ever grappled with, including calculus.

My honors thesis was also a challenge: how to develop a reasonable hypothesis that would bind together the myriad differences and few similarities between Italian and German and Austrian Baroque architecture? I ended up focusing on the churches of Francesco Borromini in Rome and Guarino Guarini in Turin—both priests were also master architects and geometers. I tried to figure out if, in order to burst forth from the static geometrical forms of the Renaissance and create a new architecture of motion, they had used the mathematics of change that were being simultaneously developed by Newton and Leibnitz. My advisor, Henry Millon, introduced me to Adolf Placzek, the librarian at Columbia University's Avery Library, the finest architectural library in the world after the Bodleian at Oxford. Millon asked Placzek and his staff to grant me access to the building manuals of the period (mid-seventeenth century), including reproductions of Borromini's original drawings in the Albertina Library in Vienna and corresponding texts on Guarini. This introduction to Avery Library, Adolf Placzek, and those ancient volumes was Millon's greatest gift to me. My friendship with Dolf Placzek continued up until his death in 2000 at age eighty-seven.

Between Thanksgiving and Christmas, I brought Henri to New York to meet my parents. My mother still held that things and people European had an edge over most things and people American. She and Hans thought Henri was fine, charming, well-mannered, and cultivated. They were not at all perturbed by his being married, given his declared intention to become unmarried as soon as the academic year was over. My mother's law practice was morphing from international law to marital law and trusts and estates. If Henri needed a divorce to make me a decent woman, my mother was there to assist.

During Christmas vacation, I saw many of my New York-based Spoleto friends. These were musicians, managers and administrators. Almost all were gay. That word hadn't yet come into parlance, but it sounds so much better than whatever pejorative terms were then in use. I only minded in the case of Bill Crawford, who was wildly handsome in his preppy way, with his open button-down shirts, tweed jackets with suede elbow patches, and slightly nasal marbles-in-the-mouth manner of speaking. Bill was so knowledgeable about music and such good fun that I refused to believe he was gay. Plus, he kept talking about Fiorella, her beauty, and how he worshipped her. That certainly was proof. No?

Being back in Providence in mid-January was yet another unhappy return. There were finals in medieval art—taught by guess who?—and in medieval history, taught by a young scholar and faculty member who was also having a fling with an undergraduate.

But he was unmarried, and very serious about her. She was correspondingly scholarly and serious about him. I was tiring of my role as mistress of my medievalist. I felt guilty about our betrayal of Henri's wife yet also longed for both recognition and concrete evidence that their separation was in the works. Henri was full of talk. But the only action he took was to tell Barnaby Keeney, president of Brown University, about our affair because he was afraid if word got out, he would be knocked off his tenure track.

Man to man, Keeney assured him that his future was secure.

Maybe they even had a little chuckle about it.

I was becoming increasingly depressed, drinking too much, in way too deep. One evening I cracked. I insisted on meeting and talking with Henri at some very inconvenient time for him. I blasted the full fire of my humiliation and attendant rage into his scrawny face. "Hell hath no fury like a woman scorned." You bet. I was scorned and scarred and burned, and I wanted him to feel my pain. I shouted and hollered and sobbed. He tried to reassure me that he was doing his best to extricate himself from his marriage. He promised that his wife knew of his plans to divorce at the end of the academic year. I pointed out that updated temperature charts were regularly replacing those previously on display.

I returned to my room at Andrews wracked with sobs, my chest heaving, my breath short. In despair, I called my mother for comfort. She said she would get the first plane to Providence in the morning and we would talk to Henri together.

My mother was coming to Providence to sort out my pathetic love life?

Hard to believe.

Yet she knew even better than I that since my departure from *Stone Horse* three years earlier, my psyche, not to mention my sense of self, had been badly broken. In the intervening months, we had talked about the consequences of living with, loving and counting on someone as damaged as Howie. Over the course of their ten-year marriage, his philandering and drunken rages had nearly killed her physically and spiritually. While to her credit she had never trashed Howie while I was little, she now began to share some details from her own experience by way of comforting me. She also knew I would benefit from professional help, as she had, to get my internal ship righted. I agreed to see Herbert Spiegel, her former psychiatrist, when I was back in New York.

I picked my mother up at Providence's Theodore F. Greene airport in the late morning. We drove directly to Henri's apartment where he received us cordially and then took us both to a civilized lunch at the Biltmore Hotel. Henri and my mother got on beautifully. Henri carried on about his plans to bring me to Princeton in the fall, and she listened approvingly.

On the way to the train station after lunch, she said, "He's a very interesting man. Be realistic, Bunny"–still her pet name for me–"being the wife of a distinguished medievalist at Princeton would be wonderful for you. You'd meet hundreds of interesting people. You'd thrive in that environment. You could continue your own studies and support him at the same time. This would be far better suited to your temperament than charging forward to prove yourself in a field as difficult as architecture."

I was speechless. When we got to the station, I managed to get out of the car, open the passenger door for her, thank her for coming, and kiss her goodbye.

As her train pulled out, I found myself wound up in a ball of fury, directed not at my mother but at Henri. Henri was nothing more than a romantic con man. Now he'd conned both mother and daughter. I returned to my room at Andrews and howled. When I had exhausted myself, I went in search of Ralph Watson, whom I found studying at his apartment. As soon as I arrived, he put his books away as though he were harboring contraband, got out glasses and ice, scotch for him, gin for me, and we drank and played backgammon late into the evening. As Andrews's curfew approached, I wove my way back to my room and wept myself to sleep.

Ayn Rand came to lecture on campus two days later. Like most aspiring architects, I had adored *The Fountainhead*, and pretended to adore *Atlas Shrugged*, although the message, spun out over so many hundreds of pages of tiny print, lost some of its punch. Nutball fascist though Ayn Rand may have been, no man was telling her what to do. And no man was going to tell me, either!

All my art history professors, including Henri and especially Henry Millon, wanted me to give up architecture and pursue an academic career in art history. They wanted me to apply for a Wilson fellowship and were sure I would be awarded one, given my academic record. William Jordy was particularly emphatic about what a fine architectural historian I would make. He made it clear that women had a very rough time in architecture. Few of them made it out of school, far fewer still to careers of any distinction. Harmon Goldstone had said the same to me years before.

One evening Henry Millon came down from MIT to give a special lecture on the subject which he was currently researching—and found totally gripping—namely, the authorship of the row of rectangular attic windows that ring the dome of St. Peter's just below its spring line. Was it Cortona, Borromini, Michelangelo, or one of their apprentices, and if so, whose? This was followed by an exhaustive recitation of the sources consulted and who had to say what, when, and where on this (to me) less-than-riveting subject.

Was that what I had to look forward to if I pursued a career in art or architectural history? I was having none of it. I was determined

Part 4: La Vita Dolce-Amara

to go ahead with my plan to study architecture and not at all interested in running a socio-cerebral salon for Henri in Princeton.

At the time, the best architecture schools on the East Coast were Penn (where Louis Kahn had begun to make his mark), Yale, Harvard Graduate School of Design, and MIT. Princeton was maybe a tier below, and Columbia was at the bottom. Yale and Harvard required students to submit a portfolio with their application. Given my absence of creative talent, this was not happening. Yale and Harvard were out. Penn and MIT relied only on a student's record and recommendations. I applied to both.

Providence's harsh winter came to an end. Clumps of yellow forsythia burst forth in the yards of both historic and less-than-historic houses. I could feel myself emerging from my cocoon of self-degradation and grief. My wings were beginning to unfold of their own volition. I didn't want to be subject to anyone's idea of who I was or who I was to become, and what I could or should be doing to enhance anyone else's life. At the end of the previous summer at the Festival of Two Worlds, despite my gate-crashing the opening night party, I had made myself so useful that Gian Carlo Menotti had invited me to return the following summer on salary to assist in the coordination of the American productions. At the end of the academic year, whatever else happened, I was determined to return to Spoleto and not wait around for Henri to get divorced. Henri suggested that Spoleto could be great fun for us both. I thought not.

I continued to spend what leisure time I had either with Rich Boardman, who was very fey and funny, and/or with very tall, dark and handsome Ralph Watson, whom I found increasingly appealing. His family had lived in Washington, Connecticut, where my Armstrong grandparents had their big house. Ralph's father had a car dealership there, but the family had recently moved—dealership and all—to West Palm Beach. Spring break was approaching, and I had never been to Florida. My Armstrong grandparents spent winters in Delray Beach, just south of Palm Beach, so I wrote to my grandfather and asked if I might stay with them for a few days. I told them I had a college friend, nothing serious, just a friend, originally from WashConn (as we called it), whose family now lived in Palm Beach, so I wouldn't be on their hands all the time. My grandfather, though he rarely displayed much emotion, seemed delighted.

Then well over eighty, he picked me up at the airport and drove me to Delray Beach at an average speed of fifteen miles per hour. We drew up in front of a shabby bungalow on a small, scruffy corner lot. I took my suitcase up the path of cracked flagstones that led to the front door. There were flowering gardenias in other yards, but not in this one. There was not even an orange tree or an oleander bush or a palm tree. Just crab grass everywhere. The good news was that the bungalow was only two blocks from the beach. The bad news was that even in spring, Florida weather can be unseasonably cold and damp.

Grandmother stood behind the screen door in a soiled, ill-fitting day dress with her slip hanging below the hem. Her tangled hair had more white in it than when I'd seen her last, and her darkly tanned face was more wrinkled. Because of the warmer climate, she had forgone the lisle stockings.

Who was this woman? And why, twelve or so years before, had she refused to shake my mother's hand when they remet in New York? Was it that my mother had failed Howie as a wife? Was it because my mother was as smart as Howie and a threat to him and to her? Was it that my mother came from a family with money, more money than her family of Huguenot department store owners had amassed? Or was it because my mother and her money were tainted by her Jewish background?

I didn't know to ask these questions then, but many years later and quite separately, Howie's brother Sinc, and their cousin, Mary

Part 4: La Vita Dolce-Amara

Armstrong Eustis, both of whom I loved dearly, made it clear: because of my mother's and thus my Jewish connections, I was not quite one of them.

In any case, at this point my grandmother and I were strangers, but I had asked to stay with them and was determined to make the best of it.

Amongst the Armstrongs, much had been made of the degree in nutrition Grandmother had earned at Barnard College during the war. But the food now on offer indicated that whatever she learned about nutrition had long been forgotten. Breakfast was coffee brewed to death in an ancient percolator, toast, and jam from jars ringed or spotted with touches of mold. Lunch was tinned soup (sometimes S. S. Pierce, but generally Campbell's) and saltine crackers. Dinner was taken elsewhere, usually at the Colony Hotel or at a local country club. If they hadn't had their clubs and hotels, I think my grandparents would have died of a combination of starvation and sensory deprivation.

Midway through my stay, Ralph came down from Palm Beach to take me to lunch and show me around. The bungalow looked just as Grandmother did: soiled, unkempt, and sad. I was ashamed for Ralph to see me there. When he arrived to collect me, the Admiral was his usual formal self and Grandmother put on her grande-dame act as they exchanged pleasantries about life in "Washington Conn." Ralph, unfazed, whisked me away for lunch and an afternoon of betting on Jai Alai, where I won $380.

The next day the sun made its only appearance during my Florida sojourn, and I took to the beach. In the evening, after a day of studying on my own, Ralph collected me and took me back to his house for dinner with his parents, who were as good-looking and even more open and charming than he. Gardenia bushes in full bloom were everywhere. The house, inside and out, was everything

I had hoped my grandparents' bungalow might be. After five days of walking in the mist on the beach on my own, many hours studying in a little corner I managed to free from clutter, and multiple trips to Palm Beach with Ralph and his family to see the sights, I was no closer to my grandmother than before, but between the Admiral and me an interest in one another had taken root.

I had to get out of my affair with Henri, but I didn't know how. Maybe I didn't have the guts. Maybe the sex was good. It must have been, because I had no tolerance for unpleasant or even unsatisfying sex. By necessity, our meetings were taking second place to my school work in general and my many trips to Avery Library in particular. Preparing for finals and wrapping up my thesis created an exhausting but welcome respite from confronting my continuing unhappiness and self-loathing. By mid-May our affair was over. My thesis was accepted. I passed my finals. I was elected to Phi Beta Kappa and would be graduating magna cum laude with honors in art history.

Best of all, I was accepted at MIT and Penn for architecture. I would start at Penn in the fall.

19. Spoleto Redux

SPOLETO — JUNE 1962

Steps up from the Piazza del Duomo, Spoleto.

As a staff member, I had to be in Spoleto earlier than the year before, so I skipped graduation. I needed wheels for my job, so I sold El Al to Joyce Reed before leaving Providence and bought a black VW convertible that I collected upon arrival in Rome and drove (top down, heat blasting) up the mountain to the apartment I had been invited to share with Giada, Giulietta, and Fiorella. It was just below Palazzo Campello, accessed through a picture-book, cobbled courtyard off the steep and narrow street. Spoleto was gnawingly cold at the end of May, but this year I was prepared. I was allocated the largest room, which surprised me. The year before it had been Fiorella's cousin's room. Her cousin was Pia Lindstrom, daughter of Ingrid Bergman. Bergman had been married to Fiorella's uncle, Roberto Rossellini. Pia and Fiorella were close. However, Pia wasn't returning this year, which is why I had been given her room. The others stayed in the smaller rooms because they had been too lazy to change.

We had a very small kitchen with no fridge. We never had

breakfast at home. That's what the cafes with those giant espresso machines were for. When we had supper at home, I learned to make spaghetti sauce from scratch by sautéing an onion, then adding nothing but tomato paste, salt, pepper, and grated Parmigiano. We bought fresh bread daily, and when the weather got hot, we kept the butter from melting by leaving it under a small but steady stream of icy tap water. We had our wine bottles refilled regularly from the casks in the bar fifty meters down our narrow street.

Gian Carlo Menotti's vision for the festival was courageous and inspired. He wanted to bring life and art to every nook and cranny of this stunning hill town. Just before our arrival that year, the American sculptor David Smith populated the ruins of a Roman amphitheatre, just off the Piazza della Libertà, with twenty-two metal forms and figures. Some were eight or nine feet high, and all were fabricated in and from the remains of an abandoned steel factory in Voltri, near Genova. Later in the season, Alexander Calder's giant stabile, "Teodelapio," was shipped to and installed in the piazza in front of the train station at the bottom of the hill. In the squares throughout the town, there appeared large and small works by eleven other sculptors, including Henry Moore and Beverly Pepper. In addition to the two main theatres, which were used primarily for opera, dance, mainstream drama, and chamber music, many venues for smaller, more experimental works as well as art galleries sprouted up in basements and abandoned warehouses all over town. Artists were engaged to design sets. Film directors like Visconti directed operas. Elia Kazan directed a play that his wife Molly had written. Roberto Rossellini directed a play that had been translated into Italian and was based on the correspondence between George Bernard Shaw and Mrs. Patrick Campbell.

My favorite work by an artist working outside of his own box was Saul Steinberg's "set" for Rossini's *Il Conte d'Ory*. *Ory* was

Part 4: La Vita Dolce-Amara

performed in concert format in the Teatro Caio Melissa. Hidden in the wings way upstage were tall vertical rollers, one on each side, with a huge canvas stretched between them. Throughout the performance, wild and kooky illustrations of the narrative by Steinberg scrolled from stage left to stage right across the rear of the stage. Steinberg's continuous cyclorama was even more dazzling and witty than Rossini's music.

There was a new group of students under Camilla Pecci-Blunt's less-than-comforting authority. Roger Fritz was on hand again. I was glad to see him, although I was never sure what he was doing there; he didn't have an official role with the festival, but he, plus camera and light meter, were definitely a fixture. Roger told me he was thinking of changing his name to Roger Armstrong-Fritz, as he thought this reference to Anthony Armstrong-Jones, photographer and then-husband of Princess Margaret, would add cachet to his persona and enhance his career. We fell into bed once or twice early in the pre-season, again more for warmth than for the joy of sex.

The regulars from the previous summer were also there: Bill Crawford and Gerry Fitzgerald, who wrote for *Opera News* on the administrative side; Tommy Schippers, conductor; Albert Fuller, harpsichordist; Bobby White, tenor/countertenor; Shirley Verrett, soprano; George Shirley, tenor; and Lili Chookasian, contralto. Of the singers, Lili was my favorite. Discovered by Tommy Schippers, she had sung Herodias in *Salome* the summer before and was to sing Clarissa in *The Love of Three Oranges* this season. She was a Mother Earth goddess: short, squat, funny, and smart, with a velvet-smooth but powerful voice. Lili had a huge mouth painted bright red, sparkling dark eyes, and a mop of wavy black hair. Star though she was, she reveled in being the happy suburban wife of George Gavejian, a successful Armenian rug dealer, and the mother of three. Lili could and did laugh about anything, onstage and off.

That year's American productions had a new group of actors and actresses, and there were new directors as well. Daniel Selznick, the son of David O.; plus Elia and Molly Kazan and Edward Albee were on the scene. Then there was Mildred Dunnock, who had been head of the theatre department at Brearley before my nemesis, Gladys Bowen, took over. There was Orazio Orlando, a gay matinee idol from Naples with straw-colored dyed hair and a huge smile, who spent many hours at the foot of my bed wringing his hands and otherwise gesticulating in Italian about whatever pulled at his heartstrings. But a young unknown actress, Marcia Stillman, was the most mysterious. She was short, frail, pretty, with thick, dark, shoulder-length hair that half hid her face and her sunken eyes. Marcia usually looked as if she were about to burst into tears. Once, when a group of us were having a coffee on the main drag, Lili characteristically called her on it.

"What's the matter, Marcia? You look ill."

Marcia turned slowly to Lili and in a stage whisper replied, "I have tired blood." Having "tired blood" subsequently became Lili's byword for anyone in any kind of mental or physical distress. I wanted to befriend Marcia. She seemed interesting and needy. Her family lived near mine at 61st Street and Park. We should have had enough in common to bring us together. But Marcia was either too ephemeral for me, or I was too base for her. When I tried to talk to her, I felt her slipping through my fingers. Roger Fritz was fascinated by her. Slowly, using both his camera and his personality, he drew her out, and in so doing, fell headlong in love with her, casting his long-term girlfriend Crista aside. He tended her as one would a sick and dying bird. It was what she needed.

Clifford David, also from New York, was tallish and robustly built,

Part 4: La Vita Dolce-Amara

with smooth, light-olive skin, and dark hair; he had a hearty laugh and a booming voice, both onstage and off. Clifford was full of himself and his talent but with a naiveté that was winning. He admitted to being the main squeeze of a slightly older, married society matron in New York who took good care of him in all ways. Soon after his arrival, Clifford attracted the attention of Pia Lindstrom, who had come to Spoleto during the pre-season weeks after all. She and Clifford fell for one another big time. Pia decided she wanted to stay on in her old room (my new room), but Giada, Giulietta, and Fiorella honored the deal they had made with me. Pia had to find other digs. She was not happy and never failed to give me a malevolent look whenever we met.

Visconti showed up to begin work on *Carmen,* with the same lead singers who had sung *Salome* the summer before: Shirley Verrett as Carmen and George Shirley as Don Jose. Ernest O. Mondorf's sublime paintings, which served as sketches for the sets, were broken down and otherwise transformed by Renato Marozzi and his crew into backdrops, legs, and borders. On the first night of Visconti's return, he was seated at the bar at Il Pentegramma, surrounded by his entourage, most of whom I knew at least by name, and some, like Roger, with whom I was on closer terms. I leaned over Roger, who had the diminutive Marcia tucked under his wing, and ordered a rum and coke with ice. When it arrived, Visconti acknowledged me for the first time.

"Eh! Signorina, would you like to use my cock to stir your coke?"

Even his acolytes stopped in their tracks. That was Visconti's style. Communist aristocrat though he was, he thrived on gross vulgarity and the shock it could provoke. I knew that game well, accustomed to sprinkling my own speech with four-letter words at home. But compared to Visconti, I was an amateur. I gave him an icy stare, and eventually the din of conversation resumed.

Spoleto Redux

My job was to look after the physical and scenic requirements of most of the plays that were to be performed in English. My first assignment was to help complete the set and props for the maiden run of Tennessee Williams's *The Milk Train Doesn't Stop Here Anymore*, or *Il Treno di Latte non si Ferma Qui Mai Più*. We managed to complete the set, but the text was in sorry shape. Ticket sales for opening night were poor, and staff members were ordered to attend to flesh out the house. By the time the curtain went up, Williams was drunk. Throughout the performance, he sat in one of the first-tier boxes taking periodic swigs from an open bottle of Scotch between audible groans. Anna Magnani, who had starred opposite Burt Lancaster in the film of Williams' *The Rose Tattoo*, and whom I adored, sat by his side, whispering words of encouragement and consolation. Seeing Anna Magnani up close was worth every minute of that otherwise excruciating evening.

One of the American plays on the season's roster was *The Love Nest* by Deric Washburn, who later went on to write the screen play for the *The Deer Hunter*. It happened that Deric's parents were Pittsburgh friends of my mother's brother, Mac, and we had each been instructed to look the other up. Thanks to Mac's coming out to Chicago and seeing me through Howie's funeral, I was better disposed towards doing as he suggested than I would previously have been. When Deric and I finally did meet we took to one another instantly. He was a Harvard graduate, three years older than I, with dirty blond, wavy hair, a broad smile, and a nicely articulated body.

It was fun dishing our respective families over lunches and dinners, in and around the countryside, and in and out of bed. He drank a lot, and so did I. Unfortunately, Deric had a serious girlfriend in New York to whom he would be returning as soon as the run of his play was over. He was sure that I could understand. At least he was honest, and he was neither married to his inamorata nor was she

Part 4: La Vita Dolce-Amara

about to walk through the door of his Spoleto rooms. Also unfortunately, I wasn't good at casual sex, although I did try from time to time as I had with Roger. To enjoy sleeping with someone I'd have to become seriously interested in him, even reviewing his potential as husband material. I was very attracted to Deric, and, having deemed his husband potential excellent, I persuaded myself that I was falling in love. Guys are good at not doing that. They can fuck for fun and then go back home to their lovers-in-waiting.

Why couldn't I do that?

One day, while I was crossing the Piazza della Libertà, I glanced down into the amphitheatre at the metal figures of David Smith and I saw amongst them a very familiar silhouette, a stooped figure with shaggy hair: Henri. And, of course, he saw me. In a flash, he climbed up the steep stone risers to greet me. All of the self-confidence I had managed to amass since my arrival in Spoleto departed. I held onto the railing for support.

"What are you doing here?"

"I have been here several days, following you about," he replied.

"You've been following me? You know where I live and work?"

"Yes, I do. I even know where you have coffee in the morning and dinner at night."

I was speechless. He looked down at his feet, waiting for this to sink in, and then continued in the same flat tone, softened by his Franco-German accent, "I am still very much in love with you, and I have come to bring you home with me."

No, please, no. Make this go away! I shouted silently to some invisible knight in shining armor who I hoped would come to my rescue. But almost immediately I collected myself and responded as calmly as I could.

"No, that isn't going to happen. I'm not coming home with you ever, whatever, whenever. I bet you are still living with your wife and trying this out just for a lark!"

"She and I have separated," he replied calmly.

"I am still not returning with you or to be with you," I choked out. "I have work to do here. Then I am going to Rome with my friends and after that to architecture school in the fall. All very much on my own." I was building up some steam. It began to feel less scary. "We are finished," I continued, gaining momentum, "We were finished months ago, long before I graduated." I paused. "Please go away. Please, please, leave me alone," I said, but my voice came out more a plea than a demand.

"No, I will not go. Not now. Whether you return with me or not, I intend to spend some time with you here," Henri declared.

"I don't have time to spend with you. I am working every day and every evening," *and spending my nights with someone other than you,* I wanted to add. "There are no days off." I turned on my heel and left him standing on his side of the railing.

After a week of being stalked, I agreed to meet him for a meal outside of town and there finally persuaded him that I would not be returning with him. I would not be seeing him again. He had the grace to believe me this time and departed Spoleto as stealthily as he had come.

I didn't see Henri again until six years later, when we met at a charity party in New York. He and his wife had adopted a little girl. She and I were not introduced.

Towards the end of Deric's time in Spoleto, The Parents arrived. They were taken with him and loved his same-block-in-the-parish connection to my mother's brother, which made Deric's imminent departure from Spoleto all the more painful. After three wonderful weeks of work, talk, and lovemaking following alcohol-saturated dinners, I drove him to the station at the bottom of the hill and waved hello to Calder's *Teodelapio* and goodbye to Deric. I did my best to entertain my parents until their departure two days later. It was gratifying to share with them the architecture, shops, and restaurants of my newly-adopted Umbrian hill town; show them firsthand what I had been up to; flaunt my improved Italian; and introduce them to my new friends, Giada and Fiorella.

Fortunately, there was lots of work to distract me from the residual anxiety caused by Henri's appearance and the gnawing pain of my failure to wrest Deric away from his full-time girlfriend in New York. None of what I was doing had the substance of assisting Beni Montresor on the sets of *Vanessa*, but it was all interesting, as were the artists. And my friendship with Giada and Fiorella was deepening. Giulietta I knew less well, as she spent most of her days and nights dealing with the press. There was a steady stream of their various friends coming up from Rome for a night or two here and there, and all of them seemed to take to me as well.

I missed Deric. More accurately, I missed having a boyfriend. But there were few candidates in Spoleto. Almost every male on the scene was gay. Many handsome specimens in the circles of Visconti, List, and Menotti were bisexual and had serious girlfriends, but they all also seemed to know the rules: When the big man calls, the girls are set aside and the young men flock to service him. Towards the end of Visconti's stay in Spoleto, he asked Roger Fritz to ask me if I wanted to come with the rest of them to Sicily later that summer to be an extra in the filming of *The Leopard/Il Gattopardo*. I was flattered to be asked (if only indirectly), and it would have been a unique experience, but I knew I couldn't handle being part of Visconti's entourage. I had the wit to decline, but my next move in the sex-and-romance department was not much of an improvement.

Spoleto Redux

Giada and Giulietta's friend Freddie, who had driven me to Florence the summer before, made several short appearances during the festival and one longer visit at the end. During those final days, we palled around in an amorphous group that included Giada, Giulietta (when she could break free—she seemed always busier than we), Freddie, Bill Crawford, Orazio Orlando, and Jojo and Marco Patriarca (a brother and sister duo, also from Rome). I found Freddie as appealing as I had before in every way, and spent time with him during his final visit, conversing in a mix of his not-great English and my not-much-better Italian. I could sense he was depressed because Giulietta wasn't paying him much heed, and I knew he was off limits, but I must have failed to convey this knowledge to Freddie because one of the last nights we were all in Spoleto, he and I ended up in bed together though I cannot remember how.

I do remember thinking I had died and gone to heaven. This man I had lusted for wanted me?

It was the best ever. It was the real thing.

Except it wasn't. At least not for Freddie.

The next days were spent putting the festival to bed, after which our group dispersed. Most of the Italians, including Freddie, returned to Rome, and I drove west to meet The Parents at the Argentario. They had booked us into Il Torre della Calle Piccola, a new luxury hotel comprised of small, stuccoed cottages nestled into a carefully landscaped, arid, and treeless hillside outside of Santo Stefano. There I was treated to three days of sun, sea, and reading, followed by after-dinner drinks under the stars and dancing the Madison endlessly in long lines with upscale Italian youths and jetsetters. I was so relaxed that I was able to discuss with The Parents my burgeoning misgivings about going to Penn to study architecture in the fall. For all my talk about becoming an architect,

Part 4: La Vita Dolce-Amara

I loved all aspects of working in the theatre. To my surprise, The Parents were receptive.

"See how you feel when the summer is over," said my mother. "We can discuss it further when you get back to New York. You can always apply for deferred admission." This from my mother, who was adamant that we three girls each have a real profession?

Giada had invited me to return with her and Giulietta to their apartment in Rome. Their brother was away for the summer and I could have his room. I loved Giada and Fiorella as I loved my Andrews Sisters, and I admired Giulietta, although she was more aloof. I felt that I belonged in their midst in a way I rarely had felt with friends at home. Why? Although these girls were bright, hard-working, well-educated, well-travelled, well-read, and stylish, each in her own way, they were nowhere near as wild or free as I. They seemed not to sleep around at all. Nor did they drink as I did. What felt so good? Was it an affinity of class, money, culture? Was it a mix of the magic of working in theatre and the thrill of being admitted to a society and culture to which I had not been born but to which I aspired?

As for Freddie, besotted as I was, I had to get myself under control. Whether Giulietta wanted him or not, by virtue of the depth of his desire and need for her, and their families' shared history, he was hers. One-night-stand or no, he would never be mine. Plus, I was staying in Giulietta's house, and I had to behave.

In Rome, we were the same group as the previous summer, plus some newcomers. I took a great shine to Margherita Boniver, a tall, slender, outspoken blonde who was pursuing a career in politics. She, too, spoke nearly perfect English, as her parents were in the Italian foreign service. She had spent time in America and England growing up and seemed more liberated than my other Italian friends. I could speak more openly and freely to Marghe than to anyone else in their circle and on any subject. Giulietta was away visiting friends during this time, so Freddie returned to Milan, which was a good thing. His absence kept me out of trouble, although I constantly replayed the memory of our night together in Spoleto. I was obsessed. But I had been obsessed before. This was familiar territory.

Apart from agonizing over Freddie, those days in Rome were idyllic. Giada and I wrote letters or did errands in the morning. Midday we drove to their country club within the city, which seemed to be patronized exclusively by the Beautiful People of Rome, all in the world's tiniest bathing suits. The club had tennis courts and a swimming pool, with an adjacent bar and restaurant. Lunch was served by the pool, where buffet tables groaned with platters of prosciutto and salumi, tomatoes stuffed with risotto, zucchini ripieni, salads of various lettuces, cold fagiolini, artichoke hearts, cheeses, and bread. Sometimes we would catch sight of Giada's father playing tennis or her elegant, slender, white-haired mother having drinks with friends. Day after day they picked up the tab for me. There was no way I could repay them. Most evenings we convened in small groups for drinks at someone's parents' apartment and then went out to eat in their neighborhood. Those evenings we each paid our own way.

During the absence of both Giulietta and Freddie, Giada and I took side trips, once to Ostia for the day, then with Marghe to Cerceo on the coast just south of Rome to visit Fiorella at her family's summer place. The distances were short, most everyone had a car, and so friends like Orazio and the Patriarcas came and went as well. When Giulietta returned to Rome, right on her heels came Freddie, back from Milan.

Ferragosto, the middle of August, when all Italians (and most Europeans) go on vacation, was approaching. The plan was to go to Sardinia. None of us had been there. At the last minute, Giulietta decided she wouldn't join us. Freddie was devastated, a state as familiar to him as obsession was to me. The group was to be Julian, a long-faced British journalist; Marco Patriarca, who had taken a shine to me and was a close friend of Julian; Marghe, the political peroxide blonde; Giada, the strawberry blonde; and me, the only one with dark hair and olive skin. Marghe, Freddie, Giada, and I took off at the crack of dawn in two cars for Civitavecchia, where we were to catch the car ferry to Sardinia. Julian and Marco never showed up, so it was only the four of us. We docked at Olbia on the northeast coast of Sardinia in the early evening and found a small, affordable hotel. Marghe and I shared a room, and Giada shared a room with Freddie.

The next day we checked out of our hotel and drove north past Arzachena to explore the beaches along the Costa Esmeralda. The water was a brilliant green and the phantasmagorical rock formations defining the coastline came straight out of an Yves Tanguy landscape. The Aga Khan had not yet begun his "development" of this brilliant and immaculate landscape. The forms and shapes of the rocks and the saturated greens of the water were hallucinatory and pristine. No one was there. Not a soul.

We returned to Olbia in the evening and checked to see if Julian and Marco had come in on that day's ferry from Civitavecchia. They had not. My guess is that Julian persuaded Marco that chasing me was hopeless and they decided not to come. We got our old rooms back at our hotel, but this time Giada and Marghe shared a room. I am not sure whose idea this was, but as soon as the door to our room was shut, Freddie reached for me before I reached for him. We tore off each other's clothes, covered each other's bodies with kisses and made love into the night, he whispering small endearments to me in Italian, and I responding in kind. In the morning, when we met the others for coffee, we acted as though nothing had transpired. Giada was, after all, Giulietta's sister.

Another beautiful day driving north. From Palau, we drove to the tiny town of Santa Teresa Gallura, just west of the northernmost point of Sardinia. There were no hotels there, so we found a family to rent us rooms for the night. This was common practice in remote locations and in resorts on crowded weekends or during holidays. We could only find one room. Marghe and Giada took the twin beds and Freddie and I slept side by side on inflatable mattresses on the cold tile floor. Freddie and I couldn't keep our hands off each other even though Giada and Marghe were in the same room. When we thought they were asleep, we each slipped a hand inside the other's bedding and caressed one another silently. As we became more excited, our breaths became shorter and faster and surely loud enough to wake the dead. We were shameless as well as thoughtless. There was no stopping us.

And so our band of four travelled in and around the north of Sardinia for another week. By day we explored its jagged hills, terraced fields, spectacular lakes, and tiny towns. We visited churches and historic sites. We met up with friends of Giada and Marghe who were also on vacation, and with people who had never before seen an American. By then I was so tan compared to my fairer friends that one local asked if I were related to Louis Armstrong, "*Louis chi suona la tromba*"—the only American he and his friends could think of. Others, because I was wearing my mid-length hair in braids, assumed I had to be a Native American. I was flattered by both suggestions.

Nights and early mornings Freddie and I spent together, indulging our reciprocal physical passion. And we talked. Freddie was not just physically appealing. His air of poetic melancholy was magnetizing to me. Even though his course of study was engineering, he was sensitive to all forms of art and beauty and to the complexities of human emotion, although our mix of languages wasn't sophisticated enough to allow us to explore these areas in depth. Best of all, he had a winning sense of the ridiculous and could be funny. We laughed a lot, but there was melancholy just behind the laughter. Often, I supposed, he was thinking long and hard about his love for Giulietta, and maybe hers for him, and he may have been uncomfortable about what we were up to.

Our last stop en route from Chiodi to Golfo Aranci was Lago del Coghinas, a stunning, smallish lake with miles of pristine, unpopulated shoreline in the middle of nowhere. From there, we returned to Olbia, boarded the ferry to Civitavecchia, and drove back to Rome. Giulietta had already returned to Rome, and on our return to their house, she held court in her bedroom. Freddie took his place at the foot of the pedestal on which she lived in his mind and heart, and he hung on her every word. Although I was also in the room, also listening attentively to Giulietta tell of her travels, to Freddie I was absent.

After a respectful interval, I withdrew to my room across the hall, threw myself onto the bed, and gave in to my misery. It wasn't just about Freddie, although that was a major component. The arguments for and against my going to architecture school in the fall were playing with increasing strength and volume, like a Baroque continuo under the more lyrical themes and variations of the summer. The thought of turning up at Penn in September was making me nauseous with fear. I didn't have the guts, the smarts or the talent. I was only going because I had been talking about being an architect since I was ten. Penn would soon prove me a fraud who thrived on the glitz and glamour of theatre but couldn't design her way out of a paper bag, much less draw one. The Fashion Group and Spoleto had proved to me that I had a decent work ethic. Brearley and Brown had proved to me that I could do research and write analytical prose, but how much research and analytical writing was Howard Rouark doing in *The Fountainhead*? This was harder stuff to resolve than rejection by Freddie. Rejection was familiar. So I buried my head in the pillow, blocking the continuo as best I could, and I relived the last ten days, beach by beach, bay by bay, bed by bed, wallowing in the pleasure I had had and in the sadness of knowing I would not have it again.

The next day I met up with Marghe. She knew what was coming better than I. She invited me to come with her to the Argentario for the weekend. I was to leave for good that Sunday anyway and was happy to get out of Giulietta's sight, although I held nothing against her, nor did she seem to hold anything against me, for which I was thankful. I packed all my things and early the next morning, before Giulietta had emerged, I bid goodbye to Giada and her generous parents, loaded my bags into the VW and took off.

At the end of the weekend, Marghe drove me to the airport. I was leaving the VW with her for the winter. I flew from Rome to London, playing the time in Sardinia over and over and over, again and again. At Heathrow, I hired a car and drove south to the open arms of my Aunt Shirley in the New Forest—my second mother and my second home.

Shirley had a knack for making me feel worthwhile. I talked nonstop about the wonderful experiences I had had in Spoleto, my time in Rome, and our various side trips, especially to Sardinia. I skipped the part about falling insanely in love and sleeping with my Roman host's boyfriend. But I was able to talk to Shirley and her husband Vernon about my reservations about going to architecture school in September.

"Lale, de-ah"—Shirley always addressed me as Lale de-ah, as though the de-ah were part of my name—"Barby has driven you so hard. She was equally driven by her father, Clarence. But Clarence is not your father and you don't have to follow in her footsteps."

Part 4: La Vita Dolce-Amara

"I do, I do," I almost wailed. "I have always been a disappointment to her and to my father. I've never been smart enough for either of them. I never achieved the academic rewards they earned. And now I am thinking of giving up on my goal of becoming an architect, a professional, to work in the theatre!"

"Lale, de-ah, that's rubbish," Shirley retorted. "You're very bright and very attractive. The theatre is a wonderful place to be when you are young." Turning towards her husband, she went on, "Remember, Vernon, when I did the can-can at a show for you, Leslie Howard, David Niven, and the other RAF pilots at the base back in 1940? I kicked so high I fell backwards off the stage! Lucky I was wearing proper knickers." Vernon chuckled proudly.

"Soon enough, if you are as lucky as I have been," she continued, "you'll find the right man. You'll get married and settle down, and this will all be behind you. Then your husband and your family will be the most important considerations in your life. You don't need to have a career just because Barby has one. Look what her career has done for her! She didn't intend it, but for much of your childhood, she simply left you out!"

From the mouth of a rightwing English equestrienne. Shirley wrapped her strong arms around me and allowed me to weep for a few moments on her soft shoulder.

"There, there, my poor darling. You have everything on your side. You'll be just fine."

While I knew getting married was far from all I wanted from life, finding someone I would love and who would love me was high on the list, maybe even higher than becoming an architect. Comforted by her kindness, her unexpected take on my mother, and her faith in me, I dried my tears, polished off the remains of my sherry and went in for a supper of "bubble and squeak" and summer pudding.

20. Der Spiegel

NEW YORK — SEPTEMBER 1962

Façade of the Old Metropolitan Opera House at Broadway and 39th Street.

My return to the city began badly. I had not acknowledged the death of The Parents' beloved Chow, Chiu Mo Ling. My mother had written me that she had died, and I hadn't called (transatlantic calls were expensive), nor had I written a letter of condolence.

"Christ, I was in England," I protested," and on my way home anyway! And after all, Mo was only a dog!"

"That was no excuse. You know how much Mo meant to us."

From there a long downhill slide seemed inevitable. I was convinced I shouldn't go to Penn, but if I gave up on architecture, what then? I wasn't an actress. How otherwise does one get "into the theatre"? I had extricated myself from my sordid affair with Henri only to get caught up with Deric, and then far more seriously with Freddie, neither of whom wanted anything serious of me.

As if my body wanted to compete with the declining state of my psyche, scabby lesions were breaking out all over my skin, one or two or three new ones every day. Those close together became patches. The patches were getting angry as they grew larger. I wore long sleeves, and my skirts hid the burgeoning blossoms on my legs. Only my face was spared this disfigurement. No one noticed.

The tenant who had lived on the floor separating Judy's, Pago's and my apartment from The Parents' duplex finally moved out. Over the summer my mother had hired d'Argout Fergusson, her team of decorators, to install an inside spiral stair to connect the apartment above to theirs, and to do up the front room for Pago and the back room overlooking the enormous roof terrace for Judy. By this time Pago had transferred from Chapin to Brearley to be one of us.

As compensation for my having been kicked out of the room that Edward Wormley had designed for me, the fourth-floor apartment was to be mine alone. I was allowed to choose my own colors and fabrics for the furniture and finishes and did my best to reproduce what I had loved about our previous apartment at 145 East 62nd. I was given a brand-new bottle-green velvet Tuxedo sofa, two easy chairs, a French quasi-Louis XVI, marble-topped writing table and two blond wood Biedemeyer side chairs, which, although antique, I found very beautiful. I had the walls of the front room painted patent-leather green. My mini piano remained in the corner by the windows, and there was already a five-foot kitchenette built into one wall, over which d'Argout Ferguson had installed a full-height curtain to close it off years before. Neil Ferguson, who had been an architect before meeting and teaming up with Pierre d'Argout, knew of my professional aspirations and sold my mother what had been his drafting table. It consisted of two stacked banks of flat files with a white Formica top that hinged for drawing on a slope. Even though I was paralyzed by the idea of going to Penn, I was glad to have something belonging to Neil, from whom, over time, I learned a great deal.

After further discussion, The Parents and I agreed that I would write to Penn and ask to postpone my admission for a year, live in the apartment upstairs, and see if I could find a course that would introduce me to the rudiments of set design.

Relating the particulars of my emotional decline was more difficult. Although The Parents freely discussed all manner of sexual exploits and deviations that occurred amongst their friends, we never talked about sexual feelings and desires of our own, neither mine nor theirs—a good thing, because most children are uncomfortable even thinking of their parents having sex. I knew that my mother was fairly repressed—because she had told me so repeatedly (as I squirmed)— and that her enjoyment of sex had been limited, despite her love for Hans.

My mother had encouraged me to see a shrink soon after I had departed from *Stone Horse*. Since I was a little girl, my mother had been telling me about psychiatry and its workings. Both she and Howie had undergone years of analysis after their divorce, and hadn't they both been the better for it?

My mother? Yes.

Howie? Maybe? No, probably not.

I was ready for anything that could reverse the slow rotation of my downward spiral. Two days after my return, I went to see my mother's erstwhile psychiatrist, Herbert Spiegel. He was of medium build and bald, with a ring of very short dark hair around the back of his head. He sported a small, Hitler-like moustache and wore bowties. While his appearance wasn't compelling, I felt comfortable with him. I figured since he already knew what my mother had had gone through with my father, I'd be off to a head start and would be done with the process in short order.

Wrong.

In the meantime, Hans caught sight of the lesions on my lower arm.

"What the hell is that?" he exclaimed, and gently pulled up my sleeve to reveal an array of pillowed red spots and angry patches.

"I don't know," I confessed, a tinge of fear in my voice. "They began to appear when I was in England and seem to be getting worse. I have them almost everywhere." He asked to see my legs, which were more bespotted than my arms.

"Well, I know exactly what they are," he said. "They are secondary syphilitic chancers."

"What?"

"You've got syphilis. We need to put you on antibiotics immediately."

"No, I do not have syphilis!" I protested, remembering his insistence that I carry a truckload of antibiotics to Spoleto that first summer for just this purpose. "You have a disgusting mind to think I could have syphilis. You are sick, and you are wrong!"

Problem: Hans was a urologist. Urologists deal with venereal disease. Who, if not Hans, would know what a syphilitic chancer looked like?

I hadn't yet written my thank-you letters to Giada and Giulietta or to their parents for all that they had done for me. I could imagine including in my effusive gratitudinal remarks that their parents might consider sterilizing the room I slept in and all their toilet seats because I had contracted syphilis.

To Giulietta I might have written, "*Thanks so much for all you and Giada did for me both in Spoleto and again by so generously sharing with me both your home in Rome and your friends...*" [not to mention Freddie]. "*I have a bit of news: Somehow, somewhere, sleeping with God-knows-whom in Spoleto, I have contracted syphilis. This is bad only if you and Freddie sleep together.*" [Something that was never ever discussed in that set of upscale Italians, not even between Freddie and me]. "*If you do, please get yourself tested for syphilis. I am sending the same message to Freddie. I understand syphilis is now easily treated with antibiotics. I do apologize for this inconvenience, Love, Lulù."*

I made an appointment to see Dr. Rudolph Baer, the Viennese dermatologist whom I had been seeing since early childhood for minor complaints. The following Monday I sat opposite Dr. Baer at his mahogany partner's desk and blurted out the story of my lesions: when they started to appear, that they were multiplying at an alarming rate, and finally Hans's insane suggestion that I had syphilis. He said softly, "Ve vill take a look to see."

I was shown into his examining room. I undressed and put on a robe. He came in, opened the robe, went over me thoroughly, closed the robe over my splotchy flesh and took my hand gently in his.

"I am sorry to say you have either syphilis or psoriasis. Let's hope it's syphilis because zat's curable."

Great! I thought. *"Let's hope its syphilis." Are you kidding? And what the hell is psoriasis?*

"You mean Hans might be right?" I stammered.

"Ya. He might be right."

"And what is psoriasis?" Dr. Baer went into a short explanation of a skin condition which could look similar to mine. In most instances, the causes of psoriasis were unknown. There were no tried-and-true treatments, and no drug company had spent the money to develop a cure, because psoriasis had not proved fatal.

"How will you know which it is, Dr. Baer?"

"You vill have a Vasserman test and zat vill give us ze answer." A nurse arrived to draw my blood.

Tuesday morning Dr. Baer called. It was psoriasis.

He asked for our drugstore's phone number so he could phone in a prescription for cortisone ointment to be topically applied, and

Part 4: La Vita Dolce-Amara

suggested that I sit in the sun whenever I could. Vitamin D from the sun was known to help in some instances. I was to return in three weeks.

For the rest of the month and into October, all I seemed able to do between my thrice-weekly appointments with Herr Dr. Spiegel and my once-every-three-weeks appointments with Herr Dr. Baer was make meaningless engagements with friends to distract myself from the questions that were plaguing me.

When I was on my own and not playing records, I listened to classical music on WQXR. One day the New School for Social Research ran an ad promoting its theatre arts program, which included set design. I raced downtown and registered for the introductory set design course. Classes were to begin the next week and were to be held during the day on Tuesdays and Thursdays. I also signed up for life drawing on Wednesday evenings. Whether I was to be a set designer or an architect, I had to learn to draw. My teacher, Raphael Soyer, the Russian-born painter and printmaker (of whom I had not heard at the time), liked my approach to the human figure, so I wrote him off immediately. What did he know? I attended very few of his classes.

Another shot in the foot.

Through Clifford David's New York main squeeze, I learned about and volunteered to work for the Writers' Stage, a brand new off-off-Broadway production company that had rented a tiny theatre on the north side of East Fourth Street. There was nothing on the outside of the building to announce its presence. As I knew about lettering and alphabets, I offered to make them a proper two-sided sign. They gave me a sheet of letterhead with their logo, and I bought two four-foot-square Masonite panels and enamel paint. I drew a grid over the tiny logo and the same grid on the panels, and over a weekend I transferred the image of the little logo to both sides of the four-foot-square sign. For the short period it took to make the signs, my misery was abated.

Between classes at the New School, I continued to do menial jobs for the Writers' Stage. I helped build the set for the first production and in so doing met and became friends with the young Andre Gregory, whom I grew to like and admire along with his wife Chiquita. But I felt none of the excitement or pride in belonging that I had felt in Spoleto. The Writers' Stage was underfunded, uninspiring, and unappealing. The East Village was no Umbrian hill town either. After a few months of being underutilized and unappreciated, I made myself scarce. My withdrawal went unnoticed.

In set design class, we were to design a set for Garcia Lorca's *Blood Wedding*. The mechanical drawing I had learned at RISD stood me in good stead, but my design for the set was less than ordinary. It was a literal room, set square to the proscenium. It had a floor cloth of large square terra cotta tiles; flats that defined white plaster walls, topped with dark crown mouldings; correspondingly dark wood-paneled doors, casings, and base mouldings; and heavy, carved Jacobean furniture like that in my grandfather's apartment at 1000 Park. It was my idea of a Spanish interior. The instructor suggested I set the whole room at an angle to the proscenium to give it some life. This helped, but in fact my design had not a spark of flair, nothing of the ephemeral that can make scenery so evocative. The best you could say was that it was as somber and lugubrious as the play itself. I despaired. Perhaps neither set design nor architecture was in my future. Nonetheless, I persevered.

Like most people first experiencing therapy, I couldn't understand why I had to do all the talking. Why no soothing explanations of why I was where I was and why I was so unhappy? Why no pearls of wisdom that would guide me to a better place? Why, for this,

Part 4: La Vita Dolce-Amara

did I have to pay a monstrous hourly sum? Spiegel had an answer to that one: If the treatment didn't cost a significant amount, the patient would not value it. The only other direct answer he gave came after several weeks, maybe months, of my sitting in an easy chair opposite him (I refused to take to the analytic couch), with me talking, sometimes weeping, and him listening.

The question: If I have so much going for me—looks, education, smarts, drive, a solid and caring family, and money (which I enjoyed, yet of which I was ashamed)—why am I such a mess?

The answer: When one has so many attributes, one has many more choices than most people. The more choices one has, the harder it is to make the right choices.

I had neither center nor focus. I felt that I was being covered with thick layers of batting through which eventually neither air, nor light, nor sound would penetrate, and that the weight of these layers was pressing me down into a dark and murky place from which there might be no escape. I could hardly get up in the morning and was constantly on the verge of tears. The spots and scabby lesions persisted. Nonetheless, I dragged myself up to Spiegel's office three times a week and to Dr. Baer every three weeks.

From Dr. Baer I learned that treating psoriasis with tar had proved helpful, but was not a cure. I started applying Zetar ointment to my lesions and stank like a fresh asphalt road.

From Dr. Spiegel I learned that mine was an old wound and had been with me for years, that it had been inflicted early on in my childhood, principally (but not entirely) by my father, and was deepened by his subsequent actions. I would have to acknowledge that however much I had loved him and tried to please him, he was largely responsible for this wound and, thus, undeserving of my love. I would have to give him up. Because Howie had treated me in this manner, I had come to assume that this was the sort of behavior I should expect, and so I sought relationships with men who would treat me in like fashion. It was a pattern that I would have to break if I were to move on.

All of which made perfect sense.

I talked a good game in Spiegel's office. I had provided the material from which these conclusions were drawn. But that was it. Talk. Nothing was getting through the layers of batting between me and the world around me. Nothing offered a way out of the quagmire in which I was submerged. A diagnosis is not a cure. I had only ever been comfortable alone with my mind when I was working or studying or, in earlier years, painting. But without some focus, some center, not even this source of relief was available. I was depressed, very, but I was not suicidal. I pressed on.

Spiegel suggested that for me to become "whole," I would have to examine my feelings for and my relationship with my mother with the same scrutiny that I was trying to apply to Howie. My mother, however difficult she may have been, and however much we may have fought, was brilliant and stylish, funny and generous. She'd had a horrible childhood and had to be forgiven for any emotional inadequacies, certainly by me, for whom she had done so much. Sure, she and my father drank a lot. So did Hans. So did all their friends. So did I, and my friends. Drink was embedded in our culture. It was our reward for getting through another day.

No, I couldn't imagine dissecting my relationship to my mother. I felt no need.

But Spiegel may have been right. Maybe this writing is part of that process.

In the middle of November, Roger Fritz arrived from Munich. He had come to visit Marcia Stillman, who lived with her mother on 61st Street and Park. His intent was to propose to her. We all

Part 4: La Vita Dolce-Amara

met up at the Spoleto Ball, which was held in the ballroom at the Plaza. I dressed to the nines and was escorted up the grand stairs to the ballroom by the very tall, very blond, very Southern Gerry Fitzgerald, who wrote for *Opera News*. We were seated at dinner with Roger and Marcia, and her sister and her sister's husband, the photographer Bruce Davidson, all of whom were very lively—including Marcia. I danced nonstop with Bill Crawford, who had attended the same sort of dancing schools as I had and was a brilliant lead. For that evening at least, my depression lifted.

Thanksgiving came soon after. Dagmar got the big table out and added leaves to it to accommodate our guests. She cooked and Elsa served. Hans usually invited a couple of strays, generally foreign urology residents who had not been invited elsewhere, and I liked this tradition, even though it sometimes made for stilted conversation. However, my mother could—and did—talk endlessly on any subject, from international affairs to ornithology (although she hated birds), so no one needed to speak unless he or she felt like it. After this particular Thanksgiving dinner, I returned to my flat upstairs, looking forward to Roger and Marcia's coming over after their Thanksgiving with her family. Two or three other Spoleto friends showed up, but Roger and Marcia did not. I was disappointed. I wanted to know how things were going and if Roger had proposed.

Two days later Roger telephoned. His voice was thin and hoarse.

"So where the hell were you on Thanksgiving evening?" I asked.

"Marcia jumped out the window. She's dead." Roger said.

"No, Roger. Be serious."

"I am serious. We were having Thanksgiving lunch in the early afternoon at her mother's. Her sister and Bruce were there as well. Marcia excused herself from the table. She went down the hall and jumped out of one of the bedroom windows. She landed in the alley between the apartment building and the church next door."

"No, no," I gasped. "Was there any warning?"

"No. Nothing beyond her usual moodiness. When she got up from the table, no one thought anything about it. Only when she didn't come back, I went to look for her and found the open window. I went to the window, hardly daring to look down. But I did, and there she was, on the pavement."

"Oh, Jesus," I said. "Where are you now?"

"I am still at the apartment. May I come see you?"

"Yes, of course. Come now, at once." Thus began days and days of handholding and otherwise helping Roger understand why this had happened and why he was not to blame himself. Many members of the New York Spoleto community joined the effort to get Roger back on his feet. Gian Carlo invited him to stay indefinitely with him and Sam (and their entourages) in Mount Kisco, an environment in which we were sure Roger would feel at home and find comfort.

Tired blood.

Blood wedding?

No wedding.

No Marcia.

Dead tired blood.

Despite December being the darkest month of the year, and despite the tragedy of Marcia's death, some light was at last making its way through the layers of batting that were weighing me down. I am not sure whether my hours with Dr. Spiegel were starting to pay off or whether it was because of a lunch I had with Henry (Hank) Potter, a friend of The Parents, or both.

During the fall, The Parents became acquainted with Hank and his wife Lucille. Hank was very much their sort. He had gone to St. Marks and then to Yale and married Lucille, who was from (yes)

Part 4: La Vita Dolce-Amara

the same block in the parish. After a few years in New York, where Hank was a theatrical producer, he and Lucille went to Hollywood, where he became a movie director. His most famous film was *Mr. Blandings Builds His Dream House* with Cary Grant, Myrna Loy, and Melvin Douglas. (His star on Hollywood's Walk of Fame is on the sidewalk opposite 6633 Hollywood Boulevard.) In the late '50s, he and Lucille returned to New York, where he was pursuing his passion for field-training Labrador retrievers and for writing eccentric treatises on Sherlock Holmes for an organization called The Baker Street Irregulars. The Parents thought Hank might help me get into the theatre, so I was invited to have dinner with them, more than once. Hank and Lucille were livelier than most of The Parents' friends. Lucille was attractive in a natural sort of way, which I admired—loose, greying, shoulder-length hair, minimal makeup, comfortable clothes. Hank was mid-height, boxy, with close-cut hair and a roundish face. Both had twinkly eyes. Over time, Hank asked me a bundle of questions about my education, my interest in theatre, my experience in Spoleto, my ambivalence about architecture, and my growing sense that I wasn't going to be any good at set design. I was touched by his concern. They invited The Parents and me to a cocktail party at their house. As I was leaving, Hank said, "I have an idea which I would like to discuss with you over lunch, just you and me. Would you be free sometime next week?"

"Of course!" I said.

The next week we met at P.J. Moriarty's, a toney Irish pub on the southwest corner of 61st Street and Third Avenue that was distinguished from other such establishments by a little electric train that ran around the entire dining room on a track attached to the walls just below the ceiling. It didn't run continuously. You had to ask the waiter to run it. I asked to have it run every time I set foot in the place. This time was no exception. We ordered our lunch and Hank began.

"You have spent all those years wanting to be an architect and preparing to be an architect. Yes?" Hank asked.

"Yes."

"So what if half your reason for choosing architecture was to impress your mother when you were little? We all make some choices for reasons like that. You aren't alone. Right? You took all the prerequisites required to get into architecture school and you got into two of the best. Yes? Then you spent two summers in Spoleto where you got roped in by the apparent glamour of the theatre, but you worked hard and you liked it. Maybe better than liked it. Right?" He stopped while the waiter brought us our food.

"Now you've had a taste of working backstage for a two-bit off-Broadway production company and you've learned that theatre is not quite so glamorous. In fact, unless you are an aspiring starlet or an ingrained techie, it can be tedious and unrewarding. And you've tried your hand at set design but think that what you came up with is too literal. Right? So far, so good?"

"Yes, yes. Right so far. Please go on."

"Not until you eat something." I shoveled some food into my face and Hank continued.

"Why not go ahead with the architecture and specialize in theatre design? You say you may not be creative enough to be a good architect? Maybe you aren't. I wouldn't know. But what counts in theatre design is not what a theatre looks like. What matters is that the building has to work for the performers, the crew and technicians, and the audience—three equally important groups with totally different interests in the process and the final product. In addition, once the house lights go down, the design of the theatre

Part 4: La Vita Dolce-Amara

interior mustn't be so creative that it upstages or otherwise detracts from what's happening on stage. Are you with me?"

"Yes, very much so."

"Then eat!"

"Okay. How about you eat, too?"

He took a few bites and continued. "If you are good at solving problems, you'll know how to make theatres that work. You'll be a natural. Very few young architects coming out of grad school will have the experience in theatre that you have. What do you think?"

I was floored. I hardly knew this man, but he had me completely figured out, and had created, from what I felt was chaos, a clear path for me to follow, a direction to pursue that was in synch with who I was, what interested me, and what I wanted to be. I wonder if he learned about architecture from directing *Mr. Blandings Builds His Dream House*. Probably not.

Re-enter John Everett Lippmann.

The first time I had seen John Lippmann was at the John Hay Library at Brown in my freshman year. Sandy Bull had come to visit me and brought with him his good friend from the Woodstock School. John had just dropped out of his second year in college in Peoria, Illinois, and was hanging out with Sandy, who was studying music in Boston and furthering his acquaintance with all manner of narcotics. I thought John was the ugliest young man I had ever seen: tall, gawky, with a smallish head, a simian face partially obscured by coke-bottle glasses, flanked with large jowls set atop a thick and furry neck. I couldn't believe that Sandy could have dragged this creature to our get-together. But he had.

John Lippmann and I met again from time to time thereafter, either with Gael McManus, who had also gone to Woodstock, or with Sandy, and John and I slowly became fast friends. John lived with his family on Central Park West. He was the son of Zilla Hymes, a founder of the New Dramatists Guild, from whom John acquired his looks, and Alfred Lippmann, a successful advertising executive who resembled an aristocratic Bob Hope, from whom John acquired his grace. Although John was less than handsome, he was very well coordinated, astonishingly lithe, and very funny. While he was dyslexic at a time when this affliction was barely recognized, his visual sensibilities were extraordinarily refined. While I was dealing with my depression, John was working for Grey Advertising. We fed each other's interests and enthusiasm for all things visual, edible, and potable. He loved my sense of design, which I didn't know I already had, and was particularly taken by my calligraphic skills. He gave me small freelance lettering jobs to do for Grey while teaching me everything he knew about typography and graphic design. Every so often he would invite me out for lunch at some smart restaurant. He would drink two or three martinis and I would down two Bloody Marys. I couldn't imagine returning to work with all that booze under my belt. But I wasn't the one who was working.

During that same period, I also became seriously interested in opera. Working on *Vanessa* had opened the door. I had been dragged to opera at City Center in my teenage years; now I wanted only to attend performances at the Met, which I deemed "the real thing." This was the old Met at 39th Street and Broadway, in the heart of what was then the Garment District. I rarely had enough money to buy two tickets, nor did I know many people interested in paying their own way. So I went on my own. I concentrated on Mozart, Verdi, Rossini, and Richard Strauss, seeing many operas for the first time and some that I had seen before but had not appreciated. I still couldn't manage Puccini; I couldn't get beyond the horror I'd felt as a child at the outcome of the final act of *Madame Butterfly*. I enjoyed "Wagner lite" (*Die Meistersinger* and *Tannhauser*)

Part 4: La Vita Dolce-Amara

but after standing through most of *Götterdammerung*, I gave up on ever being comfortable with *The Ring* or *Parsifal*. I was determined to introduce my sisters to opera. Step one was to buy tickets for Judy and me to a New Year's Eve performance of *La Traviata*.

At a party just after Christmas I had met Oswald Johnston, the older brother of Johnst, my first serious love. Oswald was the first male I had met in some time that ignited a spark in me. He was on vacation from Yale, where he was getting a doctorate in English, and wanted to see me before he went back to New Haven.

"Might you be free for New Year's Eve?" he asked.

"No, I am taking my younger sister to *La Traviata*. But maybe you'd like to stop by for a drink after the opera, even though it will be quite late?"

"Yes, I'd like that. What time do you think?"

"Around midnight."

"That would be fine. See you then."

The doorbell rang. Oswald climbed the two flights of stairs, looked deeply into my eyes (through both our myopic lenses), and embraced me warmly. I had the lights low, a bottle of cognac and two brandy snifters ready. We sat at opposite ends of the green velvet sofa, and the phone rang. It was my mother.

"We can see the lights are still on in your bedroom, and we heard footsteps on the stairs. It's very late. What's going on?"

"I got back from the opera a while ago. Judy is downstairs."

"Yes, we know. But is someone with you?"

I hesitated. "Yes. I met Bob Johnston's brother Oswald a couple of days ago, and there was no chance for us to see each other before he goes back to Yale, so I asked him to stop by for a drink."

"At this hour, you are entertaining a man in your apartment?"

"Yes. I am twenty-two, after all."

My mother passed the phone to Hans who continued, "If this

Oswald Johnston is so important to you that you have to meet him at this hour, then we should all get to know one another. Your mother and I will be right up."

With some embarrassment, I explained to Oswald that my parents were on their way and I was sorry our evening might not be as we had imagined. Within minutes, The Parents arrived in their bathrobes, with their two new Chow dogs, each on a leash, and their own brandy bottle and snifters. They sat down on the two easy chairs opposite us, as though their arrival at 12:45 a.m. was totally appropriate. Hans then started in on Oswald as though he were asking for my hand in marriage. Where was he born? Who were his parents? Where did he live? What schools had he attended? What were his interests? What was the subject of his thesis?

When Hans felt he had garnered enough information, he stood up. "It's a pleasure to meet you, Oswald," he said. "But it's very late and I think we should all be leaving. Come, Barby. Come, Suki. Come, Ching." He helped my mother to her feet, gathered up the leashes, the cognac, and their glasses, and ushered my mother, the dogs, and Oswald to the door.

"Happy New Year!" Hans called out gaily as they all descended the stairs.

Happy New Year, indeed!

Propelled by the new direction that Hank Potter had given to my career, I called the Columbia School of Architecture to find out if there were any courses I could take to prepare for my enrollment at Penn the following fall. I was told this was an unusual request and I would have to talk to Dean Kenneth Smith in person. I made an appointment to see him and took the subway up to Avery Hall on the Columbia campus. Dean Smith was a tall, bald, thinnish, and slightly stooped older gent who was an engineer, not an architect.

Part 4: La Vita Dolce-Amara

Although the nominal dean of the school was Charles Colbert, an architect from New Orleans, Dean Smith seemed to be running the show. He greeted me cordially enough, but was a man of few words.

"There's no such thing as signing up for one or two classes. You will have to make a full application, which will include your academic record and a portfolio. You want to take just one or two classes? Maybe we can work this out, but you have to submit a full application."

"And a portfolio? Just for one or two classes?"

"And a portfolio. Here's the application. We need to have everything within a week if your request for the spring term is to be considered."

"Thank you, sir," I said, and took my leave.

A portfolio?

Okay, what the hell. It was just going to be a few classes, so I wouldn't make a fool of myself at Penn. I went to work on the portfolio. I had images of my calligraphy done at RISD. Also from RISD, I had examples of my drafting—photographs of a 3-D model I had made of a Maltese cross, indicating the principles of two-point perspective, and one or two barely-passable life drawings. I had photos of the lamp I had made from the poem George McCully had written to Emily. I had images of some architectural paintings from my high school years, and the series of quasi-Chinese miniature watercolors representing the Creation which I had done for Walter Feldman's class at Brown. And I had the drawings and the model for the stage set. I organized this material, bound it, telephoned the registrar at Brown, who agreed to send my transcript to Columbia by special delivery, and completed the application. Six days later, I hand delivered the application and the portfolio to Avery Hall.

January was a month of waiting. My spirit had lifted somewhat, but the psoriasis was stubbornly persistent. There were now more angry spots and dots than there were ugly patches, which was better than the reverse, but still not pretty. I caught up with Marilla van Beuren, whom I hadn't seen for several years, and deepened my friendship with John Lippmann, who started me on a paying calligraphy job for Revlon, which was a welcome distraction. Lipp was fast becoming my closest friend.

Earlier in the fall, I had been smitten by Cesare Siepi singing *Don Giovanni* and became even more deeply so when I met him at a cocktail party at Big Lorna Livingston's and discovered he had the endearing (to my ears) Northern Italian affliction of being unable to roll his r's (same as Freddie). When I saw he was singing Figaro in *The Barber of Seville*, I took Pago, who was just twelve, to a matinee, which she professed to enjoy (though I am not sure she has been to the opera since).

I started seeing Oswald on a regular basis. His family was sufficiently eccentric that he had not been put off by The Parents' performance on New Year's Eve. When his studies permitted, Oswald would come in from New Haven and stay with his widowed father, Oswald Sr., at 941 Park. Oswald took me to a series of cocktail and dinner parties in Greenwich Village, which were populated by various New York literary luminaries. As much as I enjoyed rubbing shoulders with celebrities, I wasn't well enough read to appreciate the company Oswald was keeping, and said company had little interest in me. On the other hand, Oswald had opened up yet another sector of New York that I was beginning to know. My New York was coming to be much more than the one in which I'd grown up. It was an exciting place to live. The thought of moving to Philadelphia, which I likened to Providence, was becoming less appealing. But Penn was the best school in the East, and I had been admitted. So Philadelphia it would be.

The call from Columbia came. I was to meet with Dean Smith

immediately. Once again, he cut right to the chase. "Good morning, Miss Armstrong. You have been approved to take classes here this spring so you can go to Penn in the fall."

"That's wonderful, thank you, sir." My stomach churned with relief and excitement.

"But I have another proposition for you."

"What is that?" I asked.

"You have an excellent academic record. Adolf Placek has given you high marks." Placek? I had totally forgotten he was just downstairs at Avery Library and might speak for me. "If you can get through the second half of the first year of our program without having taken the first half, we will waive the first half and you can go onto the second year next fall."

"I don't understand."

"What I am saying is, enroll with us here at Columbia for our full program starting now. If you can make it through the second half of first-year studio, which we think you can, based on your portfolio, we will waive the first half and you can go on with the present first-year class to second-year studio in the fall. You have all the art and architectural history and humanities credits you need. However, you will be a course behind in the structural sequence. The present first-year class took Statics in the fall and is taking Strength of Materials now. You will have to take Statics now and Strength of Materials over the summer to catch up. Do you understand?"

"I think so, Dean Smith. But it is a lot to consider. May I go home and discuss this with my parents and then get back to you?"

"Yes, but make it snappy," he said gruffly. "The spring semester starts in nine days."

"Yes, sir."

It had never occurred to me to go to Columbia. There was no Louis Kahn there to lead us into the future of architecture, no

Paul Rudolph with his brutal concrete vocabulary, who was dean at Yale. In fact, there was next to no one other than Kenneth Smith at Columbia. On the other hand, Columbia was in New York, not Philadelphia. I wouldn't lose the time I had spent trying my hand in theatre and set design. And maybe I would do better at a lesser school. Maybe Columbia would be slower than Penn to discover how little talent I had. Maybe I could more easily scrape by at Columbia.

On Wednesday, February 6, 1963, I joined the undergraduate class of aspiring architects at Columbia University. Some of us already had bachelor's degrees. Many did not. I was the fifth girl in a class of around thirty-five. Better yet, a bonus I hadn't even considered: because Hans was on the faculty of Columbia College of Physicians and Surgeons, my tuition was free.

21. Getting On

NEW YORK — FEBRUARY 1963

Avery Hall, Columbia University—home of the Graduate School of Architecture, Planning and Preservation.

The design studios were on the top two floors of Avery Hall and had windows on all three sides. They were flooded with light like my senior homeroom at Brearley. I was shown to a large wooden drafting table that was to be my home base and introduced to a fellow student who accompanied me to Construction, our first class, which didn't seem too daunting. After class, I set up my parallel rule (I had only used a T-square for drafting at RISD) and stowed the rest of my equipment: mechanical pencils; skinny boxes of leads; triangular architectural and engineering scales; thirty-degree, forty-five-degree, and adjustable triangles; a protractor; a compass; a handheld lead point sharpener; white erasers; an erasing shield; a roll of masking tape; and an eighteen-inch roll of yellow tracing paper. I found something to eat on Amsterdam Avenue and returned at 2:00 p.m., in time for the first meeting of first-year studio, second semester.

A new lounge space had recently been carved from the attic above the studios. There, our half of the first-year studio class convened to receive from our critic (or teacher of design) the "program" for the project we were to execute during the first half of the semester. (The other half of the class received their assignment from their critic elsewhere.) A solidly built, middle-aged man in a slightly rumpled grey suit, unremarkable tie, and white shirt brought the session to order. He had a pleasant face; a beak of a nose; and heavily-oiled, wavy, silver hair, with a long forelock that he repeatedly pushed back from his forehead as he spoke. Everyone knew who he was, because they'd had had him the previous semester. He distributed copies of the multi-page program for our project. We were to design a new beach club on an ocean site in Westhampton Beach, toward the eastern end of Long Island. The program contained information about building on beach-front property; the behavior of the ocean, tides, and currents in that vicinity; and a digest of local zoning ordinances and applicable building codes. It listed the spaces to be included and the number and sizes of these spaces, which ranged from a single large multi-purpose assembly space to many tiny bathing cabanas. And it noted the special considerations or requirements for each type of space, such as its need for extra height, for special equipment, or adjacency to another space or spaces.

Terrifying.

After announcing the basics of the project, Mr. Silverhair started to go through the material in detail. My stomach tightened further. I couldn't understand what he was talking about. Nothing. Not because he was foreign and had an accent but because his sentences didn't seem to have verbs and nouns in the right places. They didn't go from A to B to C. He spoke with great excitement but in an irregular rhythm of random phrases and snippets. I kept trying to match the printed words in the program with the words spurting erratically from his mouth. I got nowhere. All the other students seemed rapt.

I couldn't wait for this nightmare to end. No such luck. Studio lasted from 2:00 to 6:00 p.m. three times a week, Monday, Wednesday, and Friday. It wasn't yet 3:00 p.m. We were to return to the studio, and he would come by our desks and answer any further questions, one on one. By the time he reached my desk, I was visibly shaking. There was no way I was going to be able to do this. No fucking way.

"You must be Miss Armstrong," he said when he arrived at my desk. "I am Alexander Kouzmanoff, first-year design critic." We shook hands.

"Pleased to meet you, sir," I choked out.

Professor Kouzmanoff looked none too pleased to meet me. "I understand I am to take you on and get you through this year even though you haven't had the first semester Design Studio."

"That's what Dean Smith said." Although he wasn't rude, he was so clearly unhappy that this task had been laid on him that all I wanted to do was to apologize for disrupting his teaching routine and vanish.

"Well," he said, matter-of-factly and without rancor, "I guess we'll both have to make the best of it."

Although I wanted to be sick every time I came to Studio for the next few weeks, I slowly learned to make sense of the way Kouzmanoff talked, to learn from him how to organize the program elements so I could try different ways of grouping them that might result in a rational plan, and, eventually, the beginnings of three-dimensional building forms. I watched with awe how he'd take the roll of yellow tracing paper from a student's hand, lay it over whatever he or she had drawn or sketched, and rework it this way and that within the context of what the student was trying to do, not the way he, Alexander Kouzmanoff, might do it were it his design. He was a genius as a teacher. A favorite among students, he was known as "The Kouz."

I didn't assimilate well with my fellow students, who were already a tightly-knit group. Maybe they thought I was an imposter. Maybe I found them unsophisticated. Maybe both. While Design Studio was brutal, the course work (Construction, Graphics, Statics and Urban Sociology) was less than challenging. Attendance was mandatory. On the theory that sharing problems and seeing each other's work would help develop our design skills, we were supposed to be present for the full length of the studio sessions. Many students practically lived in the studio. It was their home.

It was never mine.

I spent as little time as possible at school. I was too ashamed of how badly I sketched out my thinking, and of the thinking itself, to want anyone to see my work. While I made an appearance at every studio session, I only stayed when I knew it would be my turn for a crit from The Kouz or when we all had to pin up our sketches and drawings for a progress crit (an agonizing experience). This pattern of absence enabled me to maintain some contact with my Spoletini friends and spend occasional weekends in New Haven, although my enthusiasm for Oswald was on the wane. I reduced my sessions with Spiegel to twice weekly, and my psoriasis continued to flourish. I struggled with design late into most nights at the drafting table my mother had procured from Neil Fergusson. There I felt safe.

Over time, I made a few friends. The first was Gil Boro, who reminded me slightly of John Lippmann, although he was better looking. Gil had a deep voice and a husky laugh, and he found almost everything funny, including failure. Gil wasn't one of the design stars, so I wasn't intimidated by him. Another guy I related to was Dan Hollis. Dan was tallish, thin, with dark disorderly hair and olive skin. He had a boyish quality, enhanced by a chipped front tooth. Like Gil, he was Jewish, but hailed from Omaha and had the accent to prove it. He was clearly very bright and probably more talented as a designer than Gil or I, but he was mentally all over the place. Dan could also laugh at anything, but his laughter was tinged with irony and sometimes sadness, as though he knew something that we did not. I also liked Stanton Lyman, a diminutive young man with a heavy Boston accent. Stan prided himself on being curmudgeonly, and swore he ate lemon and ground glass every morning to maintain his ill humor. He thought the architecture of Mies van der Rohe was God given, and every project Stan designed was executed in Mies's elegant steel-and-glass vocabulary. Of the four other girls in the class, the stars were Peggy Woodring and Elizabeth Spang. I was close to neither. Nor was I close to the male stars, Bernie Cywinski and Ben Mendelsund. If design can be likened to poetry, they were our class poets. But it would be a while before I would think of the design process as akin to writing poetry.

My finished drawings for the beach club were less than stellar, but adequate. I passed. Our second design project for the spring semester had something to do with theatre. With The Kouz's unflagging help, I did slightly better. The program elements and their requirements were familiar to me, as Hank Potter had said they would be. Still, architectural design was a totally new language, in which I was neither gifted nor even facile.

The previous fall, while still in academic limbo, I had renewed my friendship with Marilla van Beuren. In the intervening years, she had not gone to college but had taken courses in public health at Columbia and then married an "appropriate young man" from the Newport set who turned out not to be so appropriate, as he was a drunk and physically abusive. She had also become ravishingly beautiful in an understated way, with her tall, athletic build, perfectly proportioned torso, and dark bobbed hair framing her long, aristocratic face. She had been divorced for some time when we re-met, and was seeing a new man, Jan Bubela, a hunky, tall, dark, smarmy Hungarian jetsetter. Jan was my first exposure to Euro-Trash. Marilla—gorgeous, loaded, and lost—was easy prey. They (she) had bought a large apartment in an elegant pre-war building on Sutton Place and she was fixing it up, no expense spared. God only knew what Bubela was doing—some kind of banking? The wedding was to be at Grey Craig on Saturday, June 15. No big deal. Second time round. Would I come? Of course.

Romantically, I wasn't doing much better than Marilla. By mid-semester, Oswald and I had run out of steam, and a tall, WASPy young man from the fourth-year studio started to hang around my desk. Chris was tall and thin, my kind of attractive, especially when accompanied by intelligence and literacy—plus he spoke better French than I did. Good thing, because upon graduation he was headed to Fontainbleau to study architecture with Nadia Boulanger. (I thought then that only musicians went to study with Boulanger.) Chris was also reputed to be a gifted designer with a fine hand. Apart from the French, I had none of his skills, and was hoping some of his attributes might rub off on me. Chris thought himself a Lothario, and one afternoon he left a long-stemmed dark red rose on my drafting board. I didn't pick up on the Lothario aspect, I just saw the rose. I fell like a stone.

Der Rosencavalier!

Bedding me took no time at all. But it turned out that Der Rosencavalier had a firmly entrenched Fräulein Rosencavalier elsewhere, and I was just a diversion. He was sexy and very good at stringing me along, which made for a miserable spring. After Columbia's graduation, Der Rosencavlier took off for France.

Soon after, as if as a reward for getting through my first semester at Columbia, my mother's friend Edgar Kaufmann invited me to come, sans parents, to Fallingwater for a weekend. Over the eight years since my first visit, I had become close both to Edgar and to his companion and friend Paul Mayèn, and I was honored to be invited there on my own. On the appointed Friday, I went to Edgar's apartment at 450 East 52nd Street, where I was introduced to John and Betty McAndrew, an older couple who would also be weekend guests. We were driven to Newark Airport, from which we flew to Pittsburgh, courtesy of Edgar. In Pittsburgh, we were met by a driver and arrived at Bear Run after 11:00 p.m.

John and Betty were as charming and intellectual as Edgar. John trained as an architect but became a museum curator early on. He had curated the Museum of Modern Art's first exhibit on Fallingwater upon its completion in 1938, which is presumably how he and Edgar became acquainted. By the time I met the McAndrews, they were living part-time in Venice but were both active in the house's restoration and preservation. The conversation over the weekend ranged from art to art history to architecture, ancient and modern, and also included literature, politics, and world affairs. Although laced with keen witticisms, it was so elevated that it was almost exhausting. I felt very much out of my league. But Edgar and Paul were consummate hosts and assured me in their way that I was holding my own. Being at Fallingwater again was like living a dream.

Marilla's wedding to the Hungarian hunk took place the following weekend. Going from Fallingwater in Bear Run, Pennsylvania, to Grey Craig in Middletown, Rhode Island, was going from one sublimity to another. The commodious library at Grey Craig was packed with close friends and family, many of whom I knew. Marilla and Jan were facing the clerical officiant, who had his back to the carved marble mantle at the center of room. I scanned the hundreds of leather-bound books that lined the floor-to-ceiling shelves flanking the chimney breast and between the tall windows, and wondered about their content. When I looked back at the fireplace, I noticed that Rembrandt was looking at me.

There was a self-portrait of Rembrandt van Rijn over the mantle!

My eyes scanned the room for further treasures. On an easel to the left of the mantle there was Rembrandt's *Hundred Guilder* etching, and on another to the right was an etching by Goya so dark that I couldn't make out the subject. All this art in this room, and I'd noticed none of it before. Why? Because in previous years I had never dared raise my eyes above my shoes. Anyway, back then I wouldn't have known a Rembrandt from a Picasso. What else was in the house that I'd never noticed?

Marilla invited me back to Grey Craig the summer after she and the hunk had separated. The van Beurens had cocktails in a little paneled sitting room off their bedroom. The portrait of Mr. van Beuren's mother standing in front of their house in Boca Grande, holding her favorite Pekinese in her arms, still hung over the fire place, but this time I noticed a small Sisley, a Signac, and an Utrillo interspersed between other canine portraits on the other walls. I was gobsmacked and wanted to know all about how they had come to be there.

After dinner, both Mr. and Mrs. van Beuren staggered up the stairs to the attic to dig out the files relating to the procurement of the art. I learned that the large, sprawling landscape over the sideboard in the dining room was a van Ruysdael. There was a bill of sale for a Franz Hals portrait that I finally found hidden in the gloom over the door to the servants' wing, and another for a Fragonard which I never located.

The biggest news of all was that years after its acquisition, the Rembrandt self-portrait had been pronounced a fake. The Knoedler Gallery had offered to take it back and restore to the family the funds they had paid for it. But the van Beurens decided they rather liked it anyway. And so it remained. We strolled down the long glass gallery that led from the dining room, passed the ballroom and the Chinese Room, and went into the library to have another look at

Part 4: La Vita Dolce-Amara

the Rembrandt. It was stunning. As we were leaving to return to the little sitting room for highballs, I picked a leather-bound book from one of the shelves to have a look, then another, and a third and a fourth. The van Beurens had had their children's prep school and college notes and papers leather bound for posterity. These were the volumes that kept company with Goya and with Rembrandt!

In order to join the second-year class in the fall, I had to take Strength of Materials over the summer at City College. CCNY's Strength of Materials was more intense and difficult than Columbia's, as it was geared towards engineers rather than architects, but Dean Smith felt certain I could manage it. Little did he know of the blood and sweat I had expended to get through Intermediate Calculus. Strength of Materials (CE 110) began in mid-June and ended eight weeks later, in early August. It dealt with such concepts as Hooke's Law (stiffness in springs); tension, torsion, compression, shear, bending, moment, compound stress, deflection, buckling, and experimental elasticity (whatever that was)—all things relating to the behavior of materials used in construction. The material covered was interesting, but the process of learning it was tedious and exacting. We met for three hours several mornings a week. There were mountains of homework, full of the kinds of calculations that I always mangled by reversing digits and dropping decimal places. That I spent most nights drinking with my friends and was hungover most mornings didn't help. We did our endless computations using slide rules. I had a twenty-inch K&E mahogany-and-faux-ivory slide rule, like the one Howie had had when I was a little girl in Boston. Mine was a gift from Hans. It had fewer functions, but enough for my purposes, and it was a sleek and beautiful instrument. The closest I got to a conversation with anyone in my class was when one young man asked if I thought my twenty-inch slide rule would get me extra credit for extra decimal places.

Over the summer, Deric Washburn reappeared. His girlfriend was no longer in the picture and he had some interest in picking up where we had left off. Drink was a big component of our relationship, and this has dulled my recall of the specifics of our reunion. But we must have resumed sleeping together, otherwise we wouldn't have had so many summer dinners with The Parents, who liked Deric (same block in ...). Just before I was to take the final exam at CCNY, Deric and I had yet another boozy dinner with my parents. My mother seemed to need just one more "divvy" before heading downstairs, and I trailed behind to haul the platter of cold meat, the bowl of salad, and the little jar of dressing out of the fridge. Hans was probably going through a mood shift, which often occurred between drinks and dinner. He'd make (more or less) perfect sense through cocktails—that is, if my mother gave him a chance to speak—then, after dinner, he would expound insane theories about people or art or politics or science or whatever. My sisters and I wrote this off as Hans demonstrating how clever and brilliant he was: our own mad scientist and poet. It didn't occur to me until I was way older that the madness was the work of drink.

Deric was beginning to feel quite at home with The Parents, maybe more so with them than with me. That evening, when Hans and Deric came downstairs to table, Hans filled our wine glasses almost to the brim and then started questioning Deric, much as he had done with Oswald Johnston. Who was he, really? And what were his life goals in addition to writing plays? The questions were posed gently at first, then at an accelerated pace, like shots from a semi-automatic weapon, in a tone that became more strident and combative. At this point my memory has checked out. But the entry in my Featherweight diary for Friday, August 2, reads:

Part 4: La Vita Dolce-Amara

"Deric came over around 8:00. All went well, then ALL-TIME HORROR SHOW. Time to leave!" ... and find a place of my own.

Five days later, I passed the final in CE 110, and had goodbye drinks with Deric, which made me both nervous and sad, as I figured (correctly) that I'd never see him again after the recent evening with The Parents. I flew to Rome to spend the Ferragosto holidays with Giada and Giulietta and their friends. I also wanted to visit Milan and its cathedral, about whose bizarre geometry I had written for Henri's class, and to see the Guarini churches in Turin, about which I had written in my honors thesis.

During the spring, I had reconnected with Adolf Placzek, who persuaded me to expand my thesis—on the interrelationship between the development of mathematics and architectural form to cover periods before and after the Baroque—in lieu of taking run-of-the-mill humanities courses, a certain number of which were required to fill up my dance card. I was honored to work with Placzek again, and the administration approved the substitution. Like others before him, Placzek was hoping I would become a scholar rather than an architect and was convinced the thesis I was pursuing was of academic merit and worthy of publication. I loved Placzek for his modesty and erudition and even more for his warmth and humor. Over the next few years, under his direction, I wrapped up the Middle Ages and the Renaissance, but found that my hypothesis fell apart after the 17th century. Mathematics had become far too complex, and likewise its embodiment of divine principles. And the origins and metaphoric significance of architectural form and proportion, at least as expressed in ecclesiastical architecture, were too diverse to analyze and quantify in this manner. I was sorry to let Dolf down.

GETTING ON

ROME AND MILAN — AUGUST 1963

I stayed once again with Giada and Giulietta, and Marghe restored to me the use of my VW. Giada, Giada's new beau, Giulietta, Freddie, and the Patriarcas made a plan for us to go to the Argentario. Our little holiday was like a continuous loop from a bad Italian movie. Giada and her beau had rarely been able to spend serious time together, so they wanted to be alone but felt guilty about it. Giulietta wouldn't give Freddie the time of day, and Freddie was despondent. I tried to comfort him while attempting to keep my own obsession with him at bay. Lots of sitting in restaurants and cafes waiting for someone to show up. Angry words when they did or didn't. Probably not much sex going on either. After a week, I left them all in Port Ercole and took off on my own, driving my VW, top down, for Milan. Freddie arranged for me to stay at his parents' house, which was not far from the Ippodromo San Siro. He would be coming the next day. A housekeeper would be there to receive me, as his parents and brothers were in the mountains. Very kind. I accepted. None of us stayed in hotels if we could help it.

Even though it was Ferragosto, Milan, unlike Rome, was bustling. The stores were open and alive. The Duomo was squat, unlike its lofty northern Gothic counterparts, but just as complex and majestic. Low-cost housing, to accommodate the families coming to Milan from all over the country to partake of the industrial boom in Northern Italy, was sprouting up everywhere. The buildings were full of color and invention—balconies projecting here, angled roofs there—unlike the brown brick, faceless blocks of our low-income projects in New York.

The night Freddie arrived we went to a trattoria in his neighborhood for dinner. When we returned to his house, he led me directly to his room and we fell into bed as we had first in Spoleto and then

Part 4: La Vita Dolce-Amara

in Sardinia the year before. We made love for hours before we slept, and then again in the morning. Although Freddie did not talk about "us" or where I fit with regard to Giulietta, he was far from silent. We joked and laughed and loved. I was taken by Freddie's sprawling two-story house, which was organized like a small Roman villa around a central landscaped courtyard. My favorite feature, other than his bedroom, was the commodious, all-white bathroom we shared: white marble tiles, oversized white plumbing fixtures, heavy chrome faucets and valves. It was larger than my bedroom at home, with a floor-to-ceiling window, sheer white curtains blowing in the summer breeze, and narrow French doors opening onto a Juliet balcony overlooking a lush green side street.

The next night Freddie's father came back to town for a day of business. We were to have a cold supper at home, prepared by the housekeeper. I had been told Freddie's father was a formidable presence, stern and severe, more Prussian than Italian–unsurprisingly, as his mother was German. Although the war was long since over, Freddy's father remained a fascist and was proud of it. I was told he spoke no English and had little time for the frivolous side of life. It was he who had pushed Freddie into engineering. Freddie seemed apprehensive about our spending an evening together. But how bad could it be if he was Freddie's father?

We convened in the family living room around 8:00 p.m. Freddie introduced us, and I apologized for my tentative Italian. Signor Roccati was tall, portly, and yes–imposing. White hair slicked back off his forehead, very Prussian at first glance. He asked me what sort of aperitif I wanted, or would I prefer something stronger, a whiskey perhaps? Before I could answer, he went on to ask about American cocktails. Had I heard of the "martini dry"? Yes, I had. I explained in my best Italian that it was mother's milk in our family. Could I make one for him? Yes, indeed. All I needed was decent gin, dry vermouth, ice, and either a lemon from which to cut some peel or a supply of olives. Like a kid on an adventure, Freddie's father led me to the kitchen, where we foraged for the ingredients. I found three stem glasses and put them in the tiny freezer to chill while I extracted a few miniscule ice cubes from the doll-sized rubberized ice tray and mixed the drinks. The gin loosened Freddie's father's tongue and he talked to us about politics, particularly Italian politics (about which I understood very little), his role during the war, the trends in industrial growth in the north of Italy vs. stagnation in the south, and so on. It was a wonderful evening. Even Freddie enjoyed himself.

Freddie and I spent five gorgeous days in Milan. For the weekend we drove to Venice. Freddie had never been. Giada told us to stay at the Hotel della Fenice, next to the Teatro della Fenice, which had not yet burned to the ground. She said that's where all the musicians and theatre people stay when they come to Venice. Our room was bathed in lemon-yellow light and overlooked a small canal barely wide enough for two gondolas to pass. We had yet another magical pair of days, wandering the streets and the Campi of that extraordinary city (which I hadn't appreciated at all when I was there with my mother, Jane Carey, and the poodle ten years before).

On our return to Milan there was a stack of messages for Freddie from Giulietta. He was preoccupied. I was upset.

Why didn't we talk it through? In part because I knew Freddie's obsession with Giulietta was a life commitment and also because my Italian wasn't good enough to express the subtleties and complexities of how I felt. In Italian, I was a nice girl, semi-cultured, sort of amusing, but I had no edge. I couldn't curse as I cursed in English. You need to know a language well to understand, maximize, and enjoy the effect of blasphemy and smut. Saying "shit" in Italian meant nothing to me (although I loved the word "stronzo" which means "a piece of shit," a word often used in Italian to describe a

Part 4: La Vita Dolce-Amara

person). Without being able to express my unhappiness, which was not jealousy but sheer pain, I took off in my VW for Turin to see, at last, the Guarini churches of my thesis.

Turin has been called the Boston of Italy. But its scale is very different. Boston's historic center is diminutive. Turin, although not a big city, is grand, more like a small Paris. It is Bostonian only because it is austere in spirit compared to other Italian cities. I knew no one in Turin to stay with, so I booked into the Pensione Europa near the center of town.

The next day I took in the gently undulating façade of the Palazzo Carignano and revisited Guarini's two most famous churches, both chapels buried in the midst of larger building complexes. They were everything I had expected them to be. The chapel of San Lorenzo, the dome of which was allegedly modeled on the Alahambra in Seville, was a marvel of distended parabolas intersecting to form an organic tracery of light and form. The geometry of the dome of the Santissimi Sidone, which houses the shroud of Turin, generates a lacework of shapes that could have been created by Gaudi, had Guarini's overriding geometry been less rigid.

Freddie wasn't home when I got back to his house in Milan. He returned later in the evening and told me Giulietta had asked him to come to Rome to see her. He was leaving in the morning but would be back on Sunday. I could stay on as long as I liked.

If I'd been able to speak my mind in Italian, I would have said something like:

You dumb fuck! You are going to throw away the kind of time you and I have had together and are capable of having in the future because Giulietta wags her finger? Don't you get it? She's just toying with you. She doesn't want you, but she doesn't want anyone else to have you either. You know what you are to her? You are her stop-gap, her safety net. She can do anything she likes with anyone she likes because she knows that in the end you'll be there! She whistles, you come like the old dog you are. Asshole!

However, my tongue was tied. I repaired to my room, slept alone, and took off the next morning for Santa Margherita Ligure, the resort town east of Genoa, where I had first fallen in love with Italy. It wasn't quite as sweet as I remembered it, so I drove on to Portofino, which had not changed perceptibly other than having become even more chic. I checked into a modest pensione, got to my room, and checked my wallet to see how much cash I had remaining for this little junket. I found I could only afford the hotel, maybe a drink, but definitely no dinner. There were no credit cards then, only travelers' cheques. I had left my stash back at Freddie's. Fortunately, I had enough gas to get back to Milan. If I was going to eat, I was going to have to get picked up by someone who would buy me dinner but not require any additional services. I'd never done anything like this before. So I wandered around the little town, looking for a not-overly-upscale café with a bar, where I could sit nursing the one drink I could afford in hopes of being joined by some respectable type who would eventually stake me to a meal.

My situation was further complicated by a new and growing physical discomfort. I wanted to pee, but when I got to a toilet, nothing would happen, but the nothing happening stung like hell. But I didn't have time to worry about that. I found the right sort of bar, ordered an extra dry gin martini on the rocks, and wrapped my legs tightly around the shaft of the bar stool in hopes that my grip on the stool would relieve the stinging ache.

It didn't.

Well before I'd finished my decoy drink, a nicely dressed man in a raw silk shirt and pleated linen trousers, maybe ten years older than I, medium height, medium build, thinning brown hair, nothing special (which was good) asked if he could join me. You bet!

We talked. I did my bit about being an American, having worked in Spoleto, now studying architecture in New York and in Italy on holiday. Eventually he asked if I were free for dinner. Oh, yes, I might be. In fact, yes, I was.

Over dinner my companion asked how I had first come to Italy and I told him about my crossing on the *Andrea Doria*, how much I admired the design of the ship and how I wept when she went down. He visibly opened up. He was from Genoa himself and was a family friend of Piero Calamai, the *Andrea Doria*'s captain both on her maiden voyage in 1953 and again when, in July 1956, she collided with the *Stockholm* and went down in Nantucket Sound. He said that Calamai, who had been fifty-eight at the time of the sinking, admitted to having made errors in judgment that fateful night. Once the *Andrea Doria* was hit, Calamai knew immediately that she was going down. However, he also knew not to pull the abandon-ship alarm as he was legally obliged to do because she was listing so far over to one side that half her life boats were submerged and inaccessible. To avoid panic, Calamai chose to wait, in hopes that other ships would soon arrive at the scene to help with the evacuation. They did. Calamai's commitment to the safety of his passengers and crew during the evacuation was cited as exemplary. He made certain that every passenger and crew member was off the ship before he himself would leave. My companion told me that Calamai's shame was so great that he had wanted to stay on board and go down with the ship, but his officers would not let him.

Despite the sinking, Calamai was praised for his leadership, but he never went to sea again. He lived holed up in an apartment overlooking the harbor of Genoa, sustained by periodic visits from friends like my generous dinner companion until his death in 1972.

Despite the unexpected pleasure of the evening, my night at the pensione was hell. The urge to pee was excruciating, and my ability to do so decreased further. As the condition progressed, I'd find a toilet and pass a drop of two without satisfying the spasmodic urges that my bladder was generating. In the morning, I drove back to Milan through pouring rain, legs clenched together, arriving midday Sunday. No sign of Freddie. I took my urinary affliction as a sign that the time had come to return to New York. There was no place for me in Freddie's life in Milan or elsewhere. Hans was in the urinary business. Surely he could put me out of my misery if I could get there fast enough. Without mentioning my affliction, I told Freddie when he eventually returned that I was flying home the next day and arranged for Marghe to collect my car again for her use over the winter. We slept apart.

The Alitalia flight was swift and uneventful. The passengers clapped when the wheels touched down, and I clapped with them. I felt emotionally drained but also relieved and proud. I'd gotten the monkey off my back.

NEW YORK — SEPTEMBER 1963

I was back at 242 East 62nd by late afternoon on Labor Day. Hans was home and not at the hospital. I described my symptoms the minute I got inside the door.

"Cystitis," he pronounced immediately, and went upstairs, returning with a vial of dark brown pills from his medical bag of tricks and a glass of water. "Honeymoon cystitis."

"What is that supposed to mean?"

"Take this now. It'll stop the burning."

"What is it?"

"Just take it. It's Piridium, an orange dye that neutralizes the acid in urine so it won't irritate you as you void."

It took effect immediately.

Part 4: La Vita Dolce-Amara

About a week after my return, I received a letter from Freddie announcing his imminent arrival. He had been working for Honeywell in Milan, and they were sending him to Toronto on business. From there he would come to visit me on the weekend in New York. He wasn't quite sure when this would happen but it would be fairly soon. Maybe the very next week.

All my resolve, my pride at having cut loose, disappeared. I was ecstatic and couldn't wait. The monkey was back, chirping and chattering away and spitting his lousy peanut shells into the air all around me.

My parents refused to have Freddie stay at the house even though they had met him the summer before, knew he was important to me and was aware that I had been invited to stay at his parents' house in Milan. Fine in Milan, but in New York, young unmarried men did not sleep under the same roof as young unmarried women. They engaged a room for Freddie (and paid for it) at the Beekman Tower Hotel at 49st Street and First Avenue, not far away.

Freddie called to say he'd be flying to New York on Friday, September 27, the day after school began. I was beside myself with excitement. I collected Freddie at the airport at dusk and drove him, top down in my latest Hillman Minx, across the Triborough Bridge, down the East River Drive, and straight to the Four Seasons bar in the Seagram Building for his first dry martini, straight-up, on American soil. Freddie was appropriately impressed. We had an all-American steak dinner at Downey's Steak House, repaired to the Beekman Towers for a drink on the terrace of the Elbow Room, and fell into bed in his room. On Saturday, we spent the day sightseeing. We never made it back to the Beekman that night, but slept instead in my bed in my apartment. This time I had the wit not to turn the lights on.

We spent a rainy Sunday at home with The Parents. Mid-afternoon

I drove him back to LaGuardia for his flight to Toronto—devastated yet again. But mid-week he called from Toronto, saying he'd be coming back the next Friday. I didn't tell The Parents this time. I just snuck him into my apartment. I took him on a tour of Bloomingdale's, as I wanted him to experience American retail at its most garish. We went to the Museum of Modern Art and then up to the top of the Empire State Building. After dinner with Spoleto friends, I took him downtown to hear Thelonius Monk. I had never cottoned to jazz, but Monk is different, especially solo Monk.

It was perfection being with Freddie in my city and sensing him take pleasure in what I most loved about New York. Our rhythm together was easy and natural, except when one of us (usually he) got melancholic. But by the Sunday of that weekend, I lost it. I couldn't believe that, once more, this was all about to end, again. He could say nothing to comfort me. I knew the game and he knew the game. I was inconsolable. By mid-afternoon I was in such a state that I couldn't wait to take him to the airport so I could begin the process of grieving and then healing, yet again.

I began fixating on the concept of repeating patterns, something that Spiegel was trying to get through to me. Four times in a row, I had fallen for guys who belonged to someone else: Henri, Deric, Chris, and Freddie (not to mention Dan Kushner). Each relationship had put me through my own personal hell in a different way. Didn't I see the pattern? If I did, I ignored it. As soon as Freddie beckoned, I opened my arms so I could be flattened yet again. When and how would I learn to make better choices?

Freddie called from Canada the next day to be sure I was all right. He was gentle and caring on the phone. That was half the problem, Freddie was no *stronzo*.

SUMMERS 1958 AND 1959

Shirley Simmonds, my third cousin once removed, but more my "second mum."

Manor Farm, the Simmonds farm in the New Forest just south of Southampton.

Ramsbury Manor, country estate of Lord and Lady Rootes in Wiltshire.

Hans, Pago, and me on the boat from Naples to Ischia, 1959.

Judy, Hans, and Pago on the same trip.

BROWN & MATRIMONIANA

Susie Ross and Tom Gatch dancing in Brownbrokers.

I am singing the torch song I wrote for Brownbrokers, *"C'est le Complex d'Oedipus Rex."*

John Lippmann comes to visit.

Emily Arnold, bride 1.

Joyce Reed, bride 3.

Elizabeth Diggs, bride 2.

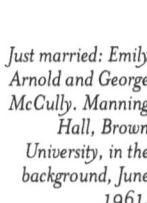

Just married: Emily Arnold and George McCully. Manning Hall, Brown University, in the background, June 1961.

Susie Ross, bride 4.

355

SPOLETO 1961

Zeiss Contaflex duel lens reflex camera given to me by Hans.

Newly arrived student of set design hard at work.

Group photo of 1961 students at the Festival of Two Worlds, Spoleto. Gian Carlo Menotti is in the back row, fourth from the right.

Samuel Barber and Gian Carlo Menotti with Eleanor Steber, who played Vanessa in the original production of **Vanessa** *which opened at the old Metropolitan Opera House in January 1958.*

TRANSITION

The Admiral and Howie, battling serum hepatitis, waiting for a train in Florida shortly before Howie's death in 1961.

Left: Gael McManus on the beach on Fire Island. Right: John Lippmann on the same beach.

Photograph taken Nov. 24, 1963 by Norman McGrath of the crowds swarming the capitol on the official Day of Mourning following John F. Kennedy's assassination.

NEW YORK AND NEWPORT

Marilla van Beuren jumping "Who Dat?"

Daphne Hellman at her harp.

Grey Craig, the van Beuren family house in Middletown, RI, as seen from the driveway.

Driving through the arch at the left of the photo above, you soon enter a gravel courtyard. The main house is to the right and the kitchen and servants' wing is to the left.

MRS. SOMEBODY

Judy and Marilla following Hans and me into St. Elizabeth's Chapel near Skylands, where I am about to marry Huey.

Huey and I emerge. The deed is done.

My mother and her brother, Mac, at the wedding reception back at home in New York.

Pago, Huey, and me licking my fingers.

Vanessa, Huey's and my daughter, and me at Sandy Walcott's Little House in Norfolk, CT.

With The Admiral at his 95th birthday party.

Sinclair, Louie's and my son.

Lafcadio, Huey's son, on the beach on Fire Island. Photo by John Lippmann.

Hans and my mother at my wedding to Louie.

John Lippmann with Sinclair and his and Judy's daughter, Sarah.

James Taylor and Carly Simon, among my first clients, at my 38th birthday party.

J. Sinclair Armstrong, Uncle "Sinc." Part brother, part uncle, and one of my best clients.

Kirsten Childs, close friend and business partner.

Hellie, Dewey's and my daughter, born subsequent to the time frame of this memoir.

EARLY WORK

Interior, the Grand Opera House, Wilmington, DE, with James R. Grieves Associates.

Pool House for Mr. and Mrs. George Backer, King's Point, Long Island, NY.

Elevated pavilion and bridge addition to Martha's Vineyard summer house.

Expansion to "dormitory" or east building, Top Masthead, Chappaquiddick Island, Edgartown, MA.

Part 5.
CHARRETTE

22. Repeating Patterns

NEW YORK — OCTOBER 1963

294 Riverside Drive, originally the home of William Baumgarten. My studio apartment was to the right of the entrance.

It was generous of my parents to give me an apartment in their house, but the situation wasn't working. I had to get out of their house.

My Andrews Sister Emily Arnold and her husband George were looking to sublet their studio apartment on the ground floor of a turn-of-the-century townhouse at 294 Riverside Drive for a year while they went abroad on George's Fulbright. I moved uptown. My mother was angry and hurt.

I felt bad, but I had to do it. And maybe being on the West Side, near Columbia, might encourage me to spend more time in the design studio.

Emily's apartment was fully furnished and equipped. All I took with me were my clothes, my drafting table with its hinged white Formica top and its base of flat files, and my drafting stool. These I placed right next to the large casement window that overlooked Riverside Park. The rent for this elegant room, the smallish foyer, and the narrow kitchen and dingy bathroom, both at the rear, was ninety-five dollars a month. Although I was mired in misery about Freddie and the continuing presence of the monkey (not to mention the mess of all those peanut shells), moving uptown on my own provided a significant lift. I loved the graceful proportions of the main room, its stone mantle and fireplace, and its eccentric, if shabby, furnishings. I loved looking through the filigree wrought-iron grille at the huge trees in Riverside Park and through them to the Hudson River. I loved having a real kitchen in which to practice my budding culinary skills and being able to have friends over as I pleased.

The course work at school was manageable, but design continued to plague me. Most architecture critics, including those assigned to our second-year studio, were practicing architects who taught on the side as adjunct professors. Few had much teaching experience and fewer still had real teaching skills. You learned from them by doing things their way. I was struggling to organize the program components and generate a reasonable plan for our first project. Our critic, Norman Hoberman, strode up to my table, looked at my layouts and said, "Miss Armstrong, you have nothing there!" and strode off. I was flattened, because he was right. There *was* nothing there.

At a nearby desk, Manuel Gerade, a student from Israel whom I had been ignoring—I thought him to be a self-important womanizer—overheard Hoberman's comment. Before I had a chance to pack up my belongings and flee the studio, he dragged his stool over in one hand and carried a roll of yellow tracing paper and a soft 6B pencil in the other.

"Let's see what you have," he said, in a slightly English accent. I didn't have the energy to tell him to push off.

"I just can't get a plan that works," I moaned.

With much the same skill that The Kouz had, Manuel lay a piece of tracing paper over my drawing and pulled together from my bits and pieces the beginnings of a viable plan.

"See what you can do with that, and then we'll see what we can do in elevation."

Over the next few weeks, Manuel continued to help me, and thanks to him I turned out a passing project. Manuel was clearly interested in our having more than a student-teacher relationship, but I was not interested. He was shortish, with a round face, and cocky as all hell. Not my type. Certainly no competition for the memory of Freddie.

John Lippmann and I continued to share our love of things visual, edible, and potable. We made dinner and played backgammon at my new apartment regularly. Lipp was fascinated by the design process that I found so difficult. When a project was due, we students spent days and nights in the studio and/or at home, *en charrette,* preparing the drawings and often a model to be presented to a final jury. In nineteenth-century Paris, the École des Beaux-Arts used to send around to the ateliers of the teachers of architecture a *charrette*, a small two-wheeled cart, to collect the drawings of its students and bring them back to the École for review. Often students would jump onto the *charrette* as it rumbled through the streets to add finishing touches to their work. Hence the term *en charrette*, which signified the last spurt of a student's effort before letting go of their project. Over time, *charrette* has evolved to its present meaning: an intense period of work involving focused and sustained effort that results in the realization of a particular project goal within a given time frame.

The guys in the class asked their girlfriends (some of whom became wives) to work on their presentation drawings and models. I had no man in my life, much less one who would stoop to help a girl *poché* her plans (*poché,* also Beaux Arts French, means applying

Part 5: CHARRETTE

color or shading between two lines) or apply Letraset (stick-on letters that came in a variety of sizes and fonts) to title her drawings. But Lipp's belief in me hadn't wavered. When a project was due, he would join me at my new apartment (accompanied sometimes by Sandy Walcott, my friend from Brown), and we would *charrette* into the night, not only *pochéing* and applying Letraset, but also wrapping heavy white vellum trace drawings around boards and gluing together models.

FRIDAY, NOVEMBER 22, 1963

News of President Kennedy's assassination ripped through the studio. Like everyone everywhere in the country, maybe in the world, we were stopped dead in our tracks. Bang. Blood everywhere. President Kennedy dead on arrival at the hospital. Lee Harvey Oswald shot by Jack Ruby soon after. Where to go? Who to talk to? Who would understand and help us handle our loss, our grief, which was of course everyone's loss and everyone's grief?

Lipp, Gael, and I had planned to get together over the weekend with some casual friends they had met recently at a rugby match in van Cortlandt Park. Despite the overwhelming events that now dominated our awareness, it was harder to dismantle the plan to meet than it was to proceed. We were all like zombies. About eight of us, including an English rugby player, convened at my apartment. We ate and drank with reserve, occasionally referring to the stunned sadness we were each feeling and its cause. We felt very close to one another. In near silence, we played Monopoly for most of the evening. The rugby player stayed the night. We slept together, although we barely knew one another. We were so involved in each other's response to Kennedy's assassination that it didn't feel frivolous or disrespectful. We stuck together as a group that whole weekend, moving from one person's apartment to the next, talking, drinking, eating, following the news on the radio or on TV, if there was one.

In early December, I invited Manuel Gerade to a performance of Bach's *Mass in B Minor* by way of thanking him for his design assistance. I knew he liked classical music, and I had never heard the *B minor* live. We went for coffee afterwards. He spoke softly and intelligently on many subjects, including himself. I found him very interesting. Maybe I had been wrong to give him such short shrift.

Manuel had been raised in South Africa during World War II. He had served in the Israeli Army, spoke several languages and knew classical music inside and out. He could whistle any Rossini overture to perfection, in key and in tempo. Manuel was funny and clearly bright, and he had already shown himself to have good design sense and an equally fine hand. That he was a self-acknowledged womanizer was intriguing, because he was physically unglamorous. When I joined the class, he was going out with the most well-heeled of the five women in our class. But that didn't last long. Maybe her Park Avenue parents went berserk about her seeing an Israeli, however cultivated he was. That may have been why Manuel turned his charms on me. The combination of his help with design and his love of classical music undid me. Ten days after hearing the *B Minor Mass* together and three days after an evening listening to Brahms symphonies at my uptown apartment, Manuel whistled me into bed. And it was nice.

I continued my two sessions a week with Spiegel. Though I didn't seem to be making much progress, Spiegel constantly reminded me that analysis took time and commitment. I also saw Dr. Baer periodically for my psoriasis, which was gone from my torso, though patches and blotches still thrived on my elbows and legs. Dr. Baer had a theory that because the cold winter air closed down the pores

Part 5: CHARRETTE

of the skin, the cortisone ointment that I was applying topically wasn't getting deep enough into the skin to do much good. He suggested that I apply the cortisone, wrap my legs in plastic wrap, and then put on opaque stockings to conceal the wrap. I was willing to try. The sores soon became less angry in that semi-tropical environment. It seemed that the remedy might be working.

One cold snowy day, I decided to walk the fifteen blocks north and two blocks east to school. I donned woolies and boots and started up the service road that runs parallel to Riverside Drive. The snow was about a foot deep, and many sidewalks had yet to be shoveled. After about six blocks, my legs felt like icicles. Yet my feet, which always get cold before any other part of my body, were warm. I ducked into the lobby of a nearby apartment building to inspect my frigid legs. The sweat generated by the plastic wrap had frozen and there was a thin layer of ice between the wrap and my skin. I waited for it to thaw and pressed on, walking until the thin layer of sweat froze yet again, at which point I headed into another apartment building lobby for another thaw. When I got to school, I headed straight for the ladies' room and removed the wrap. Enough.

In the course of the winter term, between assignments, Manuel and I listened to music together and went to the opera. We spent most evenings and nights at my place because the bathroom in his shared apartment on West 106th Street and Manhattan Avenue was infested with cockroaches. I did most of Manuel's engineering and math homework while he continued to turn out sensitive and beautifully presented solutions to our design studio assignments. Under his aegis, I struggled on with my own solutions and presentations. He told me more about his family, his heroic father, his intellectual mother (the granddaughter of Heinrich Heine), his sister, and their house in Herzliya, an upscale suburb of Tel Aviv. He conveyed to me the miracle of Israel's existence and the vision and fortitude of the people who had made it possible, and then he added that when we married and returned to Israel to live, I would have to convert to Judaism.

Married?

Convert to Judaism?

Manuel was the least observant Jew I'd ever met, and that's saying a lot, as (excepting the Sokoloskys) none of the Jewish families with whom I grew up in New York, including the Lippmanns, was observant. Furthermore, my father, having been forced to participate in what he deemed the hypocritical rituals of the Episcopal Church as a youth, had loathed all forms of organized religion and refused to have me christened. My mother had been raised by her erudite father to be areligious, partially because of his own intellectual leanings but also in recognition of the Jewish origins of his stepfather, Uncle Willie. I was religion-free and proud of it. I wasn't going to take on someone else's non-faith so as to live in a desert somewhere, however exhilarating. I wasn't going to be pushed around like that by any country, however brave and new.

The situation resolved itself when a bunch of us from school, including Gil Boro and Liz Diggs, my Andrews Sister from college, now twice-divorced, went to Killington, Vermont, for a spring ski weekend. On Saturday, when it was too icy to ski, Gil and I went for a walk. That evening, after plenty of booze, Gil told me that Manuel had whistled Liz Diggs into our bed while he and I were out. I was furious with both Manuel and Liz, but also relieved. There was no further discussion of the long term. However, it was easier for us to stay together until the end of the semester than not, at which point, because his money had run out, Manuel had to return to Israel to finish his degree at the Teknion in Haifa.

Part 5: CHARRETTE

FIRE ISLAND — SUMMER 1964

Once the school year ended, I took a bottom-of-the barrel job in the city, drafting for an architect who had gone bankrupt and was now designing very ordinary tract houses for aspirants to Hamptons living. James Leroy Riley and his dogged draftsman, a silent John Wayne type, were collectively so broke that they were occupying a portion of the cluttered and dusty Madison Avenue architectural offices of Cass Gilbert, Jr., the aged son of Cass Gilbert, Sr., who designed the Stanford University and Oberlin College campuses and the George Washington Bridge, among other treasures of American architecture. Riley couldn't pay rent, and he couldn't afford to pay for the additional drafting help he needed to grind out enough ordinary house designs to crawl out of his bankruptcy. As a girl in a man's profession, I couldn't get a paying summer job anywhere else. So I agreed to work for him for the experience, and he was willing to teach me what he knew, which was quite a lot.

John Lippmann persuaded me to take a share in a three-bedroom weekend house in The Pines on Fire Island, one of a long string of sandbars that protects the southern shore of Long Island from the ravages of the Atlantic. The Pines is almost at the center of Fire Island and adjacent to Cherry Grove, then (and now) a kitsch community of almost exclusively male and female homosexuals. The Pines was to Cherry Grove what Bergdorf Goodman is to Target. The Pines was colorful and sometimes chic. It still had a mix of straights and gays, although the gays were in the clear majority. Our house was not far from the ferry landing and the Boatel, an open-air restaurant and night spot where all the action took place. The other shareholders were friends of Lipp and of Gael McManus, who had been working for *Glamour* magazine since graduating from college. Most of them worked in the fashion industry.

My roommate was to be Annette, a glamorous German model who seemed excessively enthusiastic, first over her success at teaching me her technique for cutting up and chopping an onion (which I still employ), and then at the prospect of sharing a double bed with me. This made me nervous. I quickly looked for somewhere else to lay my head. I was introduced to another shareholder, a shy, slight, and quiet young French fashion photographer named Hillary Parterre (English mother, French father). Hillary looked a little bit like Gene Kelly, but with real hair. Hillary, known as Hill, had laid claim to a double mattress in a loft space with minimal headroom that overlooked the open living room. Although the ventilation was minimal and access was only by ladder, it promised to be a safer haven than bedding down with Annette. I explained the circumstances to Hill, and he graciously agreed to take me in.

Weekends in the Pines were the best. The moment we stepped onto the ferry in Bay Shore, amongst throngs of well-bronzed and elegantly attired men, (some) women, and designer dogs, we felt liberated: no work, no parents, no responsibilities. Fire Island was about the sea, the sand and scrub pines, the sounds of red wagon wheels being dragged along the elevated board walks, and laughter coming from people gathered on expansive decks or from behind screen doors. That summer the "Supes" reigned supreme. The Stones and Beatles were new and young enough still to be compared to the Dave Clark Five and the Monkeys. Petula Clark's "Downtown" was ubiquitous, trumped only by Mrs. Elva Miller's own quirky off-key version of the same song. We drank (too much), ate (lots) and enjoyed every aspect of what the Pines had to offer. Lipp and I were inseparable. We had each come off lousy relationships, he with a tough blonde about whom I knew very little but didn't like and I with Manuel.

Gael's admirer, Norman McGrath, an elegant Anglo-Irishman

Part 5: CHARRETTE

about seven years our senior, came out to visit. Norman was in transition from being a structural engineer to becoming an architectural photographer. My sisters Judy (twenty-two) and Pago (thirteen) came out from time to time, as did dreamy, disconnected Dan Hollis from our Columbia class. Dan brought with him a sheaf of spectacular abstract drawings he had made over the summer—just form and color, having nothing to do with architecture. Regarding architecture, he was peddling his Equal Volume Theory, whereby all rooms in a building had to have the same volume, regardless of their function. None of this made sense, but his nonsense was part of Dan's charm.

In fair weather, Lipp and I walked along the beach to explore the architecture and cultures of the communities to the east and west of us. We'd make up stories about the people in each hamlet: the young families of Sea View and Kismet; the Lily Pulitzer-clad WASPs who inhabited the oversized, shingled beach houses in the gated community of Point o' Woods; the chorus boys, window dressers and diesel dikes of Cherry Grove; the promiscuous, drunken, druggy and largely heterosexual artists and writers of Water Mill and Davis Park. We'd stop at one or another community, grab lunch, and then get back in time for late afternoon Bloody Marys, more rounds of backgammon, and people-watching at the Boatel. Then we'd go back to the house to commence further drinking and preparing and eating dinner with our housemates. Later in the evening, we might return to the Boatel, where we would assess the corporeal and sartorial merits of who and what was displayed on the Meat Rack. Then home: Lipp to his bedroom at the back of the house, and I up the ladder to my berth beside the sleeping Hillary Parterre.

Hill kept very much to himself, both in our shared bed and outside. I have never had any illusions about being sexually irresistible, but there is nothing to pique your interest like being consistently ignored by an attractive man lying beside you. And so about halfway through the summer, on my return from yet another late evening at the Boatel, I tried my charms on Hill. And it was working! But my diaphragm was in my kit in the bathroom downstairs and that meant stumbling down the ladder in the dark without waking anyone, into the bathroom, light on, installation, light off, up the ladder and then ...? To hell with that, it was only once, and I knew, because I had gone through puberty so late, that there was something wrong with me anyway. Pregnancy wasn't going to happen. Not to me.

And so Hill and I had a lovely coupling that Saturday night and on one or two subsequent Saturday nights (those times I took the proper precautions). We also went out in the city from time to time, but there was nothing serious building between us. Hill, having been unable to leave his mark on New York, sailed back to France on *Le France* at the end of July.

A week after Hill set off, I was certain that I was pregnant. My period was overdue, my breasts were swollen, and my moods were all over the place. There was no way I was having a baby, any baby. I knew nothing about children other than Pago. I was not prepared to raise a child. I had only just emerged from a family that had been ill-prepared to raise me. I had no one to talk to about my situation. My college friends were mostly married, and we had never talked about sex and procreation anyway. The three girls I knew who had gotten pregnant by mistake had married immediately. That was not happening to me. I liked but didn't love Hill, and he didn't love me. What's more, he had gone back to France, and I had to finish architecture school in New York. I knew no one who had had an abortion. Visions of young girls near death or dying on the kitchen tables of illegal abortionists didn't have much appeal. And I knew abortion was legal in some other countries, Israel in particular; Manuel had proudly boasted about it. Maybe I could get to one of those countries.

And yet, I was also thrilled and shamefully proud. If I were in fact pregnant, I was a real woman after all. Never once did I connect this pregnancy with a dream I had had at least once a year for three years in a row. In these dreams I would be diagnosed as having some sort of terminal illness—breast cancer, in one or two versions—and be desperate to have a child before I died. I would embark on a frenetic, ultimately fruitless search for someone for whom I cared sufficiently to conceive the child. I would awake stunned by the depth of this need, which was so unexpected and incomprehensible, given my family's general apathy to children and my own professional aspirations.

I made an appointment to see Dr. Hans Lehfeldt, the gynecologist who had provided me with a diaphragm a few years before, to have a pregnancy test. (Over-the-counter instant pregnancy testing devices wouldn't be available for decades.) I explained the mess I was in and also my pride and joy if, indeed, I were pregnant. Dr. Lehfeldt had written a paper on this very subject: "Willful Exposure to Unwanted Pregnancy." He thrust a copy of it into my hands and, in his fiercest Prussian accent, commanded me to take it to his waiting room and read it immediately. All of it. It was about women like me who might or might not have had access to birth control but who, for whatever reasons, doubted their femininity and went so far as to allow themselves to get knocked up as an affirmation of their sexuality.

Hans Lehfeldt was way ahead of his time.

When I returned to his consultation room, he said that he would first give me an injection, a sort of morning-after cocktail, that might result in an early miscarriage. In the meantime, we discussed my options. I soon found out that he wasn't the only gynecologist who had to leave Germany because of the Nazis. He had colleagues all over the world, some in countries like Israel, where abortion was legal. I told him that I had enough resources to get to Europe and pay the fees, which would not be excessive because the procedure was fairly simple and, more important, legal. If the injection did not achieve its intended purpose by noon of the following day, I was to take a vial of my urine directly to the lab for a rabbit test, which was then the only early way to confirm a pregnancy.

Two days later, Dr. Lehfeldt phoned me to tell me that I was indeed pregnant and asked me to come in to refine my plans. Where to go? Abortions were legal in the U.K. only if a woman was declared by a licensed psychiatrist to be psychologically unfit to bear a child. Dr. Lehfeldt had a colleague in London, Dr. Bauer, to whom he would send me. Dr. Bauer would fix me up with a shrink whom I would have to persuade that I was mentally and physically unfit to give birth (which was hard to imagine, given how proud I was to be pregnant). Dr. Lehfeldt also had a good friend in Tel Aviv, but even then, I knew the world was small, and I reckoned that the professional elite of Tel Aviv might be smaller still. More likely than not, Dr. Lehfeldt's Israeli colleague was best buddies with Manuel Gerade's parents. I wasn't ready to go to Israel, a country I'd never visited, and end up schmoozing with Manuel and his family under these circumstances. Together, we decided that I'd shoot for London, and if I failed to convince the shrink that I couldn't possibly bear this child, I would have to go on to Tel Aviv, where all I had to do was avoid the Gerade family.

By then Hill had settled in Paris, and I called to tell him my news and my plan, more as a courtesy than anything else. He was kind and gentle, surprised and sad. He agreed to come see me in London if I were successful in having the procedure done there, and he graciously offered to pay his share of the costs.

I called my childhood friend Eo (now called Allison) Coudert. who was firmly established in London in the garden flat of a lovely Regency terrace house in Bryanston Square with her husband, Ed Gottesman, and their baby daughter, Polly. Ed was honing his legal skills in international law and Allison was earning her doctorate at the Warburg Institute on seventeenth-century alchemy. As our stories were not dissimilar, and as there wasn't a judgmental bone in either her or Ed's bodies, their warm response to my call for help and support should not have been surprising.

Next, I had to figure out a reason for going abroad on such short notice that would satisfy The Parents' curiosity. I couldn't tell them the truth, however liberal they pretended to be. They were both convinced I was wild and "oversexed," and I couldn't imagine how to counter that impression under the circumstances. Also, Hans was a respected urologist at Columbia College of Physicians and Surgeons, and I didn't want to compromise his reputation by asking for his help. Fortunately, my parents had met Hill and liked him (he was French, after all), so I told them Hill had invited me to visit him and his family while he was photographing the fall collections in Paris and then I'd be going on to see my friends in Rome before returning to school in September. As I'd learned my love of fashion from my mother, I hoped they would buy in and that they would be happy for my good fortune. They were indeed, and couldn't quite believe that I had signed up to do something so worthwhile by their standards. With that done, and introductions to doctors in London and Tel Aviv in hand, I flew to London and soon settled into 25A Bryanston Square.

Repeating Patterns

LONDON — AUGUST 1964

Fortune was with me, as Dr. Bauer's London office was open even though it was mid-August. I saw him the day after I arrived, and I saw the psychiatrist he recommended the following day. The appointment with the psychiatrist didn't go so well at first, as he thought I seemed more than fit to give birth. So I cranked up some heartfelt hysterics on the spot. Okay. He was convinced and signed the papers authorizing the procedure. Two days later, Allison and Ed dropped me off at the West Hampstead Clinic, a private facility housed in a graceful Edwardian terrace house on a leafy tree-lined street. Everything inside and out was white, soft, silent, and, to the extent possible, comforting. I was given a sedative at 12:30 and an anesthetic at 1:00. At 4:00, I came to and was told all had proceeded without complication. Allison and Ed came back in the evening with champagne, which we drank with both sadness and gratitude.

Hill came to Bryanston Square from Paris to visit on Sunday and was thoroughly decent. His mother had told him he was cruel not to marry me. But we both knew I had done the right thing. The snuffing out of a life, however small, did not come easily. While I did feel relieved, I also felt intensely empty and depressed for some time.

As the sadness and gloom abated, I realized I had to tidy up my life and stop getting involved with hopelessly unsuitable men who were wrong in so many different ways. I had already had enough therapy to recognize my conformance to a destructive set of patterns and expectations set in place by the distorted relationship I had had with my father. I was wasting boundless energy attaching myself to people as hopeless at human relations as he had shown himself to be with the two women whom he had married and the one who was his daughter.

Part 5: CHARRETTE

How to break the pattern? I was approaching twenty-five and, as my mother reminded me regularly, still unmarried. I did want to marry and have children, fully as much as I wanted to be a practicing architect. I wanted a partner, a lover and best friend—someone who would understand and maybe even appreciate my coming from such a strange and varied background, someone who would forgive me for having inherited money, for being ambitious professionally, and at the same time for being so insecure. I wanted someone to complete me, to make me whole.

ITALY AND ISRAEL — AUGUST 1964

When I had fully recovered from the abortion, I went on to Rome, where I learned that Freddie was in Sicily on business and he and his brothers were spending the weekend in Catania. Impulsively, I flew down from Rome to Taormina for one day and night, to his complete surprise. He hadn't received the cable saying I was coming. I was there to see if his hold on me remained the same, hoping that it did not. As always, if Giulietta weren't in the wings, he was thrilled to see me. We had a romantic dinner under the Sicilian stars, danced as closely as was decent and then went to his room, where I lay half-naked on his bed. But I wouldn't sleep with him. I thought I was exerting massive self-control and would therefore be forever free of my desire for him.

When I returned to Rome, feeling falsely proud of having resisted my insane attraction to Freddie, there was one further chapter I wanted to close. Although I was no longer interested in Manuel, I was curious to see, however briefly, what the miracle of Israel was all about, especially now that I was no long concerned about discussing a mutual ob-gyn connection with Manuel's parents. I went to the office of El Al Israel Airlines on the Via Veneto, and while waiting to book a very expensive roundtrip ticket to Tel Aviv (I hadn't quite reckoned how far Israel was from Italy), I learned how Italians spell out their alphabet, both face-to-face and over their fuzzy telephone wires:

A	Ancona	B	Bologna	C	Como
D	Domodosola	E	Empoli	F	Firenze
G	Genova	H	(H)otel	I	Imola
J	Junior	K	Kappa	L	Livorno
M	Milano	N	Napoli	O	Otranto
P	Pisa	Q	Quebec	R	Roma
S	Savona	T	Torino	U	Udine
V	Verona	W	Washington	X	X Ray
Y	I greca	Z	Zebra		

This made my future time in Italy so much easier. No more questions about how five consonants could be strung together without an intervening vowel in the middle of a name that wasn't Polish or Czech. No further need to explain that Armstrong in English is the same as *braccia* (arm) and *forte* (strong) in Italian. I could just spell it *così*: Ancona, Roma, Milano, Savona, Torino, Roma, Otranto, Napoli, Genova. *Che meraviglia!*

Manuel's parents were out of the country and sent regrets that we couldn't meet. But Manuel and his sister, Naomi, were gracious and enthusiastic hosts. I soon learned that Dr. Lehfeldt's Israeli colleague was among their dearest friends and had delivered both Manuel and Naomi shortly after his arrival from Berlin at the beginning of the war.

Israel was very much smaller then than it is now. The Six-Day War was three years in the future. The Israelis were bursting the

Part 5: CHARRETTE

seams of the small and awkwardly-shaped parcel of land that they had claimed. There was tension everywhere—between Arabs and Jews, Palestinians and Jews, the energetic European Jews and the lethargic North African Jews, the religious Jews and the secular Jews. And yet everyone seemed to live peacefully side by side. How the Israelis had coaxed agriculture and urbanity out of that arid land and fostered such a rich and seemingly non-sectarian culture was every bit as astounding and exciting as Manuel had suggested.

My time there was short, and I had unknowingly come during the Rosh Hashanah holiday, so access to many places was restricted. We couldn't get to Jerusalem, but we went all over Tel Aviv and its environs and to Haifa, where Manuel would shortly be finishing his architectural training at the Teknion. My greatest wish was to see the real Negev, not just the desert around Tel Aviv. So on the last day of my stay we got up at dawn and drove his parents' car south to Be'er Sheva and then straight across the Negev to the southern tip of the Dead Sea. The sun was searing, the air hot and motionless, the sky cerulean blue, the horizon tinged in orange, the rugged dusty terrain a rocky mix of lunar whites and greys. There were always mirages ahead but not a car or a creature in sight. Every mile or so there would be a miserable little conifer, no more than a few feet high, struggling to assert itself against its hostile and forbidding surroundings—and succeeding. The joy and strength of life can and will overcome.

Around midday we arrived at what had been the city of S'dom (Sodom) and got our first glimpse of the flat and lifeless Dead Sea. We had the first half of food and drink we'd brought from Herzliya and then drove north along the western shore and up the steep mountainside to the ruins of the Roman city of Masada, situated high up on a large mesa on the Eastern edge of the Judean Desert overlooking the Dead Sea. The excavation of the site was in full swing, but it was not open to the public. We had the rest of our picnic outside its gates, and then proceeded further north along the Dead Sea Highway to the kibbutz of Ein Geddi, located smack up against the hostile West Bank border. The fences defining its borders were patrolled by armed young Israeli soldiers, male and female. Within these fences, the land was as green and fecund as its surroundings were not. Members of the commune welcomed us with dates, honey, and water as they scurried to and fro, tending to the orchards, fields, and livestock that produced its bounty. It was a harmonious miracle of human energy and conviction. I wanted to take root then and there, to be part of such a process, as have so many others before and after me. But Manuel reminded me that we had a long drive back to Tel Aviv, and it was already late afternoon.

On the trip back to Tel Aviv, the colors of the Negev were hallucinogenic: brilliant purples, oranges, pinks, and reds fighting for time and space in the western skies as the setting sun turned the lunar day into lunar night.

When I got back to Rome, the space and colors of the Negev were still playing havoc with my mind and with my psyche. I didn't linger. I took the first plane I could get back to New York. I wanted immediately to start breaking down the patterns that were still preventing me from choosing the right someone with whom to share my life.

23. Huey

NEW YORK — SEPTEMBER 1964

333 West 70th Street— my first architectural project.

I had to move again. The McCullys were coming back from Belgium and wanted their apartment back. I found a new apartment around the corner, a fifth-floor walk-up at the rear of a brownstone on 101st Street just in from Riverside Drive. Gael McManus agreed to room with me, which reduced the pain of the higher rent. She took the little room off the living room, and my room was in a newly built enclosure over the rear extension. It was tiny but light streamed in through the single-glazed band of windows facing south and east. I bought a pull-out sofa-bed that, when extended, just cleared the drafting table. It was my aerie, and I loved overlooking the gardens between 100th and 101st Streets. I bought a narrow, late-eighteenth-century antique Italian trestle table which we set in the glazed alcove at the south end of the living room. It served as a combination writing desk and dining table. Gael and I were ready for the fall season to begin.

School recommenced in late September. My classmates assumed

I would fall on my face in Design Studio without Manuel to do my design and drawing for me. But Manuel had never done my design work or my drawing. What he had done was help me figure out how to do my own work. By copying or otherwise adapting some of his drafting and drawing techniques, little by little I had begun to develop my own hand. I was good at lettering, so instead of using Letraset, I hand-lettered my drawings in a simple font. It wasn't much, but it was mine.

That fall we had a course in exterior building materials, and in the spring the course covered interior building materials. The sequence was taught by Jan Hird Pokorny, an architect who was to become as important to me and to my professional life as anyone including Harmon Goldstone and Adolf Placzek. Jan Pokorny was born in 1914 (as was my mother) in Brno, in what was then Czechoslovakia. He trained as an architect and fled the German occupation of Czechoslovakia at the start of the war. On arrival in New York, he took a Master's in Architecture from Columbia, joined the faculty, and married an American architect and took her name, Hird, as his middle name, which I found touching and respectful. They started an architectural practice together in 1946 but were divorced before I had the good fortune to be in his class. Pokorny had the gentle manners of an old-school European, though at that time he was just in his early fifties and had not yet begun on the course of historic restoration and preservation that defined his later career. He was then a committed modernist, though with a deep respect for the past and its preservation.

Building Materials wasn't like Strength of Materials. It didn't teach us how much weight you could pile up on one material or hang from another, nor did it teach how much torque a third could withstand before collapsing. It taught us about the many qualities of a particular material: its variations in color, texture, density, and dimensional stability; how and in what context it is best used and why; and how it behaves in response to light, moisture and thermal changes. We listened, took copious notes and then asked questions, which Professor Pokorny answered with grace, never diminishing or undermining the effort of the student presenting. My professional goal soon became to work for Jan Hird Pokorny Associates, and it nearly happened.

Early that fall I met Huey at a party given by my old friend Mike Janeway. Mike had known Huey at Harvard. Huey was tall and handsome, big-boned and muscular. His almost black hair was side-parted and combed off his large, fair-skinned, and slightly asymmetrical face. His nose was big and straight; his smile was broad. He was loud, funny, full of exaggerated gestures, and irresistibly charming. He spoke in sentences that weren't quite complete and weren't easily parsed, but he got his meaning across just fine. From the moment we met, he was super attentive. I was flattered. I had met his oldest brother on the *Cristoforo Colombo* when I was fifteen and had had a huge crush on him (though he hardly noticed me). Huey was six months older than I. He had had a shotgun marriage in 1961 and his son, Lafcadio, was now three. Huey had been unable to graduate with his class in 1961 because he was so dyslexic that he couldn't pass the foreign language exam. So his father gave him $8,000 to take his new family to Paris for a year in hopes that Huey could somehow absorb enough French, just by shopping for food and going to French films, to pass Harvard's language exam, which he did a year later. He and his wife had been back in New York for almost two years. Things were going poorly. He was seeking to separate. Could he take me to dinner?

"Are you still living with your wife?"

"Yes. But I am working on finding a place of my own."

"Then the answer is no. Absolutely not."

Huey called me regularly to update me on the progress of his separation and to see if I had changed my mind about dinner. I had not. Finally, I agreed to have lunch with him. What harm was there in that? He told me more about himself, his marriage and his love for his son. In Paris, he seemed to have full responsibility for Lafcadio's care while his wife advanced herself in the world of arts and letters. The pattern persisted on their return to New York. Huey seemed battered, but, clown that he was, he put on a smiley face, laughed, and got everyone to laugh with him. He was touching and compelling, as clowns can be.

Huey seemed smart, loved art, and was friendly with everyone. For all my efforts to be standoffish, I thrived on his attention. I was particularly taken by his devotion to Lafcadio. I wished I had had a father like Huey. By late October I could cook well enough to pull off inviting The Parents to dinner. Gael and I could seat six at the Italian trestle table. She invited her friend and then suitor, Norman McGrath, now a full-fledged architectural photographer. I invited Huey. Norman had been in Washington at the time of President Kennedy's assassination and on the following Monday, the official Day of Mourning. He brought as gifts to Gael and me extraordinary large-format black-and-white photos of the tightly-packed, grief-stricken crowds swarming in and around the steps of the Capitol, each face sharply defined, frozen in horror, sadness and disbelief. A photographer himself, Hans appreciated how well Norman had captured the crowd on that solemn day. The evening was off to a good start.

Huey couldn't resist an audience, and when he saw that The Parents might be a challenge, pulled out all stops. They couldn't get enough of him. Where had I met him? Cortesi? My mother knew of a Mrs. Cortesi who was a member of the Colony Club. Could that be Huey's mother? Married with a child? No matter, that can be taken care of, my mother assured me.

Although Huey had charmed The Parents and won the hearts of all of my friends, including Lipp and Gael, I refused to have anything serious to do with him until he physically moved out of his and his wife's apartment. This happened within a matter of weeks, and by December we were very much involved.

Huey was different from anyone else I had cared for. Attractive as he was, he was not my type physically, but new love can get past that. He was warm and funny and self-effacing, and although by his own admission the least accomplished of the three Cortesi brothers academically, he was by far the best athlete and the most charming. He loved to eat, drink, and entertain as I did. He wasn't put off either by my alleged intellect or my background. I didn't have to explain about Willie de Rham's dancing classes nor single-sex private schools. He had gone first to Collegiate and then to Milton Academy, where all the men in my father's and my stepfather's family had gone. Huey took me in hand and steered me around to meet his friends and to visit museums and galleries to revel in the contemporary painting that he so admired. He settled me and made me steady. His love smoothed many of my jagged edges. I was tickled that Huey was one-quarter Italian but could barely mumble a word of the native tongue. I would be his interpreter if we went to visit the Italian side of his family. And if we ever married, I would have an Italian surname!

My mother was beside herself when she confirmed that Huey's late mother had indeed been a member of the Colony Club. It didn't hurt either that his mother's family had amassed a fair fortune in railroads and that Huey's grandfather had had his own private railroad car to take him from Washington, DC, to his summer house in Narragansett, Rhode Island.

I was convinced, as much by his love for his son as by his love for me, that Huey represented a significant departure from the inappropriate and/or unavailable men to whom I had previously been attracted. The pattern was breaking if not broken. My parents' enthusiasm for Huey further kindled my determination to make this a permanent arrangement. They would be off my back, at last, about my being twenty-five and still unmarried. But that imagined outcome was still in the future. Although Huey now had his own apartment and we were very much an item, and although he had a regular schedule of weekends with his son, he and his wife had to face the long and painful negotiation of a separation agreement, custodial terms for the care of Lafcadio, and the finality of divorce. And I still had a year and a half of architecture school to complete.

Was I patient about all this? No.

The longer Huey remained married, the longer he conformed to the pattern I was trying to kick. So I kept the pressure on. It wasn't easy for either of us. He was doing the best he could.

Schoolwork was once again a welcome distraction. Our second design project that fall was a mixed-use hotel-cum-office building. It was all about fenestration—openings. The size, number, and arrangement of windows was going to give the mass of the building its definition and its character. The distribution of windows on the exterior skin had to relate to the plan and function of the smaller fixed modules—the hotel rooms, with their interior bathrooms, closets and shared support spaces—as well as to the open-floor areas for the office space. It was a new sort of puzzle, one I was able to solve. I got a B+ in Studio and Environmental Design, and A- in everything else. Things were looking up.

In February we were assigned the design of a public housing project that was to be between 125th and 135th Streets in Harlem. The large site was to have multiple apartment buildings, a community center, and limited on-site parking. Our critic was Percival Goodman, architect, urban theorist, and, with his brother Paul, co-author of *Communitas*.

I hated the faceless brick projects that were appearing all over Manhattan (some of the very first were designed by Harmon Goldstone's father, Lafayette Goldstone). More were appearing daily on sites cleared for urban renewal on the Upper West Side and in East Harlem. In principle, it was commendable to tear down block after block of filthy, overcrowded, airless and lightless tenements and replace them with higher building blocks set back from the street and apart from one another in a landscape of grass and trees, winding pathways, play areas for kids, and benches for the elderly. But things weren't working as planned.

People took no pride in the apartments in these projects. One person's unit was no different from another's. The public areas, with their sterile finishes, were cold and forbidding, and they nurtured crime. There were no shops along the street, no stoops on which old and young could sit to survey the passing pedestrian traffic and help keep order in their neighborhood. There was no neighborhood. It was all as Jane Jacobs had predicted in her landmark book *The Death and Life of Great American Cities*.

I had admired the Finnish-American architect Eero Saarinen ever since I had studied his work at Brown. Every building Saarinen did was different, among them The Kresge Auditorium at MIT, the Yale Hockey Rink, the archway in St. Louis, the TWA terminal at Kennedy Airport, the John Deere & Company Corporate Headquarters in Moline, Illinois. Each had a different purpose and aesthetic, and each explored and advanced a different aspect of architecture: a particular structural system, an approach to site planning, a use of materials. Each pushed one sort of envelope or another. All are works of art.

In 1961, Saarinen was commissioned to design two new residential colleges at Yale to be named after Samuel Morse and Ezra Stiles, respectively. He was given an angular site adjacent to the Neo-Gothic college buildings designed by James Gamble Rogers and built in the mid-1930s. I would stare at the Saarinen colleges for hours when I spent weekends at Yale with Oswald Johnston. I couldn't believe how anyone could come up with two building complexes that were so contemporary yet fit so well with Rogers's Neo-Gothic, that combined such innovation in plan (hardly a right angle anywhere) with such dignity and intimacy of scale.

Many planning components determine the size and massing of an apartment building. Areas of consideration are the number of vertical cores (stairs and elevators), the length of corridors accessing the apartments, whether these are single- or double-loaded (apartment units on one or both sides), and the depths of the apartment units themselves. Others are the distribution of apartments by size: studio, one bedroom, two bedroom, etc. How many of each? And within each apartment, how is the size and layout of the common living space affected by the number of bedrooms? What is the minimum size of a single and a double bedroom? Is there sufficient wall space for furniture placement? Some of these considerations are determined by local building codes, some by the program, some by economics, some by common sense, some by default.

My approach was to arrange a series of long buildings, not too high, with angled facades on the site so as to define exterior play and recreational spaces at ground level. Each building had multiple cores from which short corridors extended at various angles. A person could easily identify his/her own apartment from the outside, and once inside had a relatively short trip through public areas to home. While every unit in a vertical line of apartments would be the same, no more than two vertical lines would be the same in any one building. The apartment lines would be combined in a different order to create different-shaped buildings. With those concepts in place, I went to town, planning each and every apartment line. There must have been seven or eight. I felt like I was back in fifth grade, doing imaginary floor plans for myself and my friends. I loved it. And, it turned out, Goodman loved it too.

The presentation drawings for the project were challenging, as there were almost no right angles. Making the model was worse. When I suggested Huey might help with the presentation, he left Gael's and my apartment in a huff. But Lipp was there for the duration of the charrette. Even Gael joined in during the wee hours of the final morning. The jury convened on a cold Thursday in March. I made my presentation in front of the class and the jurors—architects who were critics for other studios or from outside—and before anyone could speak, Goodman came out with a stream of praise for my solution.

I learned from the Harlem Housing project that I cared much more about how people live—how they feel entering and leaving their building, going from their living room to their bedroom, cooking and bringing food from their kitchen to the table where they eat—than I did about designing theatres.

Sometime in the middle of our work on the Harlem project, Dan Hollis had his first psychotic break. It happened in the studio. Two of our classmates took him to the psychiatric ward at nearby St. Luke's Hospital. Dan never returned to school. He stayed in touch with Gil Boro for a while. He had more breaks after he returned home. Then we lost him. Several years later, Dan returned to New York and joined the army of homeless men wandering the streets, wearing a filthy, ragged, patchwork coat of many colors, uttering strange verbal sequences, and making little cramped drawings that would now be called Outsider Art. His smile, now full of discolored teeth, remained winning. He always seemed to know where to find me, and I was always glad to see him.

That summer I started my first paid architectural job, working for Warner Burns Toan & Lunde, a New York firm concentrating on institutional and hotel design. Dan Toan, a partner, was on the faculty at Columbia, so Columbia students were often given summer jobs. I was put to work on the schematic design for a new building for Hofstra University. I wasn't drawing or designing so much as researching—analyzing and diagramming the program elements of this complex building so that when the actual designer began to work, he or she would get the functions right. I loved being in a real office again, working with people of all ages and levels of ability. I loved coffee breaks and lunch breaks. Most of all, I loved the work.

Huey thought it was sort of chic that I was studying architecture, but he wasn't at all pleased that I planned to continue working once I was done with school. His estranged wife had wanted to work, too, and look what had happened to that marriage. But I was determined. He eventually capitulated, with the understanding that once we were married (and by then we were planning to marry), I would work but also fulfill all my wifely obligations as cook, hostess, hausfrau, and mother.

No problem. That's how I had been raised.

For the summer, Lipp found us a new and improved weekend house on Fire Island. This summer we'd be sharing with a smaller group that included Gael; Huey's good friend from prep school, Neilson Abeel, and his wife Erica; and my sister Judy. We brought along Huey's son Lafcadio, going on four, every other weekend. I couldn't get over how much fun it was to have him with us and to look after him. This year the house was way east of the ferry

Part 5: CHARRETTE

landing and the Boatel, and nearer the ocean. The neighborhood was quieter and less trashy. I have a vivid memory of a handsome, darkly-tanned guy sashaying down the boardwalk in a pair of Lily Pulitzer-type, full-length drawstring pajama pants, shirtless, his nipples connected by a thin gold chain. Ouch.

Montgomery Clift moved into the house catty-corner from ours. It was a small thrill to catch a glimpse of his handsome, depressed, booze-sodden face from time to time.

Our house was nothing more than a flat-roofed cigar box on stilts, subdivided into three bedrooms, two baths, a living room with the kitchen at one end, and a ginormous deck where everything happened except when rain forced us inside. It was another glorious summer of food, drink, sun, reading, laughter, long walks, and endless backgammon. Body surfing was Huey and Neilson's favorite pastime. Huey could bark like a seal and was, in fact, built somewhat like a seal, with a thin layer of subcutaneous fat all over his body that allowed him to stay in the ocean for hours.

In August, Huey's divorce came through. My mother went into high gear. At last she had a wedding to plan. Poor Huey. None of us gave him a chance to catch his breath. Least of all me. None of us thought he might need to. Least of all he.

EAGLE VALLEY, NEW YORK — OCTOBER 2, 1965

Huey and I and seventy-five others convened at St. Elizabeth's Chapel, where we were married on a warm and sunny October morning. The chapel, near Skylands, was where my mother and Howie had married twenty-eight years earlier. I was afraid being married there might be bad luck, given that their marriage had folded after ten years, but Huey and I loved the setting and the sense of tradition, and so we proceeded. Albert Fuller played the organ and Bobby White sang. Marilla was my matron of honor. My two sisters were my bridesmaids. Hans gave me away. Mike Janeway was Huey's best man, as he had introduced us. The Cortesi family and two generations of Huey's mother's family turned out in force, which was very decent of them, since they'd probably been to his prior wedding four years earlier.

My parents staged a sumptuous buffet lunch back at home at 242 East 62nd Street, and the guests were everywhere—in the little patio between the dining room and the library on the ground floor, in the library, the living and dining room, and on the huge terrace above my parents' bedroom. Daphne Hellman and her jazz harp trio played, as she had at my "coming out" tea. My mother's and my old friend Hedy Giusti-Lanham held forth on the ground-floor patio about how well connected I was with Giada and Giulietta's family in Rome. Huey's mother's family, who were of the highest stratum of Washington society, had known Giada and Giulietta's parents from their days in Washington and were not believing a word of this story, since Hedy was the sort one didn't believe under most circumstances. All of a sudden there was a commotion inside. Daphne stopped playing, and in swept Giada's father. He kissed my hand, then embraced me, exclaiming, "Cara Lulù, how beautiful you are! I am in New York for only a few minutes, but Giada and Giulietta told me I couldn't come back to Rome if I didn't stop by to pay my respects to you and your new husband and bring this little token of our love and best wishes."

He handed me a small, beautifully wrapped box. He said it was a bit of silver that had been in the family. It was an antique silver mustache brush in the shape of a pig with little bristles along the back; it still sits on my bureau. He turned around and caught sight of the line-up of Washington matrons standing with their jaws hanging open. He kissed their hands *seriatim* and warmly embraced the men, calling them by name.

Part 5: CHARRETTE

"Ah, Violet, and Dora, Sam and Ben, what a joy to see you all, and Hedy, too. You look wonderful, all of you. I had no idea Huey was your nephew! What a handsome fellow, and what good fortune for all of you, that he and Layzlie have found each other!" He was gone as quickly as Old St. Nick disappears back up the chimney on Christmas Eve.

Huey and I cut and distributed the cake. We danced with family and friends. I changed out of my hard contact lenses and my super-simple long-sleeved ivory wedding dress, and back into my glasses and street clothes. We were showered with handfuls of rice as we descended the steps of our house and into the car that drove us to the airport. We spent a honeymoon weekend at the Ambassador East Hotel in Chicago—which was all the time I could take as I was still in school.

I was at last a married woman—Mrs. Alexander Cortesi—and thus, in my mother's very non-feminist view, finally complete.

Just before we were married, Huey and I had moved to the top floor of a brownstone across the street from where Gael and I had lived. My mother sent out engraved Tiffany announcements stating that we had married on October 2nd, in St. Elizabeth's Chapel, Eagle Valley, New York, and were "at home" at 323 West 101st Street, New York City. Albert Fuller couldn't stop laughing over the idea of Tiffany engraving anything with a West Side address so far uptown. Neil Fergusson helped me with a few aspects of the interior decoration. In my view, architects did not do furniture, curtains, and throw pillows. Especially not female architects. Especially not this aspiring female architect. I had a lot to learn.

It was my final year and I was liking school better, and found that design was beginning to come to me, although I was hardly star material. Huey enjoyed the challenge of learning about computer systems, which were a new concept at that time, and then selling them for the Bunker Ramo Corporation. With his charm, he could sell anything to anyone. We cooked, we ate, we drank, we entertained, we worked, we laughed, and, occasionally, we argued—but only rarely. We shared all our joys and our fears, all the details of our childhoods that made us feel inadequate, and we promised to love and support each other and help each other build on our many strengths.

In the spring semester I completed my thesis project—a science library for Brown University, a project Warner Burns Toan & Lunde had on its boards. Then came the coursework. There was a course on municipal government I had taken but completely ignored. I did attend class from time to time but understood little, and had done none of the reading. In the two weeks before the exam, I borrowed class notes from friends and crammed in as much reading as I could. To this day, in a recurring dream, I relive the panic of sitting for that exam, for which I was almost totally unprepared. It was pass/fail. I passed, barely, and was able to graduate with my classmates. It was a very close call. But I was a graduate architect at last.

My new in-laws came to my graduation.

The Parents did not. They were, as usual, abroad.

I took the summer of 1966 off before deciding where to go with my new degree. I worked on cooking, and took up tennis so I could play with Huey, who had been playing since childhood. In addition to taking full time-shares with Lipp and company in yet a third house on Fire Island—this one on the far eastern end of the Pines, which we called the "Straight Ghetto"—we spent weekends with friends in many of the hot spots on the Eastern Seaboard. We were the Hertz Rent-a-Couple: chic, charming, funny, bright,

Part 5: CHARRETTE

good cooks, and ideal guests. In August, we saw the Beatles at Shea Stadium, near the end of their second and final U.S. tour. Huey and I, along with much of the world, adored them.

Huey began a new job working with his Cambridge friend, Arnold Amstutz, to put Arnold's latest computer systems brainchild, Decision Technology Inc., on the map. I accepted a job offer from Alex Kouzmanoff and his partners, who were also adjuncts on the Columbia faculty. Their offices were in New Canaan, Connecticut, so my work routine involved a reverse commute in my latest convertible. Huey didn't seem to mind the traveling he had to do for his job, most of which was back and forth to Cambridge. In fact, he thrived on it, however much I hated his being away. For me, life as a car commuter was exhausting. I would arrive home late and drink two martinis for stress relief, followed by wine; then I'd be up the next morning, bright and early (with fuzz in my mind and blankets on my teeth), in order to drive the hour-plus back to Connecticut. But I liked the work and the people I worked with.

That winter we decided we should soon try for a child of our own, though success would require a larger apartment so Lafcadio and the newcomer could each have his/her own room. As we'd both grown up in New York City brownstones (I in a floor-through and Huey in an entire house), we looked for a house to buy on the West Side. We were looking for something that was extremely rare in that part of town: small, full of light, and without any historical significance, so I could play architect and turn the floor plan inside out to make it work for a twentieth-century working couple without destroying valuable decoration or ornament. Our friend Neilson Abeel, who was a real estate broker, showed us only two houses. The first was a typical dark West Side Victorian—not acceptable. The second one was perfect. However, it had already been semi-gutted, as it was being renovated by someone else and was not for sale. But Neilson was persistent and eventually prevailed.

The house at 333 West 70th Street was way west, overlooking the then-very-active Penn Central Railroad Yards. It felt like it was on the edge of nowhere. It had been built in 1895 as one of a row of single-family houses and was virtually sans ornament. The views to the southwest—over the yards, the elevated West Side Highway, and the Hudson River—embraced every form of transport: trains, cars, airplanes and helicopters above, and freighters and ocean liners in the distance.

The house cost $62,500, which seemed exorbitant at the time, but to wrangle it away from the previous owner we had to ante up some of the profit she had expected to realize from her own intended renovation. We begged and borrowed from both our families, took out two mortgages, and closed on a very cold day in February 1967. A clause in our main mortgage contract required us to complete the renovation, which was a total gut, and obtain the new Certificate of Occupancy by the end of the calendar year. So I had to get started. I remember going to measure the house one afternoon in mid-February, turning the corner of 70th and West End and heading straight into an Arctic gale blowing off the river and over the tracks, smack into my face. What had we done?

As soon as the Connecticut project slowed down, I quit my job in New Canaan and went to work in the city for Norman Hoberman, the critic at Columbia who had said "Miss Armstrong, you have nothing there." I had ended up liking Norman and was pleased to be hired by him. However, I was assigned to work for his seemingly insane and sadistic partner, who took pleasure in reducing me to tears by shouting at me about my drafting incompetency. I lasted at Hoberman & Wasserman for six weeks but made an important

Part 5: CHARRETTE

fellow-architect friend in Ayla Karacabey Chatfield, a woman slightly older than I. She was registered, as I was not as yet, and Turkish. She was, in fact, a graduate of Robert College, on whose board my mother then served. Ayla shared with me everything she had learned at the office of Edward Larrabee Barnes, where she'd worked previously, much of which informed the design and detailing of Huey's and my new house.

I spent the rest of the spring on the drawings for the house, learning something new and different every day. I had little confidence in myself as a designer but did know that any trendy moves I made would be soon outdated. Also, in a house that was just under fourteen feet wide inside, there was no room for big gestures, so I played it straight. Like many graduates of architecture school who hadn't worked summers in construction, I knew nothing about how things were actually built, but I knew that getting the drawings right was my only chance at realizing the clean lines and details to which I aspired. So I befriended Terry Quinn, an elderly and occasionally inebriated Irish carpenter who was working on a house a few doors down, and I integrated everything that Terry could teach me into the construction documents. I found out who Terry worked for, and in June we hired his employers to do the job, on condition that Terry would be our foreman and master carpenter.

That summer I went back to work at Warner Burns and made friends with two women architects, Eleanor Larrabee and Rosaria Piomelli, who served as role models for me when later on I despaired of any advancement in or rewards from my chosen and very male-dominated profession. On weekends we returned for the second year to the house at the east end of the Pines. The big changes were that Lipp was falling in love with my sister Judy, and in August I found out I was pregnant. I was not just proud but ecstatic.

Huey and I spent the fall in frenzied agitation, finishing up the construction on the house in order to get the Certificate of Occupancy before the end-of-year deadline. We spent far too much money eating out almost nightly while planning our elaborate housewarming party, which was to be on December 23rd, Huey's twenty-eighth birthday.

The Sixties and cultural changes of every kind were well underway, but you wouldn't know it from Huey's and my life in our new house. Although I was working through the three-year apprenticeship required before I could take the licensing exams, I was also playing the role of an upscale 1950s matron: wearing expensive clothes, eating expensive dinners, and spending expensive weekends with high-living friends—all of which we could not afford. The one significant change was that Huey's nascent interest in acquiring significant works of contemporary painting came to life—though it was ill-timed, as we were very much in debt as a result of the house purchase and renovation. But there was no stopping him, and it soon got out of hand. He was passionate about painting, and he had a superb eye. Andre Emmerich owned New York's top contemporary art gallery at 57th Street and Madison Avenue. He was assisted then by Robert Miller (who soon after opened his own equally prestigious gallery on the same floor in the same building). The two of them were like dope dealers, with Huey as their junkie. It all started with his purchase of a small painting by the Greek/American abstract expressionist Theodoros Stamos. Then Huey quickly moved into the big time with the purchase of one of the less important "Stripes" by the Washington School colorist Morris Louis. It only cost $5,500 at the time—but it was $5,500 we didn't have. We could pay over time, said Emmerich, and so we (or I) did. That was just the beginning.

During the spring I pressed on at Warner Burns. We were

Part 5: CHARRETTE

consultants to Grumman Aircraft, which was preparing its submission to NASA for the design and manufacture of the United States' first manned orbital space station. Grumman had been awarded the contract for the design and construction of the Lunar Explorer Module (LEM) that eventually went to the moon in June 1969, manned by Neil Armstrong (no relation) and Buzz Aldren, and Grumman thought it had a real shot at the space station.

Our job involved planning the deployment of various living, maintenance, and experimental work functions (as well as a giant centrifuge and docking stations for the cone-shaped space shuttles that would carry crews and supplies from earth to the station) which were to be housed within an eighth-inch-thick aluminum cylinder that was the core of the station. Our drawings were always vertical, showing the cylinder upright atop the rocket, as it would be on the launching pad where it would be assembled. But eventually my belly got so big that I had to lay both the rocket and the habitation/work cylinder on its side in order to get at everything on the drawing.

At Grumman, pregnant women were let go after their first trimester. I was near the end of my second when we began our weekly meetings out at Grumman in Long Island. Not only was I regarded as a kind of freak, but I had to pee at least twice as often as the other meeting attendees. Because the Warner Burns team had no security clearance, and there were so few women at Grumman and thus even fewer ladies' rooms, whenever nature beckoned, the meeting had to be stopped and I'd be escorted for miles through the adjacent airplane hangar where the LEM was being assembled—by hundreds of little people scurrying around in white jump suits, gloves, hoods; very James Bond—to the one ladies' room. My escort would wait for me outside, and then back we'd trek.

I was due on Sunday, April 21, and stopped work that Friday. That

Sunday, we had lunch with The Parents and went to see a movie called *Dazzled* at the Plaza Theatre on 58th Street off Madison. I went into labor shortly thereafter and then went to the hospital. I had taken Lamaze classes at Dr. Lehfeldt's insistence and was determined to give birth "naturally." Huey had refused to come with me to the Lamaze classes. It wasn't his thing.

Like most first labors, mine was intermittent and long. After a while, Huey went home. He thought one of us might benefit from sleep. I was a bit hurt but not surprised. Eighteen hours later, just before noon on a radiantly sunny spring day, while the SDS was taking over the Columbia University campus and the streets of Paris were teeming with rioters, our daughter came into this world with a head of dark brown hair, deep, dark brown eyes, and skin as dark as mine. Huey's father, who was extremely fair and looked more English than Italian, was thrilled with her coloring. "At last! A Cortesi who looks like a *wop*!" he exclaimed with glee. She was named Vanessa Lale, after Samuel Barber's opera and after me. Sam agreed to be her godfather.

Two years later our marriage came to an end.

24. Two Out of Three

NEW YORK — SEPTEMBER 1968

My kids by the doors to their rooms, photographed by Norman McGrath for his and Molly McGrath's book, Children's Spaces.

After Vanessa was born, I wanted to stop running around, stop spending money we didn't have, stop entertaining or being entertained by the latest luminary in our circle, and concentrate on making a home for my daughter, my stepson, and my husband. I also wanted to get serious about my work. Designing habitable space for orbiting astronauts was an interesting diversion, but I was interested in architecture on earth.

Huey wanted none of the above. He loved the life we had been leading and wanted more: more paintings, more dinners out, more weekends in the Hamptons, more travel abroad. He felt trapped by our new domesticity and grew moody and morose. He stopped talking to me. He started going overseas on longer and longer sales trips with his boss, in hopes of selling Decision Technology's innovative software to European financial markets. Although I had help during the day in order to go to work, I earned only five dollars more per week than we paid our housekeeper, and so I felt a failure. I was often alone with our baby on nights and weekends. I was no good at being alone. That was the baggage I came with. Huey would not cut back his trips and was increasingly surly and withdrawn. I had no one to talk to. Who would understand? Hadn't we been the perfect couple? How could I possibly complain?

I threw myself into my latest job, which was to design a new home for the American Place Theatre, underneath a plaza behind a new office tower to be built on Sixth Avenue between 48th and 49th Streets. My employer, Richard D. Kaplan, was a colleague and Harvard classmate of the sadistic partner of Norman Hoberman at whose office I had lasted for only six weeks. Richard's father, a well-known philanthropist, had set him up in business and was steering public housing projects his way. Because Richard's office was nicely subsidized, he could afford to do it well. Two of my work buddies from Warner Burns had moved to Kaplan's office. I wanted in because I admired them both and also wanted to do public housing. However, Kaplan had this little theatre project, and when he read my resume and learned of my prior experience, he hired me to be the designer. I gave the American Place Theatre my all. Given Huey's withdrawal from our relationship, I succumbed to sleeping with the project's lighting design consultant, for whom I was just a dalliance. But there is much to be said for pillow talk as an educational medium. And Roger Morgan was an excellent teacher.

At Kaplan's office, I had the first of several demeaning experiences, the kind most young women had if they ventured into a man's profession. When I was well into the project, Francisco, our job captain, quit because he thought our boss was immoral and inept. Kaplan didn't have the balls to allow me to run the job (and maybe he was right, as I was only two years out of school) and instead hired Frank, a macho scumbag whom we had met previously when he hand-delivered hard drugs to the office. Frank wore open shirts, jeans, and cowboy boots to work at a time when that wasn't done, and he had three-martini lunches with other guys in the office every day. He allegedly had a degree in architecture but he knew nothing about theatre or design. However, as my superior, he refused to allow me to attend project meetings with the client for fear of his being shown up. Kaplan supported him. I was distraught, but this was my first big design job. I couldn't quit.

I knew Kaplan was dependent on me to finish working out all the detailed aspects of the design. I contained my frustration and continued to work hard, despite the insult of Frank having authority over me. When we were near the end, Richard invited me into his office after everyone had gone home, closed the door and had me sit down,

"You are good at detail and good at money, Lale," he said. "You understand what it is to come from money."

Was my background so transparent? I thought. *Maybe it was the Gucci shoes. Maybe I shouldn't wear pearls to work, even if they were fake.*

"I need someone with your experience and understanding to run my personal life, to serve as my personal secretary," he continued. "You would be terrific, and it would be a great job for you."

"What about architecture?" I stammered in disbelief.

"It's too tough. You'll never make it. Look what happened with Frank."

"LOOK WHAT HAPPENED WITH FRANK?" I wanted to shout. *You made what happened with Frank happen!* But I was tongue-tied. Finally, I muttered that I would think about it. I returned to my desk, got my purse and my coat, and took the fire stairs down to the lobby rather than stay in the office long enough to await the elevator.

Descending the twelve flights of stairs to the street I felt sick and dirty, as though I had been violated. I knew I was over-reacting. On my way to the subway, I decided that I would have to find someone who would suit Kaplan's needs as a personal secretary so I could stay on, complete the design and, more important, get credit as designer of the theatre. I asked around and learned of a well-heeled young woman from Laurel, Mississippi, Cynthia Chisholm. Her family had supported and largely subsidized Leontyne Price in her meteoric rise to fame. Leontyne and Sam Barber were great friends. He had written *Hermit Songs* and *Anthony and Cleopatra* for her. Cynthia would understand what it was to come from money. I called her, introduced myself and told her about the job. Soon afterward, she was hired.

Albert Fuller introduced me to his best friend from Yale, Llewelyn Jones. Known as Louie, a former student at the Royal Academy of Dramatic Arts in London, he was a senior editor at *Progressive Architecture* and also president of the U.S. Institute of Theatre Technology. Louie encouraged me to join the USITT to expand my knowledge of theatre design and my contacts in the field. In that context, I began to see quite a lot of him. Huey loved all my Spoleto friends and acquaintances. Huey knew and liked Louie and encouraged me to see as much of him as I pleased, more to get me off his back than to advance my career. I soon transferred my romantic attention from Roger Morgan to Louie. In June of 1970, after Huey committed to the purchase of a second Morris Louis painting, a huge Veil, for well over $50,000—even though he couldn't come up with his share of our mortgage payment—I called it quits and asked him to leave.

Instead of coming after me with a club and dragging me back to his lair, Huey seemed relieved if not delighted to depart, and within minutes found himself an apartment nearby. We agreed he would

Part 5: CHARRETTE

take the paintings and I would take the house. It was a fair division of spoils.

I was shattered.

I was just thirty, and the marriage I had hoped would last a lifetime was over.

I went into a funk that would last four years.

That same spring, Giulietta also reached thirty and agreed to marry Freddie. I was genuinely happy for them both. Their time had finally come.

Rebound marriages rarely work, and mine to Louie was no exception. But I didn't have the guts to go it alone as a single mother. Plus, I didn't want Vanessa to grow up an only child, as I had. Louie was in his early forties, never married, and dying for a family. He was my kind of good-looking: tallish and skinny but fit, with a wonderful smile and thinning hair starting to turn grey. He wore aviator glasses. Of course he was bright and funny; that was a prerequisite. But he also was good to me and adored both Vanessa and Lafcadio, whom I continued to see when I could. And he took my architectural aspirations seriously.

Louie had some very definite ideas about how I was to craft my career and for whom I was to work to get the best results. He was good friends with Philip Johnson and Paul Rudolph and wanted me to start with either one. These men were big guns, way too big for me. I knew I was not developed enough to hold my own in offices such as theirs. I said no. I had to grow at my own pace, however slowly.

"How about Hugh Hardy and Hardy Holzman Pfeiffer?" I asked. At that time, Hugh Hardy's firm was doing one vibrant and innovative project after another, many of them theatres. Hardy had started in the theatre at Princeton as a set designer. "Hugh is a good friend of yours," I said. "It could be a fit." At Louie's behest, Hardy granted me an interview. He greeted me perfunctorily, glanced through my portfolio, then looked up and said rather smugly, "We don't hire women here. We think the presence of women is distracting and diffuses the focus on the work. We cannot make an exception for you. I wish you luck finding work elsewhere."

Thanks a lot, Hugh. Why did you waste your time and mine?

I went to work for a joint venture in which my Columbia professor Jan Pokorny was a partner. They were doing a number of buildings at Lehmann College in the Bronx and at the State University of New York at Stonybrook, on Long Island, each of which had a new performing arts facility. Louie didn't approve of my job choice, as none of the principals was well-known except Pokorny, whose reputation was based more on his teaching than on his having advanced any particular architectural aesthetic. But while the work wasn't connected to housing, it would give me a chance to design. And I hoped it would mean working for Pokorny. Instead, I worked for his lesser partner, who grabbed my ass and pressed his middle-aged body into mine whenever we were alone in an elevator. Somehow this was no more insulting than being invited to give up architecture to become a personal assistant, or being paid two-thirds of what my male contemporaries were making. I figured it was par for the course, given the career path I had chosen.

While coping with my ongoing internal sadness, seeking to create a nurturing family context for myself and my daughter, and completing the three years of apprenticeship required by the state before I could qualify for the licensing exams, I was becoming increasingly aware of the civil rights movement that raged around me. Although I am a card-carrying liberal, I always have been fairly apolitical, especially in contrast to my mother. She was an ardent

Part 5: CHARRETTE

Democrat, not because she loved blacks, the oppressed, and the poor, but because she was convinced that if government programs were not in place to take care of the unfortunate, they would break her door down and take away her goodies.

At Brown during the 1960s, Canon John Crocker had led scores of students into the South to march in protest, but I was not among them. However, while a friend from Columbia and I were working for the ass-grabbing joint-venture partner of Jan Pokorny, we flew twice to Jackson, Mississippi, in a private turboprop plane with several movement leaders, including John Doar and Renata Adler. It was the winter of 1970. Medgar Evers, a World War II veteran, college graduate, and dedicated opponent of segregation, had been assassinated by a member of the White Citizens' council in June of 1963. His brother Charles Evers took up the gauntlet, and in November of 1969, he ran for mayor of Fayette, Mississippi, and was the first African-American to be elected mayor in that state. We were flying to Fayette to meet Charles Evers and kick off the design and construction of an ambulatory health-care clinic in his brother's memory. I got the job not because of any personal involvement with civil rights but because my friend and I had taken a moonlighting assignment to design and build a fancy pool house in Long Island for George and Evie Backer, the father and stepmother of one of Huey's and my new friends. They liked our work and were themselves passionately committed to the movement, hence my involvement in the Mississippi project. It was a life-changer, and my first time living with and working for African-Americans in the South that was theirs.

Sadly, the project was abandoned for lack of funding.

During this period almost all of Richard Kaplan's staff had quit except my nemesis, Frank. He was kept on to manage the construction of the American Place Theatre, the only job Kaplan's short-lived firm ever got built. Cynthia Chisholm stayed on to manage Richard. When the theatre was completed and opened, the *New York Times* published an article about the amazing new theatre forty-five feet below the streets of New York. Credit was given to Richard D. Kaplan, architect. Frank was named as designer.

Louie was outraged on my behalf but could do nothing, even in his role as architectural critic and writer. Instead, he cheered me onwards as I began to cram for the architectural licensing exams during the fall. You couldn't call yourself an architect until these were behind you. Having a degree wasn't enough. The exams were given twice a year. I was desperate to pin the letter A for Architect on my breast after all the years of hoping, wishing, and working to be an architect. The first three days were devoted to exams in six areas: structures (engineering and math), building methods and materials, mechanical design (heating ventilating, air conditioning, plumbing, electrical design and building safety), architectural history, professional practice, and site planning. The fourth day was the twelve-hour architectural design exam. You had to pass four out of seven the first time around; otherwise, you had to start over. I passed five out of seven and had to retake the exams in building methods and materials and site planning. I took them in December, just before Louie and I were married. Later in the winter I received notification that I had passed.

JANUARY 1972

Immediately after our wedding, Sandy Walcott introduced Louie and me to her childhood friend, Russell Childs, also an architect, and his new Scottish bride, Kirsten, née Seex, an interior designer

Part 5: CHARRETTE

from Inverness, who took her degree in interior architecture at the Edinburgh Art College and trained in London. Louie and I took to them both. Kirsten and I loved to cook, and both men liked to assist. Russell had just finished Artpark in Buffalo for Vollmer Associates. Kirsten was finishing the interiors of a big house in Long Island for Richard Meier. A year later Russell announced their plan to go out on their own. They had taken office space downtown opposite the Flatiron Building for $300 a month; did I want to come in with them?

I was sick of the mediocre work Pokorny's joint venture was churning out (and of being nailed in the elevator and elsewhere by his lascivious partner), and was unable to switch so that I would only work for Jan. In the meantime, The Parents decided it was time to move to a smaller apartment, now that we kids were grown. They sold their house and bought the master bedroom floor of the Whitney House on East 80th Street off Park Avenue. It had been badly subdivided into two grotty little apartments. They asked me if I'd be interested in recombining the apartments and reproducing, in this new, compressed setting, the best features of the house they were leaving.

Yes.

And yes, I would love to join Russell and Kirsten in their new space opposite the Flatiron Building.

Louie was displeased. This was even farther from the likes of Philip Johnson and Paul Rudolph than Pokorny's joint venture had been.

In early 1973, Armstrong Childs Associates, which Kirsten nicknamed "Archie," was born. We set up shop in two rooms at the rear of the fifth floor at 174 Fifth Avenue—then a very dirty and depressed neighborhood. We shared a receptionist's desk, conference room, and resources library with two other small architecture firms. My new partners were at the forefront of the movement towards sustainable and environmentally responsible design, and brought several projects with them; new offices for the Natural Resources Defense Council, and a house in Reading, Connecticut for friends. I brought in The Parents' new apartment, a renovation/restoration of a large Italianate villa in Fairfield, Connecticut, for a friend of Louie's, and the possibility of redoing The Parents' brownstone on 62nd Street for its new owners, James Taylor and Carly Simon. I had met Joanna Simon, then a mezzo-soprano, in Spoleto, and Carly was her younger sister.

We were off and running.

Russell was an experienced designer and an excellent draftsman and illustrator. He was our team leader, the cock in our roost. He occupied the larger office together with our small staff. Most of our projects were renovations rather than new construction. Kirsten and I were the workhorses. We designed and documented all the interior work. In the small office that we shared, I started to grow into the designer I am. Kirsten and I were joined at the hip with respect to what we wanted from our lives, our friends, and our work. We both believed that women deserve the same opportunities and compensation as men, but we preferred the reward of work and good times to that of political action. Along with work, we both wanted families and children. I had my second child, Sinclair, and she had her son, Aaron, in quick succession. And we worked, cooked, and laughed through it all.

Louie was a great teacher. Through his eyes I learned to see nature and the built environment in a way that I hadn't before. He introduced me to the work of other architects and sometimes to the architects themselves. They were people I might have known had I gone to Penn, but I had no such opportunity at Columbia, which in my day had no strong design leadership. Louie taught me not to be afraid of architectural motifs, furniture, and objects from the past, but to cherish them and enjoy their juxtaposition with things new. He taught me the elements of style, and liberated my nascent sense of color. And he encouraged me both as a designer and thinker, most particularly as I developed the concept that I later turned into a book, *The Little House,* which was published by Collier Macmillan in 1979. I owe him a great debt.

But Louie was also controlling and oppressive. He was a skilled writer but a perfectionist, to the extent that little that he or his staff did was good enough to give him satisfaction and relief from self-scrutiny and criticism. He was constantly needling me about how to write my CV and how to format a proposal (both helpful), and also how to dress for a project interview, for dinner, and for bed, as well as how to wear my hair (not so helpful). He also instructed me on how to arrange flowers, how to set the table, even how to prepare entire meals all of one color—which may have been interesting and stylish for Luis Barragan, the Mexican architect, from whom Louie learned of this practice, but not for me. In the evenings I would drown out his fastidiousness with gin. He drank his share as well. Things got worse after our son Sinclair was born. After a few months I snapped. I couldn't tolerate being Galatea to Louie's Pygmalion. I was drying up inside. To compound matters, I had met someone else to whom I was insanely attracted. Irresponsible though it may have been, I wanted to breathe again, to flower.

In the spring of 1972, I drove my kids to Russell and Kirsten's weekend house in Norfolk, Connecticut. I asked Louie to move back to his old apartment off Beekman Place, which he had kept as a supplementary office, and told him I would be back in a week, and wanted him to have moved out by then.

However painful it was for him—and I know it was deeply painful—he did as I asked.

Kirsten, Russell, and I soldiered on. Along with our occasional office designs, we joined with James R. Grieves of Baltimore to renovate and restore the nineteenth-century Grand Opera House in Wilmington, Delaware. On our own, we remodeled John Johanssen's controversial Mechanic Theatre in Baltimore and renovated five disparate buildings of various vintages for the theatre and music departments at Brown University. And, of course, we did myriad residential projects for friends, friends of friends, and family members. I had a one-semester gig as an adjunct at Columbia, teaching second-year design studio. When we adjuncts were asked to give presentations of our work to the students, I entitled mine "Kitchens, Closets, and the Performing Arts." I wanted the students to know that entry-level architects with their own businesses don't start designing skyscrapers or trendsetting houses. We take whatever walks in the door, work our asses off, and are proud when our projects improve the environment and the lives of the people who inhabit them.

On a personal level, the patterns I tried so hard to break remained firmly embedded in me, though the succession of monkeys on my back had different names and wore cloaks of different colors. But I had two amazing children who brought more joy and depth to my life than I had imagined possible. I had good friends and a good life.

The grand charrette was over. I was a practicing architect at last.

I was a decent mother, and, over time, I became a very good designer.

I have loved being both.

As Meat Loaf says, "Two out of three ain't bad."

Epilogue — Barbara Song

> "When you're ready to stop, stop. If you have presented all the facts and made the point you want to make, look for the nearest exit."
>
> — William Zinsser (my stepfather's cousin), *On Writing Well*

Almost there...

NEW YORK — LATE SIXTIES

Gould Hall, Robert College of Istanbul, Istanbul.

Instead of the relationship between my mother and me becoming closer after I became Mrs. Someone, it deteriorated further. When Huey and I bought our house on West 70th Street, she didn't "get" the location or my sense of interior design, such as it was. When she and Hans came for dinner, she would wear country clothes (read: Hermes, not Patagonia or REI) and pack her jewelry in her purse so she wouldn't be robbed on their way to our perilous edge of Manhattan. Hans was ever genial, but my mother would scowl until she was able to dominate the conversation, which she invariably managed, as she was an accomplished *raconteuse*. Toward the end of the main course and two double vodkas later, she would run out of steam and direct Hans to take her home before the meal was over, thus disrupting whatever bonhomie had developed over the evening.

She rarely remembered the names of my closest friends or dinner guests unless they had reached some level of distinction in an area she valued, in which case she made them her friends and entertained them on her own. When Vanessa was born, she was delighted at last to have a grandchild, but she told me not to think of bringing Vanessa around without a nanny in tow. We didn't have a nanny. We had only a housekeeper who took care of Vanessa when I was at work and stayed to babysit some evenings.

When The Parents hired me to do the renovation of their new apartment in the Whitney House, nothing except the kitchen was to be contemporary. Not my taste, but a job is a job. My mother was pleased with the results. But when I also undertook the renovation of the 62nd Street house bought by James Taylor and Carly Simon, she threatened to sue me on the basis of conflict of interest.

JUNE 1973

At age fifty-six, Hans was diagnosed with lung cancer. No surprise, given that he smoked three packs of unfiltered Camels a day. He and my mother both gave up smoking on the spot. He was operated on; a large cancerous chunk of one lung was removed and the surgery was declared a success. No follow-up chemo or radiation. They and the Chows had just moved to their new apartment. With the threat of a lawsuit hanging over me, I saw very little of The Parents during Hans' recuperation other than to attend to details relating to the completion of the renovation.

A year later, Hans complained of pain in his gut. He returned to Columbia Presbyterian, was opened up again and then swiftly closed. He was riddled with inoperable cancer and looking death square in the eyes. My mother had terrible trouble dealing with Hans's impending departure. She didn't like being at the hospital, although she went dutifully every day, staying for an hour or so. My sisters and I took the long shifts at Hans's bedside. Even in dying, Hans was interesting and funny, full of mad theories on which he could expound freely in my mother's absence. My mother's brother Mac came up from Washington and kept her company at the apartment, where she found herself and her situation easier to manage. The evening Hans died, I held his hand as his breathing grew lighter and shallower, until it stopped altogether, just as I had done with Howie thirteen years before. I returned to the apartment and told my mother, my sisters, and Mac that Hans had gone.

I had no idea how my mother was going to manage. Hans's love and respect had given her the freedom to be who she wanted to be. She and I were no longer close. She and Hans had been drinking too much, her figure had gone to pot, and she was developing the distended belly of many hard drinkers; but being committed to drink myself, I wasn't comfortable throwing stones her way. From a distance, I grieved for her.

The next spring, I was given an award by the United States Institute for Theatre Technology (USITT) for a compendium a colleague and I had made of performing arts facilities built in the U.S. during the Sixties and early Seventies. I was to receive the Founders Award at USITT's annual convention in New Orleans, but I was still recovering financially from the excesses of my life with Huey and couldn't afford the travel expenses. A friend suggested that I ask my mother to come with me and to finance the trip. I couldn't imagine her agreeing to pay for anything of which she wasn't the focus. But I was wrong. Our trip to Louisiana broke through much of the ice that had formed between us. We were even able to talk about her and Hans's drinking. She said that in the year between Hans's initial operation and his death, he seemed to feel alternately ashamed and angry that he had succumbed to cancer, and thus felt unworthy of any sort of serious conversation or rapport with her. They both avoided any discussion of his illness and the possibility of its recurrence, much less his death and the aftermath for her. And so they drank all the more to fill their unhappy silence.

And Hans continued to smoke on the sly.

In New Orleans, my mother told me that she had begun a strict regimen for the consumption of alcohol: two two-ounce glasses of vodka on the rocks before dinner, wine with dinner (which she rarely drank to excess), and one ounce of vodka on the rocks before bed. Weekends, two ounces of vodka were added at lunchtime. To her credit, she more or less stuck to this regimen for the remainder of her life. Slowly, over time, she pulled herself back together, lost the weight she had gained, and began to see friends again.

Within a year of Hans's death, it was her turn to deal with cancer—breast cancer resulting in a brutal radical mastectomy: the breast, all the muscles of the chest below the breast and all nearby lymph nodes were removed and the ribcage was then covered with a skin graft from the inner thigh. The right side of her body was ravaged. Plywood was softer to the touch. My mother was physically shy and, by her own admission, sexually repressed. She knew there would never be another man in her life. She took increasing comfort in the formal rituals of her life: her work in trusts and estates and matrimonial law, the charitable boards on which she served, formal lunches, dinners, and trips to Europe with friends who shared her elevated standards of travel and travel accommodations. Neither my sisters, nor I, nor our children were a significant part of these rituals.

My mother had served on the board of Robert College of Istanbul since the late 1950s. She was hugely admired for her keen mind and grasp of matters affecting the operation and finances of the school, which were truly Byzantine. She was cherished for her humor, her storytelling, and her love of creature comforts and vodka, even Turkish vodka. Several other board members had had legacies, children who followed them onto the board. She was determined that one of her three daughters should follow her. My sister Judith, teacher and scholar, was the logical choice, but then there was an opening on the board for an architect, as a new complex of buildings was to be added to the 1914 Arnavütköy campus, just north of Istanbul proper. So my mother shoved and otherwise finagled, got me elected and paid my travel expenses for my initial trip. With my first sight of the Bosphorus from the terrace of the Istanbul Hilton, I was as hooked on Turkey as I had been on Italy as a girl of thirteen.

Every hour I have spent, both in New York and in Istanbul, working with Robert's staff, teachers, fellow trustees, and consulting professionals has done more for my heart, my soul, and my senses than whatever I may have done for Robert College in return. Serving with my mother for almost fifteen years gave us each a chance to know and admire one another in a context meaningful to us both and on a level footing. Our service to Robert College healed many of our wounds.

Not long after Hans departed, Uncle Mac was diagnosed with Amyotrophic Lateral Sclerosis, known also as ALS and Lou Gehrig's Disease. After four years of diminishing functionality starting from his feet and working its way up to his head, Uncle Mac died. His wife, Alverta, was a saint, and all four of his sons, and I, to a lesser extent, spent time with him and marveled at his ability to take pleasure in an ever-shrinking sphere of interests and activities. By contrast, my mother was mortified by the demeaning progress of this disease and Mac's willing imposition on others to help him through each day as his condition deteriorated. This was not going to happen to her—neither the debilitation nor the dependence. She read up on the Hemlock Society, euthanasia laws in the United States and abroad, and other Right-to-Die organizations that were beginning to take off in England in the early eighties. When the time came, she was determined to end her own life with dignity and without the suffering and humiliation that her brother had endured.

As my mother grew older, her close friends began to fall by the wayside, and she was hard-pressed to find the level of intellectual and social company she valued. She had sight in only half of one eye and was losing height because of osteoporosis. Eventually, she became so stooped that her lungs were becoming compressed and she was both short of breath and in pain. Still, she went to the hairdresser every week and was impeccably dressed and groomed. Every weekday she took a taxi to the Grand Central Building office of Satterlee, Stephens, Burke & Burke, where she had been of counsel since just before Hans died in 1974. At SSB&B, as elsewhere, she was adored for her fine mind and sharp wit. She was their trust and estates mascot and she loved the SSB&B lawyers in return. They were more family to her than we were. In spite of her limited sight, she could still read and compose a perfect legal brief. Although it was difficult for her to cross from one side of a room to the other without pausing to catch her breath, all her other systems were operating at full capacity. She weighed just over one hundred pounds and continued to drink her five-plus ounces of vodka every day.

MONDAY, JULY 31, 2000

My mother telephoned me in the morning and asked if I could come to her apartment around dinnertime and spend the night with her, as she was afraid she was no longer able to get to the bathroom and back to bed during the night on her own. I said of course, packed my overnight bag, grabbed my laptop and showed up just before her daily maid, Nuala, was to leave for the evening. I realized this was going to be a long-term need, and Nuala and I agreed to spell one another on overnight duty for the rest of the week until my mother and I could come up with a more lasting plan for the future. My mother became impatient with Nuala's and my negotiations and said the situation would take care of itself.

My third husband, Dewey, and I had separated almost a year before, following a sixteen-year marriage. But Dewey, a pulmonologist, was fond of my mother, so he continued to act as her attending physician. He stopped by on his way to his new home to check in on her and said she was fine. I thought if she was having trouble sleeping, she might want more than her usual quota of vodka and asked if that would be all right. Yes, he said, why not?

At around 10:00 p.m., I settled into one of the two Louis XVI fauteuils in her bedroom and was about to start "gassing," as we used to call our conversations, when she cut me short.

"I am not in the mood to talk tonight. I don't feel well at all and just want to go to sleep, but I will need to get up during the night and when I do, I will ring this bell for you to come to take me to the bathroom."

She took a mid-size bronze bell by its wooden handle and rang it, then replaced it on her bedside table.

"Do you understand, Lale?"

"Yes, Ma, I understand."

"You may go now and wait for me to ring."

"Okay, Ma." I kissed her on the forehead and took my leave to the guest room down the hall. She could be very imperious. This was nothing new. Fifty minutes later the bell rang. And I came in

Epilogue—Barbara Song

and took her to the bathroom and brought her back. Fifty minutes later the bell rang again, and thirty minutes after that and then in another forty minutes. We barely spoke. Around one in the morning, she asked for a shot of vodka, which I got for her, complete with rocks, and waited in silence for her to drink it. Lights out again and back to the guest room. Twenty minutes later the bell rang, and she seemed noticeably sleepier on the trip to the bathroom and back. Twenty-five minutes later, she was even more sleepy. I had to bear most of her weight on the way back to her bed. Another sound of the bell and off to the bathroom again. This time I couldn't get her off the toilet seat. I propped her up with pillows and ran to call Dewey.

"Something's wrong, Dewey, I can't get Ma to wake up and come back from the bathroom to bed. I think she's dying."

"She's fine, Lale. Don't be so dramatic. Just wake her up and carry her back if you have to. She weighs nothing."

"Okay. Bye, sorry to wake you."

I went to the bathroom. She was still asleep, propped up on the pillows, and I couldn't wake her. So I hoisted her up and away from the toilet, got my arm around her and dragged her back down the narrow hall. I dumped her indecorously on the bed. As I was arranging her, I stopped in my tracks. Her feet were turning purple. She was hardly breathing at all. I had seen this before—twice. I completed reassembling her on the bed, straightened her nightie, pulled the covers over her and held her hand as her breathing became increasingly shallow. Then there was no more.

I called Dewey. "She's dead," I said.

"She can't be."

"She is."

Strangely, I felt light-headed, almost jubilant. I knew there was little left for her to live for, and I had dreaded seeing her through a further decline that was bound to be painful and demeaning. Now she had died on her own, and we were both free. It wasn't until my sister, Judith, came the following morning and found the empty vial of sleeping pills in the trash that we realized what she had done. We destroyed the vial. She had covered all her bases. She didn't die alone. With me on hand, there could be no suggestion of suicide, which would have necessitated a police report. And more important to her, she didn't soil herself in the process.

Very tidy. Very Barbara Zinsser. A great gift to us all, especially to me.

Do I miss her?

No. She was very hard work.

Did I love her?

I did, once.

Acknowledgments

John Bowers,
writer, teacher, husband and friend, without whose love, encouragement, experience, and support this Girl Intrepid could never have done what she did.

Sara Pritchard,
writer and soul sister: my muse, my first reader and editor, and my source of courage.

Tom Wallace,
my agent and second editor, who told me mine was the best memoir of our generation that he had ever read and encouraged me to press on.

Dale Burg,
my friend, college classmate, and third editor, who tried to teach me the rules of grammar. Not happening.

David Stanford,
my final editor and steadfast guide along the treacherous pathway to publication.

Colin Rolfe and Epigraph,
who turned a plethora of visual material laced with graphic prejudices and opinions into the cohesive and elegant volume that it is.

Anthony Russell,
close friend, artist and graphic designer who depicted *Girl Intrepid* in line, color, and type exactly as I wanted her to be.

John Lippmann,
my late best friend: the first to believe in me as a designer.

My teachers: Mary Carpenter, Jocelynn Gibson, Juan Lopez-Morillas, Adolph Placzek, Alexander Kouzmanoff, Percival Goodman, and Jan Hird Pokorny.

The American Academy in Rome where I spent the spring of 2012 researching, writing, and rekindling my love of that eternal city and all things Italian.

The Maslow Family Graduate Program in Creative Writing at Wilkes University which I attended twice yearly for over a decade as John Bowers' spouse and enthusiastic groupie.

And finally the many friends who have read for me, advised me, comforted me and otherwise supported me throughout this long process, not least: Sheila Biddle, David and Mary Bowers, Elizabeth Diggs, Peter Falkner, Gloria Levitas, Church and Liné Lewis, Eddie Lewis and Mary Feidt, Emily Arnold McCully, Joyce Reed, Virginia Ripley, Laura Shaine Cunningham, Claire Tomlinson, and Jivan Wolf.

Thank you all.

Index

'21' Club, The, 24, 153

A
Abeel, Neilson, 393, 394, 398
Abramovitz, Kassie, 150, 162
Addams, Charles, 262
Adler, Renata, 410
Admiral, The. *See* Armstrong, Sinclair Howard, Sr.
Albrecht-Carrié, Claire. *See* Carrié, Claire
American Academy in Rome, 426
American Farm School, The, 30, 81
American Place Theatre, The, 405, 410
Andover, Phillips Academy Andover, 64, 65, 66
Andrea Doria, 41, 44, 58, 78, 110, 350
Armstrong, Elisabeth S., "Lis," 198
Armstrong, Elizabeth H., "Aunt Elizabeth," xi, 10, 29, 38, 53, 69, 89, 156
Armstrong, George A., "Uncle George," xi, 9, 69, 156, 186, 187, 188, 189, 250
Armstrong, James S., "Sinc," xi, 38, 198, 199, 200, 203, 239, 240, 241, 246, 247, 250, 293, 361
Armstrong, Katharine Martin LeBoutellier, "Grandmother," xi, xii, 31, 130, 156, 199, 203, 204, 247, 250, 293, 294, 295
Armstrong, Katherine, "Kittrin," 155
Armstrong, Sinclair Howard, Jr., "Howie," x, xi, xix, xx, xii–xxix, 23, 34, 37, 39, 42, 62, 69, 70, 116, 122, 123, 130, 131, 155, 156, 158, 160, 174, 186, 187, 198, 199, 201, 202, 203, 204, 205, 206, 209, 210, 212, 213, 214, 215, 217, 219, 236, 238, 240, 241, 242, 243, 245, 248, 249, 250, 251, 256, 261, 283, 284, 285, 290, 293, 301, 312, 315, 320, 342, 357, 371, 379, 394, 418
Armstrong, Sinclair Howard, Sr., "The Admiral," xi, xxvi, 31, 149, 156, 182, 199, 200, 203, 207, 239, 247, 250, 293, 294, 295, 357, 360

Armstrong, Sinclair Wallace, "Sin," xi, 140, 181, 182, 186, 187, 188, 189, 192
Armstrong, William C., "Bill," 156
Armstrong Childs Associates, 412
Arndt, Edith, 93
Arnold, Emily. *See* McCully, Emily Arnold
Athens, 81
Aunt Elizabeth. *See* Armstrong, Elizabeth H.
Aunt Lis. *See* Armstrong, Elisabeth S.
Avery Library, 287, 288, 295, 332

B

Babe. *See* Coudert, Allison Moore
Backer, George and Elvie, 362, 409
Baer, Rudolph, 317, 318, 320, 369,
Barber, Samuel, "Sam," xiv, 267, 277, 278, 279, 281, 323, 356, 403, 407
Barnard College, 10, 21, 101, 138, 294
Barcelona, 86
Barclay's Dancing Class, 18
Basinger, Anne L., xv, 33, 34, 35, 123, 124
Beacon Hill, One Primus Avenue, 3, 9, 154
Biddle, Sheila, xv, 40, 426
Big Tug, Little Tug, 73, 202
Blair & Co., 26
Bloomingdale's, 6, 353
Bok, Gordon Dennis, "Denny," xvi, 120, 121, 122, 123, 130, 131, 136, 147, 187, 195
Bold Water, 203
Boniver, Margherita, "Marghe," xiv, 306, 307, 308, 309, 311, 345, 351

Bonmartini, Count & Countess, 47, 54
Bonmartini, Francesco, 55, 148, 149, 150, 172, 174
Boro, Gil, 337, 371, 392
Boston, MA, 4, 62, 186, 326, 342, 348
Bowen, Gladys, 40, 100, 299
Bowers, John, v, 425, 426
Brearley School, The, 3, 20, 21, 34, 40, 52, 53, 68, 99, 105, 113, 114, 123, 138, 142, 147, 152, 179, 186, 256, 299, 310, 334
Brearley, Samuel, 20, 21
Brown University, ix, 138, 139, 148, 176, 179, 181, 183, 220, 226, 233, 234, 256, 258, 310, 326, 330, 368, 390, 397, 410, 415
Brownbrokers, 188, 257, 280, 355
Brunner, Heinrich, "Henri," xv, 285, 288, 289, 291, 292, 295, 302, 303, 304, 313, 344, 353
Bryn Mawr College, 20, 116, 125, 233
Buckley School, the, 100
Buchsbaum, David, 183, 223
Buffalo, NY, 42
Bull, Alexander Benjamin, "Sandy," xvi, 119, 121, 127, 135, 136, 231, 236, 262, 326
Bullmore, Andrew, xiv, 172, 173, 174, 191, 192, 196
Burg, Dale, 425
Burley, Hampshire, 48, 168

C

Cahill, Camilla, xiii, 51, 102, 103
Cahill, John T., 102
Calamai, Piero, 350

Cambridge University, 173, 191, 196
Camden, ME. 120, 130
Camp Treetops, "Treetops," 28, 172
Cape Cod, MA, xviii, xxii, 208
Cape Porpoise, ME, xix, xxiii, xxiv
Capri, 78, 196, 216
Carey, Jane, 46, 47, 54, 347
Carling, Edna, 21, 33, 135
Carol, Hurricane, xix, xxiii, xxvi, xxviii, xxix, 59, 84, 209
Carpenter, Mary, xvii, 123, 426
Carrié, Claire, xiii, 101, 102, 104, 119, 121, 135, 162, 426
Carrié, Mrs. Eleanor, 101
Cartier-Bresson, Henri, 275, 276
Casa Mila, 86, 109
Chapin School, The, 113
Chapin, Vera, 19
Chappaquiddick Island, MA, 43, 108, 156, 202, 203, 362
Charlecote, xi, 130, 157, 198, 199
Chatfield, Ayla Karacabey, 400
Chicago, IL, x, xxix, 38, 41, 71, 73, 236, 239, 249, 283, 301, 396
Childs, Dr. & Mrs. Edward P., 100
Childs, Dr. Edward P., 100, 108
Childs, Eddy, 101, 107, 204
Childs, Eleanor, 101, 204
Childs, Kirsten, xvi, 101, 361, 411, 412, 413, 414
Childs, Lucinda, Sr., 43, 44, 100, 108, 204
Childs, Lucinda, "Cindy," xiii, 43, 44, 70, 71, 100, 101, 107, 108, 124, 135, 162, 200, 228
Childs, Russell, 411, 412, 413, 414
Chookasian, Lili, 298, 299

CIA, Central Intelligence Agency, 89, 91
Claridges, 30, 165
Clark, Hedy. *See* Giusti-Lanham, Hedy
Clark, Honoré, xv, 177, 221
Club of the Three Wise Monkeys, The, 165, 166, 172, 174, 179
Cody, WY, 36
Cohn, Roy, 15
Çok Güzel, 160, 176, 266
Collegiate School, 300
Colony Club, The, 18, 24, 387, 388
Colony, Hotel, 285, 294
Colony Restaurant, The, 24
Columbia College of Physicians and Surgeons, 106, 378
Columbia School of Architecture, 329, 332, 333, 334, 374, 385, 393, 398, 399, 409, 410, 413, 415
Columbia School of Law, 12, 20
Columbia University, 102, 287, 292, 329, 338, 339, 403
Contaflex TLR, 265, 269, 275, 330, 356
Cook County Hospital, 73, 240, 246, 250
Coolidge, Clark, 225, 233, 236, 237, 239
Coolidge, Mr. & Mrs. Arlen, 225, 233
Coolidge, Sylvia, 225
Cortesi, Alexander, "Huey," xv, 359, 360, 384, 386, 387, 388, 389, 392, 393, 394, 395, 396, 397, 398, 400, 401, 403, 404, 405, 407, 410, 416, 418
Cortesi, Lafcadio, 360, 386, 387, 389, 393, 398, 404, 408

Cortesi, Vanessa, xiii, xvi, 403, 404, 408, 417
Cosmopolitan Club, The, 18, 100
Coudert Frères, 29, 90, 286
Coudert, Alexis C., 10, 29
Coudert, Allison Moore, "Babe," xiii, 10, 15, 31
Coudert, Allison Pierce, "Eo," xiv, 15, 103, 286, 378, 379
Coudert, Tracy, xiv, 15, 51, 64, 103
Crawford, William, III, xiv, 260, 268, 288, 298, 305, 322
Crisholm, Cynthia, 407, 411
Cristoforo Colombo, 44, 78, 159, 386
Crocker, John, 410
Cue Magazine, 16
Cunningham, Laura Shaine, 426
Curran, Alvin, "Al," xiv, 192, 193, 194, 195, 196, 197, 200, 211, 212, 220, 221, 222, 224, 225, 227, 228, 233, 257, 259, 280, 287

D
d'Argout Fergusson, 76, 112, 115
d'Argout, Pierre, 76, 314
David, Clifford, 299, 300, 318
Davies, Jack, 105
Davis, Richard, 98, 99
de Nobili, Lila, 270, 281
de Rham, William, 19, 388
de Rham's Dancing Class, 18, 19
Deer Creek Ranch, 36, 159
Delray Beach, FL, 243, 293
Dewey. *See* Oehler, Dewey
Diabolique, 99
Diggs, Elizabeth, "Liz," ix, xiii, 226, 227, 233, 258, 259, 262, 355, 371, 426
Dior, Christian, 30, 57, 58, 75, 129

Doar, John, 410
Domani e Troppo Tardi, 60
Drinker, Nancy, xiv, 62, 110, 116
Durbin, Barbara, 41, 70
Durbin, Johnny, 41

E
Eastern Yacht Club, xvii, xxviii, 201, 209, 213, 218
Edgartown Yacht Club, 108, 201
Edgartown, MA, xxix, 41, 43, 70, 107, 110, 156, 204, 206, 362
El Al, 197, 225, 231, 237, 295
Emmanuel College, 191, 192
Eo. *See* Coudert, Allison Pierce
Epigraph Publishing, 426
Erie Canal, 42, 43
Etnier, Vicky, 135
Eustis, Mary Armstrong and Bill, xi, 186, 187, 294
Evers, Charles, 410
Evers, Medgar, 410

F
Falkner, Peter, 426
Fallingwater, 96, 98, 109, 340
Fashion Group, The, 126, 128, 129, 130, 165, 310
Feidt, Mary, 426
Feldman, Walter, 219, 224, 227, 234, 330
Fergusson, Neil, 76, 314, 337, 396
Fitzgerald, Gerry, 322
Fitzpatrick, Louise, xii, 7, 17, 76, 158
Flying Cloud, 70, 74
Fonda, Jane and Peter, 106
Franchi, Giada, xiv, 270, 272, 276, 279, 280, 282, 296, 300, 304, 305, 306, 307, 308, 309, 311, 316, 344, 345, 347, 395

Franchi, Giulietta, xiv, 268, 272, 279, 280, 282, 296, 300, 304, 305, 306, 307, 309, 311, 316, 344, 345, 346, 347, 348, 380, 395, 408
Freddie. *See* Roccati, Federico
Fritz, Roger, xiv, 269, 273, 276, 279, 298, 299, 302, 321, 322, 323
Fuller, Albert, 298, 394, 396, 407,

G

Gaffer. *See* Lewis, Clarence McK., Sr.
Galston, Nina Moore, xv
Gaudi, Anton, 86, 109
Genoa, 45, 46, 349, 350
Gerade, Manuel, xiv, 366, 367, 369, 370, 371, 373, 376, 377, 380, 381, 382, 383, 385
Get Togethers, The, 63
Gibson, Joycelynn, xv, 134, 135, 138, 140, 141, 142, 147, 148, 152, 180, 426
Gilchrist, Joan Miller, 199
Gilmore, Lynn, 99, 100
Giusti, Goffredo, 45, 229
Giusti-Lanham, Hedy, 45, 228, 229, 230, 395, 396
Gnoli, Domenico, 255, 256
Goldstone, Aline May Lewis, 25, 26
Goldstone, Harmon, xii, 24, 26, 61, 126, 291, 385, 390
Goldstone, Lafayette, 24, 390
Goodman, Percival, xv, 390, 392, 426
Gorham-Holmes, Barbara, 168, 174
Gottesman, Edward, 286, 378, 379
Gracie Fields, 78, 79
Grand Bretagne, Hotel, 30, 81

Grandmother. *See* Armstrong, Katharine Martin LeBoutellier
Grannie. *See* Salomon, Helen Naomi
Granny Pat. *See* Fitzpatrick, Louise
Greenwich Village, 59, 127, 128, 232, 331
Grey Craig, xii, 17, 184, 339, 340, 341, 358
Gritti Palace Hotel, 46
Grumman Aircraft, 402
Guggenheim, Carlo, 55, 77

H

Haden, Charlie, 231
Hamilton, George, 19
Hardy, Hugh, 408, 409
Harrison & Abramovitz, 24
Harrods, 165, 166, 167, 168, 174
Harvard University, 62, 67, 94, 95, 102, 138, 139, 192, 292, 301, 386, 405
Hassler, Hotel, 30
Hebron Academy, 120, 121
Heinz, Drew, 256
Hektoen Institute, 211
Hellman, Daphne, 119, 135, 136, 231, 262, 358, 395
Hellman, Geoffrey, 119
Herzliya, 370, 382
Hoberman, Norman, 366, 399, 405
Holidays, The, 63
Hollis, Dan, 337, 374, 392
Hotel Sacher, 85, 87, 88
Howie. *See* Armstrong, S. Howard, Jr.
Huey. *See* Cortesi, Alexander
Hurricane Carol. *See* Carol, Hurricane

I
Ischia, 196
Istanbul, 420

J
James, Charles, 55
Janeway, Elizabeth, 106
Janeway, Michael, "Mike," 105, 109, 386, 395
Janeway, Mr. & Mrs. Elliott, 105-106, 109
Janeway, William, "Bill," 105
Johnson, Philip, 408, 412
Johnst. *See* Johnston, Robert C.
Johnston, Oswald, Jr., xiv, 65, 328, 329, 331, 337, 339, 343, 391
Johnston, Robert C., "Johnst," xiv, 64, 65, 66, 94, 328
Jones, Llewelyn, "Louie," xvi, 360, 407, 408, 409, 411, 412, 413, 414
Jordy, William, xvii, 219, 291
Joynson-Hicks, The Hon. Miss, 166, 175

K
Kahn, Lois, 105
Kahn, Louis, 291, 332
Kahn, Louis I., 332
Kaplan, Richard D., 405, 406, 407, 410, 411
Kaufmann, Edgar, Jr., 24, 94, 96, 340
Keeney, Mr. and Mrs. Barnaby, 181, 289
Knickerbocker, Cholly, 24
Knudsen, Dagmar, 12, 13, 14, 15, 92, 100, 101, 115, 117, 322
Koska, Bona di Panizza, 93
Kouzmanoff, Alexander, xv, 335, 336, 337, 338, 366, 398, 426
Kriendler, Karen, 153

Kruger, Jerry, 103, 119
Kunz, Bessie, 113, 152
Kunz, George Frederick, 114
Kushner, Dan, 210, 211, 239, 241, 242, 245, 246, 248, 353
Kushner, Dr. & Mrs. Daniel, 248, 251
Kushner, Gail, 243, 249

L
Landeck, Armin, 123
Lara, 214, 215, 217
Lawrence, Margaret, 4, 11, 16
LeBoutellier, Charles, "Grandpop," xi, 149, 156, 157
Le Corbusier, 32
Lee, Leonard, 104
Lee, Sarah Tomerlin, 126
Legendre, Bocarra, "Bo," 36, 37,
Lehfeldt, Hans, xvi, 229, 376, 377, 381, 402
Lenya, Lotte, 59, 60, 257
Levitas, Gloria, 426
Lewis, Alan Churchill Ripley Lewis, 426
Lewis, Annah Churchill Ripley, x, xi, 159
Lewis, Eddie, 426
Lewis, Liné, 426
Lewis, C. McKenzie, Jr., "Mac," xii, 26, 159, 249, 250, 251, 301, 359, 418, 420
Lewis, Clarence McKenzie, Sr., "Gaffer," xi, 7, 11, 16, 25, 26, 75, 88, 136, 158, 236, 260, 261, 311, 319
Lewis, Harold, 25
Lewis, Helen Forbes. *See* Salomon, Helen Naomi, "Grannie"
Lewis, Hyman Philip, xii, 24, 26

Lindstrom, Pia, 296, 300
Lippmann, John, "Lipp," xvi, 326, 327, 337, 355, 357, 360, 361, 367, 368, 371, 372, 373, 374, 388, 392, 393, 397, 400, 426
Lippmann, Sarah, 361
List, Herbert, 269, 270, 304
Little House, The, 414
Livingston, Linda, xiii, 53, 54, 56, 57
Livingston, Lorna, "Big Lorna," 56, 331
Loerke, William, 183
London, 48, 286, 311, 377, 378, 411
Lopez-Morillas, Juan, "L-M," xv, 259, 287, 426
Louie. *See* Jones, Llewelyn
Lukin, Sven, 229, 230, 232
Luna, Signora, 267, 274

M

Mac. *See* Lewis, C. McKenzie, Jr.
MacArthur, Arthur, 19
Maison Dior. *See* Dior, Christian
Manhattan House, 31, 32, 157
Manheim, Emily, 31, 32, 33, 64, 65, 70, 73, 162, 208
Manheim, Kate, 31, 32
Manheim, Tony, 31
Mannes College of Music, 103
Manor Farm, xii, 48, 168, 354
Marblehead, MA, xvii, xviii, 71, 130, 208, 209, 210, 211, 212, 214
Mariani, Fiorella, xv, 270, 271, 272, 279, 280, 281, 288, 296, 300, 304, 305, 306, 307
Maslow Family Graduate Program in Creative Writing at Wilkes University, 426
Marozzi, Renato, 271, 272, 300

Martha's Vineyard, MA, xxix, 42, 200, 203, 242, 362
Masserman, Christine, 38
Masserman, Jules, 38
Mayèn, Paul, 96, 340
McAndrew, John & Betty, 340
McCarthy, Joseph, 15
McConnell, Allen, 183
McCully, Emily Arnold, ix, xv, 226, 227, 233, 258, 259, 262, 330, 355, 365, 384, 426
McCully, George, xi, 227, 262, 330, 355, 365, 384
McGrath, Norman, 357, 373, 374, 387, 404
Mcintosh, Millicent, 21
McLoed, Cissie, 38, 70, 71, 73, 74, 130, 131, 160, 174, 198, 199, 201, 202, 204, 205, 206, 209, 212, 213, 215, 239, 240, 245, 248, 250, 261, 264
McManus, Gael, xv, 236, 326, 357, 368, 372, 373, 384, 388, 392, 393, 396
Meat Loaf, xvii, 415
Menotti, Gian Carlo, xv, 256, 267, 268, 272, 273, 278, 281, 297, 304, 323, 356
Merry Makers, The, 63
Middletown, RI, xiii, 184, 340, 358
Mies van der Rohe, Ludwig, 238, 245, 246
Milan, 44, 282, 283, 306, 307, 344, 345, 347, 348, 349, 351, 352, 381
Miller, Cecile, 31, 162
Milliken, Seth, 211, 212, 213, 214, 215
Millon, Henry S., xv, 258, 287, 288, 291

Mingii. *See* Zinsser, Ruby
Mingolini Guggenheim, 55, 56, 64, 144, 169
Minoletti, Giulio, 44
Miss Viola Wolff's Dancing Class, 18
Mitchell, Jean Fair, xv, 21, 22, 33, 135, 138, 147, 148, 152
Monkey Club. *See* Club of the Three Wise Monkeys
Montresor, Beni, 276, 277, 278, 279, 304
Moore, Louis de B., 10
Morgan, Roger, 405, 407
Morse, Robert, 220, 224
Morvan, Suzanne, 117, 118
Mount Athos, 81, 83, 84
Mrs. Pat. *See* Fitzpatrick, Louise
Munroe, Gretel Zinsser, xii, 113, 114
My Funny Valentine. *See* Curran, Alvin
My mother. *See* Zinsser, Barbara L.
Myers, Robert Manson, 66, 67, 68

N
NASA, National Aeronautics and Space Administration, 402
Neimark, Dr. and Mrs. Mortimer, 244, 245, 246, 249
Neimark, Hortense, 244, 246
Neimark, Philip, "Phil," 244, 246
New Forest, The, Hampshire, xiv, 48, 168, 311
New York Times, 21, 142, 144, 160, 410
New Yorker, 73, 119, 151, 262
Newport, RI, 17, 196, 338

Newton Sharp, Laurie, "Mrs. NS," 166, 168, 172, 173, 174
Niagara Falls, 43
Niagara River, 42

O
Oehler, Dewey, "Dewey," xvi, 361, 422, 423
Oppens, Ursula, 66
Orlando, Orazio, 299, 305, 307
Ortona, Egidio & Giulia, 256
Oyster Bay, NY, xvii, 10, 13

P
Pago. *See* Zinsser, Katherine
Parents, The. *See* Zinsser, Dr. & Mrs. Hans H.
Paris, x, 39, 52, 56, 57, 129, 348, 367, 377, 379, 386, 387, 403
Parterre, Hillary, "Hill", xvi, 373, 374, 375, 377, 378, 379
Patriarca, Jojo, 305, 307
Patriarca, Marco, 305, 307, 308, 345
Paul, Elliot, 52, 53
Pavilion Restaurant, Le, 24, 117
Pecci-Blunt, Camilla, 267, 268, 269, 278, 279, 281, 298
Pembroke College, 138, 139, 140, 176, 177, 181, 183, 185, 227
Pennsylvania, University of, School of Architecture, "Penn," 292, 295, 305, 310, 313, 314, 329, 330, 331, 333, 413
Perrera, Mrs. Carol, 212, 214, 215, 216
Peterson, Anna, 6, 9, 12
Placzek, Adolf, "Dolf," xv, 287, 288, 332, 344, 385, 426
Plaza Athenée, Hotel, 30, 56
Pokorny, Jan Hird, xv, 385, 386, 409, 410, 412, 426

Portofino, 46
Potter, Henry, "Hank," 323, 324, 325, 329, 330
Potter, Lucille, 324
Priester, Helen, "Hellie," xviii, 361
Princeton University, 249, 286, 292, 408
Pritchard, Sara, 425
Providence, RI, x, 139, 177, 192, 219, 233, 239, 251, 258, 262, 285, 288, 289, 292, 296, 331

R

Radcliffe College, 126, 138, 146, 147, 148
Ramsbury Manor, 169, 354
Rapf, Joanna, 224
Raymond, Odile, 29, 57
Reed, Elinor Hope, 81
Reed, Hope Williams, 81
Reed, Joyce, xiii, 226, 227, 233, 238, 250, 258, 259, 262, 355, 426
Reed, Roy, 28
Reversing Falls, 133
Resnick, Hank, 106
Resnick, Michael, "Mike," 106
Resnick, Muriel, 106
Rhinehart, Ray, 185, 186
Rhode Island School of Design, "RISD," 139, 233, 330, 334
Riley, James Leroy, 372
Ringwood, NJ, xii
Ripley, Virginia, 426
RISD. *See* Rhode Island School of Design
River Club, The, 18
Robbins, Jerome, "Jerry," 106
Rolfe, Colin, 426
Robert College of Istanbul, 30, 80, 176, 399, 419, 420
Roberts, Eddie, xiv, 185, 259, 266, 267, 269, 274, 280, 281, 287
Roccati, Federico, "Freddie," xv, 282, 283, 304, 305, 306, 307, 308, 309, 311, 313, 316, 317, 331, 345, 346, 348, 349, 351, 352, 366, 367, 380, 408
Roccati, Signor, 346, 347
Rome, x, 54, 55, 256, 266, 296, 303, 306, 310, 311, 348, 378, 380, 383, 395
Rootes, Annie, 169, 170, 171, 174, 197
Rootes, Lord & Lady, 29, 197, 354
Rootes, Sir William, "Billy," 169, 170, 197
Roque Island, ME, 70, 133
Rosen, Deena, xiv, 221
Ross, Susie, xiv, 226, 227, 233, 240, 258, 259, 263, 355
Rudolph, Paul, 333, 408, 412
Russell, Anthony, 426
Ryan, Daphne, 36, 37

S

Sacher Hotel. *See* Hotel Sacher
Salomon, Helen Naomi, "Grannie," xi, xii, 11, 25, 29, 32, 48, 75, 158, 182, 261
Salomon, William J., "Uncle Willy," xii, 158, 371
Santa Margherita Ligure, 46, 349
Schein, G. David, 15
Schill, Miss, "Shillum", 16, 53
Schippers, Thomas, 284, 298
Seeger, Pete, 119, 237
Shepheard's Hotel, 30, 31
Simmonds, Anthia, 48, 168
Simmonds, Mr. & Mr. Vernon, 48, 168, 311, 312

Simmonds, Shirley, xii, 47, 169, 354
Simmonds, Vernon, xii, 47, 169
Simon, Carly, 361, 413, 417
Sinc, Uncle Sinc. *See* Armstrong, J. Sinclair
Sky Hollow Farm, 4
Skylands, xii, 8, 11, 158, 159, 359, 394
Smith, Kenneth, 329, 331, 332, 336, 342
Smith, Sinclair, xvi, 361, 413, 414
Sokolsky, Dorothy, "Dodo," xiii, 15
Sokolsky, George, 15
Spiegel, Herbert, 207, 290, 315, 318, 319, 320, 321, 323, 337, 353, 369
Spoleto, x, 255, 256, 259, 260, 262, 264, 266, 267, 269, 272, 277, 278, 283, 285, 287, 288, 292, 296, 300, 302, 305, 306, 310, 316, 319, 322, 324, 325, 345, 353, 356, 407
St. Bernard's School, 26
St. Ignatius Loyola, 100
Stanford, David, 425
Steber, Eleanor, 356
Steinberg, Saul, 262, 297
Stillman, Marcia, xv, 299, 300, 321, 322, 323
Stone Horse Light, Stone Horse, xix, xxii, xxv, xxvii, xxix, 38, 41,70, 71, 130, 131, 133, 159, 200, 201, 208, 211, 213, 215, 217, 218, 236, 239, 240, 249, 284, 289, 315
Sturgeon Bay, WI, 41

T
Talbott, Harold, 19
Taylor, James, 361, 413, 417
Tel Aviv, x, 370, 377, 378, 381, 382, 383
Third Avenue El, "the El", 6, 17, 75, 76

Threepenny Opera, The, 59, 60, 128, 280
Tomlinson, Claire. *See* Carrié, Claire
Top Masthead, 156, 202, 203, 207, 362
Town Bull, 67
Treetops. *See* Camp Treetops
Trinity School, 105

U
Umbria, 47, 256, 268, 304, 319
Uncle George. *See* Armstrong, George A.
Uncle Willie. *See* Salomon, William J.
U.S. Institute of Theatre Technology, USITT, 407, 418

V
van Beuren, Marilla, xiii, 16, 17, 19, 28, 31, 40, 52, 53, 196, 330, 338, 339, 340, 341, 358, 359, 394
van Beuren, Mr. & Mrs. Archbold, 16, 52, 53, 162, 184, 341, 342, 358
van Rensselear, Charles, 24
Vanessa, 267, 272, 274, 276, 278, 304, 327, 356, 403
Vassar College, 10, 40, 286
Venice, 46, 47, 340, 347
Vienna, x, 84, 85, 86, 288
Visconti, Luchino, xv, 273, 274, 275, 297, 300, 304

W
Waddington, Dorothy, 126, 130
Walcott, Alexandra, "Sandy," xvi, 223, 234, 360, 368, 411
Wallace, Tom, 425
Washburn, Deric, xv, 301, 303, 304, 313, 343, 344, 353

Washington, CT, xi, 130, 198, 200, 292
Washington, DC, 395, 418
Watson, Ralph, xiv, 287, 290, 294, 295
Welling, Harriet, 238, 240, 241, 245
Welling, Mary Paul, "MP," 239, 240, 250
Welling, Mr. & Mrs. Paul, 239, 240, 251
White, Joe, 207, 208
White, Robert, "Bobby," 298, 394
Wisconsin, University of, 138, 139, 148
Wolf, Jivan, 426
Woodman, Sarah, "Sally," 150, 151, 153
Woodstock Country School, 119, 236
Woodward School, The, 4
World Telegraph & Sun, 15
Wormley, Edward, 24, 77, 92, 93, 95, 314
Wright, Frank Lloyd, 95, 109
Writers' Stage, The, 318, 319
Wyler, Ruth, 67, 150, 152

Y

Yale University, 65, 68, 228, 233, 259, 266, 292, 323, 328, 332, 390, 391, 407

Z

Zanos, Dimitri, 81
Zinsser, Barbara Lewis, "Barby," x, xii, xiii, xx, 5, 9, 23, 24, 25, 29, 30, 32, 33, 36, 37, 39, 46, 47, 48, 52, 54, 55, 58, 61, 62, 66, 67, 71, 75, 77, 79, 82, 85-91, 92, 94, 98, 100, 104, 105, 106, 110, 111, 112, 115, 124, 128, 135, 142, 155, 159, 160, 165, 170, 182, 183, 204, 205, 207, 215, 227, 228, 236, 238, 255, 257, 260, 261, 266, 272, 290, 293, 306, 311, 312, 313, 314, 315, 320, 322, 328, 343, 359, 380, 387, 388, 394, 396, 399, 409, 416, 419, 421, 422, 423, 424
Zinsser, Dr. & Mrs. Hans H., "The Parents," 112, 113, 115, 117, 118, 126, 127, 136, 143, 144, 148, 166, 176, 177, 192, 195, 197, 204, 217, 218, 221, 228, 231, 239, 250, 288, 303, 304, 305, 313, 314, 315, 323, 324, 329, 331, 332, 333, 343, 344, 352, 353, 360, 371, 378, 387, 388, 389, 395, 397, 402, 412, 413, 416, 417, 418
Zinsser, Hans, xii, 62
Zinsser, Hans Handforth, xii, 62, 63, 77, 85, 89, 94, 106, 110, 111, 112, 115, 135, 161, 195, 204, 205, 206, 211, 223, 231, 232, 239, 264, 265, 266, 316, 317, 320, 322, 328, 329, 342, 351, 354, 359, 378, 387, 394, 419, 420
Zinsser, Judith, "Judy," xii, xv, 106, 107, 110, 112, 113, 114, 115, 116, 123, 127, 136, 161, 195, 197, 221, 233, 314, 327, 328, 354, 359, 374, 393, 400, 418, 419, 420
Zinsser, Katherine, "Pago," xii, xv, 106, 107, 112, 113, 114, 115, 117, 127, 136, 143, 144, 161, 186, 228, 314, 327, 331, 343, 354, 359, 374, 375, 418, 419
Zinsser, Ruby, "Mingii," xii, 113, 114, 115, 161
Zinsser, William, 416

www.ingramcontent.com/pod-product-compliance
Lightning Source LLC
Chambersburg PA
CBHW030212170426
43201CB00006B/61